The First Suburbs

THE

First Suburbs

*Residential Communities on
the Boston Periphery
1815–1860*

Henry C. Binford

THE UNIVERSITY OF CHICAGO PRESS
Chicago and London

The University of Chicago Press, Chicago 60637
The University of Chicago Press, Ltd., London

© 1985 by The University of Chicago
All rights reserved. Published 1985
Paperback edition 1988
Printed in the United States of America

97 96 95 94 93 92 91 90 89 88   6 5 4 3 2

Library of Congress Cataloging in Publication Data

Binford, Henry C.
  The first suburbs.

  Bibliography: p.
  Includes index.
  1. Suburbs—Massachusetts—Boston—History—19th
century. 2. Cambridge (Mass.)—History—19th century.
3. Somerville (Mass.)—History—19th century. I. Title.
HT351.B54 1984   307.7′4′0974461   84-16127
ISBN 0-226-05158-7 (cloth)
ISBN 0-226-05159-5 (paper)

For my parents,
who taught me to respect the past,
but to work for the future

Contents

Illustrations

Tables

Preface

FOR A century and a half, the suburbs have promised the best of both worlds. On the one hand they offered the pleasures of nature, the security of home ownership and good schools, the satisfaction of trustworthy neighbors in a small community; on the other, the rewards of work in the city, the excitement and uplift of urbanity. Until the nineteenth century only a few rich people could combine the two, moving with the seasons between estates and town houses. But in the second quarter of the nineteenth century, businessmen and professionals sought their own democratized and cheapened version of the privilege and took up daily shuttling in pursuit of that dream.

This book began with an interest in those first commuters. I wanted to know who they were, how they decided to become commuters, and how they coped with the problems of divided loyalty. I assumed the story of their outmigration and settlement was the central theme in early suburban history.

But I found that I could not understand the commuters without dealing with their noncommuting suburban neighbors and with suburban local history. It became clear that the first commuters were not simply outmigrants—many were not even from the city. Moreover, the early history of the suburbs was not primarily the story of commuter colonization; it was the story of how suburban residents—commuters and locals—became caught up by the power of the residential community ideal. Pursuing these threads, I found myself writing a different book, moving away from a history of commuting and toward a history of community building in the suburbs.

I could not have written this work without criticism and help from many people. First on the list are two men who gave me crucial assistance in defining and redefining the study. Oscar Handlin supervised the dissertation with which I began, and he has read and improved every line of many revisions since. Robert Wiebe read and heard about more drafts than I can count, and the book reflects so many of his suggestions that he rightly deserves a footnote every second page.

Several Northwestern University undergraduates did some of the more tedious tasks of searching, counting, and coding. For patience, enthusiasm, and intelligence in that work I am grateful especially to Deborah Landau, and also to Michael Foley, Alan Gregerman, Kathi Hellerbach, Elizabeth Weal, and Rosemarie Zagari.

For critical readings and proddings, I am indebted to Beth L. Bailey, Charles J. Beard, T. H. Breen, Caroline W. Bynum, Kathleen Conzen, George Fredrickson, Karen Halttunen, Arthur McEvoy, Frank Safford, Cynthia Scott, Donald M. Scott, Joan Wallach Scott, Carl S. Smith, Conrad Totman, and Karen Winkler. They have, in various ways, kept both the manuscript and the author from coming apart at the seams. I alone am responsible for flaws that remain in the published work.

Mr. and Mrs. Leo Flaherty were indispensable guides to the Massachusetts Archives. Mr. Anthony Fiore gave me endless help in the Somerville City Clerk's office. I also wish to thank the personnel of the Boston Atheneum, the Cambridge City Clerk's Office, the Cambridge Historical Commission, the Cambridge Public Library, the Somerville Historical Society, the Somerville Public Library, the Harvard University Library, the Yale University Library, the Manuscript Division of the Library of Congress, the National Archives, the Bell Room in the National Geographic Society, the Northwestern University Library, the Newberry Library, and the Wisconsin State Historical Society.

For financial support I am grateful to the Danforth Foundation, the Harvard-M.I.T. Joint Center for Urban Studies, the Northwestern University Faculty Research Committee, and the Center for Urban Affairs and Policy Research at Northwestern.

Robert Bauer, Patricia Berry, Karen Harder, Catherine Schoenberg, Kathleen Schwartz, Joan Stahl, and Patricia Vernon typed versions of the manuscript.

Finally, I would like to thank my colleagues in the History Department at Northwestern. For ten years now, they have made it a superb place for teaching and for learning.

The dedication of this work can only begin to suggest the debt I owe my parents, or the gratitude I feel.

Henry C. Binford

Introduction
Community Development & Suburban Growth

ETWEEN 1815 and 1860 a new kind of community, the residential
suburb, appeared on the outskirts of America's largest cities. So important was this new form of settlement that it permanently changed
the meaning of the word "suburbs." For centuries the term denoted an undifferentiated zone outside the city limits, a region mingling estates, scattered
farms, waste land, dumps, and scrubby artisan hamlets. After the 1850s suburbs meant a collection of separate communities housing many city workers,
linked to the city through commuting, but often defiantly independent in
government.[1] The first residential suburbs, emerging in the Jacksonian era,
were at the heart of this transformation and played a large role in the long-
term shift from the preindustrial walking city to the mass transportation city
of the industrial era.

Nearly all accounts of residential suburbs are preoccupied with that long-
term shift and oriented to what came in the late nineteenth century and after.
These accounts treat the suburbs as adjuncts of the city and link their origins
to the beginning of mass transportation and mass commuting in the 1850s
or, more commonly, to the streetcar network of the post–Civil War period.
In answer to the question: Where did the suburbs come from? they reply:
The city gave birth to them. Swelling population, the enterprise of transportation promoters and builders, the flight of the middle class from the core began and sustained the recurrent process of suburban growth.

This book is not about the long-term growth process or about post–Civil
War suburbs. It deals with a different and earlier kind of suburb, which
dominated the growth process on the city outskirts in the first half of the
nineteenth century. Antebellum communities of this kind were both ancestors of the later and more familiar suburbs and distinctive communities in

1

their own right. They pioneered some lasting traits of the species: municipal priorities emphasizing residence over industry or commerce and stubborn determination to preserve local autonomy while making the most of city benefits. Yet they were also quite different from many late nineteenth- and twentieth-century suburbs. They were not created by public transportation or large-scale commuting, and only at the end of the period were these phenomena of much importance to the residents. Instead, those who created the first suburban communities (1820–50) were peripheral residents trying to exploit opportunities available at the city's edge—opportunities in suburban land speculation, small business, and unscheduled transportation. Few of these early suburbanites were daily commuters, but many of them sought to make a home in the suburbs while profiting from the city's nearness.

Thus this work differs from most accounts of suburban history in two ways. First, it disconnects the origins of the residential suburb from mass transportation and commuter expansion. Innovation in these spheres did not begin the change on the outskirts but occurred in the midst of it and constituted only one element in the making of suburban communities. Second, in answer to the question where the suburbs came from, this study replies: the suburbanites created them, deliberately and self-consciously, as communities suiting their needs and goals. The first suburbs were made as well as born, not just artifacts of city expansion but products of a community-building process that began in the early nineteenth century.

The main goal of this book is to place the suburb in the context of Jacksonian community development. In making a new community, antebellum suburbanites were doing on the city outskirts what many of their contemporaries were doing in other settings: the factory town, the frontier settlement, the booming river or lake port. All of these were new, and all were communities where the residents seized the opportunities of some particular locale and focused their resources, traditions, and hopes in a collective effort to develop the setting. In all of them, in this period, growth and increased interaction with the outside world forced residents to worry about and redefine the communities' goals and limits.

The suburbs, however, enjoyed advantages and faced challenges unlike those present in any other locale. Standing between city and country, suburban residents had to cope with unique and constant problems of self-definition and autonomy. Their communities were larger, denser, more diverse, more urbane, and faster growing than small towns of the country, but smaller, more specialized, and less wealthy than the adjacent city. Where would they find models for their institutions? How could they control their involvement with the city to preserve independence and prevent absorption? These questions also shaped the first suburbs.

This work examines suburban growth in Cambridge and Somerville, Massachusetts, two communities on Boston's northwestern perimeter. Through their experience, it traces the community-building enterprise of suburbanites and explores the relationship between antebellum community development, the transformation of the city periphery, and the creation of the first residential suburbs.

Antebellum Suburbs and Some Theories of Urbanization

Before beginning a study of Jacksonian suburbs, it will be helpful to clear the stage of some misleading conceptions and to place the first suburbs in their appropriate context of antebellum community growth. Three bodies of scholarship might seem to offer a proper frame for this work: studies of modern (i.e., late nineteenth and twentieth century) residential suburbs, studies of the preindustrial city outskirts, and studies of the general features of the city-country boundary or fringe. All offer insights, but none provide an adequate basis for understanding the early nineteenth-century suburban community.

Too much twentieth-century thinking about suburbs rests on a narrow and teleological conception of their origins. American city watchers, fascinated for more than a century by repeated cycles of suburban growth, have lost sight of the first stages in the process and never paid much attention to what was there before—the semirural villages on the city outskirts. Looking backward from a twentieth-century vantage, across decades of automobiles and tract developments, into years of streetcars and frame cottages, we tend to focus on the large-scale suburban sprawl of the late nineteenth century and after, and we think of suburbs as inextricably linked to mass transportation. Railroads, streetcars, automobiles "create" suburbs. We also think of suburbs as extensions of the city, built by developers and outmigrants from the center. This conception, in which all suburban history is a linear, accelerating process beginning about 1850 and leading to Levittown, has become an unquestioned article of faith in both popular and scholarly works.

But this model of suburban development is inadequate to describe nineteenth-century suburban history. It distorts the past in two ways: by encouraging a foreshortened chronology, beginning only when mass carriers allowed many thousands of people to commute, and by focusing attention entirely on the city's expansion. In this view, the late nineteenth century was "the first suburban era."[2] Earlier suburban communities were, at best, mere forerunners of the suburbs that came with the streetcar.

Even if one is concerned only with the origins of the modern suburb, the late nineteenth century is the wrong starting point. Important parts of the suburban growth process began long before and arose from sources other than mass transportation or large-scale migration. The extension of the journey to work, for example, antedated streetcars, railroads, and omnibuses, began indeed in the walking city era, and began to *change* both city and suburbs before mass carriers allowed mass commuting. Similarly, the process of speculative residential development at the edge of the built-up area, which later became strongly oriented to the streetcar network, began in the 1830s, when no one foresaw a city built around public transportation. Indeed, in the thirties, forties, and fifties, before mass transportation had much impact, American suburbs took on many of their characteristic traits. They became residentially oriented, even though the suburban area contained many non-residential interests. They became commuter-dominated, although they housed only a small number of commuters. They displayed a powerful desire for civic independence, although their interests and problems were clearly tied to those of the city.[3] In short, transportation and outmigration did not by themselves create the modern suburb, and important traits of the suburbs have roots in an earlier era.

A still more important weakness of the mass-transportation model is its preoccupation with the city's growth. In most studies, almost by definition, suburbs are extensions of or additions to the metropolis, or reflections of its "decentralization" or "deconcentration."[4] Yet next to the city there were, throughout much of the early nineteenth century, separately incorporated municipalities which contained large and growing numbers of people, and whose diverse economic activities were not simply transplanted from the city.

Insofar as scholars have considered American suburbs before the mass transportation era, they have looked for New World examples of an older European pattern—the *faubourg* or *Vorstadt*.[5] They have shown that the outskirts of colonial Boston or Philadelphia were in some ways like the outskirts of other preindustrial cities, providing housing for the poorest citizens, estates for the wealthy, and locations for depressed trades and noxious manufactures. These suburbs of the walking city persisted, presumably, until they were overwhelmed by middle-class residential expansion. This model of development also fails to describe early American suburban growth. Even in the colonial period, some of the forces that created the European preindustrial pattern were absent in North America: guild domination of a city corporation, proscription of lower-status tradesmen and artisans, confinement of certain groups to "quarters" of the city never took hold in the English colonies. In any case, the faubourg analogy does not do justice to early nineteenth-century suburbs. By then, the leading American cities were no longer, strictly speaking, preindustrial: the expansion of Atlantic trade, fueled by England's industrialization, had already begun to reorganize the ports, swelling the area of the docks and warehouses, purging residences from the realm of mercantile business, strengthening the cities' canal and road connections to the hinterland. By then, as Kenneth Jackson has shown, suburban growth rates matched and often exceeded those of central cities. By then, peripheral manufacturing zones were often producing for bigger markets in the city and beyond.[6]

By themselves then, these two models for understanding suburban development provide only a sketchy outline of a long and important period of growth in the early nineteenth century. America's suburbs did not change suddenly from preindustrial villages into residential dormitories. Streetcar suburbs of the kind so vividly described by Sam Warner did not become the dominant models for growth until after the Civil War. On the other hand, American versions of the preindustrial suburb experienced major, qualitative changes some decades earlier.

Between the erosion of American faubourgs and the rise of the streetcar suburb lay fifty years of transition—and from the suburban viewpoint, fifty years of community building. What happened in these fifty years? Studies of modern suburbs or of the preindustrial perimeter are of little use in filling the gap, but another scholarly model is suggestive. Geographers, economists, and rural sociologists concerned with the general features of city-country interaction have defined the concept of the urban fringe. Their studies help in understanding what forces were at work in the city's environs, though they do not fully explain what came between the faubourg and the streetcar suburb.

Works about the urban fringe have often drawn upon modern case studies, but unlike investigations of the residential suburb, they have not been narrowly concerned with commuter expansion. Nor have they emphasized the preindustrial qualities so common in descriptions of the faubourg. Rather, they have identified a general and mixed pattern of settlement and economic activity, which has appeared in many times and places and in which urban and rural influences interacted. One of the earliest investigators defined the fringe as "an area where most of the land uses are in a flux."[7] This fringe pattern commonly mingles scattered residences and small farms with storage and marketing facilities, noxious industries, dumps, prisons and similar institutions, cemeteries, and other land-intensive, city-related but often city-rejected phenomena. The early nineteenth-century city periphery contained many of these features, and the growth of a fringe economy was an important part of its history. As the preindustrial faubourgs evolved under the pressures of an industrializing economy, the fringe pattern was one of the first results.

In themselves, however, most studies of the fringe are of partial and limited use in explaining the historical process precisely because they are descriptive and general. Many are based largely on evidence from twentieth-century cities and take for granted a world in which the communication and transportation links between city, fringe, and country are much tighter and more extensive than those present in the early nineteenth century. Their accounts of interaction between city and country also involve ingredients and motives unknown before the Civil War: automobiles, zoning regulations, the pursuit of federal government aid. Some British and European scholars have examined the rural-urban fringe over an extended period, but their works take for granted a centuries-long buildup of land uses and a governmental framework that also differed sharply from the antebellum American pattern. The present study will explore the fringe landscape as it evolved in the early nineteenth-century United States and will identify the influences and motives affecting residents in that setting.

The Suburb as an Antebellum Urban Community

To understand how suburbanites acted in that environment, we must examine the suburb as community—not as something transitional but as a social unit, a place of life, work, and politics. Focusing on the antebellum community requires an altered perspective on the whole process of urban growth. Sociologists, planners, geographers, and other students of urbanization have traditionally looked at the whole metropolitan region as if from the vantage of a balloon. Each suburb was but one of many similar, often interchangeable pieces in a mosaic. On the other hand, central city boosters have regarded suburbs as if from the windows of the chamber of commerce. They have viewed the outlying communities as colonies.[8]

This study offers instead a suburban window on city growth, a perspective essential in understanding the early suburbs. Viewing these communities from without or from a later vantage would obscure small but significant changes in each locality: in the jobs, investments, and hopes of local leaders; in the structure and operation of local government; in the evolution of neighborhoods. Yet in the era before mass transportation, tiny areas and seemingly minor alterations—invisible from a metropolitan or central city perspective—were the ingredients of urban growth. To understand either the sequence of urbanization or the nature of suburban communities, we must look at the details of local history.[9]

Recent historians have produced vivid accounts of many different localities in the early nineteenth century.[10] Indeed, the antebellum United States was a land full of new communities. There were old ones reshaped by new technology or new positions in a regional marketplace. There were new ones built to exploit emerging possibilities for manufacturing, trade, or speculative profit. In all of these cases, changes in the larger economy or society produced a new matrix of local conditions. Local residents, using the tools of law, politics, and guesswork, tried to cope with steadily changing environments.

In-depth studies of particular places have identified important features of the urban growth experience in a variety of settings. In big cities and small, the early nineteenth-century experience involved some general features: the problems raised by growth and changing relationships with the larger world, the mixture of enthusiasm and anxiety with which the residents worried over and tinkered with their local institutions. But local variations were as important as the overall themes. The elements of urban growth came in various packages for different cities, subcommunities, and towns.

For residents of big cities, urban growth meant dramatic increases in numbers and density. In percentage terms, American cities grew more rapidly in the early nineteenth century than ever before or since. Unprecedented numbers of diverse newcomers and transients crowded within the relatively small and undifferentiated space of the old walking city. Growth also meant the specialization of business and the expansion of markets. It meant a loss of artisan control in manufacturing. And it meant friction between various working-class subcommunities: black and white, Protestant and Catholic, native-born and immigrant. By the 1820s and 1830s it meant elite fears of disorder and a variety of efforts to discipline and uplift the poor. Throughout the early nineteenth century it meant extensive revamping of local government, in order to provide services and implement reforms.[11]

In smaller urban communities, many of these phenomena appeared selectively, later, and in less potent combinations than they did in New York or

Philadelphia. Yet smaller communities experienced their own set of changes associated with crossing what Stuart Blumin calls "the urban threshold." Either because they were newly established or because they changed quickly from agricultural to commercial or manufacturing centers, they faced a problem of cohesion and self-definition. Much of the process of change in small cities involved external forces not centered in or controlled by the community: the location of roads, canals, and railroads; the expansion of big city marketing and financial networks. In response to growth and outside pressure, residents of small communities engaged in vigorous boosterism and strengthened local bonds. Leaders of such places, Michael Frisch has persuasively argued, shifted from a sense of community that was direct, personal, and informal to one that was abstract but nonetheless powerful.[12]

Almost no one, however, has examined community development in the unique setting afforded by the antebellum suburbs. Communities on the city's periphery shared some traits with communities elsewhere. They were new, full of promise and threat, experiencing the strains of growth and the crises of community identity. But in the early nineteenth-century suburbs, the matrix of local conditions differed in several ways from the circumstances present anywhere else. The suburbs were small towns immediately adjacent to a big city, not big cities or freestanding interior centers. They were thinly settled, semirural communities which were nonetheless influenced by an urban economy and inhabited by urbane citizens. They merged the traditions and institutions of an older peripheral society with the innovations and threats of the growing city.

Unlike the residents of other, contemporary small communities, early nineteenth-century suburbanites lived in several worlds at once. Their everyday communities were small in many senses of the word. They contained few people, scattered over large areas. In a period when the reach of transportation and the media was selective and uneven, many residents within a few miles of the city had little communication with the center. Some of the suburbanites' most important activities took place in village settings: town meetings, churches, fire companies. In most aspects of life they dealt with small numbers, small distances, and small group endeavors.

On the other hand, because they lived next to the city, their world involved features and possibilities unknown in more remote communities. Long before mass transportation or regular contact, the suburban economy was far more diverse, the suburban population far more varied than the economy or society of any country area. Moreover, suburban residents planned their activities and projected their futures on the basis of proximity to the city.

Throughout the early nineteenth century, many of them had jobs which kept them oriented to the city and frequently traveling to and fro—wagonmen, omnibus drivers, land hustlers, food brokers, and artisan manufacturers. A few of them, at particular points in the early nineteenth century, engaged in enterprises that were impossible anywhere except on the city periphery—developing the main entrance routes, supplying goods for immediate consumption in the city, building streetcar lines.

Thus suburbanites enjoyed growth with less density and conflict than city dwellers faced. They could modify their institutions without the pressure of demographic crises and on the basis of sophisticated models near at hand. Yet suburban development also involved an immediate, intimate, and multifaceted relationship with a much larger neighbor. As individuals and in behalf of their communities, suburbanites had to deal with a far more diverse mixture of temptations, intrusions, and threats—including the ultimate threat of annexation to the city—than did the residents of any remote small town. These hybrid circumstances—small town society and urban atmosphere—produced a unique blend of the community-building forces that were at work across the nation.

In responding to that peculiar blend, suburban residents took the first steps in creating the modern residential community. This study emphasizes the disproportionate influence exerted, in the Jacksonian era, by small numbers of affluent suburbanites. Entrepreneurs in the peripheral towns, more than central city residents, took decisive steps in shaping the physical, social, and political form of the future suburbs. They established the centers of suburban business and industry, played the major roles in expanding the transportation system, and pioneered the systematic development of land for commuter residence. In so doing, they came to perceive and define their communities as unique elements in the growing metropolitan complex. Suburban residents led the way in creating modern suburbs: commuter-based, residentially oriented, politically independent.

The tasks confronting the present study are to analyze the elements of urban growth in suburban communities and to examine the way suburbanites of the early nineteenth century both exploited and were shaped by their particular matrix of conditions. The following pages try to reconstruct the small setting and localized perception of the early suburbanites. They ask: Who lived on the city outskirts? How did suburbanites respond to their changing metropolitan environment? How did they adapt the economy and culture of the fringe to new conditions of mobility? How did their little villages become residentially oriented, commuter-dominated, and defensively independent, when they were none of these things in 1815? How did suburbanites define their communities, and how did these self-conceptions change between the expansion of the fringe and the emergence of streetcar suburbs? Statistics, collective biography, and the tracing of small group endeavors provide answers to these questions.

When considered from a suburban viewpoint, and in the context of early nineteenth-century community development, the transformation of the city periphery may be seen as occurring in three overlapping but distinct phases of change. From the Federalist era until the depression of 1837–43, the most important changes in the suburbs were associated with a booming fringe economy—a zone of manufactures and commercial activity related to the city but not requiring regular contact. The second stage began in the 1830s, when fringe growth was at its peak, and continued into the 1850s. In this period, some suburbanites promoted free bridges, omnibuses, and commuter rail lines, and thereby triggered a revolutionary change in mobility, improving ease of access to and from the city and also transforming suburban expectations about work, residence, shopping, investment, and government. In the third phase, which began with the economic recovery of 1842–43 and accelerated in the ensuing prosperity, the city outskirts became an area for commuter residence. Residential development superseded fringe pursuits as the dominant ingredient in the suburban economy. The culmination of independent suburban growth came in the 1860s, when suburban residential leaders confidently and articulately defined their communities' role in the metropolis, when they subordinated local opposition, rejected the alternative of annexation, and found their municipal program eagerly adopted by younger suburbs farther from the city.

Cambridge and Somerville as Jacksonian Suburbs

The two communities studied here, Cambridge and Somerville, were suitable examples of suburban community development because they illustrated a general pattern visible in other, similar locales. To be sure, these two had their peculiarities: unlike many nineteenth-century suburbs, they had long experience with the New England town meeting form of government. Unlike some important nineteenth-century suburbs, they were never annexed. How did Boston's suburbs compare with those of other cities, and where did Cambridge and Somerville fit in the constellation of Boston's suburbs?

Every big American city had residential suburbs before the Civil War. Every big city also changed its boundaries dramatically in the course of the nineteenth century, sometimes absorbing empty space, sometimes annexing neighboring communities. The nine United States cities that contained more than 100,000 people in 1860 fell clearly into two categories with regard to their histories of suburban growth and annexation. In one group were two cities (New York and Baltimore) that contained large amounts of territory from an early date and thus had ample room for many years of residential expansion within their own boundaries. The other group of seven (Philadelphia, Brooklyn, Boston, New Orleans, Cincinnati, St. Louis, Chicago) all had much less territory in the early nineteenth century than they had at the end. In every case, they annexed some of their first residential suburbs but found their overtures resisted by others. Proposals for annexation usually found strong support in cities but generated heated controversies in the suburbs. Some suburbanites favored annexation because they thought it would bring increased resources and improved services. Others feared the results of surrendering local control. In general, the more prosperous and mature a suburb became, the less its likelihood of being annexed.[13]

In the first half of the nineteenth century, Bostonians most often compared their territorial situation with that of Philadelphia, another old but still growing seaport. Both cities began the century within cramped borders, enclosing only about two square miles (compared with Manhattan's twenty-three). Both cities had large suburbs by the 1840s. In 1854, after a long controversy, the Pennsylvania legislature consolidated the city of Philadelphia with Philadelphia County, thus adding 127 square miles and all the major suburbs to the city in one stroke. Boston leaders tried to move in the same direction in the 1850s but were thwarted until after the Civil War, when they absorbed several suburbs but failed to annex Cambridge, Somerville, and Brookline. The city gained only minor increments of territory after 1873, as a ring of staunchly independent municipalities closed around its limits. Boston's metropolitan history differed from the experiences of other cities only in that annexation ended earlier and more decisively. Other cities, especially the younger cities of the trans-Appalachian west, continued to annex various suburbs in the late nineteenth century, but most of them confronted stubborn holdouts beginning in the 1860s, and all of them reached relatively firm limits by 1900.

In the metropolitan Boston area, Cambridge and Somerville were pioneers of the independent path of growth. They were both in the innermost ring of suburbs, a ring that originally included Charlestown, Roxbury, and Dorchester. Among these Charlestown was in some ways a special case, having a long history as an independent seaport and a former rival to Boston itself. The other suburbs all experienced explosive growth in the early nineteenth century. (By 1860, Cambridge and Roxbury were among the forty largest cities in the United States, each containing well over 20,000 people.) Roxbury and Dorchester, annexed after the Civil War, became important residential districts of Boston. Cambridge and Somerville, resisting annexation, became models for most of Boston's suburbs after 1873.

Thus these two communities illustrated one important line of suburban development evident throughout the nineteenth-century United States—the one leading to independent, residentially oriented cityhood. Each was an early but not isolated example of what suburb boosters in many places would later call "the city of homes." Indeed, insofar as their histories involved wrestling with the issues of residential growth and municipal autonomy, Cambridge and Somerville also represented an important phase in the histories of most suburbs, including those that were annexed. Struggles over annexation, whatever their outcomes, were symptoms of a strong and self-conscious localism everywhere.

Moreover, Cambridge and Somerville were different from each other and internally differentiated; they illustrate not just one but several versions of suburban growth. Cambridge, a college and farming town since the seventeenth century, became first a center of agricultural marketing and light manufactures in the early nineteenth century and then a location for factory industry and commuter residence in the 1840s and 1850s. Somerville until 1842 was the western part of Charlestown, a hilly area of pastureland and scattered farms without any village centers. It grew more slowly than Cambridge, but became a boom town with the arrival of the railroad. After 1840 Somerville quickly followed Cambridge in the transition from peripheral village to residential suburb.

The three parts of this book correspond to the three overlapping stages of antebellum suburban history and focus attention on the details of Cambridge and Somerville growth in order to illuminate the larger process they exemplify. The first and last sections deal with old and new kinds of suburban society: the middle with the changes in mobility which lay at the center of the suburban transformation. Part I traces the evolution of a fringe society that arose after the Revolution, when bridges and roads opened new gateways to the city, that flourished in the 1815–37 period, and influenced suburban expansion long after.

Part II explores a long change in city-suburban relations, centering on transportation but reaching far beyond the journey to work. Along with the rise of commuting, the years between 1820 and 1860 saw a revolution in mobility that involved individual habits, political goals, metropolitan economic and social organization, and definitions of the "city" as well.

Part III examines the suburban communities that emerged after 1842 in response to changed conditions of mobility. These first residential suburbs had many modern features: commuters, governments that provided services and amenities, and boosters who viewed their suburbs as competitive units in a metropolitan system. But every element of modernity had been shaped by a matrix of earlier suburban institutions, activities, and goals.

These communities were both prototypes for the future and reflections of the antebellum era. They were not yet fully "modern": commuting was still an elite phenomenon; it did not include the blue-collar straphangers who later rode the streetcars. Many suburban residents still saw themselves as members of small communities, not of a metropolis. The suburban towns were far from densely settled. Nevertheless, by the Civil War, suburban enterprise had produced new kinds of communities, both in reality and in the minds of their inhabitants.

PART ONE

Gatekeeping

1

Improvement Enterprise
and the
Fringe Economy

New England Glass Company Factory, East Cambridge,
in the 1820s. Detail from an Invoice, 1828.
Courtesy of the Maryland Historical Society, Baltimore.

TURNING inland from their wharves, Bostonians of the 1780s had no trouble deciding where their city ended and the countryside began. Surrounded on three sides by water, Boston had only one boundary on land, at the narrow "neck" that led southwest to the pastures of Roxbury. South of the city, across a large cove, were fishing towns that faced the harbor. Due north, across the Charles River, was Charlestown, a sister and rival port set off on a peninsula of its own (see fig. 1). To the west, beyond the huge expanse of the Charles River Basin, were hundreds of acres of salt marsh, briar thicket, and swamp on the Cambridge shore. Except for the maritime centers and a few mills, tanneries, and shipyards, the landscape of this region around the city resembled that of the rural interior.

By the 1830s the urban-rural boundary was less distinct, both physically and economically. It was even a matter for debate in politics. The change did not occur simply because Boston expanded, but rather because the entrepreneurial activities of a few Bostonians and many suburbanites created a distinctive zone between city and country. The economy of this fringe zone was neither rural nor urban. It contained some farms and some factories, but much of its vitality arose from performing chores that had to be done just outside the city: assembling, storing, preparing, and transporting goods for the urban market. In this new peripheral region, suburbanites established patterns of work, social life, and community structure that set them apart from the city, the country, and the past and laid a foundation for future suburban development. This chapter and the next concern the economy and society of that fringe area.

The special features of the fringe reflected the distinctive experience of its residents. Promoting growth on the periphery involved motives, means, and results different from those evident in Boston. Bostonians in this period worked constantly to strengthen their grip on the hinterland, bringing the resources of all New England ever more smoothly to the city's docks. Bridges, canals, factories, and ultimately railroads were their tools. By contrast, people of the surrounding towns sought to profit from their position at the city's gateways. For them, opportunity lay in roads, taverns, teaming, and the brokerage or processing of farm goods.

These efforts produced two distinct paths of growth. Central Boston, with trade expanding both overseas and inland, grew denser and more specialized. Especially after 1815, wholesalers, jobbers, and other specialized merchants carved up the realm of the older trading princes. The mercantile community built new and larger facilities for handling, storing, financing, and marketing their cargoes. With the aid of engineers like Loammi Baldwin,

Boston's elite bridged the rivers and drove a canal through to New Hampshire. With the aid of architects like Charles Bulfinch, they filled the Boston peninsula with elegant homes. Mercantile expansion and city policy both worked to create a commercial downtown, driving industry and other pursuits to the outskirts.[1]

The towns surrounding the city did not share directly in these changes. Boston's actions set terms for the suburbs, but suburban entrepreneurs followed a different path. There the small initiatives of local residents were more important than the great works and visions of the Bostonians. Traffic from the hinterland was the basis for expansion, and suburbanites were sensitive to every detail and nuance of local exchange. The suburbs also took in small industries pushed out from the city and generated others to supply city demand. The result was a city-oriented but not citified way of life.

Bridges, Bridgeheads, and Competitive Localism: Origins of the Fringe

The fringe economy flourished between 1815 and the 1840s, but its roots lay in the period between the Revolution and the War of 1812. From Federalist period improvements, the suburbs gained a twofold legacy. The physical inheritance was obvious: bridges and highways that became a skeleton for future growth. There was also a legacy of enterprise: a collection of models and procedures, of successful and failed ventures which guided fringe residents of the 1820s and 1830s.

In Charlestown and Cambridge, geography and eighteenth-century experience determined the lines of post-Revolutionary action. Entrepreneurs of that period confronted a barren landscape, but one that contained resources and models available to developers.[2] Both towns lay on a broad peninsula between the Charles River on the south and the Mystic on the north. They contained three distinct areas: the Cambridge plain, the Charlestown mainland, and the Charlestown peninsula. Most of eastern Cambridge was swampy lowland, poorly suited to farming and offering no good landing places on the river. The town center, near Harvard College, faced south across a bridge to Brighton, Roxbury, and thence Boston and west toward Watertown and West Cambridge. To the north, the Cambridge flatlands yielded to the claybeds and steep ridges of mainland Charlestown. Here too there were few inhabitants, the most important being dairy farmers along the ancient road known as Milk Row, who pastured their cows on the hills above. Most of Charlestown's people lived on the peninsula, where they had access to Boston by a ferry and to Medford by a road over the Charlestown Neck. Beyond Cambridge and Charlestown, in the rest of Middlesex County, was more territory of similar nature—divided into huge town units, sprinkled with villages, bucolic, remote, and empty.

Much of this area was cut off from the city. The main roads from the north ran through Medford and Charlestown to the ferry.[3] From the west traffic flowed through Watertown and Cambridge, across the river and around through Roxbury to the Boston Neck. So poor were these connections that no one could rely upon "normal" routes. Closure of the ferries by bad weather, for example, forced travelers from the north to circle around through Medford, Cambridge, and Roxbury, finally entering Boston from the southwest—fully an extra day's journey.[4]

After the Revolution, the suburbs offered an especially dismal prospect. Charlestown, the only large settlement, had been destroyed by bombardment and fire. Eastern Charlestown and Cambridge, headquarters for Washington's siege of Boston, were littered with the fortifications and debris of revolt. War and war debts made rural isolation worse, as towns neglected the roads and bridges. Here as in most of Massachusetts, isolation from the markets in coastal cities stifled agriculture. Farming remained extensive and unspecialized. Farmers ate most of what they grew.[5]

Yet in this backward region there were three keys to future development. The most obvious was city access: any improvement in traffic, especially the traffic that fed the city and supplied its commerce, would enrich both sponsors and suburban residents. Charlestown, Medford, and Watertown offered another model. They had prospered in colonial times as break points on trade routes, where farmers bought supplies and teamsters shifted heavy cargo from wagons to vessels. Brokers, food processors, artisans, and innkeepers clustered at these points. Post-Revolutionary developers would try to duplicate these outlying trading centers.[6]

A third, less traditional resource lay in certain large blocks of estate land. A few of Boston's eighteenth-century merchants had consolidated large seats in the suburbs: the Temple family in mainland Charlestown, the Lechmeres, Inmans, Danas, and Foxcrofts in Cambridge. All of these except the Danas were Tories and fled in the Revolution. Judge Francis Dana was left supreme in Cambridge, while the other estates were opened to sale and development.[7] A variety of speculators with a variety of schemes pursued pieces of this property.

For half a century, until the coming of mass transportation, plans for suburban economic development would be based on these eighteenth-century models and resources. Improving travel, brokering and processing country goods, and exploiting large tracts of land—these were the goals. All of them depended on better access to the city. In the Federalist era, widespread enthusiasm for internal improvements brought that access. Before 1815, Boston capital and expertise built three bridges across the Charles, linking the city with Charlestown and Cambridge; and two more across Miller's River and the Mystic, joining East Cambridge with Charlestown and Charlestown with Malden. Bostonians also built the Middlesex Canal, winding north from Miller's River to the Merrimack Valley. Suburban residents (sometimes with Boston help) launched an array of smaller, derivative ventures: turnpikes, town and county road improvements, wharves, small canals, and land reclamation projects (see fig. 2).

The first development of the suburbs was intensely localized and competitive. No overall policy shaped the explosion of improvements. Years later, in a similar explosion attending railroads and streetcars, many small ventures would be guided by a vision of the residential suburb or of metropolitan growth.[8] Early national entrepreneurs had no such overarching scheme. Instead, particular local projects, based on eighteenth-century models, absorbed their energies. The narrow interests of partnerships, corporations, and village centers were paramount in their thinking. Moreover, they were far more constrained by topography, far more limited by financial and technical resources than their descendants of the railroad era.

In these circumstances, vigorous competition and jealous promotion surrounded every bridge, every turnpike, every scrap of road. Fighting for interests that seem trivial today, rival entrepreneurs spent years pursuing partners with capital, strategic bits of land, and the patronage of town meeting, county court, or state legislature. Nocturnal sabotage and high legal reasoning became instruments of the same struggle.

The timing, location, and interests involved in these competitions laid a basis for all future suburban growth. They fixed the centers of population, trade, and industry. They created suburban villages and made them different from each other. They passed on a legacy of competitive localism to the next generation, and beyond. Four kinds of entrepreneurs, in a rough sequence, played varying roles in the promotional fray. The Boston-Charlestown seaport elite, both Federalist and Republican, built the bridges and the Middlesex Canal.[9] These were expensive, formidable ventures, incorporated by the state and backed by its most prominent citizens: John Hancock, outgoing governor; Judge Thomas Russell, Continental Congress delegate and first president of the new Boston Chamber of Commerce; Francis Dana, chief justice of the State Supreme Court; and James Sullivan, attorney general.[10] These men and their associates sought profit through funneling trade to the

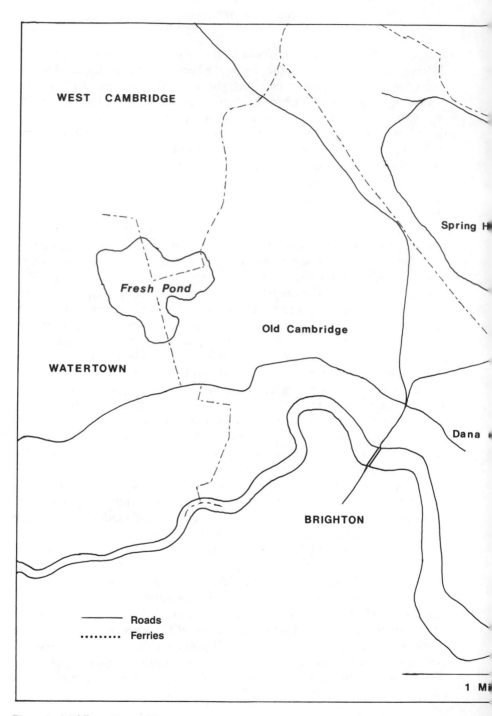

Figure 1   Middlesex County Transportation Routes in the Late Eighteenth Century

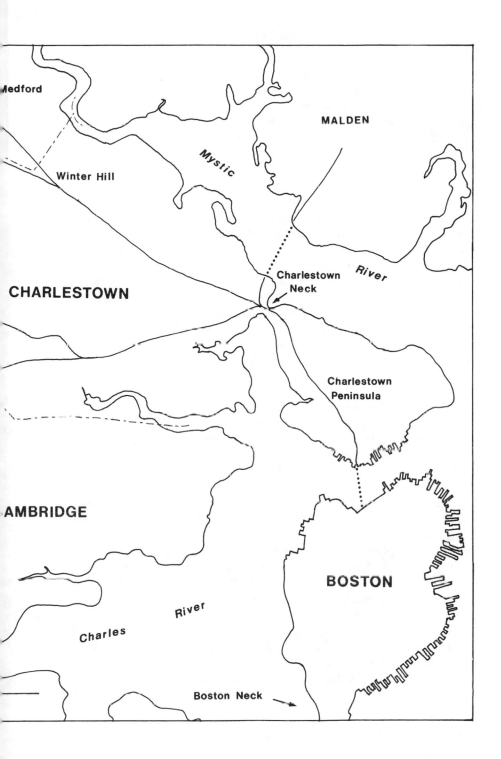

city and charging tolls at the narrow points on each funnel. Some of them owned land in Charlestown and Cambridge, but with the notable exception of Dana, they played little role in promotions beyond the bridges.[11]

The field lay open instead to landowners and traders of Middlesex County, some of whom were shareholders in the bridges. Between 1803 and 1805, hinterland entrepreneurs incorporated three turnpikes, one leading to each bridge.[12] A good example of this second entrepreneurial type was Jeduthun Wellington (1750–1838), a prosperous farmer and a legendary figure in local history. A militia colonel in the Revolution and an ardent Republican, Wellington later served eighteen terms as selectman of Cambridge, nine as her representative in the General Court, ten as committeeman of the Northwest Precinct, and a total of fifteen in lesser town and precinct offices. Three generations of Wellingtons had assembled a farm which occupied most of what is now Belmont Center, almost exactly halfway on a straight line from the West Boston Bridge to the Concord town boundary. Jeduthun added a tavern and a sawmill to the family empire. Recruiting landowners in three different towns, he laid out a turnpike running arrow straight from the West Boston Bridge to Concord—and, not incidentally, through his land. For the next thirty years, he worked indefatigably to divert traffic from the older routes to the road he clearly viewed as his and to defend its whole length from encroachments.[13]

The bridge and turnpike promoters both sought gain from the flow of country traffic. The third and fourth groups of entrepreneurs took their cues instead from the eighteenth-century trading centers and the availability of estate land. They focused on small areas nearest the new bridges, in Cambridge and on the Charlestown mainland. At the center of their schemes were short pieces of public and private road, not turnpikes, and two plans for new trading centers: Cambridgeport and East Cambridge (see fig. 2). The goals of these two groups were similar, but they differed dramatically in their membership and their methods.

Both of these plans drew encouragement from a fever of town building that swept through Middlesex after the opening of bridges. The rebuilding of Charlestown offered a prototype. Charles River Bridge, opened in 1786, gave new life to the old seaport. Through a combination of private capital and town meeting largesse, Charlestown residents replaced war rubble with widened streets, new taverns, wharves, stores, and a markethouse.[14] When bridges appeared at other points, Middlesex residents thought of duplicating Charlestown's success in entirely new settings. In Malden, directly to the north of Charlestown, bridge building sparked talk of a new town that might channel the northern trade away from Medford. Medford citizens were both alarmed and amused at this prospect. Their minister made fun of his neighbors' pretensions:

> As for the Malden miserables, they were never awake till the talk about this bridge put them in motion, like men who walk in their sleep. They now leave their corn unhoed, and their grass not cut, to carry petitions to court for a bridge . . . the distracted creatures think, that, if there should be a bridge, they shall at once commence a seaport town, have still-houses, stores and what not. And in consequence of this wretched delusion, and that neglect of business among them, which it occasions, their families next winter will have no bread, and their cattle no hay. It will be a deed, not of charity, but of indispensable justice, in Judge R[ussell] to provide for the support of the poor ignoramuses; since it is owing to his superannuated whims that their brains have been turned.[15]

Each of the two bridges to Cambridge, opened in 1793 and 1809, provoked similar visions. One group of developers—and one kind of enterprise—centered on Francis Dana, a leading backer of the West Boston Bridge. His estate included most of central and southeastern Cambridge. One of his bridge-building partners, Leonard Jarvis, bought the Inman estate next door, and these two enlisted Andrew Bordman, whose farm adjoined both estates. All three men were descendants of old Cambridge families, with roots in the First Church and long careers in town office.[16] In developing the center they called Cambridgeport, they joined with younger local businessmen. The most important were Royal Makepeace, a twenty-one-year-old storekeeper near the bridge, and Josiah and Daniel Mason, cousins who established a store, wharf, and tannery near Makepeace.[17]

Cambridgeport was in many ways a colony of Old Cambridge. It was designed to be for Cambridge what Medford and the Charlestown seaport had long been—a place where country traffic met coastal and ocean navigation. Its backers were established citizens, whose main assets were their land and their influence in the Cambridge town meeting. With good reason, the five principals called themselves the Cambridgeport "proprietors," since they owned most of eastern Cambridge. On their own, they were able to survey streets and lots, to build an elaborate network of canals, and to drain and dike scores of acres of marshland. From 1793 to 1807 their work enjoyed the collective blessing of the town. They built three bridge approaches (Main Street, Mount Auburn Street, and Harvard Street), and the town obligingly made them public roads. They donated land and money for a new meetinghouse; the town created a second parish. They sought an act of Congress making their new town a port of delivery; the town supported their application.[18]

But after 1804 a rival group, representing a fourth kind of enterprise, disrupted the unity of public purpose. Leading this new venture was Andrew Craigie, a Cambridge resident but in many ways an outsider. Craigie had purchased a Brattle Street mansion, but unlike the Port promoters he had no ancestral connection with the town. He was Episcopalian, not Congregationalist, and his backers were powerful Boston Federalists, not Cambridge landowners.[19]

Drawing on all the lessons of twenty years past, Craigie and his partners launched a coordinated effort at bridge, road, and town building centering on the last remaining site for a span across the Charles: Lechmere Point in East Cambridge. This endeavor was a tour de force, capping Craigie's long career of speculation. In secret, complicated transactions dating back to the 1790s, he had acquired nearly all the land on Lechmere Point. He then interested the Middlesex Canal corporation in the project, offering them direct access from the end of their waterway to Boston. Perhaps they might even build a towpath on the bridge, so their barges could be pulled straight across the Charles River basin to the city's docks. Seven of the thirteen original incorporators of the bridge were canal shareholders, and the canal company owned one-third of the bridge stock.[20] But Craigie, though his name was listed last, held another third of the stock himself.

Outmaneuvering two rival groups, he obtained a charter in 1807, then enticed even more Federalist money into both the bridge and a land speculation company in Cambridge. Harrison Gray Otis and T. H. Perkins, investors in Dana's earlier bridge, smelled profit in this one, too. Along with other young Federalists, they bought into Craigie's venture on terms that guaranteed the promoter a $340,000 profit.[21]

As latecomers in suburban development, Craigie and his associates faced an uphill competitive struggle, but they could follow what amounted to a blueprint for bridge, road, and town building. Craigie's land deals united strings of property holders on routes that flanked the approaches to both Cambridgeport and Charlestown. He built new roads (now Cambridge Street and Medford Street) and fought for years to gain public maintenance. Decades later, these streets would still be popularly known as "Craigie roads."[22] Sitting in the Beacon Street mansion of Harrison Gray Otis, the East Cambridge promoters designed a break-point village for Lechmere

Point along the lines of the tried formula. They included a blacksmith shop, hay scales, and a brewhouse and agreed to offer all possible inducements to wagonmen to choose the East Cambridge route over its rivals. In plans drawn by their surveyor, the salt marsh of the point became a gridwork of streets—a tiny imitation of contemporary planning in New York and Philadelphia. Lacking the support of town meetings but enjoying Federalist patronage in the state legislature, Craigie's group chartered its whole operation as the Lechmere Point Corporation.[23]

The development of East Cambridge, tightly controlled by a Boston-based corporation, contrasted sharply with the Cambridge-rooted and town-meeting-backed promotion of Cambridgeport. Not surprisingly, the Port promoters and the town saw Craigie as an intruder and resisted his efforts.[24] The ensuing struggle between rival entrepreneurs had two lasting effects: First, East Cambridge would remain alienated from Old Cambridge and the Port and oriented to Boston until the late 1820s. Cambridgeport had representation on the Cambridge Board of Selectmen from 1805 onward and for a time enjoyed a majority. East Cambridge would not be represented in major town offices until 1820 and would not be equally represented until several years later.[25]

At the same time, Craigie's Boston and Federalist connections won victories for his new village. Charlestown, Cambridgeport, and East Cambridge all tried to persuade the Middlesex County courts to leave Old Cambridge and relocate in new quarters. In 1813, when the county was controlled by Federalists, Craigie's group won out, offering land and $24,000 for buildings. In the same year he sold waterfront land to a group of Boston businessmen, who built the first of the glass factories that would later be the mainstay of East Cambridge prosperity.[26]

The second consequence of this rivalry was to reinforce the use of county and state governments as tools by road- and village-centered entrepreneurs. The core issue in Cambridge was public maintenance of Craigie's bridge approaches. Shut out from the patronage of the town, he turned first to the County Court of Sessions, which also had power to lay out roads as public ways. But from 1807 to 1809 Republicans controlled the county, and they rejected Craigie's petitions on four separate occasions.[27] Finally, in the summer of 1809, Craigie and the Federalists tried to overwhelm local resistance by appealing to the Federalist state legislature. T. H. Perkins, a member of the Federalist central committee, headed a petition requesting a state committee with power "to explore, view, and mark out new highways from the westerly end of [Canal] Bridge to communicate with the great roads into the

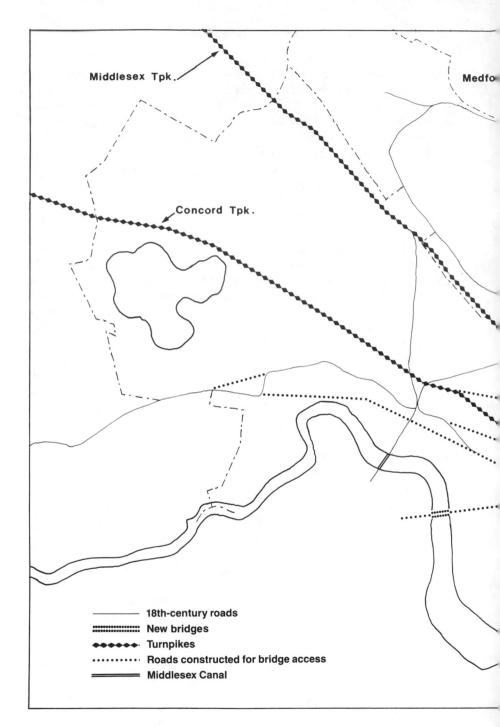

Figure 2 Major Improvements in Inner Middlesex County, 1780–1830

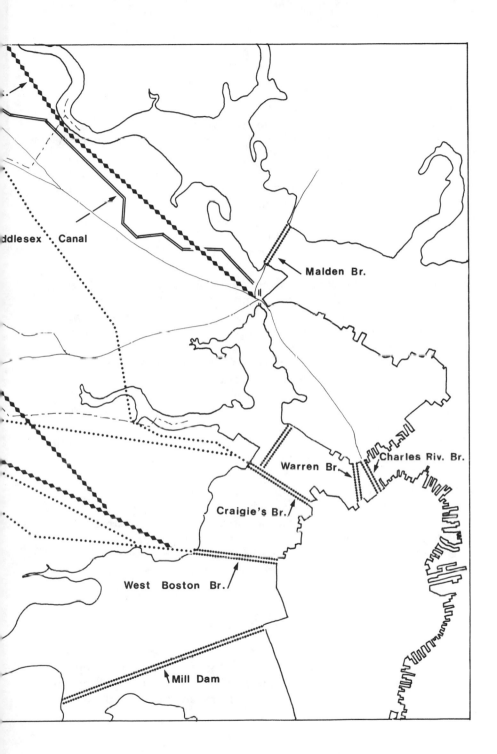

ddlesex   Canal

Malden Br.

Charles Riv. Br.

Warren Br.

Craigie's Br.

West   Boston   Br.

Mill Dam

country at such places as will best comport with common convenience and the public good."²⁸

This was a frontal assault on traditional town prerogatives. In response, Cambridge granted some concessions to Craigie but sent an indignant remonstrance to the state. This document, signed by Dana and the Cambridgeport leaders, protested that "the inhabitants of Cambridge and Cambridgeport are deeply afflicted by the incessant machinations and intrigues of Mr. Andrew Craigie, in regard to roads" and denounced the Perkins proposal as unconstitutional: "such a petition, viz., to lay out roads without number, with courses undefined, by a committee of the Legislature, your remonstrants conceive, never was before offered to any Court, Legislative or Judicial, of Massachusetts."²⁹

The echoes and aftershocks of this squabble, and of others related to it, rang through town meetings and county and state courts for another decade. The atmosphere of the village competition lasted even longer. Even when Dana and Craigie were dead, the alignments they established continued to shape the economic and political life of the suburbs.³⁰

But the first round of improvement was largely over by 1815, its achievements terminated and crystallized by the national crisis of Embargo, Non-Intercourse, and war. General financial distress crippled lot sales in East Cambridge and killed seaport dreams in Cambridgeport. Neither the county courts nor the glass company brought any appreciable benefit to East Cambridge until after the war. Bostonians, although they continued to profit from the bridges, did not make any more major investments in Middlesex County until the railroad era. From 1815 to the 1840s, they turned their attention farther afield—to textile projects and interior lands.³¹

The framework of bridges, roads, and villages was in its place; the Bostonians had withdrawn; the suburban entrepreneurs were left to struggle and speculate in a reduced arena. In the 1820s and 1830s the drama of the improvement period subsided. But the marks of that period were evident in the transformation of agriculture and industry that produced the fringe economy.

Farming and Industry in a Village Setting

Some suburban residents felt the economic crisis only as a distant event. On the heels of the various improvers were large numbers of small operators—old residents and new settlers alike—who took advantage of the improved climate of access. Massachusetts farmers, and therefore those who catered to the movement of farm goods, were to some extent insulated from commercial crisis. Most farmers enjoyed little or no contact with the state's external trade, and the handful in the inner suburbs who supplied the Boston market could rely on the city's relatively constant demand for food.[32] In Cambridge and Cambridgeport, some newly settled tradesmen seem to have prospered along the new roads. The price of land on the main roads—where country traffic passed—held steady throughout the depression, while lots on the canals declined in value.[33]

After 1815, small-scale enterprise became the basis for a new phase of suburban growth. Population data provide a crude measure. Between 1810 and 1840, the combined population of Cambridge and Charlestown nearly tripled, giving them almost 20,000 inhabitants. Many of the towns in the next ring outward—from Malden on the north to Brighton on the southwest— also grew at a steady rate. Statistics for entire towns are in one sense misleading: half the population of the two innermost suburbs lived on the Charlestown peninsula. Elsewhere the increase reflected new village settlements rather than dramatic growth in the old centers. While the suburbs kept pace with Boston's growth rate, it was the *kind* of growth, more than the numbers, that made a difference.

Throughout the Jacksonian period, suburban economic growth had two engines: farming aimed at the city market and small, city-oriented, craft-based industry. The outlines were as follows: agriculture itself moved steadily outward from the city, became specialized and labor-intensive. People in the inner suburbs took on the task of moving, selling, and processing agricultural products. A very few factories and a large number of shop industries expanded the realm of nonfarm employment.

The qualitative change in agriculture, barely hinted at by population statistics, was sharply evident in scenes along the highways. Men born in Middlesex County in the early nineteenth century, looking back in their old age, retained vivid memories of agricultural traffic, flowing incessantly along the main roads at all seasons of the year. In summer there were wagons and ox-carts piled with cheese, butter, produce, and wool, some driven by professional teamsters, some by the farmers themselves. At mealtimes, tavern yards as far north as Stoneham (9 miles from the city center) were white with canvas wagontops. Winter brought heavy teaming using sleds and pungs, stacked with beef, pork, grain, and kegs of cider.[34] From New Hampshire, Vermont, and the Connecticut Valley, drovers brought cattle and swine in many seasons, selling a few animals along the way, leaving some to be fattened in Sudbury and Concord, driving most to the Brighton cattle market just south of Cambridge.[35] By the late 1820s the pens at Brighton were receiving two to eight thousand animals every Monday, gathered from a flow that filled the roads for days in advance. The traffic distressed the country clergy, who protested "the noise and confusion of Autumnal Sabbath in Middlesex . . . the lowing of herds, the bleating of flocks, the resounding lash, and the drover's voice and whistle, discordantly mingled with the songs of the temple."[36]

Some of this movement was merely an expansion of volume within old grooves. In the New England interior, farming itself did not change until the coming of the railroad. Farmers clung to traditional implements, methods, and modes of distribution. Even the Middlesex Canal, offering a clear advantage over teaming for heavy loads, failed to change farmers' habits. Country people preferred the pleasures of tavern society and the security of personally superintending their goods.[37]

In a few areas within 20 miles of Boston, however, urban demand and improved access caused an extensive transformation of agriculture.[38] The two most dramatic changes were in the supply of milk and produce. In the past, Boston's milk came from household cows or from herds just outside the city (as in Milk Row in Charlestown). Only storable dairy products such as cheese and butter traveled more than a mile or two from producer to consumer. Improved roads pushed dairying outward. Lexington farmers in particular specialized in milk and by the 1830s had instituted daily delivery to Boston. In several towns, fresh milk supplanted cheese as the principal dairy product by 1840.[39]

At the same time, farmers to the west and northwest devoted themselves to vegetables. During the 1820s and 1830s, farmers began transporting their freshest wares to the city in wagons or on horseback almost every morning. Cultivation became intensive; draining, irrigation, manures, hired labor, and even some tenant farming became elements of West Cambridge agriculture by 1840.[40] New market facilities added regularity to the Boston end of the trade in the 1820s, and after 1835 the availability of cheap ice harvested from Middlesex ponds further stimulated the quest for freshness.

Production for the city brought radical changes in the farmer's way of life. Even with the old framework of irregular delivery, members of farm families found themselves devoting more time to predawn trips to the city. The son of a Concord farmer recalled "riding down in the night on top of the load of farm-produce, potatoes, eggs, butter—passing Harvard College in the dimness of the early morning, the great silent buildings . . . staring blankly in the fading moonlight at the sleepy farmer's boy."[41] Daily delivery pushed such trips well back into darkness. By the 1830s Lexington and West Cambridge residents were rising between midnight and 2:00 A.M. in order to reach Boston customers with milk or produce by dawn.[42]

The pressures of such schedules led to increasing use of middlemen to carry out delivery and sale. A host of specialized brokers appeared. True milkmen, who owned no herds but collected milk and sold it on fixed routes, were ranging outward from Lexington through Boston, Charlestown, Cambridge, and Medford during the 1820s and 1830s. In the same period, other Lexington and West Cambridge residents made daily rounds selling fresh cornmeal and meat.[43]

The reorganization of agricultural supply also changed land use. While land values in Lexington and West Cambridge soared, and farmers strove to reclaim waste, some older farmland on the Charlestown mainland and in Cambridge fell gradually out of use. The Milk Row district of mainland Charlestown, for example, was losing the basis of its eighteenth-century sobriquet: the outer suburbs enjoyed a competitive advantage of richer soil, which could not be overcome even with ample resources.[44]

Scattered small farms remained common in the inner suburbs in the 1840s, but commercial agriculture on any appreciable scale had disappeared. The one form of cultivation that expanded was horticulture, employing intensive method and scientific breeding, and conducted on relatively small plots of ground in Cambridge and Brighton.[45]

Instead, land near Boston furnished sites for agricultural marketing and processing facilities, which in turn became centers for related pursuits. The most famous of these was the Brighton Cattle Market, established as an outgrowth of army supply needs during the Revolution. By the early 1840s well over 130,000 animals per year changed hands every week. What began as a transient crossroads gathering had become a permanent institution, with pens, the Cattle Fair Hotel, erected in 1830, and across the street, the Brighton Bank.[46]

In 1837 the success of this main market led to the establishment of a second facility in northern Cambridge. Zacariah Porter, who had lived in Brighton and probably had experience in cattle dealing there, moved to Cambridge and joined with two partners in a development based directly on the Brighton pattern. Their market intercepted the main northwestern route of the drovers toward Brighton, at a point directly accessible to Boston via the Middlesex Turnpike. Purchasing a 17-acre lot, they built pens and a large hotel. By the 1840s, this establishment had attracted the same assortment of stables, wheelwrights, blacksmiths, and tanners that had long clustered around the older market to the south.[47] Also linked with the cattle markets in Brighton and northern Cambridge were butchers, meat packers, coopers, and chandlers. During the 1820s, all of these pursuits expanded and central- ized in the inner suburbs. By 1830 the largest slaughterhouse in Massachu- setts was in East Cambridge, drawing its supply of animals from the two markets to the west.[48]

These changes in the suburbs were related to a fundamental transforma- tion in Boston itself—a long movement toward stable, regulated channels of food supply. For more than a century Bostonians had debated the issue of a permanent central markethouse. Country producers feared regulations and preferred to seek higher returns through itinerant peddling or through jock- eying for position and haggling in the open air. Even Faneuil Hall, a gift to the city from Peter Faneuil in 1742, was hotly opposed at the time of con- struction, approved only with the proviso that no restrictions would be placed on itinerant sales, and periodically closed by town meeting votes for years afterward. Farmers and the poor remained suspicious of a market con- trolled by the city's elite. Moreover, with cattle grazing on the Common and gardens thriving in the South End, Bostonians were only partly dependent on regular outside supply.[49]

After the Revolution, however, conditions changed. The Charles River bridges increased the flow of vendors from the country and enhanced the val- ue of a fixed stall location in a market. The town and the market authorities imposed a series of increasingly stiff regulations on the use of all markets: as- signing spaces to each commodity, prohibiting infringements of territory, regulating vehicular traffic, and attempting to control the "forestallers," who exploited crowding at the market by buying cheaply at the city's outskirts and selling dearly at its center.[50]

But the pressures of food supply continued to outrun piecemeal measures, and by 1820 the neighborhood of Fanueil Hall had become unmanageable— choked with vehicles, chronically littered with trash, garbage, and animal waste, and fraught with accidents and petty exploitation. Shortly after the town became a city in 1822, such conditions allowed Mayor Josiah Quincy to gain approval for an extensive redevelopment of the area, including wid- ening streets and building the Quincy market, a set of new facilities on filled land adjacent to Faneuil Hall, opened in 1826.[51] At the same time the city's population became more dependent on external sources for food. Although cows continued to graze on Boston Common down to 1830, a movement to enclose and landscape this area gathered strength from 1815 on. New residential and commercial developments spelled eventual doom for gardens throughout downtown Boston: a quick demise for the showpiece garden of Gardiner Greene on Pemberton Hill, a process of slow elimination for the vegetable plots in the South End.[52]

Expansion of the fixed markets and decline of home-grown supplies did not put an end to the older methods of obtaining food. Indeed, the spilling of Boston's population into newly filled and unsettled areas at the edges of the peninsula probably created even more opportunities for those who sold from horse-drawn wagons, door-to-door. Contemporaries noted that retail sales of food from small shops scattered throughout the city increased dramatically in the second quarter of the century.[53] From the suburban viewpoint it did not matter: fixed markets and scattered vendors were all part of the overall reorganization of Boston's relationship to the hinterland, and all offered new opportunities to suburbanites.

Changes in agriculture interlocked with an expansion of manufacturing, which also helped to remake the map of Middlesex settlement (see fig. 3). For the most part, manufacturing on the fringe meant artisan production, not large factories. Suburban industry produced kinds of work and places of work that had not existed in the eighteenth century. It did not, in the 1820s and 1830s, produce large, lasting concentrations of low-skilled wageworkers. The industrial sector of the fringe economy exemplified the stage of growth that Franklin Mendels calls "proto-industrialization," in which organization and markets exert more influence than factory production.[54]

In this period, for example, the inner suburbs did not share directly in the textile revolution or the transfer of Boston capital into factory production.[55] A few early spinning mills tapped Charles River water power at Watertown, Waltham, and Newton. These mills were miles upstream from the area here studied, and they were soon outclassed by the massive development along the Merrimack twenty miles to the north. By the early 1840s, the Lowell mills alone produced seventeen times as much cloth and employed eleven times as many people as those of Waltham, Watertown, and Newton combined.[56]

Near Boston the textile transformation appeared mostly in the form of minor affiliated industries. A Malden dye house, established in 1803, furnished a model for two other plants in Malden and one at Watertown. A new method bleachery at Waltham probably served as a pattern for one built on the Charlestown mainland about 1823. In West Cambridge, the Whittemore family built a card factory. Each of these establishments employed, in 1845,

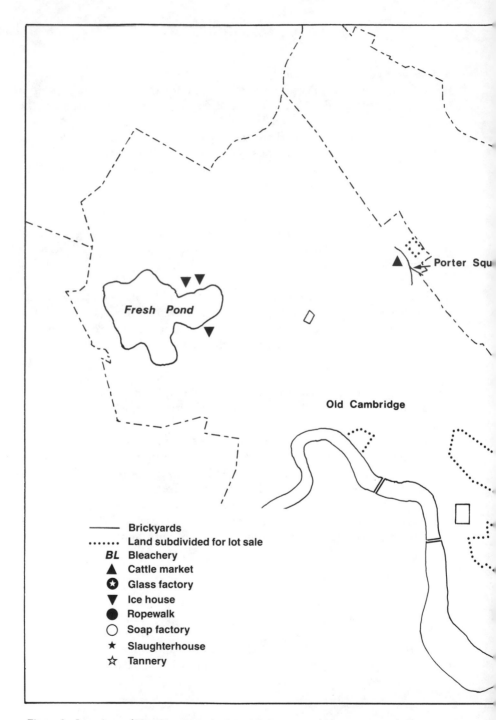

Figure 3   Locations of New Economic Activity, 1815–42

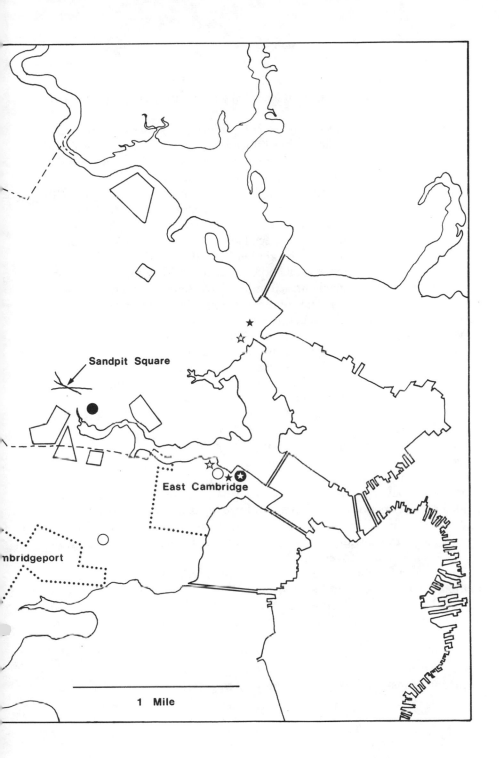

Sandpit Square

East Cambridge

Cambridgeport

1 Mile

between thirty and seventy people and produced a tiny community of workers' dwellings in its immediate vicinity.[57] They were hardly at the cutting edge of the factory revolution.

Boston capital also trickled into the inner suburban region to support three other islands of industry: the Medford shipyards, the ice-harvesting business at ponds in western Cambridge, and the East Cambridge glassworks. In the 1820s and 1830s, Medford shipbuilding became big business, but it did not involve factories or incorporation. Shipbuilding remained essentially a craft, controlled by entrepreneurs who lived and worked in the suburbs. Each of Medford's ten yards was the "shop" of a master builder, who took on a few apprentices and a great number of specialized artisans and workmen. Organized on this traditional basis, using timber floated down the Middlesex Canal, Medford yards dominated the industry. In 1845, they turned out more than a third of the tonnage launched in Massachusetts. Bostonians liked to think of these shipyards as a part of their commercial establishment, but the city merchants were really just consumers; mercantile capital was "invested" in Medford through orders placed by the Appletons, Perkinses, and Grays.[58]

The business of cutting and storing ice for export was another refined craft. Frederick Tudor, Boston merchant, established the overseas ice trade between 1805 and 1820. But his success depended heavily on the skills and labor of Middlesex residents. To oversee ice harvesting, he hired suburbanites who had already been cutting ice for their own use. In the suburbs, the business generated work in cutting, which involved large groups of unskilled workers under a foreman, and in transporting the product, which involved wagon trips to Boston. Dr. Benjamin Waterhouse, looking out his window on Old Cambridge Common in the spring of 1836, noted a stream of six-horse teams passing every half hour from dawn to dusk, pulling vehicles loaded with large blocks of ice. Some suburbanites combined work for Tudor with produce farming and ice sales to Boston market men.[59] On the whole, the ice trade made a few suburbanites rich, but it remained decentralized, seasonal, and relatively small in scale.

Only in East Cambridge were there large factories and a permanent population of wageworkers. In the 1820s and 1830s two more glass companies followed the one first lured by Craigie. By 1845 the three firms provided work for 241 people, placing them among the larger employers in the state. In East Cambridge the Boston-owned glassworks dominated the economy until the 1850s. But East Cambridge was not Lowell. Most of the glassmakers of the fringe era were proud, highly skilled Europeans, not New England farm girls or unskilled Irishmen. Moreover, the glass business could not compare in scale or resources with the textile firms of the same period. By the mid-1840s the three glass factories represented about $400,000 in invested capital—roughly the amount originally committed to the Waltham mills in 1813 and less than one-sixteenth the amount involved in the Lowell complex by 1845.[60]

Less visible than the shipyards, the ice gangs, and the glassworks, but more important for Cambridge and mainland Charlestown, was the proliferation of small manufactures in response to city demand. Ropemaking was the earliest example. Expelled from the city, ropewalks found a place on the fringe. By 1845 there were at least nine such operations in Cambridge and Charlestown, and Cambridge alone produced more cordage than Boston.[61]

Still more important were the fringe industries that came from the country. Tanning, chandlery, and brickmaking were all traditional slack-season pursuits of farmers. In the past, only small batches of output found their way to market in Boston.[62] Better access led to centralization and change in scale. Larger tanneries appeared in Cambridge and Charlestown, giving work to ten men or more and buying hides in bulk lots from the Brighton and Cambridge slaughterhouses.[63] Commercial soapmaking was traditionally a noxious pursuit that stigmatized its practitioners.[64] But on the fringe, smell became money. Animal by-products and waste from suburban abattoirs were transformed into products that cleansed the Bostonian and lighted his house. One of the first businesses in Cambridgeport, and the foundation of a family empire, was Nathaniel Livermore's soapworks, established in 1804. By 1840 a rival plant in East Cambridge was the largest soap factory in the United States, employing fifty men. Cambridge and Charlestown by 1845 made half the hard soap reported for the state.[65]

Medford and mainland Charlestown, blessed with extensive clay beds, had long been known as brickmaking centers. After 1815, a taste for brick in architecture led to an explosive growth of the industry, especially on the Charlestown mainland. By 1845 this area produced three times as many bricks as any other Middlesex community except Cambridge. And the five innermost suburbs—Charlestown, Cambridge, Malden, Medford, and West Cambridge—accounted for 99 percent of reported county output and 43 percent of the bricks made in the state.[66]

Brickmaking, more than any other pursuit, symbolized the replacement of agriculture by a fringe economy. As farming withdrew, younger members of farm families converted their land to bricks, stripping away the soil to open clay pits and drying yards. The change was dramatically illustrated by the fate of the Ten Hills Farm in Charlestown. In the 1830s it was owned by an enthusiastic gentleman farmer whose dairy cows won a national reputation. But he could not compete with Lexington's soil. In the 1840s he sold his prize herd and much of his land. On the shrunken remainder of the estate, his sons devoted themselves to making bricks.[67]

The brickyards left an indelible imprint on both the social and physical landscape. They were concentrated in three areas near transportation. One center lay on the Medford Turnpike. One straddled the Charlestown-Cambridge border south of Milk Row. The last, made accessible by the Concord Turnpike and later the railroad, was near Fresh Pond in western Cambridge. In each place the proprietors hired gangs of young, unskilled men, sometimes housed them in barracks, and swelled or shrank their number with seasonal work. New Hampshire men, farm boys from western Massachusetts, and Irish immigrants all took their turn in the yards. Insofar as the fringe produced a proletariat, it was most obvious here, in what a contemporary called "little mines of prosperity" for their owners. In many ways, bricks were more valuable than houses: the clay lands were held back from residential development until after the Civil War.[68]

Taken all together, fringe agriculture and industry produced a pattern of clustered development, an array of specialized villages in Boston's orbit. Farthest out were the areas of intensive dairy and produce farming in Lexington and West Cambridge and the industrial centers of Medford, Watertown, Waltham, and Newton. More diverse and more complex were the numerous centers in Charlestown and Cambridge.

The economic geography of this region is beyond precise description. Available statistics are crude and incomplete. The best data were gathered at the end of the period, when the railroad had already begun to influence the economy. Moreover, snapshot enumerations did not capture the pattern of seasonal and migratory work so vital to the fringe.

Yet it is clear that the changes outlined above produced extensive but subtle changes in the labor force. There were no decisive, large-scale shifts from agricultural to urban employment. A majority of those reporting occupations in the 1840 census for Cambridge and Charlestown were nonfarm workers.[69] But both places retained strong links with agriculture. If we omit areas that had never contained much farmland—the Charlestown seaport peninsula and the marshes of East Cambridge—we find 339 persons engaged in agriculture among the 1,887 listing occupations. Furthermore, farm and nonfarm work were mingled. Contemporary accounts make it clear that some of the brickmakers, soapboilers, teamsters, and provision dealers of these towns cultivated some crop as well. Those who were listed under the vague categories labeled "commerce" and "manufacturing" were often members of farming households.[70] The peripheral economy was neither urban nor rural, but hybrid.

Moreover, this fringe economy was really a collection of village economies, each different from others. The prevailing kinds of work, and the relation between farm and nonfarm sectors, varied with the subcommunities. In 1840, the dominance of manufacturing workers was greatest in East Cambridge, where they accounted for 82 percent of the reported occupations. An 1845 industrial survey indicated that most of these men worked in the glass, soap, and brush factories—steam-powered works which coordinated the activity of from twenty to two hundred apiece. Almost no one in East Cambridge worked the land full-time, and the crowding of 2,500 people into less than a square mile of area made this community almost as densely settled as the Charlestown peninsula. Its brick buildings, wharves, and smokestacks would surely have pleased Andrew Craigie and the other Boston Federalist founders.

The two outlying areas, mainland Charlestown and Old Cambridge, offered a sharp contrast. They contained no factories, no large buildings, and a population scattered over vast areas. Yet they were not traditional farming villages. Their economy involved specialized and labor-intensive production in both farming and the extractive industries, ice and bricks.

Cambridgeport, though it was not a port, had the most diversified economy in the area, based on shop industries and commerce. The bridge approaches were dotted with the taverns and stores planned by the founders. Along the river and the roads were lumber wharves, ropewalks, and soap and brush factories.

All of these places *looked* like villages of the past and the interior. Contemporary woodcuts capture a typical vignette: a junction of roads, with indistinct boundaries and deep ruts, a dusty square or common, a meetinghouse or two, some dwellings and shops, perhaps a tavern, a factory, or a bank. Each of the villages had fuzzy limits, as clustered settlement shaded off into waste and woods.

In part this was to be expected. The founders of Cambridgeport and East Cambridge, who had worked from eighteenth-century assumptions about trade, also anticipated communities on a nucleated village pattern. In 1800, Abiel Holmes, pastor of the First Church in Old Cambridge, had observed the building of the West Boston Bridge with keen interest and predicted the emergence of a "compact and populous" settlement at the bridgehead.[71] In ensuing years, new population centers in the outlying towns were described in language nearly identical to Holmes's account of early Cambridgeport.[72] Even in East Cambridge, the community of workers near the factories remained semirural in appearance—a collection of cottages and gardens near the crossroads at the bridge.[73]

This contemporary sense of physical separation was acknowledged by guidebooks and enshrined in village nicknames that lived on long afterward. The Charlestown peninsula contained not only the town center but "Mill Village" off the main road and "Neck Village" at the juncture with the mainland.[74] East Cambridge was more often called "The Point" or "Craigiesville," while Cambridgeport people distinguished their village from "Cambridge." Old Cambridge, whose inhabitants tended to chauvinism, spoke of Harvard Square as "The Village" or "Cambridge" and thought of Cambridgeport as merely "the village that unites Cambridge to Boston."[75]

Smaller communities, often lacking a definable center, were nevertheless regarded as distinct entities by neighboring residents. Thus the brickmaking community on the Cambridge-Charlestown line was variously known as "Sandpit Square" or "Brickyard Village," and the settlement near the Porter Square cattle market was called "the North Village."[76]

Throughout the region, residents linked themselves to roads and centers of work. Woburn came to contain an "East Village" and "South Village" as well as a "Center"; West Cambridge residents realigned themselves into north and south communities, along the two main roads, and a Watertown textile mill gave birth to "Tin Horn Village," named for the proprietor's manner of rousing his workers in the morning.[77]

Especially in these more remote places, the persistence of wasteland and country solitude reinforced the sense of discrete, semirural communities. In the summer of 1842 an English traveler was surprised to find "uncleared forest" at Boston's northern doorstep. One year later, a small boy on a hill in northern Malden was able to hear the rumble of traffic over Malden Bridge—5 miles to the south.[78] Even in the innermost suburbs, the upper windows of houses offered vistas miles in extent: from Charlestown, the hills of Waltham and Milton; from Old Cambridge, the golden dome of the State House in Boston. In 1834, when a mob from the capital burned the Ursuline Convent on the Charlestown mainland, the flames were clearly visible to those at street level in Cambridge.[79] The various villages of Charlestown and Cambridgeport were clearly separated by tracts of orchard and woods, pleasant to strolling adults and invested with superstitious meaning to venturesome children. Roving small boys, meeting their peers from the next village, defended the honor of their homes against taunts: "Pointer," "Port Chuck," or "Charlestown Pig."[80]

Beyond Cambridge and Charlestown, even the arrival of news was a leisurely matter. In many places the taverns still served as the primary information centers, and in towns on the post roads a few stores began to obtain occasional Boston newspapers. On extraordinary occasions such as the outbreak of war, at least one enterprising peddler loaded his cart with the Boston papers and traveled out through Charlestown, Malden, and South Reading, blowing a horn to attract customers.[81] By the 1830s there were two indigenous Middlesex weeklies: the *Bunker Hill Aurora* (established 1827) and the *Concord Whig* (1817). But these, like the Boston dailies, enjoyed only a limited and sporadic circulation through the mails, the stages, and the pockets of travelers.[82]

The scattered centers, the absence of dense settlement, the fuzziness of boundaries, the bucolic appearance of the landscape—all these bore a resemblance to the country. To many outside observers, the suburbs of this period seemed an economic backwater. Hardly anyone outside the fringe understood what had happened there since the late eighteenth century. Bostonians paid almost no attention: their diaries, letters, and newspapers almost never mentioned the adjacent towns. After an initial burst of investment in the bridges and in Craigie's East Cambridge venture, the most influential Bostonians abandoned the periphery. Between 1815 and the 1840s, they focused their attention elsewhere, promoting residential enclaves within the city or investing in manufactures and land distant from the city.

Even those few who did write about the suburbs, in guidebooks and official documents, revealed little comprehension of the fringe. On the one hand Boston observers viewed the inner suburbs as rustic and pastoral, presenting "a wide extent of country, with its innumerable villages and farm houses," or "a rich array of agricultural taste and beauty." On the other, recognizing fringe population growth and commercial activity, they vaguely extended Boston's hegemony, insisting that "the neighboring towns of Quincy, Dorchester, Milton, Roxbury, Brookline, Brighton, Watertown, Cambridge, Charlestown, Medford, Malden, and Chelsea . . . are component parts of the city, and are . . . associated with it in all its commercial, manufacturing, literary, and social relations and feelings." As late as the early 1840s, even the most astute Boston scholars, who knew that the periphery had somehow changed, could only describe that change in the crudest terms, lumping a few nearby municipalities into a category influenced by industry or Boston demand and leaving the rest under the heading "country towns." They ignored diversity within the towns and the complexity of relations between the city and the fringe.[83]

In fact the urban fringe was neither a backwater nor a component part of the city but a distinctive economic region. Its patterns of economic initiative, its importance as a locale for brokerage and processing of goods destined for the city, its centers of specialized, city-oriented industry were possible only within a short distance from Boston and only because of improved links with Boston. The evolution of the fringe in the early nineteenth century involved a basic shift to a more city-oriented economy, but a shift that strengthened and multiplied villages—small, mixed-activity population centers—rather than one that extended the dense settlement pattern of the city.

Moreover, by the 1830s fringe entrepreneurs and residents had accumulated several decades of experience with their version of urban growth. Most of that experience involved haphazard, unplanned, localized initiative. Of the four groups of entrepreneurs who played a role in this period, those with the biggest plans were the first to drop out. The Bostonian bridge builders and the Craigie group largely quit the scene before 1820. The most ambitious suburban developers, like Wellington, Dana, and Makepeace, often fell short of their goals or found success in ways they had not foreseen. Many turnpikes went broke; canal and port developments languished, but the villages prospered and grew. Their success had less to do with big visions than with small efforts by obscure people—land speculators, farm brokers, innkeepers, deliverymen, makers of soap and bricks.

Such a pattern of development had important implications for suburban social organization. The first surge of economic growth occurred without any guiding plan and produced an assortment of diverse villages in each suburb, but it also created a distinctive belt of economic activity intermediate between city and country. Social institutions and social interaction reinforced both the village-centeredness and the distinctive character of the region. By the 1830s, economic and social development compelled some suburbanites to begin thinking about what suburban towns had become and what they should be. Both kinds of fringe evolution—the basic shift toward a more urbanized economy and the strengthening of small, mixed-activity population centers—were enhanced by the development of social institutions and leadership groups in the village centers.

2

Village Building

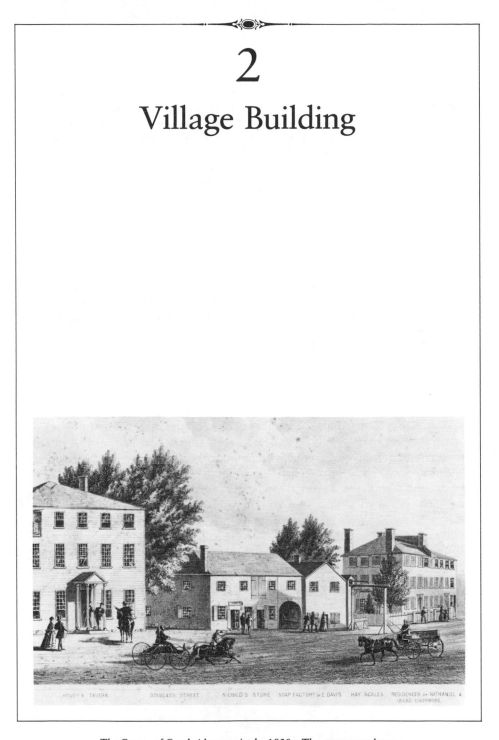

The Center of Cambridgeport in the 1820s. The structures shown
reflect the mingling of industry and agricultural brokerage on the fringe,
and the prominence of the Hoveys and Livermores.
Courtesy of the Cambridge Historical Commission.

I N THE 1820s and 1830s, only a few entrepreneurs could hope to see the broad outlines of regional change, and they saw them imperfectly. Most residents of the Boston periphery lived in much smaller settings. For them, the fringe economy was not an arena but a set of conditions: villages to live in, jobs to take, opportunities to seize. In each of the nascent villages they pursued what seemed to be narrow and traditional activities. They set up taverns, shops, and smithies. They founded churches, fire companies, markets, and banks. They nurtured local elites—small groups of dignified property holders with standing in the locality and careers in town office. In creating these village-centered social patterns they drew on old models and seemed to be reproducing little New England town centers all through the suburban "frontier."

But the resemblance was deceptive. Just as the fringe produced a distinctive economy and a unique body of entrepreneurial experience, so too it produced a distinctive path of social evolution. In the 1830s all of the fringe villages, and the towns that included them, were social entities different from those that had existed in 1800. They were unlike communities distant from the city, unlike neighborhoods within the city, unlike each other, and growing more different over time. For small communities away from the city, growth involved simpler changes and more distant forces. Rural towns contained an extensive hinterland oriented toward a common village center. Rural towns that changed into something else—a commercial center like Kingston, New York, or a milling and industrial center like Rochester—might differentiate internally, but they still stood at the center of a rural universe and depended much more heavily on links to that universe than did Cambridge and Somerville. External forces such as traffic from a canal, an absentee factory owner, or a stream of migrating people might transform such places. But such forces remained distant, in many ways outside the social life of the community.[1] On the fringe, by contrast, each town contained several close-set centers, no one center was dominant, residents of the hinterland around them were oriented in several directions at once, and the newest centers had little hinterland at all. In addition, all of the peripheral centers lived in the shadow of the much bigger center across the river. As the fringe diversified and more residents became economically and socially involved with the city, there was good reason to think the suburban towns had lost their integrity as communities.

On the other hand, the fringe villages were not urban neighborhoods. Cities of this period saw dramatic increases in density and the beginnings of spatial differentiation, as the rich, the workingmen, the blacks, and then the immigrants clustered in particular districts and established churches and other local institutions. City dwellers were accustomed to districts that were crowded with people and thick set with organizations, where the reference points were clear cut and the opportunities for friction were many. From the 1820s through the 1840s, many episodes of controversy and violence between whites and blacks and native and immigrant citizens centered on local institutions like taverns and churches or on territorial boundaries such as those between wards, municipalities, or the turfs of rival fire companies.[2] But the density gradient dropped off sharply outside the city core. The fringe also saw growth and differentiation, but it took the form of village proliferation within a large and lightly populated territory. Even in factory-based East Cambridge, the persistence of wasteland, water, gardens, and empty lots made density a relatively useless term until the late 1830s. Nowhere in the Jacksonian suburbs could residents define their communities in the ways that city dwellers did: by reference to a contiguous but alien population, a sharp boundary between land uses, or an area marked out by municipal authority.[3] By the same token, nowhere on the fringe did residents have to deal with problems of constant crowding and friction.

Too complex and multinucleated to be rural, too diffuse and vaguely defined to be urban, fringe society produced unique and unprecedented patterns of demographic change, social organization, and leadership. The experience of living in fringe society determined how suburbanites thought about their collective goals, how they responded to the city's expanding influence, and especially how they responded to mass transportation. Clearly, we need to know more about the growth and structure of these villages. What kinds of people lived there? Where did they come from? Who put down roots and who moved on? What did it mean to be a member of the community? Could the process of inclusion take in newcomers or transients? How did village residents form organizations and choose their leaders?

I will argue that, in the era before mass transportation, *before* the suburbs had much regular contact with the city, fringe society took on three attributes that strongly shaped the behavior of peripheral leaders and the nature of the evolving suburbs. First, the population became more diverse. Fringe village growth attracted several kinds of newcomers, some with interests linked to the country, some with experience and jobs in the city. Second, suburban social organization became more complex. A multicentered society produced overlapping patterns of membership. Many individuals belonged to more than one "community," and different groupings had different boundaries. Third, suburban leadership became more specialized and powerful. While village elites resembled those of the past, in fact, they placed new men in old positions. Unlike the leaders of eighteenth-century towns, the stewards of fringe society represented a broader range of interests, goals, and talents.

All these changes produced urbanism without density, uniformity, or large numbers of people. They also produced urban growth along a slower, more relaxed timetable than those imposed on big cities and industrial centers. Yet fringe growth was in its own way problematic. Suburban towns were fragmented, deprived of cohesion around a single center. Each village followed its own largely unpredictable path of development, laying the basis for conflicts of interest between the several centers. In some ways Boston threatened to absorb some villages and some suburbanites. Thus, beneath the superficial pattern of smooth growth and proliferating villages, fringe development created large problems of self-definition that would surface from the 1830s to the 1850s.

Village Demography

Demographic trends and local variations strongly shaped the social character of the antebellum suburbs. In the first four decades of the nineteenth century, villages were dominant. Village population changes, village institutions, and village-centered patterns of membership and leadership were the most important influences on suburban social life. For some, the community also involved broader ties of loyalty that transcended village centers. Only occasionally and for a few did community involve townwide loyalties or activities. Later, as the village centers were submerged in a general pattern of growth, their importance would decline. The institutional centers of social life would be scattered more evenly through a larger built-up area. Some suburbanites would refocus their community attachments toward tiny, cohesive residential districts. For some the municipal community and its subdivisions would become more important. For all, the outlines and ingredients of community in the 1850s would be different from those of the 1820s.

The basis of this pattern of social evolution lay in population shifts of the early nineteenth century. In the fringe period, uneven and unpredictable growth created very different conditions for community development in the several parts of the suburbs. Table 2.1 indicates the overall trends among the several communities here studied. The population of the whole Cambridge–mainland Charlestown area doubled between 1820 and 1840 and then tripled between 1840 and 1860. On the eve of the Civil War, more than 34,000 people lived in an area that had contained only about 4,000 in 1820.[4] But

Table 2.1

Village Population Growth, 1820–60
(noninstitutional population)

Period	Mainland Charlestown (Somerville)	Old Cambridge	Cambridgeport	East Cambridge
1820 Total	—[a]	1,296	1,360	384
Increase, 1820–30		414	728	1,533
Percent gain		32%	54%	399%
1830 Total	1,154	1,710	2,088	1,917
Increase, 1830–40	319	270	1,395	620
Percent gain	28%	14%	67%	34%
1840 Total	1,473	1,980	3,483	2,537
Increase, 1840–50	2,067	1,920	3,817	1,463
Percent gain	140%	97%	110%	58%
1850 Total	3,540	3,900[b]	7,300[b]	4,000[b]
Increase, 1850–60	4,485	2,487	5,272	3,101
Percent gain	127%	64%	72%	78%
1860 Total	8,025	6,387	12,572	7,101

SOURCE: Recompilation of manuscript census data. Omits McLean Asylum, Cambridge Jail, Cambridge Almshouse, Harvard College.

a. Charlestown data for 1820 are recorded in a peculiar way. Discrimination of mainland and peninsula proved impossible.

b. Estimates based on sample data.

there were huge discontinuities between villages, especially in the period 1815–40. Previously, newer centers were insignificant. After 1840, village growth patterns evened out and blended together.

For a whole generation, therefore, the villages were very different places. The western areas—mainland Charlestown and Old Cambridge—grew very slowly until 1840. With fewer than 2,000 persons apiece, these communities remained comparable to the towns of the country. Cambridgeport, on the other hand, quickly outgrew older communities. Already on a par with Old Cambridge by 1820, it continued to acquire more people each decade than it had in the decade preceding. By 1840, this one village in Cambridge was not only larger than its neighbors but more populous than most towns in the state.[5] East Cambridge, a tiny hamlet in 1820, caught up in ten years, but never quite matched Cambridgeport in simple population growth after that boom.

From the viewpoint of suburban residents, separate *paths* of growth were even more important than differential rates. In the fringe era, more than before or after, the villages differed in population structure, in degrees of population stability, in the relation between stable residents and transients, and in the kinds of people they attracted. The differences were not just a function of distance from the city, and the history of each village was not just a passage from rural to urban status. In these and other ways the growth of the fringe did not conform to standard notions of urban-rural demography.

Demographers have often held that rural areas are characterized by large proportions of children and old people, whereas city populations are swollen by people in their "productive" years; that urbanized populations contain more women than men and more single-person households; and that city populations are more transient, are affected by heavy in-migration of young adults, and probably feature a large number of households with boarders.[6]

Under fringe conditions, the alleged demographic symptoms of urban or rural status appeared in strange mixtures. Age profiles, household characteristics, and patterns of migration and stability all indicate that the fringe villages combined some features of long-settled farming towns with other traits characteristic of the newly settled frontier or the dense metropolis. The particular circumstances of each village, not its place along some simple rural-urban continuum, shaped its population.

The populations of western Cambridge and Charlestown, growing very slowly, settled on ancient family farms in the oldest village center and displayed some signs of rural "maturity." Here there were large proportions of old people, especially elderly women (fig. 4). In Old Cambridge there were

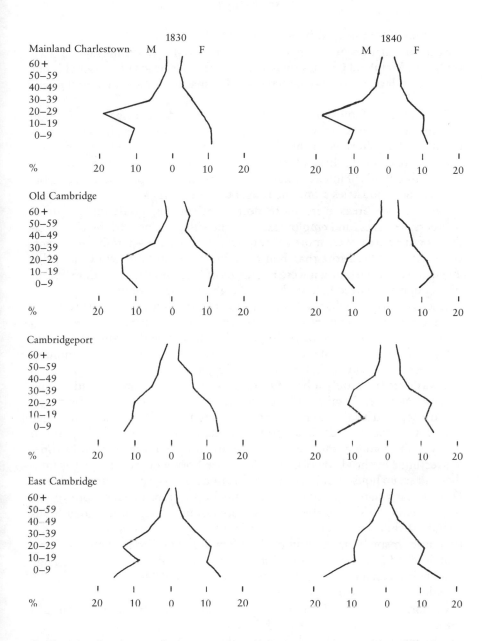

Figure 4   Age Profiles for Four Fringe Villages

many households headed by women (table 2.2), apparently the widows of farmers and artisans whose names had been linked with Cambridge for two centuries. Mainland Charlestown held fewer female heads of households but did exhibit the supposedly characteristic dominance of males in a rural population.

A closer inspection, however, reveals the impact of fringe urbanization even in these western communities. The decline of family farming was apparent in a striking shortage of children. About half the households of Old Cambridge were childless. Instead, these communities attracted young adults to fill the labor needs of intensive agriculture, ice and brick production, and the various shop industries along the routes to Boston. As a result, the sparsely settled western areas were more dominated by big households, full of boarders, servants, and employees, than the villages closer to the city. Residents of these areas were more likely to live in large units—families augmented by extra adults. More than half the adult males in both Old Cambridge and mainland Charlestown were not heads of households; more than a third of the population lived in households of eight or more people.

Just as the "rural" villages showed signs of urban influence, so the two new centers of Cambridge were oddly countrified. The evolution of East Cambridge resembled in some ways the growth of towns on the frontier, in some ways the factory towns of a later period.[7] It was in the beginning a community of young males living in large households, a tiny village where almost no one was over sixty, only a handful of households were female-headed, and factories attracted immigrant labor. Some of these traits of a rapidly growing, dense, industrial center persisted until the forties. But East Cambridge moved in some regards *away* from the classic urban-industrial pattern. Many of the young in-migrants to this community, both the skilled Europeans recruited by the glassworks and the native-born workers, arrived as families and set up housekeeping in a proliferating array of small frame cottages. From an early date, such households made East Cambridge far more youthful than either Boston or the suburbs more distant. Seven of ten households contained children under ten, and an increasing proportion of the population lived in small, apparently nuclear families. The "boardinghouse" pattern declined over time, so that East Cambridge came to have fewer large households than any other suburban community. By 1840, only two of every ten adult males were not household heads.

Cambridgeport, socially as well as economically, combined traits found in the other communities. By 1840, this largest and most rapidly growing community was four decades old. The founders and their spouses were now in their sixties and seventies, giving Cambridgeport a mature age profile. Even

Table 2.2

Population Characteristics of Four Fringe Communities, 1820–40

Characteristic	Mainland Charlestown[a]		Old Cambridge			Cambridgeport			East Cambridge		
	1830	1840	1820	1830	1840	1820	1830	1840	1820	1830	1840
Household composition											
Number of households	177	236	225	263	337	226	343	665	70	372	529
Percent female headed	7%	9%	31%	28%	22%	11%	15%	13%	13%	10%	10%
Number of adult males in population[b]	384	503	370	434	505	344	502	926	125	538	596
Male household heads as percent of adult males	46%	47%	42%	44%	52%	55%	58%	62%	35%	62%	79%
Percent of households containing children under 10	71%		48%	48%	56%	75%	65%	66%	80%	72%	72%
Household size Percent of all households containing											
1–4 people	36%	34%	41%	38%	41%	33%	34%	48%	39%	46%	47%
5–7 people	31	38	31	27	31	36	36	34	24	39	42
8 or more	34	28	28	35	28	31	29	18	37	14	11
Sex ratios											
Males per 1000 females	1250	1176	815	913	913	886	903	849	1043	1070	987

SOURCE: Data from the manuscript census schedules, recompiled by villages. Omits institutional population and a handful of black householders, for whom age data were not compatible with those available for the rest of the population.

a. Data for 1820 not available; see notes to table 2.1.

b. "Adult males" are those aged over 16 in 1820, those aged over 20 in 1830 and 1840.

in 1830, one household in ten in Cambridgeport contained three genera-tions—about the same proportion as in Old Cambridge, and far higher than in East Cambridge.[8] But Cambridgeport's sustained growth brought in large numbers of young adults, continuing the youthful bulge in its age profile. As in East Cambridge, many of these young people had children and established small households, increasing the proportion of adult males who were house-hold heads and reducing the prevalence of big, augmented units.

These differences between village populations were still further complicat-ed by patterns of growth and mobility. Rates of increase alone indicate heavy in-migration to all of these communities, and everything we know about oth-er places in this era would lead us to expect many departures as well.[9] But the flow of population, influenced by local conditions, was not everywhere the same.

Census records for the period before 1850 allow us to follow the move-ments of household heads, but not those of the whole population. Many pioneering studies of geographic mobility have therefore focused on later decades.[10] These post-1850 studies have all stressed the transience of nine-teenth-century populations and have discovered relatively uniform rates of turnover in a variety of settings and times. Yet many of these studies have employed crude rates of persistence for large aggregates of people, and most of them have dealt with populations affected by heavy foreign immigration, an accelerated shift to factory industry, and the increasing availability of lo-cal and long-distance mass transportation. A detailed examination of data stretching farther back in time suggests that, in an earlier period, population mobility varied enormously between localities.[11]

Overall persistence rates for the household heads of Cambridge and main-land Charlestown declined with population growth (table 2.3), so that by the 1850s they approximated the rates found in other places. But a finer break-down (table 2.4) reveals large differences between the several centers in the twenties and thirties. In the fringe period, the male householders of Old Cambridge were an extraordinarily stable group. Well over half of those present in 1820 and 1830 were still there ten years later. East Cambridge, on the other hand, was an unusually volatile community. In a pattern resem-bling that of new western towns later in the century, two-thirds of the house-holders vanished within ten years.[12] Cambridgeport and mainland Charles-town fell characteristically in between.

What explains these early differences? It might seem at first that they are artifacts of the data, data that are biased because they deal only with house-hold heads, omitting large numbers of young dependents. Other recent stud-

Table 2.3

Crude Persistence Rates for All Household Heads,
1820–50

(persisters as percent of initial total N)

Village	1820 (N)	1820–30	1820–40	1830 (N)	1830–40	1830–50	1840 (N)	1840–50
Mainland Charlestown	—	—	—	177	39%	17%	236	35%
Old Cambridge	225	46%	29%	263	49	27	337	51
Cambridgeport	226	50	25	339	41	27	662	37
East Cambridge	70	30	9	370	31	18	528	34
Cambridge Total	521	45	25	972	39	22	1,527	39

SOURCE: Linkage of manuscript census records. Omits blacks, for whom age categories were different in 1820 and 1830.

Table 2.4

Persistence by Age and Sex for Four Fringe Communities, 1830–50

	1830 (N)	1830–40	1840 (N)	1840–50
Mainland				
Charlestown				
M 50+	41	34%		
40–49	39	51		
30–39	45	44		
20–29	33	30		
Total	158	41%	215	34%
F 50+	15	*		
20–49	4	*		
Total	19	*		
Old Cambridge				
M 50+	56	54%	73	56%
40–49	48	60	74	60
30–39	55	73	72	44
20–29	30	33	43	50
Total	189	58	262	53
F 50+	52	25	45	49
20–49	22	27	30	33
Total	74	26	75	43
Cambridgeport				
M 50+	89	43%	127	32%
40–49	73	48	114	39
30–39	84	44	210	42
20–29	44	40	127	34
Total	290	44	578	37
F 50+	20	25	45	24
20–49	29	24	39	44
Total	49	24	84	33
East Cambridge				
M 50+	53	40%	74	39%
40–49	63	38	94	28
30–39	123	28	181	40
20–29	93	32	123	37
Total	332	33	472	37
F 50+	15	*	21	*
20–49	23	*	35	*
Total	38	*	56	*

SOURCE: Linkage of manuscript census records.
*Not significant.

ies have shown that young males were the most transient group in the population.[13] We cannot trace the movements of these people, and there were clearly more of them in Old Cambridge than in East Cambridge. Perhaps, therefore, the same high rates of turnover prevailed everywhere, but were hidden in Old Cambridge.

This was not the case. Even if *all* the "invisible" young males were as transient as those in East Cambridge, the overall rates of turnover for the villages would remain about the same, because the stability of Old Cambridge and the transience of East Cambridge were apparent at all ages.

These variations, then, were not statistical artifacts, but reflected real differences in village structure. The tendency to move or stay, for example, was clearly related to the size of households (table 2.5). In all four communities, men who headed large units were much more likely to persist, and large households were more common in the west. Moreover, in all four communities, those who stayed for ten years were likely to stay for twenty; in East Cambridge as in Old, more than half of those who had been resident for a decade would be there after another.

All of this evidence suggests that, for those over thirty, stability was a permanent condition, a putting-down-of-roots reflected in the gathering of a large household.[14] The western areas contained more people who had sunk those roots; East Cambridge contained few. Fragmentary evidence about employment supports this conclusion.[15] In the western areas and to some extent in Cambridgeport, the long-term residents were those who owned farms, taverns, or shops and housed their workers; who converted farmland to brick- and ice-making, surrounding the ponds and clay beds with barracks for their help; sometimes those who took in young workers as lodgers. In short, the persisters in these regions were those who ran the big households that were fundamental productive units in the economy.

So were they also in East Cambridge. The tavernkeepers, grocers, managers, and some skilled workers from the glassworks—these stayed for many years, built Greek revival houses that still adorn some East Cambridge streets, and assembled large households like their western neighbors. But in East Cambridge the most important unit of production was the factory, not the household. While more East Cambridge men were householders, few of them could make those households central points of the economy. Few of them could sink the kind of roots that were possible for a larger number in the west, and therefore, in the words of an East Cambridge resident of the twenties: "but few young men find it for their interest to remain here long."[16]

Transience was only one factor shaping village populations. The more transient new settlements were also the fastest growing. High turnover, rein-

Table 2.5

Persistence by Size of Household, 1830–40,
for White Male Household Heads

Size	Mainland Charlestown		Old Cambridge		Cambridgeport		East Cambridge	
	1830 (N)	1830–40	1830 (N)	1830–40	1830 (N)	1830–40	1830 (N)	1830–40
1–4 people	48	29%	51	47%	83	37%	142	28%
5–7 people	51	33	54	57	113	45	136	31
8 or more	59	58	83	65	93	48	52	56
Total	158	42%	188	58%	289	44%	330	33%

SOURCE: Linkage of manuscript census records.

Table 2.6

Stable Household Heads as Percent of All Household Heads
(white males only)

Village	1830 (N)	Present ≥ 10 years	≥ 20 years	1840 (N)	Present ≥ 10 years	≥ 20 years
Mainland Charlestown[a]	—	—	—	215	51%	14%
Old Cambridge	189	68%	30%	262	70	24
Cambridgeport	290	60	19	578	45	14
East Cambridge	330	37	2	472	46	14

SOURCE: Linkage of manuscript census records.
a. Calculations for 1830 are not possible without 1820 data.

forced by strong currents of in-migration, meant that the stable householders occupied a different role in the population of each village. As of 1830, two-thirds of the householders of Old Cambridge had either been there for ten years or would be for the next ten (table 2.6). But in East Cambridge, barely one-third had been or would be ten-year residents. The long-term residents of Cambridgeport did not bulk so large in the population as they did in Old Cambridge, but because the Port was the largest of the fringe villages, there were more such long-term householders—nearly two hundred in 1830—than in any other community.

In simple demographic terms, these four villages all represent variations on a theme enunciated by recent historians of other places. In each, there was a core of stable residents and a large body of transient people. Some scholars, finding this pattern characteristic of most towns in Jacksonian America, have suggested that the stable core *was* the community, that the rooted, long-term residents dominated local institutions through a kind of interlocking directorate, while a vast floating population swept constantly through the towns.[17]

But demography was not the sole determinant of community. The institutional structure and leadership patterns of the fringe drew in not only the stables, but some kinds of newcomers and transients. A simple, two-part model—established core and fluid mass—does not adequately describe early suburban society. Rather, village growth produced several levels and types of inclusion. To understand how these appeared and how they shaped the long-term development of the suburbs, it is necessary to retrace the formation of suburban social organizations in the sequence of their appearance.

Fringe Society and Leadership

The most basic units of fringe social organization were households, kin-groupings, and economic partnerships. All of these were influenced by early nineteenth-century population change. Between 1800 and the 1830s, the suburban villages came to include five overlapping but analytically distinct categories of people. There were first the old farmer-artisan families. As time passed they intermarried with a second group: prosperous fringe entrepreneurs, often migrants from the country, who pursued rural-linked occupations. A third group, very small but very important, included Boston merchants and professionals who bought suburban estate property. People from these categories, in various combinations, came to dominate the fringe elite.

In addition there were two other kinds of village residents, more numerous and obscure. The fringe economy attracted young opportunity-seekers—teamsters, innkeepers, building tradesmen—who were often transient and rarely chosen to leadership posts, but who joined various organizations and dealt actively in real estate. Finally there were the extreme transients. Every list of suburban residents, whether it be the census, the roster of a church, or the roll of taxpayers, contains names that never appear in any other record of the area. Many of these seem to have been casual workers, whose main influence on fringe society was their *lack* of influence. Throughout this period the fringe produced no organized or stable working class and very little class-based activity—no unions, no strikes, no indigenous riots. The lack of working-class activity was probably as important for the suburbs as its presence was for contemporary Boston and Charlestown or for the smaller and more densely settled industrial suburbs of Philadelphia. From the middle-class viewpoint, the first two generations of suburban life were trouble-free. When "trouble" threatened, it met a strong response.

Of these five kinds of suburbanites, the most visible were the first two, joined in large, intermarried households. Skimming local records, it would be easy to gain the impression that a few families ran the towns. The same names—Livermore, Hovey, Tufts—appear again and again. These names represented not only families but economic partnerships. Recreating on a tiny scale the patterns that had once dominated Atlantic trade and were beginning to link the seaboard economy with that of the interior, these family networks exerted a strong influence on suburban society. They stretched between and beyond the villages, into the country and into Boston. They promoted the "colonization" of Cambridgeport from Old Cambridge and of mainland Charlestown from the western farms. The combined efforts of these families, in villages that were essentially quite small, were so influential as to make them institutions of a sort—basic units of society. A few examples will illustrate the patterns.

By the 1820s and 1830s, the founders of Cambridgeport, many of whom were still active there, had produced a second generation reaching maturity. The Mason clan, so ubiquitously involved in the early partnerships with Dana, Makepeace, and others, was even more numerous in the third decade of Cambridgeport's history than in the first. In 1830, there were at least five related Mason households in Cambridge, containing 36 people, and owning among them a tavern, wharves in East Cambridge and Cambridgeport, shops, and many tracts of land held for speculation. If we include the men married by Josiah Mason's numerous daughters, the family contained five selectmen, a future alderman and a future mayor of Cambridge.[18]

The Masons were intermarried with the Livermores, whose family empire was smaller but farther reaching. Nathaniel Livermore, pioneer soapmaker of Cambridgeport, arrived from Waltham with his wife and children in 1804. One son, John, joined him in the business, and both grew wealthy making soap for the city. A second son, Isaac Livermore, built an even more successful career on Boston-suburban-hinterland linkages. Beginning as a clerk in a Cambridgeport dry goods store, he became a dealer in wool from the west and a heavy investor in suburban real estate. By the early 1840s he had taken a partner in Boston and his standing among the city's commission merchants was sufficient to make him a member of the building committee for the new Boston Merchant's Exchange in 1841. Richard Henry Dana, who was a contemporary of Isaac Livermore and who envied his success, captured the Cambridgeport entrepreneur's personality in a diary entry of 1847: "L. is a shrewd man, and rather inclined to management, but not dishonest."[19]

Also prominent among Cambridgeport gatekeepers were the Hoveys. Thomas Hovey (1740–1807) was the descendant of a long line of Middlesex farmers, artisans, and innkeepers. Four of his nine sons carried these old family occupations to Cambridgeport about 1799. They bought land on both sides of the causeway to the West Boston Bridge, erected a tavern and a provision store, opened a smithy, and cultivated a farm. The second generation further expanded the interlocking family businesses. Two of the sons opened a nursery, whose fruits had acquired a national reputation by the 1840s. Meanwhile, their cousin opened a bacon-curing plant, and another cousin provided a Boston outlet, securing a stall in the new Quincy Market from the time of its opening in 1826.[20] In the 1830s, Cambridgeport contained at least seven related households of Hoveys, and these held more young men who would rise to eminence in the 1840s and 1850s. Moreover, a

Mason married a Livermore, and a Livermore married a Hovey. All three families were prominently represented in Cambridgeport throughout the first six decades of the nineteenth century, and the chains of offspring, siblings, cousins, and in-laws flowed on into the twentieth.

By far the most varied and extensive kin network was that of the Tufts family of Medford, Cambridge, and Charlestown. Tufts University, in what was once western Charlestown, stands as a reminder of their land, wealth, and zeal. But in the nineteenth century they were known for brickmaking, agricultural processing, and the brokerage of nearly everything that passed from country to city. Peter Tufts of Milk Row was the eighteenth-century consolidator of large family tracts near the Medford-Charlestown line. His sons dispersed through the Charlestown peninsula and mainland, acquiring additional land at various locations. Two of them were among the early investors in the Charles River Bridge. Another became head of a large family of farmers on Winter Hill.[21] The eldest son moved to the peninsula and became a cordwainer, and *his* sons expanded the business into tanning, butchering, and oil processing. By the fourth generation, in the 1840s, Tufts entrepreneurs were among the wealthiest men in the county, combining all the old family trades with a mill at Charlestown Neck and grain dealing in the city. Some of these men built lavish homes on the mainland, invested in real estate, and turned some of their property to brickmaking.[22]

The career lines evident in the Livermore, Hovey, and Tufts families represent extremely successful examples of a process repeated in other families and in individual cases. Again and again, new suburban opportunities attracted the offspring of old Middlesex families or young men from the rural north and west. Individuals frequently took up several callings in different places. Younger brothers followed their pioneering elders to new locales, and marriage wove new webs of alliance. Some of these family stories encapsulate the history of the region. Eighteen-year-old David Sanborn walked from New Hampshire to Roxbury in 1813 and found work on a farm. Within a few years he moved to mainland Charlestown, became a dealer in milk, and married Hannah Adams Stone, descendant of five generations of Stones and Tuftses. In due course, David's younger brother Robert appeared from New Hampshire, married Hannah's sister, and the Sanborns inherited their father-in-law's farm at Sandpit Square. They made bricks where cows had grazed. In the 1840s and 1850s they and their children operated stores on the square, built houses, taught in the schools, and served as officers in the fledgling town of Somerville. Daniel, one of the sons, turned to surveying and attained national fame after the Civil War as producer of the Sanborn maps, which traced, in fine detail, the growth of America's cities and suburbs.[23]

Stable, numerous, and cooperative, these big, interlocking households showed how family enterprise and fortunate marriage might quickly blend newcomers with old residents to produce a powerful establishment. Yet it would be wrong to think of suburban society as merely a network of stable families or of suburban leadership as a kind of kin-based oligarchy. The influence of the big families was obvious, if only because they could field so many people in a relatively small arena. But there were also newcomers who enjoyed stature without large family enterprises and people who joined the community without becoming stable residents.

Throughout the early nineteenth century a few Bostonians, often semi-retired, followed the long tradition of suburban estates. In the outer suburbs wealthy men built a handful of true country seats. Harrison Gray Otis thought of buying "a box in the country for a summer residence" as early as 1797 and did so in Watertown in 1808. In 1836 the China merchant John P. Cushing laid out the most elaborate estate in the area on a site near the Otis property. With 120 acres and a staff of more than twenty, Cushing's Bellmont impressed even visiting Englishmen.[24]

In Cambridge and Charlestown, the Bostonian estates were less grand, but their owners were year-round residents who took an active part in developing the suburbs. Long Wharf merchant Benjamin Bigelow, for example, moved to Cambridgeport before 1810 and in 1818 bought the mansion and grounds of the Inman estate. His younger partner Isaiah Bangs, who married Bigelow's daughter and joined him in suburban land ventures, also followed his employer by moving to Cambridgeport a few years later. Both men became town officers and backers of suburban business.[25]

This mingling of old residents, successful country migrants, and semi-retired Bostonians had a strong impact on suburban patterns of membership and leadership. In the eighteenth century, rural New England society had been based on a few basic organizations and a small number of leaders: the parish and its committeemen, the church and its deacons, the town meeting and its selectmen, here and there a corporation and its directors. Most of the leaders were drawn from a small pool of prominent men who held multiple offices, served long terms, and generally acted as stewards of all town affairs.[26] Jeduthun Wellington, the turnpike promoter, exemplified this older pattern of leadership. The nineteenth-century fringe produced many churches, many local organizations, new kinds of corporations, and expanded town governments. These all resembled their predecessors, but were subtly altered in form and membership by new conditions and new people.

In the fringe era, the churches were central institutions of village development. They focused zeal in a period of strong doctrinal contention. They were expensive: church buildings were far larger and more costly than most houses, shops, or schools. They were inclusive: unlike every other organization, they took in women and children as well as men. All these conditions would change after 1840, when reform organizations and party politics assumed more importance in the suburbs, when municipal and commercial buildings grew larger, when many suburbanites were less village-oriented. But until the 1830s, the churches were uniquely important.

It was not surprising, therefore, that meetinghouses were among the first fruits of fringe prosperity. In 1800 there were three churches in all of Cambridge and Charlestown. By 1840 there were twenty-eight in Charlestown and twelve in Cambridge. Only a handful of towns in the state could boast so many spires, but then only a handful could claim the mixture of fervor, resources, and growing population found on the fringe.

In part, this proliferation of suburban churches simply reflected a regional process—the breakup of Congregational orthodoxy throughout New England. It happened that Charlestown and Cambridge harbored two of the most talented and stubborn defenders of the old order: Jedediah Morse (1761–1826) and Abiel Holmes (1763–1837), respectively. In each case their refusal to bend the ways of old churches encouraged the secession of new ones. Between 1800 and 1820 Morse lost parts of his flock in the formation of the Baptist, Universalist, Unitarian, and Methodist churches of Charlestown. And Holmes, having suffered some losses to the Unitarians and Baptists in Cambridgeport, was ultimately expelled from his own pulpit and forced to form a new orthodox congregation, the majority of the First Parish having gone over to Unitarianism.[27]

Such divisions were occurring everywhere. But most towns could not afford more than one or two meetinghouses and did not hold large numbers of each dissenting group. In rural communities the first quarter of the nineteenth century saw protracted battles over use of meetinghouses and town halls, ingenious time-sharing solutions, and sometimes too many heavily mortgaged churches.[28] On the fringe, however, rapid growth allowed sectarianism to reach logical conclusions.

For these reasons, the overall pattern of church building roughly followed that of population growth (fig. 5). An explosion in the teens and twenties was followed by a lull in the thirties and then a second wave of expansion from the forties onward. Church building reflected and reinforced the "backwardness" of mainland Charlestown and the early maturity of Cambridgeport. The west in general was institution-poor. With no churches until the 1840s, residents of mainland Charlestown and western Cambridge were forced to continue the rural custom of long walks to Sunday meeting, some-

Year	Mainland Charlestown (Somerville)	Old Cambridge	Cambridgeport	East Cambridge
1800				
			1807: Congregationalist	
1810				1813: Methodist
			1817: Baptist	
1820				
			1822: Universalist	1823: Universalist
			1826: bank	1827: Congregationalist
			1827: Evangelical	1827: Baptist
1830		1829: First Church schism		
		1832: bank		1831–37: bank
1840				
			1841: Methodist	
			1842: Evangelical	
	1844: Congregationalist	1844: Baptist	1842: Episcopalian	
	1845: Baptist		1846: Unitarian	
		1849: Catholic		
1850				
		1851: bank		
		1851: Congregationalist } North Cambridge		
		1852: Baptist	1852: Congregationalist	1853: bank
	1854: Universalist			
	1855: Methodist			
1860				
	1862: Episcopalian			

Figure 5 Chronology of Churches and Banks

times even into neighboring towns.[29] Church communities for them were huge, fuzzily defined areas.

Religious innovation and church founding centered in the new eastern villages. The issue of Unitarianism, for example, split the Old Cambridge church in 1829, but Unitarianism had long since taken hold in the Cambridgeport congregation, founded in 1807. That first Cambridgeport church was followed by gatherings of Methodists in East Cambridge in 1813 and of Baptists and Universalists in the Port in 1816 and 1821. Lest matters get too far out of hand, some Cambridgeport citizens invited Lyman Beecher to preach and launched a conservative reaction of Evangelical Congregationalists in 1826. All of these churches were thriving well before the Holmes affair reached its peak in 1829.[30]

But churchgoing was different from church building. Tradition and doctrine as well as demography shaped churches, influencing patterns of attendance and leadership. The new village churches, especially in Cambridgeport, attracted people along old routes, brought newcomers into traditional roles, and quickly elevated some newcomers to places of influence.

In the past, there had been two large fields of church attendance in the area, both determined by the ancient highways.[31] The northern field drew from the hilly parts of mainland Charlestown and centered on churches in Charlestown and Medford. The southern field drew from the Cambridge plain and the south slopes of mainland Charlestown and centered on Old Cambridge. The founding of new villages did not at first change these fields. Old churches continued to pull from a wide area. New congregations carved out sectors within the old territory: Cambridgeport dissenting churches drew from central and western Cambridge; East Cambridge attracted some people from the south part of mainland Charlestown.

Down into the 1830s, the structure of suburban society was strongly influenced by family connections to the First Church in Old Cambridge. Despite the hiving off of towns, parishes, and dissenters, the old church remained regional. In Old Cambridge itself, 60 percent of the 1820 household heads had been baptized, married, or owned the Covenant in the First Church.[32] Residents of western Charlestown continued to appear in the church records in the 1830s. The colonization of Cambridgeport, too, was reflected in links to the mother church. In 1820, one in five of all Cambridgeport householders, and 25 percent of those over 45, had either passed under the hand of the First Church minister or had brought children there for baptism. Some of these had come even after Cambridgeport became a separate parish. But East Cambridge and the eastern parts of Charlestown had slender connections to the old church. Only eight of the seventy East Cambridge householders left their names in First Church records, and only two of these had been baptized there.

Even if they no longer went to the First Church, many suburbanites of this era would still walk a long way to hear the Word rightly preached. Sectarian preferences, combined with the leadership of some widely married families, extended the reach of some new churches beyond their home villages. The Baptists, for example, were the first of the dissenting groups to organize formally as a church. The founding group included storekeepers and artisans from Old Cambridge and several of the Hoveys of Cambridgeport. They searched for land in a hostile environment and settled on a lot in the Port. But the first two deacons were from the old village, as were many of the congregation. In the late 1830s, about a third of the pews were purchased by Old Cambridge residents, including the two boxes held by Josiah Coolidge, who owned a large estate on Brattle Street, and the balcony pew of Addam Lewis, a black farmer from far northern Cambridge.[33]

The Universalists were more localized. With the support of the Mason family and one of the Charlestown Tuftses, they built a meetinghouse in lower Cambridgeport in 1822. Of the 34 men who incorporated the church, at least 27 were residents of that vicinity. But the congregation came from a wider area, and one of the first deacons was Samuel Watson, whose northern Cambridge farm was three miles from the church.[34] In a similar fashion, the Third Congregational church was organized by tradesmen in East Cambridge but chose Robert Vinal, of Sandpit Square on the Charlestown mainland, as its deacon.[35]

These attendance patterns were shrunken, specialized, but recognizable derivations of the old First Church model. The Cambridgeport churches, absorbing parts of the old territory, also pulled young people and newcomers into something like the traditional kinds of loyalty. Few old residents were involved in their establishment. Even among the mainstays—the Baptist pewholders, the Universalist incorporators—a majority were in their twenties and thirties, and a substantial number were not from families present at the preceding census. Yet despite the general tendency of young people to leave town, those who attached themselves to a church were more likely to stay: two-thirds of the known Baptists and Universalists remained for more than ten years. These were, then, new churches that took in new people, but settled many of them permanently into old-fashioned habits.

The same seems to have been true of those who were not mainstays, but merely members. Of all the new Cambridgeport churches, the First Evangelical Congregational church was the most volatile and the least connected to Old Cambridge society. It was in large part the creation of Dr. James P. Chaplin, M.D., who migrated to Cambridgeport from Groton in 1805 and practiced there until his death in 1828. Chaplin was a kind of neighborhood shepherd who took numerous patients into his household and offered his wagons to ferry neighbors to Sunday worship. He was an early convert to Lyman Beecher's Trinitarian revival in Boston and with the aid of family, patients, neighbors, and a fleet of vehicles, swept some of that enthusiasm into Cambridge. From meetings at his house came a church, a "first-born child of the great awakening in Boston," in 1827.[36]

The ministers of this congregation, being eager for conversions, kept extremely detailed records of their flock. Between 1827 and 1839, 64 men and 143 women joined the church. Of these, only 11 had any previous connection with a church in Cambridge, but 108 transferred from other churches outside the town. More than half of those who joined in this period transferred out again, usually to some other church far away. But amid this fluidity there were clear signs of a stabilizing process: 70 percent of those who left did so within nine years of their arrival; of those who remained for ten years 67 percent were members until they died.[37]

In East Cambridge, the churches could not gain such a stable following, even among those with powerful devotion. Eight people played leading roles in establishing the Methodists and a second Universalist church in the late 1810s and early 1820s. All of these founders were gone by 1830. The Second Baptist Church, set up by Bostonians as a mission to the factory workers, found transience a threat to its existence and survived only because of the dedication and donations of two East Cambridge tradesmen.[38]

The combination of long-distance drawing power with varying degrees of instability among the congregation produced strange patterns of leadership. In all the villages, a few men who served as deacons bore a heavy responsibility for long-term maintenance of the churches. The deacons were a curious group, whose main shared characteristic was respectability. Age, employment, ancestry, place of residence, place of work, or length of time in town were not necessarily important; practical ability, reliable behavior, and long-term commitment were the desired traits. For example, the First Parish in Old Cambridge, following its split with Abiel Holmes, chose two new deacons. The first was Abel Whitney, a cabinetmaker from western Massachusetts who settled on a farm near the future site of the cattle market in northern Cambridge, and the second was Sidney Willard, professor of Hebrew at Harvard and son of President Josiah Willard.[39] Altogether, twenty-seven men served as deacons of the churches in Cambridge between 1808 and 1842. At the time of election, they ranged in age from 25 to 70. Some had been born in Cambridge. At least two had been there less than five years. Some lived next to their churches; some lived miles away.[40]

In choosing these stewards of their congregations, suburban residents might rely on a young man's credentials or an old man's record, but they demanded both financial and social competence and took quite seriously the scriptural injunction that church deacons should be "men of good report, full of the Holy Ghost and wisdom."[41] Stephen T. Farwell, for example, migrated from Fitchburg to Old Cambridge when he was twenty-six, became a clerk in a store, joined the First Church, and almost immediately became a lay leader, first as superintendent of the Sunday school and then as deacon at the age of thirty-two. He was aided in this rapid progress by the reputation that preceded him: his father was a deacon in Fitchburg and his uncle a deacon in Cambridgeport, he had already performed church work in his native town, and he had been singled out from childhood as an exemplar of sobriety.[42] Sound business sense and gravity of demeanor were frequently mentioned as characteristics of the good deacon. In the village context the title was of great significance until well after the Civil War and was synonymous with integrity, good manners, and earnestness.[43] Those chosen to the office felt that acceptance was a weighty matter, not to be undertaken without a kind of semipublic soul-searching.[44] Once accepted, the office was a permanent responsibility. Of the 27 Cambridge deacons 22 held office until death. Of the five who resigned, three had served more than ten years.

The churches, then, were village-centered but drew some members from afar. They absorbed newcomers and raised a few to stature as deacons. While they reflected the differing stability of the villages, they seem to have been part of the stabilizing process that made some into long-term residents. For all these reasons, they chose leaders whose backgrounds were diverse, but whose reputations, behavior, and dedication were exemplary—men who not only led but embodied the long-term interests of the community.

The fire companies, outwardly so different from churches, were also a means of inclusion and elevation. In the fringe era, they functioned in a manner roughly analogous to that of the religious bodies, but they took in a different membership and their "modernization" was more obvious.

As in the case of the churches, there were traditional precedents. Volunteer engine companies had existed in Old Cambridge and in central Charlestown, as in many other towns, since the colonial era. Town governments and sometimes private corporations supplied the equipment and paid expenses; menfolk of the vicinity gave their labor. These organizations were partly utilitarian and partly aids to good fellowship. Their members were frequently young and given to raucous behavior. A company including many Harvard students was disbanded in 1822 after it flooded a college building, and an early West Cambridge company, made up of employees in the Whittemore card factory, drew wry comments from older citizens:

> They had meetings on the first Tuesday in every month, except in winter, about an hour before sunset, when they would race with the machine about the Common, and exercise its power in vain attempts to play over the vane of the meeting-house. Its members were thus excused from military duty.[45]

Cambridgeport produced a company along these lines in 1803, even before it had a church. The men of mainland Charlestown, after a failed attempt in 1831, secured one of the town's engines in 1838, and assembled a company based near Sandpit Square—the only organization to appear on the mainland before it became Somerville in 1842.[46]

But by the 1830s, the suburban fire companies were not altogether like those of the past. In some important respects, they had moved closer to an urban form of organization recently adopted in Boston. The old-fashioned fire societies were wholly inadequate to the demands of nineteenth-century city conflagrations. In 1825–26, after a lengthy battle with the forces of tradition, the reform mayor Josiah Quincy had succeeded in establishing a fire department. The city council abolished the volunteer companies and assumed control over the choice of engineers and firemen.[47]

In 1832, Cambridge took a step in the Boston direction, setting up a fire department under the selectmen, who were to appoint members and officers of the companies, and a Board of Fire Engineers to oversee the whole. In practice, however, the Cambridge fire department of the 1830s was a blend of old practices and new forms. It absorbed some old societies and encouraged new ones, so that by 1833 the town had six engine companies—two in each village—and a hook and ladder company in Cambridgeport. The members were unpaid, organized themselves on an essentially volunteer basis, elected their officers, and submitted their rolls to the selectmen for routine approval. Throughout the thirties, the selectmen accepted all the names put to them, confining their oversight to the appointment of the Board of Fire Engineers and the passage of numerous regulations prescribing care of the engines, prohibiting out-of-town excursions for competition with neighboring fire companies, and the like.[48]

Thus organized, the fire companies were ideally suited to the needs of young men who wished to gain a foothold in the community, and also took in some who were merely passing through. In 1835, the seven Cambridge companies contained 279 men. Almost all of these were in their twenties and thirties, and a few were in their teens. Three-fourths of them had not been heads of households in 1830, and more than half were not children of the 1830 householders. A small number were truly mysterious transients, whose names appear on the rolls for a year or two, never to be seen in any other record. In fact, very few people remained firemen for long: less than 20 of the 279 were still attached to the fire companies five years later.[49]

Yet most of these young men passing through the companies remained in the town. Like those who joined churches, firemen were more stable than their neighbors, more than half of them remaining for at least nine years. There were the usual village variations in the rates of persistence (between 40 and 50 percent for East Cambridge and the far northwest; about 60 percent for Old Cambridge and Cambridgeport), but in general, joining a fire company was likely to be a first step in joining the community.

It could also be a step toward leadership, but along a different path from that which led to becoming a deacon. The elected officers of the fire companies included new arrivals and established families—young Hoveys, Livermores, and Tuftses. When the selectmen annually chose the Board of Fire Engineers, they almost invariably picked men in their thirties who had recently been fire company officers.[50] Those who had been engineers were commonly called to more weighty office. Twelve of the thirty men who served as engineers from 1833 to 1840 were later chosen to be selectmen, aldermen, or city councillors of Cambridge. But of all the engineers, and all the 279 firemen of 1835, only three were ever in their lives made deacons of a church.

The Masons and the Odd Fellows served some of the same social functions and also provided another means of integrating promising newcomers to the communities. A Masonic Lodge was organized in Cambridgeport in 1805, and young Isaac Livermore, clerking in a dry goods store, made a point of joining soon after he came of age.[51] Twenty-four years later, at about the same age, future congressman Anson Burlingame arrived from frontier Michigan to study law at Harvard. He had joined the Odd Fellows while in Detroit and obtained a visiting card before leaving for the east. He presented his credentials to the Friendship Lodge in Cambridgeport almost immediately on arrival, and during his time as a student the Odd Fellows served as a key link in obtaining the speaking engagements that helped to launch his political career.[52]

In addition to these religious and fraternal-political organizations—and overlaid upon them—was a third kind of membership and leadership centering on economic institutions. Small towns of the eighteenth century had few organizations devoted solely to the business needs of the community. Unlike the churches and fire companies, the groups that sponsored markets and banks could not look to a continuous body of village tradition. Nevertheless, like the older societies, economic organizations of the fringe period evolved from simple models toward more complex, urbanized forms.

In 1812, hoping to profit from traffic over the new bridges, 34 Old Cambridge residents formed a partnership to build a markethouse. This group exemplified the first stage of the inclusion process.[53] It had strong roots in Old Cambridge society. All but one were associated with the First Church, and five were or would be among its deacons. Most were long-established and permanent residents. They averaged 47 years of age, and while 9 would die in the next ten years, only one would leave town. There were several tradesmen, a president and three professors of Harvard, a county judge, a registrar of deeds, and 11 past or future selectmen. But this assembly of notables also included several prosperous newcomers who had arrived within the preceding decade, some through marriage into the old families.

Like the churches and fire societies, this group was a model for slightly different organizations in later decades—the local banks. Until the mid-1820s, all financial transactions—loans, deposits, discounting paper—had to be carried out in Boston and on Boston's terms. Suburban shopkeepers, manufacturers, and landowners sought their own institutions, which they undertook not only as business ventures but also as aids to community independence.[54]

But starting a bank was a far more specialized, costly, and delicate task than organizing a church or a fire company. Any new bank required backers with strong personal reputations, capital, and some experience with finance. In the small, highly fluid villages of the fringe, finding the right combination was no small endeavor. Banking made strange bedfellows: promoters sought men who could concentrate the wealth and stature of their communities. Because few suburbanites had any extensive financial background, the handful of Boston-employed residents was crucial. While none of them were bankers, they did include merchants, brokers, and publishers who were acquainted with the workings of credit and exchange.[55]

Between 1825 and 1832 six banks appeared in the inner suburbs—three on the Charlestown peninsula and one in each Cambridge village. Only three of these survived the financial crisis of 1837–42. These three included one bank in Charlestown, the oldest of the lot, and those in Cambridgeport and Old Cambridge. Their success was directly related to their ability to gain a foothold in their immediate localities. The experience of the Cambridge banks illustrates the pattern.[56]

In 1826 the legislature chartered the Cambridge Bank, earliest outside central Charlestown, to locate in "the town of Cambridge, and village of Cambridgeport."[57] Like the First Baptist Church, this was a joint enterprise of the Old Cambridge–Cambridgeport elite. Among the twelve men who incorporated the bank and formed its first board of directors were five from Old Cambridge, three of whom had been founders of the markethouse fourteen years earlier. The expansion and diversification of that elite, and the prosperity of Cambridgeport, were reflected in the difference between markethouse and bank. The markethouse proprietors had required only the town's permission to use a parcel of the common lands and had purchased $10 shares to defray a total cost of $329.94 for construction *and* maintenance. The bank promoters obtained a state charter and raised $150,000 to capitalize their operation. The salary of their messenger alone was greater than the whole cost of the market.[58]

This was not a traditional partnership or even just a "country bank." But neither was it comparable to the big banks of Boston, whose capital ranged from $500,000 to $1,800,000.[59] The Cambridge Bank was not intended to rival Boston but to serve the interests of two suburban villages. Its founders were scrupulous in representing those interests. There were six incorporators, three from each center, and nine directors, three from the old village, six from the new. The guiding spirit and first president was Dr. James P. Chaplin, who was at the same time beginning to import Beecher's revival from Boston. But in banking, Chaplin was catholic: his associates included four deacons—Congregational, Unitarian, Baptist, and Evangelical—and a warden of the Episcopal church. Of the nine directors, three lived and worked in Old Cambridge, three in Cambridgeport, and three lived in the Port but worked in Boston.[60]

This first Cambridge bank dramatized the close relationship between Old Cambridge and Cambridgeport, the maturity of the younger center, and the growing importance of a few residents who worked in the city. It was an unequal partnership, with the Port dominant. It did not include any representatives of western Cambridge, mainland Charlestown, or East Cambridge. It joined the interests of the Harvard Square–Main Street tradesmen with those of a few veterans of Boston commerce. From the old village, the bank took the markethouse model; from Boston, the experience of a new element in the population; from Cambridgeport, a needed environment of economic growth.

In 1832, four of the five Old Cambridge partners in the bank split away to incorporate another in Harvard Square. The Charles River Bank thus completed the circle of colonization and recolonization between the villages. It brought to Old Cambridge many of the same traits that characterized the first bank: a varied but prestigious board of directors, a combination of long-established residents and very fresh arrivals (one resident for less than a year), and a merger of local business interests with the experience of a few who worked in Boston.[61]

Both of these ventures were successful: descendants of these banks do business in Cambridge today. East Cambridge, lacking a diverse group of stable leaders, could not duplicate the pattern. The Middlesex Bank, chartered in 1831, was a creature of the glass manufacturers and their nonresident Boston associates. Of the six incorporators, at least four were managers of the New England Glass Company and two were Bostonians who never lived in East Cambridge. The bank itself was an affiliate of David Henshaw's Commonwealth Bank in Boston. Middlesex bank president William Parmenter was an agent of the New England Glass Company and a rising Democratic politician. He made use of the bank, through questionable procedures, to advance his own interests and those of the glassworks while denying loans to other East Cambridge businessmen. Both his bank and the Commonwealth were among Andrew Jackson's "pets," and both failed in the crisis of 1837–38.[62] Thereafter East Cambridge had no other bank until 1853.

All of these fringe institutions were different from their antecedents and showed the effects of differential village growth and selective urbanization. The changes were subtle, undramatic, unplanned, and localized. There had been a multiplication and modification of traditional patterns rather than an introduction of radically new forms. But taken all together, these alterations had produced a new social landscape in the suburbs. More organizations, differentiated from each other, and shaped by village peculiarities, meant new modes of inclusion and new networks of leaders.

"Belonging," for example, was now a more complex matter than it had been. In the western parts of Cambridge and Charlestown there were few local organizations: no churches, no fraternal lodges, no banks; only the fire companies at Porter Square and Sandpit Square. In East Cambridge there were many more groups to join—more ways to be, at least for a while, a part of an organized local community. But the population was so transient, the economy so dominated by factory employment, and the influence of Boston-oriented manufacturers so large that East Cambridge organizations had only a small basis. A few energetic and devoted residents kept them going. Cambridgeport, with some help from Old Cambridge, produced the most stable, most diverse, and most innovative organizational structure. With strong links to the old village society, a mixed economy, four churches, a Masonic Lodge, and the region's first bank, the Port was clearly the most flourishing community of the 1830s. Here there were organizations that helped to root newcomers, that served some transients, and gave high standing to a few, whatever their background.

Yet even in Cambridgeport, and more so in other areas, the array of organizations could accommodate only a diminishing fraction of the population. Available records suggest that, once established, suburban organizations did not grow much larger during the 1830s. Making generous assumptions about church membership and assuming constant turnover at the known rates, we may estimate that all the churches of Cambridge could accommodate about 3,000 people during the decade, and the fire companies about 500 (table 2.7). But we can also estimate that nearly 6,000 adults lived in the town at some time during the decade. Especially in the Port, rapid growth provided the basis for healthy institutions, but it also provided ever larger numbers of those who were never included. Membership might take in all kinds of residents, in different ways and degrees, but many residents were never members at all.

At the other extreme of society, an oddly similar process occurred. The overall pool of suburban leaders became larger, richer, and more diverse. Inclusion on the basis of intermarriage, credentials, status, or needed talents brought in old residents, newcomers, and transients and a wide range of experience. But by the 1830s, there were many more leaders in one field who never led in another. The extent of specialization over the long term is indicated in figure 6, which shows the degree of overlap between Cambridge leadership categories on the basis of lifetime careers. In more than a century before the founding of the second parish in 1808, only 131 men held the most prestigious posts of the town. All but two of the deacons were selectmen as well. If we add the bankers, the 34 years from 1808 to 1842 produced almost as many leaders as the previous century. But in the nineteenth century, multiple office holders were a shrinking minority.

In the fringe period, there were some survivals from an earlier era. Jeduthun Wellington, the West Cambridge turnpike promoter and long-term town servant, was in his eighties, and his land was no longer in Cambridge. But he still presided over his farming empire, and his voice (as we will see in chap. 4) would be heard again in politics. Moreover, there were newer leaders who resembled their predecessors in a superficial way. Levi Farwell, for example, was deacon, selectman, and bank incorporator in Old Cambridge. Isaiah Bangs combined the same posts in Cambridgeport.

But Farwell was a new arrival and proprietor of a large store, and Bangs was a Boston Long-Wharf merchant. Each spoke for a set of interests that were not represented in eighteenth-century Cambridge. Their associates in

Table 2.7

Estimates of Institutional Capacity in Cambridge,
1830–40

Institution or Population Group	Number	Known or Estimated Initial Membership	Estimated Loss	Estimated Gain	Total Membership (Net + Loss + Gain)
Churches[a]	11	2,200	880	880	3,080
Fire companies[b]	7	231	208	208	439
Adult Population[c]					
Old Cambridge	—	959	384	544	1,503
Cambridgeport	—	1,068	534	1,449	2,517
East Cambridge	—	1,006	604	841	1,847
Total	—	3,003	1,522	2,834	5,867

a. Assuming 200 members each; 40% loss and 40% gain. Omits Harvard Chapel.

b. Assuming 90% turnover.

c. Adults = male + female aged 20 and over. Assumes losses of 40%, 50%, and 60% for Old Cambridge, Cambridgeport, and East Cambridge, respectively.

the new leadership pattern were still more clearly connected to modern concerns. There were "instant leaders" like Charles Coffin Little. Born in Maine, he came to Boston and found, at age twenty-two, a job as clerk in the bookselling firm of William Hilliard, long-time Old Cambridge resident, deacon of the First Church, and incorporator of the Cambridge Bank. In 1827, when he was twenty-eight, Little became a partner. Two years later he married Hilliard's daughter and bought a house in Old Cambridge. Within a year he helped to organize the Charles River Bank. Within six years he had been chosen both selectman and state representative. By 1847, when the Boston firm became Little, Brown, and Company, he was deeply involved in land speculation in Cambridge. In the 1850s he would be a major promoter of gas and water companies, railroads, and ultimately the streetcar.[63] There were even transient leaders, like Deming Jarves of East Cambridge, an incorporator of the New England Glass Company and manager of its works. Jarves served East Cambridge as assessor, selectman, and state representative even though he lived there for only five years.[64]

The days of Jeduthun Wellington, when there had been one church and one town center and a simple array of loyalties, when the same men prevailed in economic, religious, and political affairs, were over. Some suburban residents, watching the fragmentation of the old communities, thought the time had come to redraw the urban-rural boundary. The several villages were moving along different paths, and the long history of Massachusetts towns offered many precedents for such a situation. In the past, communities that grew different socially or economically had often become legally distinct as well. In the 1820s and 1830s some suburbanites looked to these precedents and suggested a new line between urban and rural territory. They advocated the separation of mainland Charlestown and of Old Cambridge as farming towns on their own and the annexation of eastern areas to Boston (see chaps. 4 and 7).

In the 1840s there was indeed a massive reorganization of suburban municipalities when mainlanders split off from Charlestown to incorporate Somerville and residents of Cambridge and the peninsula obtained city charters. Yet neither of these changes involved the simple city-country split envisaged by some a decade before. That kind of division was impossible, for two reasons: the first, implicit in the preceding chapters, was that an urban-rural line proved difficult to draw. City influences were already at work throughout the region. Only in the far western parts of mainland Charlestown and Old Cambridge could one find large tracts of farmland, and these held few people. Everywhere else—on the peninsula, near Sandpit Square, in

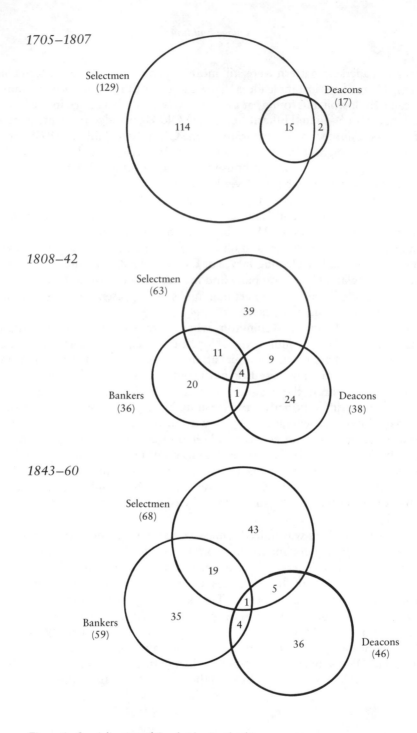

Figure 6 Specialization of Cambridge Leadership

all three villages of Cambridge—were many citizens for whom the farm town model was irrelevant. Their communities and their personal loyalties were neither urban nor rural but many-layered and diverse. Residents of each center had local loyalties, but they also had ties to other villages, to the traditions and commerce of the country, and to the city, where some found work. For the majority of suburbanites, separation of a rural sector was not the answer.

There was a second and more important reason for the failure of an urban-rural division. Fringe growth had not only fragmented and diversified the old peripheral towns, it had also set them apart as units from the city and the farming towns further out. In both directions, toward city and country, the economic and social boundaries were soon to be redrawn in a new and unprecedented fashion. From the mid-1830s to the mid-1850s, rapid changes in travel habits and government organization heightened the importance of the municipal communities as opposed to the villages. These changes came in three stages. The first, which had roots in fringe conditions, brought a revolution in mobility, opening regular, reliable contact with Boston to an important segment of the suburban population. With this change, and partly because of it, came a reconstruction of local government. Recognizing both the conditions of the fringe and the opportunities created by transportation, the men who created Somerville and citified Cambridge turned municipal corporations into tools of community enterprise, explicitly devoted to interests that were neither urban nor rural. The final stage, wholly unforeseen in the 1830s, brought the influence of a new constituency to bear on suburban society and suburban government, a constituency made up of those who worked in Boston, lived outside, and became dependent on public transportation. Small in numbers, but energetic and wealthy, the commuter bloc accelerated the reorganization and redefinition of peripheral towns into suburbs.

PART TWO

Walking & Riding

3

The Mobility Revolution Begins

VIEW OF THE NEW ATHENÆUM, AT CAMBRIDGE, MASS

Omnibus on Main Street, passing the Athenaeum,
in Cambridgeport, early 1850s.
Courtesy of the Boston Athenaeum.

AMONG fundamental changes in nineteenth-century urban life, the shift from walking to public transportation was at least as important as the spread of work in factories, and the two kinds of change were in many ways similar. The revolution in mobility, like the one in industrialization, did not begin with complex technology, did not occur all at once, and affected some places and some people far more quickly than others. Like industrialization, the mobility revolution accelerated and changed character in the late 1840s and 1850s, when urban mobility came to involve corporate organization, sophisticated equipment, and large numbers. Although relatively few people worked in factories before 1860, and relatively few rode omnibuses, trains, or horsecars, the organized activity of these few gradually changed the habits and expectations of the whole society.

Between the 1820s and the 1850s, the revolution in mobility changed the pattern of community building in the suburbs from one based on small, road-centered villages and irregular contact with the city to one based on continuous, predominantly residential settlement and routine daily movement through the metropolis. For residents of Jacksonian cities and towns, the significance of this change stretched far beyond the innovations in transport technology which have fascinated many historians. The overall change took place in every mode of travel from walking to commuter trains. It involved new possibilities as much as new devices: a lowering of barriers and costs to moving about; an increase in the variety and reliability of carriers; a new set of expectations about possible journeys; and ultimately a new vision of how the city would grow, how its parts would fit together.

Suburban residents experienced two aspects of this transformation of mobility that were uniquely related to their history and their location. First, they played a crucial role in beginning the change. Given their long experience as brokers, processors, and gateway entrepreneurs, suburbanites had a strong and continuous interest in better access to the city. By the 1830s they also had clout: fringe expansion gave them capital, talented leaders, and votes. Moreover, suburban residents saw a possibility that Bostonians were slow to recognize: the systematic development of land for commuter residence through a combination of public and private means. Until the mid-forties, peripheral residents, not Bostonians, led the way in promoting local transportation, changing their careers and habits to take advantage of it, and adapting local government to a new set of assumptions about future growth.

A second uniquely suburban aspect of the transformation was the rise of a commuter presence. Between 1830 and 1860 the mobility revolution reordered the population and interest groups of the suburbs. Of the original five groups, the smallest and newest contained the Boston merchants. This

84

group, grown larger, more diverse, and very different from its origins, would be dominant by 1860. Gradually the merchant stewards would become demanding commuters, slowly pushing aside the old farm families, the young opportunists, and ultimately the fringe entrepreneurs.

This chapter and the two that follow concern three elements of the mobility revolution: its beginning as a change in the habits, expectations, and apparatus of travel; its role in triggering a reformation of suburban government in the 1840s; and its maturation into mass commuting after 1845. The first stage in this process was a lowering of the barriers to regular movement between Boston and the suburbs. In 1820, any such travel required time, energy, money for tolls, and still more money if one used a vehicle.[1] The barrier of expense remained high until the 1850s, but by 1845, time and energy were no longer required. For those who could afford it, the realm of daily movement now reached far into Cambridge and mainland Charlestown. Because a small but significant number *could* afford it, the relationship between city and suburbs changed substantially.

The Walking and Riding City

The walking city of the early nineteenth century was actually several cities—with different boundaries for different purposes. Long before mass transportation appeared, many individuals were accustomed to occasional long trips, and a few were involved in routine travel. The shift from walking to riding was revolutionary because it combined distance and regularity. The exceptional trip became ordinary; the range of ordinary trips expanded. The initial pressure for removing these various limits of walking mobility arose from the fringe, and arose naturally from its economic and social interests.

When the errand was important and the time ample, walking could take early suburban residents over extensive territory. Farmers, shoemakers, and tanners from the far distant suburbs customarily brought their wares to Boston on foot. Country storekeepers acquired stock the same way. Down to the 1840s, churchgoers and women marketing or visiting commonly walked from Cambridge and Charlestown to the city. Special occasions produced uncommon efforts. Two young men of Woburn, attending a lecture series at Harvard, spent a term walking sixteen miles daily for the purpose.[2] Nathaniel Hawthorne, at Boston's Independence Day celebration in 1838, encountered whole families who had stretched the walking city to its limits:

> Late in the evening, during the fire-works, people are consulting how they are to get home,— many having long miles to walk: a father with

wife and children, saying it will be twelve o'clock before they reach home, the children being already tired to death.[3]

Extension of the city's economic reach also involved some people in regular trips. Suburban innkeepers of the 1820s and 1830s geared their business to the needs of professional teamsters and crack stage lines. Long-distance teaming brought huge vehicles, traveling in groups at announced intervals, taking goods on commission, and keeping to set timetables. The last stop on these trips was usually at some tavern in the suburbs where the drivers could rest and arrange their wares, and from which they might journey into Boston, complete their sales and return within a day. Along with the teamsters came the long-distance stagemen employed by highly competitive companies and straining to outdo their rivals in speed and regularity.[4] In the inner suburbs, transportation of farm produce, milk, bricks, sand, lumber, and eventually ice made work for short-haul teamsters, some of whom employed extra drivers and ran wagons in and out of Boston several times daily.[5]

Ordinary people, through energetic walking or for purposes of business, might thus expand the city when time and resources allowed. For a few members of the elite, who always had time and money, energetic walking and driving might expand it further and more consistently. Until the 1830s, stamina and a flexible schedule were as important as money. Ill-kept and unlighted roads were often impassable and sometimes unfindable, especially in darkness or bad weather. In the words of a contemporary, "people walked at night by faith."[6] The career of James Shuttleworth, India Wharf merchant and Cambridge resident in the early nineteenth century, illustrated the rigors of daily travel. With ships at sea, a business that centered on midday meetings with other merchants, and a servant to drive his carriage, he enjoyed maximum freedom of movement. Yet he once nearly died on the way home, losing his way in a storm, and once he had to abandon the trip for fear of being blown off the bridge.[7]

By the early 1830s, it was possible for a few people to pursue schedules that might daunt a modern commuter—but only a few, and only those who did not need much sleep. Josiah Quincy, leaving office as mayor of Boston in 1829, became president of Harvard. Living in Old Cambridge, he retained an office in Boston and went there almost every day. In order to do both Harvard's business and his own, Quincy rose at 4:00 A.M., finished off college affairs in the morning, drove his own chaise to the city about noon, and returned for dinner.[8] Elias Phinney, gentleman farmer, attorney, and clerk of the Middlesex County court in East Cambridge from 1831 to 1849, lived the whole time on his farm in Lexington. He drove the round trip every workday for eighteen years and claimed that his duties and his travel took from sixteen to twenty hours daily.[9]

Occasional exertions by the majority, business trips by a few, uncommon regimes for the elite marked out the boundaries of the pre–mass transportation city. All of these interests fed the process of change from the 1820s on. The first initiatives came into suburban efforts to shake off the burden of tolls at the bridges, beginning in Charlestown and spreading to Cambridge from 1823 to 1836.

Charlestown's experience with free bridges was immortalized in the Charles River Bridge case, which was nine years in litigation, involved famous men, produced Taney's landmark Supreme Court decision, and raised issues not settled for several years more. The Warren Free Bridge Corporation, chartered by the state in 1828, built and opened a toll-free span next to the original Charles River Bridge. During the ensuing legal battle, the old bridge went bankrupt, and the new one proved expensive to maintain. The state, seeking a general solution to the problem of bridge funding, finally compelled Charlestown to assume ownership and to provide a fund for repairs.[10]

In the beginning, however, this and other free bridge movements were not matters of constitutional law or state policy. They were manifestations of suburban enterprise. The campaign in Charlestown, which began in 1823, and one launched in Cambridge in 1836, both reflected the interests of the fringe. In each case, elite leaders using populist rhetoric whipped up support for an extension of the walking city. The initial Charlestown agitation sought to end tolls for pedestrians. Its backers consistently portrayed the struggle as one of workers and tradesmen against the rich proprietors of the Charles River Bridge. Even the governor, who opposed a free bridge, nevertheless offered concessions to "the laboring and business part of the community," suggesting that their plight might eventually be relieved by state support of the bridge, to be defrayed by a continued toll on pleasure vehicles.[11]

The advocates of the new bridge were hardly laboring men. Their leaders were all descendants and members of the Charlestown mercantile-trading elite. But their interests also required access to Boston, and they were backed by what a legislative committee called "a strong wish in the community for free avenues to the city."[12]

In Cambridge, the prime mover in a similar venture was the ubiquitous Isaac Livermore. Along with two other Cambridgeport land speculators, he formed the Hancock Free Bridge Corporation in 1836. Their movement simmered for ten years, restrained by a shortage of capital in the depression of 1837–42 and by the state's desire to avoid mistakes made in Charlestown, but in 1846 Livermore obtained a second charter authorizing his corporation to buy the two existing Cambridge bridges, to amass a maintenance fund from continued tolls, and then to surrender both bridges and fund to the state. This procedure took twelve more years, climaxing in a huge celebration in 1858.[13]

The Suburbs Discover Mass Transportation

Freeing the bridges was a long-term project, mounted by established citizens with a large and lasting interest in the collective prosperity of the fringe villages. As in the founding of banks, the leaders were businessmen of the Charlestown peninsula and Cambridgeport. Like the banks, the bridge movements involved a flexing of suburban muscle, using corporations and other forms of public authority to advance their interests vis-à-vis the city. It took them years to chip away the barrier of tolls, but they could afford to wait, and the *expectation* of free crossings helped to change the climate for other kinds of enterprise. By 1836 it was likely, by 1846 certain, that all the bridges would one day be free.

Even while tolls stayed high, another group of suburbanites reduced the barriers of time and energy, through the introduction of scheduled public vehicles—coaches, omnibuses, and commuter railroads. Each of these early mass carriers appeared because fringe residents bent long-distance transportation to serve their particular needs. In beginning this process, the young opportunists—men with a small stake seeking quick returns—led the way.

Taverners, stablers, and teamsters of the suburbs had long been acquainted with the overland stages. During an explosive growth of staging between 1800 and 1830, men of the suburban towns served the passengers, built the vehicles, repaired them, and sometimes owned shares in the stage companies. The larger suburbs had their own daily stage connections with Boston before 1820. The Old Cambridge line, a typical example, operated in a manner identical to that found in the longer runs: the driver stopped in front of a designated tavern at each end of the line and sounded a horn to summon passengers. A traveler might also book passage in advance, just as he could for overland runs, leaving his name at the local tavern, being picked up at its door in the morning and taken directly to any address in central Boston.[14]

In the mid-1820s, citizens of Roxbury, Charlestown, and Cambridge took the radical step of instituting coaches every other hour. The two main figures in beginning such "hourlies" on the north side of the river were both young opportunists of a semitransient variety. Alson Studley, a resident of the Neck Village trading community, arrived there as a young man in about 1825, but disappeared about 1840. Ebenezer Kimball, also a young migrant, ran a tavern in Cambridgeport, bought land, joined the fire company, purchased a pew in the First Baptist church, and invested in the northern Cambridge cattle market, but vanished before 1840.[15]

Both of these lines quickly found a pool of demand, bought more vehicles, hired extra drivers, and attracted rivals. By the early 1830s an assortment of vehicles ran into Boston from the three Cambridge villages and from Neck Village in Charlestown. That decade saw the introduction of omnibuses, the first vehicles designed specifically for local service. Early versions resembled elongated stage coaches, but featured a door at the rear and seats placed along the sides instead of crosswise. For the courageous, more seats were provided on the roof, bringing total capacity to about twenty. The first true omnibus in the United States was built from French plans and began service in New York in 1831. The first omnibus in New England appeared on the Old Cambridge–Boston run, making its maiden trip on Harvard's commencement day in 1834.[16]

From the mid-1830s until the coming of the streetcar in 1856, through good times and bad, coach and omnibus proprietors continuously expanded their operations. In 1840 the Charlestown omnibuses ran every 15 minutes, and 8 vehicles provided half-hour service to Old Cambridge and Cambridgeport. Equipment and routes changed hands rapidly among the semitransient proprietors, while competition and consolidation produced ever larger partnerships that carved up the suburban territory. Studley bought out most of the lines from Charlestown and East Cambridge. In 1849 three Cambridgeport men formed the Cambridge Stage Company, which acquired all the lines through the Port and the old village.[17]

Competition also reduced the cost of the ride. During the late 1830s and early 1840s all the omnibus proprietors offered fare reductions through the sale of tickets in package lots. In this "commutation" of fares they borrowed a device from the turnpikes and steamboats. Within a few years, railroad and streetcar companies carried the procedure to higher levels of refinement and introduced the word "commuter" to the language. But the omnibus firms laid the basis. With package tickets, the cost of a round trip dropped below 25 cents on all the routes in Charlestown and Cambridge.[18]

This was a booming business, but it had its limits—both as a business and as a system of transportation. Several of the proprietors, combining omnibus operations with taverns and stables, became prosperous men. A few used coaching as a springboard into the streetcar business.[19] But they were exceptions. Most of the omnibus owners were small-scale operators, who made money but never entered the circle of major suburban entrepreneurs or leaders. Of the thirteen men who owned coaches or omnibuses between 1831 and 1849, a majority were residents for less than ten years. Only one ever held a major office under town or city governments. Only one ever became a bank or corporation director, and none ever served as deacon of a church. Conversely, the largest suburban landowners and businessmen—like Livermore, C. C. Little, or the Hoveys—never engaged in the omnibus field.[20]

Moreover, the coach-omnibus network was inefficient, a patchwork of "lines" rather than a transportation system. Some of its flaws were obvious from the start, some became more serious with the growth of demand. Its management was unstable; it was expensive; it served only the most populous villages in the suburbs; and it encountered the same impediments as walking or private carriages: tolls, bad roads, weather, and traffic.

Given all these limitations, the omnibus could not replace walking or driving. In a sense it was an improved version of the private vehicle, a better mode of conveyance for well-to-do people on flexible schedules. The relationship between old and new carriers was evident in a Cambridge vignette of the 1830s. Throughout that decade, Josiah Quincy remained loyal to the old order, driving his chaise daily along the road to the city. Since he habitually rose at four, he frequently dozed at the reins on the way home, relying on his horse to follow the familiar path. This sight of Quincy's vehicle was not a welcome one to Cyrus Morse, coach and omnibus driver between Old Cambridge and Boston for more than thirty years. Morse was a man who cherished swift, safe, precise driving. For many Cambridge residents he symbolized the omnibus era. Years later they remembered his dignified presence and his team of six matched horses. Morse dared not complain to the Harvard president, but the meandering chaise continually tested his patience and his skill in avoiding an overturn. Frustrated, he turned to Quincy's servants, pleading in vain for their help in taking their master's driving out of his incompetent hands.[21]

By itself, the coach-omnibus network did not work a revolution in travel. Yet it did provide a regular means of mass access to Boston, and it demonstrated a substantial demand for the service. This pool of demand, so quickly seen and exploited by suburban opportunists, eventually became visible to the lofty Bostonians who backed the first railroads, but not until suburban residents forced them to look at it.

Railroads Discover the Suburbs

Trains, as first conceived, had little to do with the suburbs. Like the bridge and canal projects of the preceding generation, the first railroads were meant to be links to distant markets and resources. They were gigantic ventures, backed by the wealthiest and most powerful men of Boston, who devoted years to their vision of hinterland connections.

Four railroad lines, all aimed at remote goals, traversed the inner Middlesex suburbs. Only two of these actually passed through Cambridge and mainland Charlestown, but these communities were affected by the route choices and policies of all four. The Boston and Lowell, opened in 1835 as the first passenger railway in the state, joined Boston to the Merrimack Valley textile mills. It was, in E. C. Kirkland's words, "an adjunct to an existing industrial development."[22] The Boston and Worcester, opened in stages from 1834 onward, aimed first at the Connecticut River Valley and then at Albany and the West. After a delay during the nationwide depression, competing lines entered the fray. To the west, Fitchburg businessmen launched a rival to the Worcester, a railroad that would give their city its own "access to deep water."[23] The Fitchburg Railroad opened on a route through Cambridge and mainland Charlestown between 1843 and 1845. To the north, the Boston and Maine entered competition with the Lowell and finally obtained its own access to Boston in 1845.[24]

In the ten years between the opening of the Lowell and the arrival of the Maine, managers of all four railroads experienced a wholesale change in their thinking about local passengers. The men who built these lines had dreams of Vermont produce, Lowell fabrics, and New York wheat. They had no initial interest in local travelers. Yet between 1839 and 1845 they rebuilt their facilities to encourage suburban travelers, introduced specially designed and scheduled commuter trains, developed an array of commutation tickets, and plunged heavily into advertising and selling suburban house lots.

This change occurred for two reasons: first, the railroads immediately found an unexpected demand for passenger accommodation, especially in the suburbs. Second, the economic depression of 1837–42, which caught some companies with their lines half-built, gave peculiar importance to a nearby and obvious source of revenue. With their visions of distance temporarily clouded, railroad men had more reason to examine the experience of omnibuses and to bend to appeals from suburban customers.

Still, Bostonians were remarkably slow and stubborn in responding to suburban pressure. They knew from long observation of the turnpikes that their roads would have a selective impact on the areas they passed through. Outlying residents knew it, too: surveys and plans for the first railroads touched off struggles in the hinterland. Towns competed to be included on routes, and within towns, tradesmen in the village centers, who supported railways, vied with each other and with suspicious farmers, who saw the trains as a tool of Boston domination.[25]

But for the first railway entrepreneurs, benefits to country towns were a secondary consideration—an additional argument used to bolster their petitions for incorporation. They continued to resist local passenger demand for some time. The Lowell, for example, built its lines on a route which avoided existing population centers. Early trains ran straight through, without stopping from one end to the other, on a schedule suited to the needs of Bostonians having business at the mills. Engineers and managers of the railroad sought speed and proudly recorded improvements in their "time" for the nonstop run.[26]

But residents along the Lowell and every other railroad pressed for accommodation. From 1837 on, the Worcester received requests for season tickets at reduced rates. These petitions were rejected, since the managers did not wish to make "separate contracts with each regular customer."[27] The attitude of the early railroad entrepreneurs was evident in the opinions of Nathan Hale, leader of the group that promoted railroads in Boston from the 1820s on, publisher of the *Boston Daily Advertiser*, and president of the Boston & Worcester. Summarizing the achievements of Boston railroad enterprise down to the fall of 1839, he portrayed the new routes as "channels of intercourse between Boston and the interior country," whose most important effect would be felt when they reached even further inland, and when they made connection with the projected Cunard steamship line to Liverpool. Hale's consideration of passenger fares was governed by his orientation to long-haul traffic and his lasting assumption that "very few will get in or on the trains at Needham or Newton."[28]

Yet after 1837, demand appeared in ways that even Hale could not resist. In that year the Lowell established its first intermediate station, opening a makeshift office in a Woburn shoe store. Within two more years the manager had permanently altered the schedule to include regular stops for "way passengers." In 1839 the Eastern Railroad became the first Boston company to adopt season tickets. The first trains over the route of the Fitchburg, intended to carry ice from Fresh Pond in Cambridge, provoked calls for passenger service all along the line. Within a year the managers instituted all-passenger trains and began to make intermediate stops at the north Cambridge cattle market and the bleachery in Somerville.[29] And by the beginning of 1844 they frankly admitted changing their policy:

> The passenger business was deemed of little moment when our road was chartered, and no suitable provision has ever been made for it. But such numbers have desired and patronised regular trains, that the same have been adopted with success; and when proper depots and arrangements shall be made therefore, there is every reason to anticipate a very considerable gain from this source.[30]

Moreover, a small but increasing number of Hale's railroad associates were themselves suburbanites. James Hayward, who helped to plan the Lowell, the Maine, and other companies, moved to Cambridge about 1830. The aging promoter Royal Makepeace, still seeking opportunities after years of effort in Cambridgeport, was a member of Hale's original group of railroad agitators. In 1831, Isaac Livermore and Benjamin Bangs of Cambridgeport were among the early subscribers to the Worcester. Livermore also backed the Fitchburg. In 1843 Hale finally took a strong initiative toward the new market. Following the lead of other companies, he instituted an all-passenger "Newton Special" train, serving only suburban stations.[31]

Once they recognized a pool of demand, railroad men moved quickly to enlarge it. The Fitchburg promoters found new riders with every station they opened, and ticket sales outstripped their predictions even in the dead of winter. The lesson was not lost. In building the rest of their line they completely reversed the original railroad policy. Delaying their construction schedule, they deviated from the initially surveyed route in order to bring "facilities to important towns of business and travel." Their guide, as they expressed it in January 1845, was "a policy of running for dense population and business villages."[32]

Abandoning their resistance to "separate contracts," the railroad companies now borrowed and improved the device of commutation from the turnpikes, steamboats, and omnibus lines. When the Maine pushed through its extension to Boston in 1844–45, it adopted the entire panoply: suburban depots, special trains, and package and season tickets. Reading their reports, one would think they had invented local travel. They were proud of the "beneficial effects" their railroad conveyed:

> in the accommodations it affords to a large population who had heretofore been debarred from rail-road conveniences; in the increased value of property in the towns through which it passes, and the opportunity it affords to the crowded population of the north part of

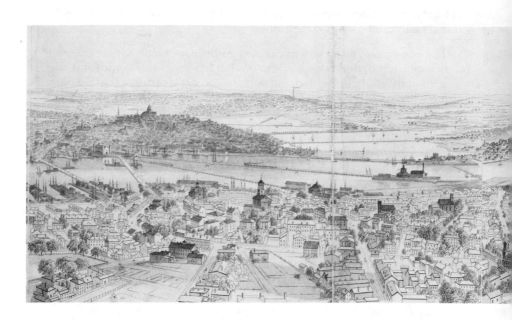

the city, to avail themselves of a conveyance into the country, where lands and buildings are cheap, in comparison with other sections of the country in the vicinity of Boston.[33]

Fittingly, the best chronicle of this change appeared within Nathan Hale's own family. His son Charles was two years old when the Worcester opened its first stretch of track.[34] Like many small boys, Charles enjoyed watching the trains, and he grew up with a suburban perspective on the railway. From the windows of his family's house near the tracks, he watched his father's railroad grow. Being the son of a newspaper publisher as well as a railway president, he decided to report what he saw. For five years, from his eighth to just after his fourteenth birthday, he issued 148 numbers of a handlettered newspaper, the "Rail-Road Journal of the Boston and Worcester R.R.," laboriously done in pencil on manila paper. Cribbing extensively from his father's *Daily Advertiser*, adding drawings, anecdotes, and comments of his own, he compiled a record of suburban service from 1839 to 1844.

Early numbers of the journal were filled with descriptions of long-distance trains. But in the 1840s Charles Hale's accounts, which undoubtedly drew on his father's conversation, contained more references to railway activities

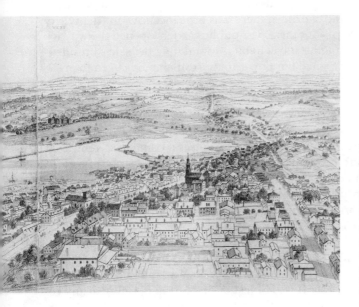

View of Boston, Cambridge, and Somerville from the Bunker Hill Monument in Charlestown, 1850. Note the extensive network of railroads and the scattered pattern of the suburban settlement.
Courtesy of the Boston Athenaeum.

affecting Newton. When the Newton Special appeared in the spring of 1843, he trumpeted its advantages to his home community. For months thereafter he gave emphasis to the special in his observations on schedules and equipment used, and he interviewed the train's conductor about "commutation tickets." In the spring of 1844 he noted the use of the special to sell house lots owned by the company. And in July of that year he succinctly described the commuter's daily regimen, which the Boston and Worcester now sought to encourage. Commenting on a change in the Newton Special timetable, he noted that:

> By this arrangement, persons residing out of town, & having business in the city are enabled to come in in the morning train at 7: Go out at 12 to dine: Return at 2; and go out to sleep at 5¼ or 7.[35]

The City of Occasional Riders

The omnibus and the railroad, shaped by suburban pressures, in turn shaped suburban habits and expectations. By themselves, the new facilities made only small changes in metropolitan society. They were too expensive and served too limited an area. At this period, too, before Irish immigration compounded Boston's land shortage, there was little incentive for many city residents to move outward. But these first public carriers opened the way for a revolution later, by changing travel habits, stimulating the sale of residential lots, and enlarging the small but powerful Boston-employed group in the suburban population.

Very quickly, coach and omnibus stretched the realm of occasional journeys. Package tickets, usable at any time, were suited to the needs of shoppers and men on business errands. In the early 1830s, observers spoke of the omnibus as a tool of such intermittent travel, not as a commuter vehicle. It was "the businessman's convenience and the man of pleasure's luxury."[36] Wealthy Bostonians used public transportation to extend their visits and vacations. The train, especially, became a new kind of pleasure carriage. Coach and railroad proprietors tried to spread this practice, encouraging middle-class summer outings to suburban hotels and cemeteries.[37]

But even for the elite, public carriers remained one of many options. Harvard faculty members like Henry W. Longfellow and John Gorham Palfrey were frequent guests at Boston dinner tables. The omnibus covered their route, but they often chose to walk. For less affluent people, riding in any vehicle still smacked of luxury. When George Ripley, merchant of Boston, arranged for his sister to come in from Newton for the opening of the new Quincy Market, the morning ride in the stage coach was clearly a special part of the occasion. Other suburban residents booked passage on the stage for unusual events and were impressed by the flourish with which "the horses, for city display, whisked up to the door." But even on major occasions, public coaches were too expensive for many. In 1843 a Malden farmer's son lost the chance to hear Daniel Webster speak at the dedication of the Bunker Hill Monument because his father could not afford the fifty-cent round trip fare.[38]

Nevertheless, the riding habit spread. A woman who grew up in Cambridge later recalled rides on the omnibus in 1842. Her fellow passengers—Harvard faculty and Cambridge businessmen—had already adopted the commuter custom of reading newspapers while they rode. Throughout the 1830s and 1840s, suburban residents viewed the increase in riding with fascination and distaste. Charlestown and even Old Cambridge were now increasingly visited by all kinds of city intruders—coaches, chaises, people on horseback—even on the Sabbath.[39]

In this changing environment of travel, a few suburban landowners began to divide old farms and estates into large house lots. These sales began in the mid-1830s, flagged during the depression years, and revived in the early 1840s. By the middle of that decade, residential subdivision had produced two clusters of new settlement near the omnibus and railroad lines. One of these, along the road between Old Cambridge and Cambridgeport, arose from the division of the Dana estate in the 1830s. Another, along the Fitchburg railroad in mainland Charlestown and northwestern Cambridge, appeared when several old farms were platted in the 1840s (see fig. 7).[40]

In addition to these systematic subdivisions, a number of small operators in Cambridgeport stepped up dealings in house lots. In peculiar alliances, Boston merchants, local tradesmen, and young opportunists began a kind of residential promotion that would shape suburban growth for decades to come. They built side streets off the main arteries, and petitioned the town for public maintenance. They pooled resources to buy land for long-term speculation. They persuaded town authorities to change the name of the old Concord turnpike to the more seductive "Broadway."[41]

These residential promoters were often new arrivals and fast movers. Francis Bowman, a typical example, arrived in Cambridgeport in the early 1830s. Within five years, while he was still under forty, he helped organize a movement to reform the Cambridge schools and joined Livermore in incorporating the Hancock Free Bridge. Within a few years more, he became a state senator, led the group that created the new town of Somerville, and served as a member of its first board of selectmen.[42]

True "commuting"—daily journeys from suburban residence to city work using public carriers—arose gradually out of irregular travel and suburban lot promotion. Before the mid 1840s there was no massive out-migration of transit riding Bostonians. Throughout the early nineteenth century the mercantile elite was notoriously citybound, venturing into the suburbs mainly for entertainment, retirement, or burial in Mount Auburn Cemetery (opened in 1831). Improved roads encouraged summer rentals of suburban farmhouses, and the very rich had their estates, but many Bostonians continued to think of peripheral residence as a kind of rustication—a cheaper expedient when one could not find or afford suitable housing in the city. Newly arrived or financially embarrassed people might live in the environs, but the city was the place for active and successful men. J. G. Palfrey, dean of Harvard's Divinity School, who had many friends in Old Cambridge, clearly regarded life amidst Boston society as the most desirable goal, and treated his Cambridge estate as a secondary alternative.[43]

Even those who wanted to live in the suburbs sometimes gave up in disgust. William J. Hubbard, a young Boston attorney, made an effort in the mid-1820s, when he married the daughter of James P. Chaplin, physician and bank president in Cambridgeport. On land acquired from his father-in-law, Hubbard built a home for his bride in 1827–28. But within three years he moved back into Boston, never to return, "for the sole reason that only twice a day was there any public conveyance by which he could reach his office, and if detained later than four o'clock P.M., must come home on foot or hire a public conveyance, costing not less than a dollar."[44]

Instead of true commuters, the suburbs gained what might be called "transitional" commuters—who could afford omnibus or railroads but were not transportation-dependent. Many owned vehicles; many walked in good weather. This expansion of the Boston-employed group of suburbanites drew in two kinds of men: previous suburban residents whose work arose from the fringe economy's city linkages and Bostonians who were well-to-do but not wealthy—wholesalers and other specialized merchants rather than shipowners or textile magnates.

In the 1830s, there was nothing dramatic about this change, either for society or for the individuals concerned. They were a tiny fraction of both the suburban population and the Boston work force. Moreover, for both kinds of Boston employees, entrance to "commuting" involved an extension of old practices. For previous suburban residents, going to work in the city was a part of fringe expansion, when those who processed farm goods opened outlets for selling them. For Bostonians, moving to nearby Cambridgeport continued a separation of home and workplace that had already begun within the city. The West End of Boston, at the city end of the bridge to Cambridge, had become fashionable in the 1820s. Observers noted that merchants were moving there, "not for the sake of business, but to get out of the way of it."[45] In the 1830s, this movement spilled over the bridge into Cambridge.

Yet the transitional commuters soon became a revolutionary force in the suburbs. They joined the interests and leadership patterns of fringe and city, mobilizing the resources of each in a way that would never quite be repeated. They worked in the city and carried city institutions to the suburbs. They were unusually active in suburban society. They owned enough land to allow speculation, and their holdings were geographically concentrated.

The unusual position of these early "commuters" is indicated in table 3.1. This table is based on a search of the 1841 *Boston Directory* for the names of all 1,527 white male suburban householders. It provides a minimum estimate of transitional commuting, since there were surely Boston workers omitted from the directory and new suburban residents omitted from the census. But given the cost of access to the city and the employing capacity of

Table 3.1

Characteristics of "Transitional" Commuters, 1840

Commuting population	Mainland Charlestown	Old Cambridge	Cambridgeport	East Cambridge	Total
Number of white male householders	215	262	578	472	1,527
Number of known Boston-employed	10	12	61	14	97
Boston-employed resident in same place in					
1830	—	2	18	2	22
1850	8	7	37	8	60
Occupations					
Dealers in Agricultural goods or derivative products	6	1	16	1	24
Specialized merchants	1	1	26	2	30
Professional-clerical	1	7	8	3	19
Other	1	2	8	5	16
No data	1	1	3	3	8
Tax data, 1840[a]					
Number owning real estate	N.A.	5	32	6	43
Number owning horse and carriage	N.A.	5	17	2	24

SOURCE: Linkage of Manuscript census records with *Boston Directory*.
a. Cambridge Tax Rolls (microfilm), Cambridge Public Library.

the suburbs, the total population of the Boston-employed was probably not much larger than the 97 here identified, nor very different in social status.[46]

The 97 known Boston workers were a new, young, but lasting element in the suburban population. In 1830, 75 percent had not been suburban householders, but 60 percent would still be there ten years later. Eighty percent were under 50; half in their twenties and thirties. They also represented a distinct part of the Boston work force. More than half were specialized merchants, who had succeeded an older generation of general traders as the mainstays of Boston commerce. These were people at the growing edge of the city's economy. Among them were a few Cambridgeport pioneers and their children: Isaac Livermore, whose wool business had become a basis for venture in railroads and Democratic politics; the Hoveys, whose nursery supplied their "agricultural warehouse and seed store" in Boston. There were also newer arrivals who dealt in commodities made in the suburbs—soap, oil, hides, brushes. Still others dealt in markets that were about to be transformed by the railroad: grain, dry goods, and hardware.[47]

These men were in several ways different from the semiretired merchants of the preceding suburban generation. Benjamin Bigelow had been fifty-three when he bought the Inman mansion twenty years before. The new settlers were less mature, less omnicompetent, and less rich. Even the biggest taxpayers in the 1840 group—Josiah Quincy and Isaac Livermore—were not as wealthy as the Brattle Street estate owners in Cambridge and not nearly as wealthy as the Boston elite of merchants and industrialists.[48] But the wealth of the 1840 Boston employees was concentrated. Two-thirds of the 97 lived in Cambridgeport and adjacent Old Cambridge. At least 20 of them owned big lots carved out of the old Dana estate between the two villages. Only 11 percent of the Cambridgeport householders were Boston-employed, but these men owned 25 percent of the assessed property in the village.

With energy, property, and talents, the new wave of Boston employees slipped easily into suburban leadership. In Cambridge, the 80-odd commuters furnished 22 long-term stewards: selectmen, deacons, bank directors. Ten more of the commuter group would eventually serve on the school committee or the city council.

In all of these respects—youth, stability, concentrated property, and active leadership—the transitional commuters differed from the majority of the suburban population *and* from a later generation of true commuters. They also shared two strong interests: a desire for better access to Boston and a taste for city amenities. Along with the land speculators and suburban tradesmen, and building on the achievements of the young opportunists, they worked to strengthen the city-suburban connection.

Indeed, by the late 1830s the relationship of city to suburbs had already changed. The free bridge advocates, omnibus proprietors, railroad constituents and developers, intermittent riders, and Boston workers all reshaped the interchange. So far, these boundary changes were uncoordinated, selective, and rudimentary, affecting a few areas and few people. The suburban villages remained distinct and different, still separated by physical obstacles and localized habits. Most Bostonians and most suburbanites had little regular interest in each other.

The full impact of the mobility revolution and the transformation of villages into suburbs came with two developments of the 1840s and 1850s. First, the various suburban interest groups joined to strengthen local governments, remaking them into agencies of an explicitly suburban, residential kind of growth. Second Irish immigration and crowding in Boston pushed large numbers of true commuters into many parts of the suburbs, making residential growth for a time the most important focus of suburban society and government.

4

New Model Communities

Home of G. G. Hubbard, commuter and suburban entrepreneur,
in Old Cambridge. Constructed in 1850.
Courtesy of the Alexander Graham Bell Association
for the Deaf, Washington, D.C.

N O SINGLE event marks the end of the fringe, or the beginning of modern suburbs. But a turning point of sorts came between 1841 and 1846, when residents of the Charlestown mainland split off to become Somerville, while Cambridge and the peninsula became cities. The reconstruction of suburban government brought together all the forces and interests that created the fringe and blurred the urban-rural boundary. Struggles over municipal forms compelled suburban interest groups to articulate their positions and to organize support in unprecedented ways. The outcome marked a victory for suburbanites with a conscious vision of the residential suburb.

The events themselves are famous for the wrong reasons. They are legendary parts of suburban local history. The separation of Somerville has been portrayed repeatedly as a revolt of farmers against the domination of city folk on the peninsula.[1] In Cambridge, the recollections of famous men have created the impression of a bucolic village around the old Common, struggling against the domination of the bustling commercial and industrial centers to the east.[2]

This chapter will argue that the new forms of suburban government, like the new facilities of transportation, were at the center of a longer process, in this case the "modernization" of government. Most twentieth-century Americans think of local government as a provider of services: schools, police and fire protection, street repairs, transportation, utilities, and a host of others—all generated and managed by "city hall." In the eighteenth and early nineteenth centuries, when fewer people lived in cities and cities offered less, local governments were far more important as tools of enterprise and mediators of conflict than as managers of a service empire. In New England, the word "town" did not call to mind a building full of functionaries; often it was not even connected with a particular building. Town officers served part time without pay, and their realm of activity merged into the sphere of private funding and action. In this context, the town was less a thing that governed than a reservoir of legal power, a body of land held in common, and a forum for resolving disputes. It shared responsibility with other local organizations, with the county, and with the state. In some ways the church and its deacons, the corporation and its directors had as much "governing" influence as the town.

The complex passage from this older kind of local government to the modern city occupied many decades.[3] In 1820 all the local governments of Massachusetts were legally towns, but Boston was well on the way to developing a city bureaucracy. In 1822 it adopted a representative city government. By the Civil War the Boston municipal establishment would have been familiar in outline to a modern observer: an imposing city hall, officials chosen through organized partisan battles, a large budget, and squadrons of salaried personnel who dispensed services.

The suburban governments followed their own peculiar path of modernization but did not arrive at Boston's result. The new governments of the 1840s were an intermediate step, a mixture of old and new: they were better able to provide services and set policy, but they were also created as improved tools of enterprise and stronger arbiters of conflict. Local officers, though they had more work, more power, more carefully defined duties, and sometimes new titles and salaries, continued to be stewards as much as managers. Until the late 1850s, informal procedures, "standing," and private authority remained keystones of suburban government.

This long-term perspective provides the only coherent explanation for the events of the 1840s. If we consider the whole period 1830–50, we do not find a conflict of farmers and city folk. We do not even find two consistent sides. Rather, we find suburban residents of various kinds in their first struggle with a lasting set of issues. They wanted governments that would aid improvements, but they also wanted governments that would remain small and cheap. They wanted governments that would be accessible to rival entrepreneurs, but they also wanted governments that would monitor the competition, setting an orderly course toward the future. They wanted governments that would be efficient, but they also wanted governments that would be informal, allowing a few men of standing—volunteer stewards—to order the affairs of the community. These goals were not easy to reconcile. In the attempt, suburbanites first bent town forms to meet the pressures of urbanization, then bent city institutions to fit town desires.

Village Government

The government of early nineteenth-century towns was in many ways a system of rituals. It involved uncodified laws and customs, unspoken relationships of deference and responsibility, unrecorded bargains and decisions. Resting at bottom on conversation, common knowledge, and tacit acceptance of rules, such a system was extremely flexible but ultimately fragile. In the long run it was undermined by several changes: too many people, a breakdown of deference, a need for precise accounting and specialized skills.

But the first pressures of fringe growth appeared in familiar forms, and suburban residents showed remarkable skill in adapting traditional institutions to meet them. Like most folk institutions, their ramshackle system of government offered built-in resilience: a *tradition* of tinkering and innovation, a long-standing practice of representing all areas and interests in choosing leaders, an assumption that men of standing would both cooperate and compete at the same time, and a strict devotion to procedures for handling and appealing arguments.

Theoretically, the town was a simple democratic organization, in which all important decisions were made in an open meeting of qualified voters and executed by officers elected for the purpose, especially the selectmen. Two hundred years of innovation produced a complex set of institutions within the town framework. Towns had wide latitude in choosing limitless numbers of standing and special committees. By 1800 some of these, such as the school committees and overseers of the poor, amounted to independent departments with authority to draw on the treasury and with a habit of reporting separately to the town meeting.[4]

Towns also possessed numerous options for coping with the dispersion of population. Funds for schools might be apportioned among districts, and by application to the state distant settlements might be incorporated as parishes to support their own churches. Each of these subjurisdictions could elect its own officers and conduct certain parts of the town business independently of the town meeting.[5]

In practice, the town apparatus did not provide either purely democratic control or a fully defined municipal administration. Rather, town authority might be used by whatever citizens were able to exert enough influence in town meetings. Depending on attendance, the granting of the town's favors might change from one meeting to the next, and unsuccessful applicants— like Craigie in his battle for Cambridge Street—might turn to other reservoirs of power, such as private incorporation, or seek redress through appeal to the county or the state.[6]

In keeping with these traditions, suburban towns absorbed the first pressures of fringe enterprise and population growth. Road-centered interest groups sought the aid of town and county in making their highways straighter and smoother. When several of the turnpikes proved financial disasters, their backers persuaded local authorities to shoulder the burden of maintenance. Even though the roads themselves were unprofitable, their investors sought to protect the value of related facilities—hotels, mills, landholdings—by keeping open the lines of access.[7]

New centers of population needed new schools, but this, too, was a familiar problem for which accepted solutions were at hand. To cope with scattered population, Charlestown and Cambridge created new school districts.

Both also shifted management of the schools from the selectmen to separately chosen boards. To cope with village diversity, they developed hybrid school systems. By 1830, the Charlestown peninsula and the three Cambridge village centers all had year-round primary and grammar schools. The Charlestown mainland and northwestern Cambridge still operated on the rural plan, with schools taught by women in summer and men in winter, and varying their schedules to suit local conditions.[8]

Conflicts, too, were handled in traditional ways. In the 1820s and 1830s, more churches, more villages, and more contact with Boston all led to strenuous arguments that drew in every suburban interest group. Three examples, each different but each calling forth a traditional response, were the Old Cambridge controversy over Reverend Abiel Holmes between 1827 and 1829; the townwide battle over enclosing the Cambridge Common (1829–32); and the anti-Catholic riot on the Charlestown mainland in 1834.

The disputes over Holmes and the Common illustrated methods of resolving and appealing internal disputes, methods that depended heavily on the leadership of the town stewards and on mutual acceptance of procedure. In the churches, eminent laymen usually played a crucial role in disciplining wayward members. An offender might be visited by pastor, deacons, or a committee of members. If he remained recalcitrant, the church might act as a body to excommunicate him or, as the Baptists put it, to "withdraw the hand of fellowship."[9]

In the Holmes dispute, the parishioners tried to turn this kind of group discipline against the minister himself. The central point at issue was the refusal of Holmes, then sixty-four and in the thirty-fifth year of his ministry in Cambridge, to invite Unitarians to preach from his pulpit. Ultimately he was dismissed, but he formed a new church, and the conflict ended after a bitter lawsuit over the title to church property. Yet the most interesting feature of the controversy was its length. A tiny group of people took two years to decide they could not agree. Moving with great formality and discretion, Holmes and his parish exhausted every means of reconciliation. Six times they repeated the sequence of protest, parish meeting, vote against Holmes, and rejection of the parish request. Each side clearly believed that, given time, the hand of God and the pressure of the community would bring the wayward to right thinking.[10]

In both scale and procedures, this was a village dispute—a private argument among a small number of the pillars of Old Cambridge society. The maximum number of votes cast in the parish meetings was 124. Most of the debate involved a dozen-odd householders around the Common. Close relatives took opposing sides, but their differences received little notice beyond the parish.[11] Within this small arena, however, everyone followed the rules. Long polite letters, memorials, and carefully ordered meetings were the framework. The leaders were men of unimpeachable character. For the dissidents, the main spokesman was Israel Porter, keeper of the most important tavern in Cambridge and director of the bank, who, at eighty-nine, had been a parishioner long before Holmes's arrival. Holmes's supporters countered with a remonstrance headed by Major Jonas Wyeth, owner of a large piece of western Cambridge, one year older than Holmes himself, and descendant of a family that had belonged to the First Church since 1645. In parish meetings where both sides appeared, there was consistent and unanimous agreement in choosing the same man for the essential post of moderator.[12]

Furthermore, before, during, and after the parochial controversy, participants on both sides were pursuing other local interests which sometimes brought them into alliance. Several of the leading figures in each faction were tradesmen in the Old Cambridge village, and some were among the proprietors of the markethouse built in Harvard Square in 1812–13. By the late 1820s the house was deemed an obstacle to traffic, and in March 1827 the proprietors named a committee to seek a new site. This body included both Holmes's most steadfast supporter and one of his main opponents. These two continued to work together in behalf of the market throughout their dispute over the church.[13]

In the civil arena, where problems might transcend a single organization or area, the same kinds of dispute-settling mechanisms were carried to a high degree of refinement. Guidance by the notables, strict adherence to rules, and long cycles of pressure, litigation, and appeal were the central ingredients in public conflicts as in parochial. The selectmen, as stewards of the whole town, played a key role. Cambridge and Charlestown, like most towns since the eighteenth century, sought to broaden the base of these leaders by allocating offices geographically. Charlestown habitually chose one of its selectmen from the mainland; Cambridge gradually chose men to represent all three villages.[14]

Obviously these mechanisms were delicate. Being informal and to some extent extralegal, they required mutual goodwill and roughly equal numbers on opposing sides. Throughout the 1820s and 1830s, this informal system produced a peculiar tension: town residents clung to the democratic meeting, where each group had a chance to bid for public sanction; but at the same time they worried about the ability of "the substantial citizens . . . to keep proper control."[15]

In normal times, town government involved a constant low level of disorder and a strong elite presence. The open meetings, in which all officers were elected and all major decisions made, were ill-attended, chaotic, and subject to domination by dissident groups. Even the annual election meetings, the most important gatherings of the year, attracted only a fraction of the voters. Those who did attend made the meetings social as well as civic occasions. An early nineteenth century Malden resident remembered that "Town Meeting commenced early in the morning and lasted all day . . . There was plenty going on. . . All sorts of games, everything else you can think of, were carried on during the time the meeting was in session, or while they were not doing anything. The people were outside."[16]

Underlying every aspect of town affairs was the possibility that some men or some groups might disobey the rules. In Cambridge and Charlestown moments of intense partisan or religious feeling, or of strong rivalry between villages, broke down the balance. By commandeering town meetings, or appeal to the county and state, a small group might acquire unusual power. For almost any reason discontented voters could reduce a town meeting to impotence. Often such factions arose from remote and underrepresented parts of a town and sought some redress of grievances. Knowing they could not muster enough votes in a large meeting, they descended unexpectedly and raucously on a small one. Those frustrated by town government sometimes turned to violence. Since the eighteenth century sabotage had been a common feature of struggles over roads and bridges, and it figured in the development of Cambridge and Charlestown.[17]

Yet until the 1830s such "breakdowns" were of no lasting consequence. They were an expected part of competition, and they were momentary even when grievances were strong. The town continued to be both an ally of competitors and a judge of the competition. In the suburbs, the peak of its success came in resolving a conflict between Old Cambridge and both of its eastern neighbors between 1829 and 1832. This affair began over the issue of whether to improve the Common, but it quickly ramified in ways that revealed the divergence of the three villages. By 1830 it involved all the most influential men in town, and settlement efforts went far beyond the initial issue.[18]

In the early 1820s, following trends elsewhere, some of the landowners near the Common began a movement to fence it in, converting a dusty waste into a landscaped public park. This was at first a cooperative venture among neighbors, who proposed to make the changes at their own expense. But they needed public authorization, since the Common was not only town land but a nexus of roads whose legal boundaries were unclear.[19]

The sponsors of enclosure were Old Cambridge notables: Deacon William Hilliard, tavernkeeper Israel Porter, attorney and poet Francis Dana (son of the judge), and Harvard College steward Stephen Higginson, who had already been active in landscaping and tree-planting projects within the Harvard Yard. These leaders sought support from their most prominent neighbors for their petition to the town: Higginson's small son Thomas Wentworth Higginson was dispatched to acquire the signature of seventy-five-year-old Benjamin Waterhouse, whose study windows opened onto the Common.[20] Finding the town meeting indifferent and being uncertain of their legal footing, the backers of enclosure won support from the state legislature. An act of 1830 authorized the work but required that the new boundaries of the enclosed Common and the roads around it should be laid out by two special commissioners. These were duly appointed by the governor in June 1830 and held hearings at Israel Porter's tavern early in August.[21]

At that point a storm broke over the project. The proposed plan for the improvement required small detours in the routes of two of the principal bridge approaches: the old Concord Turnpike and the "Craigie" road from Watertown to the bridge in East Cambridge. Landowners in both East Cambridge and Cambridgeport, having struggled for years to secure and maintain these routes and being accustomed to fight for the tiniest advantage of directness, raised vehement objections in identical petitions to the state commissioners. They were joined by Jeduthun Wellington of West Cambridge, who at eighty was still vigorously defending the turnpike he had promoted 27 years earlier.[22] When the commissioners authorized the improvement as planned, the conflict shifted to the Cambridge town meeting, where a movement to seek repeal of the act produced the largest town meeting in Cambridge history in the fall of 1830. But here too Old Cambridge was victorious, and strenuous arguments ended in two votes allowing the project to continue.[23]

Old Cambridge won the enclosure fight, but the new villages won in the long-term reconciliation. The controversy itself showed the way to a healing compromise. At the October meeting, angry citizens had filled the Old Cambridge meetinghouse to capacity. The November meeting, which decisively approved the enclosure of the Common, also considered a petition for a new town hall to be located in Cambridgeport. Resorting to traditional town procedure for mediating differences, this meeting named a nine-man committee, composed of three men from each village and including the most vehement supporters and opponents of enclosure. A favorable report by this body led to two more committees, one to develop plans and one to oversee construction. These committees were also balanced geographically, drew on both sides of the Common issue, and incorporated men of high standing in their respective communities.[24]

Having settled their differences, all three villages now joined to defend the enclosure of the Common in Old Cambridge. Jeduthun Wellington, who, of course, was not a party to the town hall deliberations, refused to give up his effort to preserve the Concord road. In the spring of 1831 he mounted a campaign for redress from the legislature, filing a petition signed by 107 supporters and timing it to coincide with petitions (which he probably helped to engineer) from the town meetings of West Cambridge, Watertown, Waltham, and Lexington. Wellington contended that enclosure forced travelers "to pass the said Common, in their travel to and from the city of Boston, by a circuitous route, considerably increasing the distance," and that their rights were "impaired, not . . . to subserve the interest of the public, but to gratify the taste for ornament of a few individuals."[25]

When the matter came up for consideration, he found that his former partners in road building had deserted him, and his movement encountered the powerful opposition of a united Cambridge. The committee that considered Wellington's proposal received a remonstrance from Israel Porter and 72 others, including most of the surviving promoters of the enclosure movement. But more tellingly, it also received a remonstrance containing 297 signatures gathered in Cambridgeport and East Cambridge and including many of the leading *opponents* of the initial enclosure attempt. These documents were backed by the Cambridge selectmen acting on instructions from the town meeting. And yet another remonstrance came from West Cambridge friends of the enclosure, who insisted that Wellington's forces had manipulated the town meeting there, gaining its support "by the importunities and management of a few individuals."[26]

In the face of such opposition, Wellington's appeals to state and county fell flat. By the end of 1832 the matter was settled: Wellington and the interests he represented had lost; Cambridgeport was henceforth to be the seat of the town hall and the center of Cambridge politics; and Benjamin Waterhouse could spend his declining years in pleased contemplation of "the handsome enclosed Common" now visible from his study.[27]

These events confirmed not only the strength of town government, but the new power of commercial and professional men in Cambridge villages. Once Wellington's kind of road-centered enterprise had been paramount on the Boston periphery. Now a different kind of improvement, centered on enclosed parks and public buildings, gained town approval. The shift reflected a change in population and leadership. All nine members of the "reconciliation" committee that considered the new town hall were men who had been born outside of Cambridge, had arrived there in the early years of the century, and had built careers on the basis of the emerging suburban economy. They included four storekeepers, two lawyers, one glass company official, one professor, and the Harvard steward who had been the main backer of Common enclosure. All were landowners, but none had ever been farmers.[28]

A final test of this modified town system, which revealed both its strengths and its weaknesses, came in the summer of 1834. An anti-Catholic crowd, drawing most of its members from Boston and Charlestown, burned the Ursuline Convent on the Charlestown mainland. This riot was in one sense a "city" event, a spillover of urban antipopery, but it happened in the suburbs and drew in suburban residents. One of the main agitators against the Catholics was a brickmaker and teamster who lived near the convent. The nuns and their students were rescued by local farmers, and suburban authorities were the first to cope with the event.[29]

In the most important sense, town government failed. At least two of Charlestown's selectmen were at the scene, but their personal appeals could not calm the crowd, and they balked at calling the militia. With the town's firemen conspicuous among the rioters, the convent burned to the ground. Efforts to identify offenders and affix blame foundered in a sea of conflicting testimony and general anti-Catholicism.[30]

From the viewpoint of middle-class suburbanites, however, town government responded in certain important ways. In reasserting public power, mobilizing right-thinking citizens, and, in general, closing the barn door, the local stewards did their ongoing job. Amid rumors that angry Catholics would take their revenge against Harvard College, Cambridge selectmen mounted a "patrol watch," stationed men at alarm bells, sent "criars [sic] through the streets" to call an indignation meeting (which duly condemned mobs), named a committee to seek a "military power" in Boston if needed, and authorized two of their number "to remain in session through the night."[31]

These were panicky actions, but they were based on normal procedures and led to permanent changes. The selectmen asserted their customary roles as stewards and spokesmen of the town. They used the town meeting to mobilize other leaders and to solidify and express majority opinion. They delegated tasks to committees. When the emergency ebbed away, some of the tightened apparatus remained. Within a month the selectmen, "at the request of the sheriff and many inhabitants," set up a regular "patrol watch" in East Cambridge, and hired official bellringers in each village. Thus Cambridge acquired its first municipal police and its first alarm system.[32]

111

The Limits of the Town

The First Church schism, the Common–road–town hall controversy, the convent riot, all illustrate the adaptation of traditional town institutions. But in the 1830s there were also three forces at work that would highlight the limits of the town system and create a strong constituency for change. These were, first, the rapid adoption of expensive city institutions by a coalition of Boston-oriented citizens and suburban landowners; second, the alienation of western residents, who paid for services benefitting the east; and finally, the frustration of some residents, especially the Boston-employed, who found town government disorganized and inefficient. These forces, acting in both Charlestown and Cambridge, produced the new governments of the 1840s.

These events should be viewed against the background of *successful* adaptation of town forms. They should also be seen in a larger context of regional and national events, which did not cause suburban changes but did, no doubt, influence their timing and nature. Between 1840 and 1845 many Americans enthusiastically took to new kinds of organized activity on an unprecedented scale. Emerging from their first national depression, merchants used the railroad to probe new markets. The "divorce" of corporate and governmental power, far advanced but not complete in the 1830s, opened the way for novel uses of the corporation. The two major political parties were now "mature" in Massachusetts and many other states, as they demonstrated in the election of 1840. A rough party balance in Massachusetts gave occasional influence to small, quickly organized, ad hoc, and splinter groups. In politics and out of it, reformers turned evangelistic energies and techniques—perfectionist ideology, mass meetings, petitions, national and regional coalitions—to reshaping the moral community.[33]

All of these developments had direct and indirect consequences in the suburbs. Among the Boston-employed suburbanites were people like Livermore, leaders in the process of railroad promotion and market redefinition. The whole effort to free the bridges and the battle over Cambridge Common versus the turnpikes were ingredients in the redefinition of corporate power. Cambridgeport became a hotbed of temperance and abolition excitement, the scene of mass meetings that drew reformers from the entire region. In a symbolic change, the First Evangelical Church gave birth in 1842 to another Cambridgeport revival-based congregation, this one devoted to immediate abolition of slavery, not conservative religion.[34]

In a less obvious way, these national and regional changes in the role of organizations shaped the role of local government. The new town of Somerville and the new city of Cambridge were created by entrepreneurs who were expanding their activities in the wake of depression. The new civic charters represented a novel use of the *municipal* corporation. The struggles over reorganization involved political maneuvering, mass organization, and petitioning on a scale never before seen in the suburbs.

Long-term frustration and an appropriate context influenced new governments in both Cambridge and Charlestown, but because they had different histories, the paths to change and the results were not quite the same. The outline was as follows: In Cambridge there were two overlapping arguments, one between "improvers" and fiscal conservatives and one between Old Cambridge and the two newer villages. The city charter represented a defeat for the farmer-artisan interests in Old Cambridge and a compromise on the improvement issue. In Somerville an early agrarian separatist movement failed, but a coalition of fringe entrepreneurs and Boston employees, centered on Sandpit Square, won independence from the mainland and set up a new town corporation.

The whole sequence of events began in Cambridge, and the key initiatives came from four young, Boston-oriented residents. All four arrived in the 1820s and 1830s, slipping rapidly into the new suburban elite. All were educated, mobile, and worldly; all were acquainted with the business and professional circles of both Boston and Cambridge. James Hayward, the most important of the four, graduated from Harvard in 1819, became tutor and professor of mathematics and a landowner in Old Cambridge. His knowledge of surveying led him into railroad promotion throughout the state. He carried the same skills and zeal into planning the enclosed Common in 1830 and conducting the first systematic survey of Cambridge streets in 1838. The career of Reverend Thomas Whittemore also stretched beyond the local arena. He came to Cambridgeport as pastor of the First Universalist Church in 1823. Leaving that post in 1831, he served the town as selectman, representative, and member of numerous committees, and the Cambridge Bank as president. Joining Hayward in railroad promotion, he became president of two Boston railroad companies and director of others. The other two improvers were younger men from East Cambridge: William Parmenter, glassworks manager and Democratic politician, and Ephraim Buttrick, attorney and dealer in land.[35]

These four led a modernizing campaign through the Cambridge town meeting. Between 1830 and 1838 they borrowed institutions and rhetoric from Boston with remarkable speed. Far in advance of any pressing need, Cambridge acquired services and amenities only recently introduced in the city. The enclosed Common, copying Boston Common, was only a first step. Next came a fire department, modeled on Mayor Quincy's Boston reforms. When Quincy set up the Boston fire department in 1826, the city had 50,000 people packed into its little peninsula. Cambridge, whose 7,000 residents were spread through a far larger area, established a department in 1832.[36] The following year, at the instigation of Hayward and the others, the town meeting voted to reorganize the almshouse and to investigate building sewers.

In 1834, when residents of Old Cambridge and Cambridgeport asked for new schools, Hayward suggested and chaired a committee which proposed revamping the entire school system. He noted that the growth of population in "three separate villages" made the continued proliferation of school districts an inefficient response. "Such a system is to be tolerated only in country towns, with a scattered population, in which it is practicable to bring the children together only in small numbers. It is certainly time that the town of Cambridge should avail itself of its local advantages."[37] Following the committee's recommendation, Cambridge became one of the first towns in Massachusetts to abandon the district system. Instead, the town was divided into three large wards, and the school committee began to group children into "grades" by level of achievement, setting a goal of stratifying the entire school population into as many such levels as possible.[38]

For Hayward, the mathematician and surveyor, the disorderly, ill-marked streets and roads of Cambridge were especially vexatious. Approaching this problem, too, he found reforms in Boston and support from his neighbors. In the early nineteenth century it was already fashionable for Bostonians to criticize their seventeenth-century street pattern. In 1824–25, Mayor Quincy, seeking to promote health and traffic, won backing for a general survey of the streets. His arguments were echoed by the petitioners for enclosing Cambridge Common, who complained that the roads crossing that space were "constantly changing their direction," making travel difficult because of the "utter impossibility of keeping in the travelled paths on dark nights, or when they are obliterated by drifting snows."[39]

In 1837–38 Hayward surveyed the roads of Cambridge. His report might have described the situation in Boston: "In the older parts of the town," he lamented, "we must be content with less of regularity, order, and symmetry, in the arrangements of the streets, public squares, and private estates, than is attainable in the more recently settled parts." After a lengthy catalog of encroachments he cited the advantages of wide streets in promoting health and guarding against fire and called for the appointment of a board of street commissioners and a committee to give fixed names to all the streets.[40]

Several features of this improvement campaign deserve emphasis. First, the Cambridge improvers were in a suburban vanguard. Even the Charlestown peninsula, which contained more people than all three Cambridge villages, adopted a fire department, school grading, police, and highway improvements *after* Cambridge.[41] Moreover, the Cambridge movement enjoyed initial popular support. It was an outgrowth of earlier, privately funded improvements like the Common; its leaders, though newcomers, fit the earlier notions of stewardship and represented all three villages. Yet the Cambridge improvers, adopting progressive measures in advance of need and acting through traditional town channels, were nevertheless committing the town to a new, specifically suburban, and expensive vision of its future.

These men, unlike Bostonians, understood the unique properties of the fringe area. Hayward, in discussing the importance of sidewalks, captured the peculiarities:

> In the early settlement of a country, or in parts of the country remote from towns and villages, there is less occasion to attend much to the margin of the highway. . . . But in parts of the country more thickly inhabited,—on the thoroughfares leading to large towns—and especially in a place like Cambridge, which is not only *cut up* into avenues to the city, but which is . . . constantly thronged, not only with strangers passing through its principal streets from the country to the city, and from the city to the country, but with a busy population of its own of nearly 8,000 persons,—it is highly important to guard from inconvenient encroachment. . . that portion of the public highway which is appropriated to the use of the many who walk.[42]

The improvers' schemes, based on this understanding of suburban conditions, implied a new policy for the town. Neither farming nor dense city settlement had a place in their dream. Small business and middle-class residence were the goals. Their task was to banish the disorderly remnants of agricultural society from the path of commerce and domesticity. Hayward complained, at the end of his catalog of street impediments, that "it is a thing not quite obsolete in this fair town, to ferment manures and manufacture all sorts of abominable composts on the margin of the public roads."[43] Country customs must give way. Enclosed parks, defined roads, graded schools—even license tags for the dogs—marked the path of growth.[44]

In place of farmers, the suburbs were to house the middle class. Hayward, Whittemore, Parmenter, and Buttrick all owned speculative lot property. Their supporters included large-scale speculators like Francis Bowman. In reforming the schools and straightening the roads, they sought to promote "building and immigration." It was desirable to make improvements before they were urgently needed, so as to make the town

> more eligible as a place of residence. This will not only add to the value of property in and about our villages, but will tend to the healthy increase of population among us, by giving us constant accessions of citizens from a class of people who will not only add to our respectability, but give us accessions of wealth, and thus diminish our public burdens.[45]

It promised an appealing community in later years, but it called for more efficient management and more increase in "public burdens" than Cambridge would stand for. Improvements generated discontent from two sources: the improvers themselves became disgusted with the sloppiness of town meeting government and some of their fellow citizens came to resent the cost of modernity.

The expansion of city services and amenities quickly showed in suburban budgets. Per capita expenditure levels of both Charlestown and Cambridge rose only slowly in the early years of the century but began a sharp climb in Charlestown in the 1820s and in Cambridge in the 1830s (see table 4.1). At first suburbanites responded to rising public outlay by "improving" town finances. Town treasurers were required by law to render an annual account, a duty long fulfilled by oral reports in town meeting. As population grew both Cambridge and Charlestown adopted printed reports—first simple one-sheet summaries of the accounts, then the text of the treasurer's report, and finally in the 1830s pamphlet reports of the major town officers.[46]

But the laws governing accountability were vague, and the patchwork organization of town government allowed public money to flow through a number of independent authorities for schools, highways, care of the poor, and lesser purposes.[47]Men trained in counting houses and professional offices were naturally impatient with the expenditure of their taxes through an undisciplined apparatus. In Cambridge and later Charlestown, the improvers of the 1830s set up annually elected finance committees, which usually included the most successful business and professional men of their respective communities. These committees had no legal power and little role in disbursing funds. In practice, they were reduced to auditing the accounts and making recommendations. In performing the task, however, they drew attention to the shortcomings of town financial procedures.

All four of the leading Cambridge improvers served on the first finance committee in 1836. They returned a report that strongly recommended "a more strict system of conducting the money affairs of the town." It was shocking to them that under the existing regime the town had no records of

Table 4.1

Per Capita Municipal Expenditures, 1830–70

(in dollars)

A. Total Expenditures					
Village	1830	1840	1850	1860	1870
Charlestown	3.52a	6.06	8.39	—b	38.11
Somerville	—	—	4.87	4.32	25.07
Cambridge	1.52	3.86	6.47	7.50	24.61
B. Debt Service Expenditures					
Village	1830	1840	1850	1860	1870
Charlestown	.19	.79	.75	.77	3.68
Somerville	—	—	.29	.32	1.20
Cambridge	.05	.22	.29	.59	2.31

SOURCE: *Annual Statement of the Expenses of Charlestown* (1830 through 1870); Town of Cambridge, "State of the Treasury" (Broadside, Cambridge, 1831); *Annual Report of the Receipts and Expenditures of . . . Cambridge* (1845 through 1870); *Reports of the Selectmen and Treasurer of the Town of Somerville* (1845 through 1870). Population data from the census. Accounts of all three communities have been reconstructed according to common definitions. Debt service figures do not include interest on special loans for water, sewers, or other large capital improvements, or payments into sinking funds.
a. Charlestown expenditure date for 1829.
b. Complete data not available.

its property, its debts, or its accounts receivable, but that it did have four boards authorized to draw on the treasury at will and without coordination.[48] Year after year the finance committees were compelled to watch the outflow of money over which they had no control, and their reports reflected growing frustration. "It will be perceived," said the report submitted in March 1840,

> that the expenditures have, in almost every case, exceeded the appropriations made at the commencement of the year, and some of the Boards, who are authorized to draw upon the Treasury, do not appear to have kept them in mind, as orders have been constantly coming upon the Treasury after an appropriation has been exhausted, and the Treasurer entirely out of funds.[49]

This committee and others of the period were distressed not only by un governed expenditure, but also by inadequate provision for revenue. Local tax bills were not sent out until the middle of the fiscal year, citizens were notoriously leisurely about paying, and the means of enforcement was weak. Towns could choose collectors who were empowered to seize property in lieu of unpaid taxes, but town meetings experienced difficulty finding citizens who would accept election to the post. The end of every fiscal year saw a large outstanding balance of uncollected taxes.[50]

The inevitable consequence of revenue shortfall was mounting town debt. In both communities, town meetings voted to pay for expensive improvements through borrowing money rather than raising taxes. By the later 1820s, paving projects in Charlestown had already generated a debt greater than the annual budget. Cambridge found itself in the same position, for the same reasons, ten years later. Disregarding the advice of their finance committees and treasurers, both towns continued to spend freely and to contract new loans, without either raising taxes or making provision for repayment of existing debts. The depression of 1837–42 made matters worse. In the early 1840s, the endemic shortage of funds forced Charlestown to seek short-term loans of more than $10,000 yearly, at high interest rates, simply to meet the current expenses of the town.[51]

To the men who advocated improvements and served on finance committees, such conditions were intolerable. Nearly all of them were experienced in business, and some, as private citizens, maintained strict control over accounts many times larger than the town budgets. Yet as watchdogs of municipal finances, they were confined to making small changes in accounting, issuing ever more vitriolic reports, and festering with impatience.

The Community as Business Corporation

Town government seemed unable to provide both improvements and efficiency. It was also unable to equalize the benefits among the several villages. While the improvers festered, residents of western Cambridge and Charlestown exploded. Old families and new entrepreneurs joined in separatist movements, insisting that their areas would be better and more cheaply served by the creation of new town governments.

It was only logical that this sentiment should arise first on the Charlestown mainland, long the most anomalous part of the inner suburbs. For years mainland residents had complained that they did not receive fair return for their taxes. As town expenses rose, they complained more loudly.[52] Whatever the distribution of funds, it was clear that the peninsula paid little heed to the mainland. Describing the school system in 1827, a writer for the *Bunker Hill Aurora* gave a detailed account of facilities in the seaport and then added, as an afterthought, that "without the neck there are, we believe, five district schools, which keep during the winter." Early editions of the *Charlestown Directory*, published in the 1830s, included only a handful of mainland residents and gave them all the same address: "without the penin-sula." Guidebooks of the period sometimes ignored the mainland altogether, portraying Charlestown as if the peninsula were the whole.[53]

Small wonder, then, that some of the mainland residents should attempt to sever the connection formally, by creating a new town. Separation had al-ways been the ultimate recourse for aggrieved citizens in Massachusetts towns. Both Cambridge and Charlestown had "mothered" many communi-ties in the past, most recently in 1807, when Brighton and West Cambridge took their leave of Cambridge.[54] Early in 1824, mainland farmer Samuel Tufts and seventy-seven of his neighbors petitioned the legislature for a simi-lar accommodation. Their argument repeated earlier complaints about town benefits but laid most stress on the "unnatural connection" between the two areas. "The one," said their brief,

> is a seaport, the other an agricultural community: The one by its contiguity with Boston imitates the expenditures of the city, the other, more frugal in their habits, disclaims all such rivalship.[55]

Most of the 1824 petitioners were farmers, and their argument contained a strong defense of husbandry against "the commercial and manufacturing in-terests which . . . are preying upon the vitals of their common father."[56]

The failure of this effort led to a renewed application five years later, again headed by farmer Tufts. The second petition covered the same ground and again drew a sharp distinction between the virtues of agriculture and the ex-ploitative interests on the peninsula:

> we ought to be liable only to the charges common and incidental to a country town, and not to the great sums of expenditure which the morals and habits of a seaport town necessarily require. We ask relief from the charges of paved streets, night watches, public lamps, fire engines, and many burthensome exigencies, in all of which we have no other possible interest than that of the public at large; but to support and cancel the expense of which, a large proportion of the revenue raised from our fields, or saved from the hard and slowly acquired earnings of our husbandry, are required.[57]

These early separatists failed because of strong opposition on the main-land itself. In both 1824 and 1828, Tufts and his militant yeomen met oppo-sition from tradesmen, brickmakers, and fishermen who thought their inter-ests lay in continued unity with the seaport. Given this opposition, the legislature rejected the petitions. Agrarian separatism in general was based on a limited and obsolete conception of suburban society. Efforts to divide

Charlestown cleanly into a farming village and a port were blocked by men who were not in either category.[58]

Late in 1841, a new movement arose, centered on the landowners and Boston-oriented tradesmen. Of the six new separatist leaders, two had links to the older movement, but four had not even been in Charlestown in the 1820s. They were all part of the new fringe leadership. The most vocal were Clark Bennett, a brickmaker, James Hill, Jr., a Faneuil Hall marketman, and John S. Edgerly, a Boston grain dealer—all under forty, all recently arrived. They were joined by Francis Bowman, the peripatetic speculator and reformer from Cambridge.[59]

The first signature on their petition was that of farmer Guy C. Hawkins, who had signed the first Tufts petition as a young man and now owned one of the few large farms left near Boston. But the 1842 appeal bore the marks of vigorous recruiting by the younger men. It consisted of seven sheets of signatures, each gathered from a different area of the community. Joined together, they contained 151 names—a large and representative cross section of mainland householders.[60]

The petition itself contained none of the earlier agrarian rhetoric. It stressed convenience and economy, offering statistics to demonstrate that the area could maintain its existing services and institutions more cheaply as a separate town. A supporting petition, equally spartan in language, came fron nonresident landowners, some of them speculators who lived in neighboring Cambridge. A critic on the peninsula confirmed the businesslike character of the movement even as he ridiculed it, blaming the agitation on "the commercial character of the age" and expressing doubt that the petitioners could "maintain a Corporation" as they claimed.[61]

The promoters of the new town were not only businessmen but Whigs. In this capacity, too, they sought efficient use of local resources for local ends. During the 1830s the Democrats of Charlestown had outstripped the once-dominant Whigs. By the early 1840s Charlestown consistently supported Democratic candidates for governor and state representative. A Whig minority on the mainland, bolstered by young commuters, reasoned that separation would lead to Whig control of the new town meeting and a Whig representative in the legislature.[62]

Just as the movement changed in character, so resistance to it eroded. The 1842 petition won the support of several important residents who had been opposed in 1828. Moreover, Charlestown leaders acquiesced in the separation, having come to regard the mainland as more a liability than an asset. With energy and sophistication, Hawkins, Edgerly, and the merchant Nathan Tufts settled the complex negotiations over division of property and fixing a boundary. On 4 April land developer Francis Bowman, unanimously chosen moderator, opened the first town meeting.[63]

Somerville was one kind of solution to the issues of the 1830s: cost, efficiency, and geographical equity. But this was only a first step and left some observers with a sense that "the towns about us do not seem to be fixed right yet."[64] Old Cambridge residents took the next steps. First, at the annual election meeting in 1842, fiscal conservatives led a retrenchment effort. Passing a resolution "that the expenses of the town ought to be reduced," they turned several improvers out of office. The leader of this reaction was James D. Green, a straitlaced Congregational minister who had retired from his East Cambridge pastorate. Moving to Old Cambridge, he became a town officer, state representative, and later the first mayor of Cambridge.[65]

Retrenchment was a doomed effort. Neither the town nor the conservatives themselves wanted to make cuts in the biggest items of expense, schools and highways. Moreover, any real check on spending and debts required stronger and more centralized authority than the town provided. In the end, both improvers and retrenchers reached the same conclusion: town government was inefficient.

In the summer of 1842, therefore, Old Cambridge citizens began a separation campaign. The old village center provided the core of leadership. Heading the main petition were Harvard professors Joseph Story and Simon Greenleaf, and Harvard Square artisans Jacob Bates and George Coolidge. This and a second petition brought together many earlier Old Cambridge leaders: ministers and deacons from both sides of the First Church battle, more than half the surviving petitioners for enclosing the Common, and, near the top of the first sheet, Benjamin Waterhouse.[66] But here as in Somerville, the movement also drew strength from the young entrepreneurs. Among the separatists were several northern Cambridge real estate dealers, who had supported the Somerville campaign earlier the same year. There were also ice harvesters and brickmakers from the area near Fresh Pond.[67]

The leaders were like those in Somerville. Their petitions were similarly brief and businesslike. But the outcome in Cambridge was far different. Charlestown had agreed to Somerville's separation, but Old Cambridge met the united and overwhelming resistance of Cambridgeport and East Cambridge. In response to the 317 signatures on the separatist petitions, the newer villages mustered 748 names on three remonstrances and with their numerical advantage secured the formal opposition of the town meeting. When the legislature postponed action until 1844, the exchange was repeated. The 323 signatures from Old Cambridge met 847 names and another set of town meeting "resolves" from the east. On both occasions, the leaders of the opposition were commercial and professional men of the new Boston-oriented elite: Isaac Livermore, the Hoveys, Thomas Whittemore, Ephraim Buttrick, and William Parmenter.[68]

In the wake of separatist failure, improvers and retrenchers joined on a balanced town committee to consider reorganizing and strengthening town government. In 1845, chairman Ephraim Buttrick reported their recommendations: to make the selectmen salaried officers; to give them the powers of the previously independent assessors, overseers of the poor, and highway surveyors; to make their chairman an ex officio member of the school committee; to make one of their number chief engineer of the fire department; to pay the town clerk and give him power to audit the accounts.[69]

This committee and its recommendations were logical outgrowths of the long tradition of town innovation, but the proposed centralization was too much for town meeting democracy to swallow. The report was thrown out early in 1846. Shortly thereafter, in a rather sour annual report, the town's finance committee noted that expenditures continued to exceed the amounts allowed, that agents of the town continued to ignore requirements that they submit proper accounts, and that none of the several boards consulted the finance committee before making drafts on the treasury.[70]

At this point the only remaining option for discontented townsmen was to import another Boston institution—a city charter. In Cambridge as in Boston this was a difficult step. Distaste for the city form of government was deep rooted. Popular objections and resistance in the legislature had postponed Boston's cityhood for years. It was the last major American port to obtain a charter, clinging to the town form until 1822, when it contained more than 40,000 people, some 7,000 of whom could raise their voices in town meeting. The state, in allowing city incorporation, and Mayor Quincy, in leading the first city, went to great lengths to allay public fears. Still, many suspected that cities were inherently more oppressive and expensive than towns.[71]

In Cambridge, however, the visible strains of growth and the frustration of both improvers and economizers overrode fears. Suburban residents also ignored the fact that, in 1846, neither Cambridge nor Charlestown had more than a third of the people Boston had in 1820. In 1846, Cambridge chose a geographically and politically balanced committee to draft a city charter. A hard core of resistance in Old Cambridge produced petitions against it, but most of the former separatists had joined the move toward city status. The sentiment for division, which had once attracted 323 signatures, now drew only 108. Gone from the list were many of the tradesmen and speculators. By a referendum vote of 645 to 224, Cambridge accepted its new charter and became the fourth city in Massachusetts.[72]

With the creation of these new governments and the city of Charlestown (1847), the boundary between city and town was moved outward, in a formal sense, from Boston into Middlesex County. But the new municipalities were in reality hybrids—in both form and purpose. Somerville, though its charter made it merely a town like other towns, promptly adopted urban improvements. Within the first year, the town meeting authorized a number of large, new, modern schools. The town's one fire engine did not call for a fire department, but the selectmen did set up a board of firewards, a system which had immediately preceded the fire department in Boston. In 1845 a committee to consider a new fire engine rejoiced, Hayward-fashion, in the town's residential growth:

> by the rapid progress of converting the farms of Somerville into streets, house-lots and squares, we see on all sides the embryo workings of a large and popolous [sic] town; that . . . the enterprize and energy of our own people is exciting the industrial population of the neighboring towns and cities, and many desirable families are hoping and intending soon to escape from the dust and tumult of Boston and to enjoy the rural scenery . . . of our hillsides.[73]

Somerville's appeal, said the committee, lay in a government that combined stewardship and economy. "We . . . have put all our shoulders to the important wheels, . . . paying cash down, incurring no debt," and keeping taxes low.[74]

Conversely, the city governments of Cambridge and Charlestown embodied elements of the town form. The new charters, modeled after those of Boston, Lowell, and Salem, placed strong restraints on city officers. The mayor and aldermen had only the powers previously vested in the selectmen. The mayor was to be ex officio chairman of the school committee and the overseers of the poor, but these bodies were still elected independently. Any thirty voters could force a general public meeting, and the mayor had no veto over legislation.[75]

In justifying the city charter, the newly founded *Cambridge Chronicle* described it as a better means to old town goals, insuring a full representation of interests to save the citizens "from the inconvenience of frequent meetings and the danger of hasty action in matters demanding grave deliberation." James D. Green, the first mayor, drew praise not only as an administrator but as a good town steward, who led the "friends of Order, Temperance,

Chastity, and Religion" while in office. He was as much a deacon as a civil servant, a man who strove "to make peace and order take the place of rowdyism and disgrace."[76]

In both Cambridge and Somerville the New Model governments were a step toward city forms of administration, but in goals and structure they had strong links to the past. In both places leading citizens assumed that local government would still be government by a small elite of stewards—the mayor and aldermen in Cambridge, the selectmen in Somerville. The new Cambridge city council was viewed as a limited and structured substitute for the town meeting. Throughout the 1840s, men of standing—almost all Whigs, except for the Democratic elite in East Cambridge—controlled the council's membership by means of ward caucuses, which nominated slates. In Somerville, a Whig majority enjoyed similar control of a smaller and more manageable policy in the new town meeting.

In reconstructing their governments, suburban residents thought they were keeping the best of the old, while bending to new conditions. They were determined to have improvement, economy, a balance of interests, and leadership that was both efficient and stewardly. In fact, their reconstructed governments were interim steps, halfway houses on the path to a service-oriented bureaucracy. They had explicitly acknowledged some changes in suburban interests and goals, and they had confirmed the subtle but decisive changes in suburban leadership: the inclusion of newcomers, the new power of fringe entrepreneurs and Boston employees. These were the first steps in redefining their communities in response to growth.

Yet their New Model governments were fragile creations based on assumptions that were true in 1840 but would not remain so for long. Suburbanites took it for granted that their communities would be relatively small, with links to the city that were occasional except for the commuting of an elite minority. They thought they could count on a harmony of economic interests among local entrepreneurs and on voluntarism in public affairs. If problems arose, they put their trust in the unity and activism of the "best men," who would work out solutions in town meeting and caucus. Somerville and the city of Cambridge were built on these assumptions. Better suited to the demands faced in the 1820s and 1830s, they were not altogether ready for the challenge that would come with increased commutation after 1845.

5
Commutation

Streetcars in Cambridgeport, late 1850s.
Courtesy of the Cambridge Historical Commission.

ALL OF THE changes discussed so far—the evolution of the fringe, the first alterations in habits and institutions of travel, and the planting of new, residentially oriented communities in the fringe environment—occurred when the suburbs were still very sparsely populated and rather loosely connected to the city. Only after these developments did the great migration of commuters begin. Mass commuting climaxed and completed the shift from walking to riding communities. Yet unlike the earlier stages of the mobility revolution, the commuter explosion was largely unexpected. Suburban residents opened the way for what they presumed would be a modest number of well-heeled rail and omnibus riders, but the growth of commuting far surpassed their expectations. Between 1845 and 1860 the number of Boston workers living outside the city rose from a few hundred to more than ten thousand. In Cambridge and Somerville the hundred-odd transitional commuters of 1840 became six hundred by 1850, and at least fifteen hundred by the late fifties.

Later observers could see that this migration was part of a wholesale reorganization of the city, accelerated in the 1840s by rail-based marketing, factory production, and the arrival of immigrant labor. What had been a trickle of Boston employees into the fringe became a flood to the suburbs because "push" factors in the city joined the "pull" forces already at work. Warehouses, larger offices, and railroad facilities displaced housing in the central city. Landlords crammed thousands of Irish immigrants trapped by their poverty into slums created from middle-class housing.[1] Prosperous Bostonians fled these changes and joined the pioneers of the 1830s beyond the city limits. A growing commuter constituency encouraged new transport innovations culminating in the streetcar, which became a symbol for the whole process of urban deconcentration.

Yet contemporaries and later historians, fascinated by the overall dimensions of the change, missed subleties and variations in its timing and impact. Mass commuting, for example, created a new distribution of population in the suburbs. Although commuters still concentrated in a few residential areas, the clumps were much larger and more numerous, spreading through and between all the suburban villages. A larger number of the new commuters were dependent on public transportation; they did not own vehicles and lived beyond walking distance. They were more diverse in background and employment, had no previous connection with suburban society, and worked in jobs that had nothing to do with the fringe economy.

Moreover, circumstances peculiar to the 1850s gave the commuters a prominence they would never have again. They made up a larger proportion of the inner suburban work force than at any other point in history. And since the cost of travel remained high until the coming of the streetcar in the late 1850s, they continued to be well-to-do. From 1845 until the mid-fifties, the suburbs experienced mass commuting but not commuting by the masses.

Suburbanites knew more about these details than Bostonians, but the migration involved so much irregularity and so much unpredictability that no one took it all in or saw its implications fully until it was well underway. Instead, Bostonians and suburbanites indulged in a vague fantasy of growth, which masked the true characteristics of change in the suburbs.

The Migration
Promotional Dream and Economic Reality

Starting in the mid-forties, the commuter migration drew notice as an unprecedented phenomenon. In the absence of either experience or hard data, residents throughout the region were free to indulge in speculation. A few interested parties—first the suburban entrepreneurs, then the Boston railroad men and realtors—encouraged a vision of suburban change that ran well in advance of reality. Reading contemporary accounts, one might well imagine that the whole business community was flocking to suburban homes.

Boston writers, having ignored the suburbs for decades, suddenly became conscious of the number of "Bostonians" who lived beyond the city limits. This outlook extended the views of the merchant elite, who for years had considered anything connected with their commerce to be properly part of Boston. Since they built the railroads to link their wharves to the interior, they tended to think of all riders on public carriers as men of the city. The mobility revolution, in this view, emanated from and centered on Boston. The editor of the *Boston Directory* for 1846 estimated that "2,000 persons daily arrive and depart by Rail Roads, and all other conveyances." Noting the dramatic rise in suburban population, he asserted that "this increase is made up chiefly of men doing business in Boston and who, with their families, reside in these towns."[2]

Boston and suburban speculators fed this dramatic but vague notion of the change. When the railroads finally committed themselves to the commuter trade, they did their best to promote a migration. They cut fares, sold lots themselves, and ran free special trains to carry prospective buyers to new subdivisions.[3] By 1850, railroads and realtors both churned out propaganda in behalf of suburban living. "Somerville, Medford, and Woburn," read an advertisement for the Boston and Lowell, present many delightful and healthy locations for a residence, not only for the gentleman of leisure, but the man of business in the city, as the cars pass through these towns often during the day and evening, affording excellent facilities for the communication with Boston. Convenient tenements can be obtained at reasonable rates, which, together with the low price charged for the Season Ticket, make it an object of economy, as well as health and happiness, to reside in these places.[4]

The land developers responded by stressing the excellence of transportation. Ads for suburban lots summarized the appropriate schedules for trains or omnibuses. By 1850 such literature portrayed a land where every lot was a country paradise, yet all were "within a few minutes' walk of the station."[5]

More disinterested observers noted the connection between Boston changes and suburban migration. In 1849, the directory summarized contemporary thinking in pointing out the increased use of omnibuses:

Within a few years this convenient mode of conveyence has come into extensive use in Boston and vicinity. The increase of business having made inroads upon private dwellings, together with the influx of foreign population, have induced many to remove to remote parts of the city, or to neighboring towns; hence the great demand for this class of conveyance, a demand which seems to be abundantly supplied, as the crowded streets will testify.[6]

It was up to the mayor, speaking in 1848, to synthesize the traditional Boston outlook and the new vision of mobility in one grand, chauvinistic appraisal:

The population of Boston is supposed to be 120,000, but in estimating our numbers in order to provide the facilities for business, it is but just to add those persons who daily resort to our City, who spend here most of their waking hours, and occupy streets and warehouses in the same way that they would do if, as in other cities, their families resided within our territorial limits . . . I think that we may say, that, during business hours, Boston represents a population of from two to three hundred thousand souls, and this is daily increasing.[7]

This was a businessman's fantasy. Boston would not receive a daily influx of 80,000 to 180,000 for at least another decade. But in the context of other judgments it was an understandable dream. Even the crude data gathered at the time reveal a striking and rapid increase in daily traffic across the city's boundaries. Three surveys, taken in 1826, 1847, and 1851, suggest the magnitude of change (table 5.1). Still, all of these contemporary speculations

Table 5.1
Surveys of Traffic, 1826, 1847, 1851

Means of transportation	1826		1847	1851	
	Vehicles	Persons	Persons	Vehicles	Persons
Pedestrian	—	4,910	—	—	26,197
Horseback	—	131	—	—	251
Carriages, coaches, and wagons	5,009	—	11,150	13,689	30,906
Railroads	—	—	15,073	1,695[a]	28,357[a]
Total entering and leaving on land	5,009	5,041	22,223	15,384	86,484

SOURCE: *Bowen's Boston Newsletter,* 14 October 1826, II, 177; Nathaniel Dearborn, *Boston Notions* (Boston, 1848), 221; "Travel to and from Boston," *Hunt's Merchant's Magazine*, 25 December 1851, p. 759.

a. Omits railroad freight cars and men riding them, who are included in the total.

were Boston-centered and indiscriminate. They did not clearly distinguish between long-distance travel, irregular business trips, and commuting. They overemphasized the new migration. They ignored its significance for the suburbs.

To trace the commuter migration more precisely and to place it in the context of larger trends in travel and suburban growth, I have employed four kinds of quantitative data. (See the Appendix for a full description.) Samples of *Boston Directory* listings for 1846, 1851, 1855, and 1860 provide information on the spread of commutation generally. Data on the directory population include workplace and residence information for all persons (4,434) listed in the 1851 directories for Cambridge and Somerville. The linked population (3,056) includes all persons who appeared both in the directories and in the 1850 census schedules. These names have been traced backward and forward in time through a variety of census, directory, taxation, voting, and membership records for Boston and the suburbs. Because the directory and linked populations are inherently biased, they have been measured against a sample population of 502 households (2,617 people) drawn systematically from the 1850 census for Cambridge and Somerville.

These data reveal a significant increase in commuting but a selective and gradual spread of the practice. Of the more than 25,000 names in the *Boston Directory* for 1846, approximately 1,500 (6 percent) were listed as residents of the suburbs (table 5.2). By 1860 the estimated commuter population surpassed 10,000, and the commuter proportion of the listings had tripled. These are minimum estimates; the directories probably underlisted commut-

Table 5.2
Suburban and Boston Residents Listed in the Boston
Directories, 1846–60

Place of Residence	1846	1851	1855	1860
	A. Sample Data[a]			
Suburbs	96 (6%)	222 (11%)	445 (17%)	674 (18%)
Boston	1,396 (86%)	1,635 (81%)	1,988 (76%)	2,808 (75%)
Uncertain	127 (8%)	162 (8%)	183 (7%)	262 (7%)
Totals	1,592	2,019	2,616	3,744
	B. Extrapolated estimates for all Boston listings (rounded to nearest 100)			
Suburbs	1,500	3,600	7,100	10,800
Boston	21,900	26,200	31,800	44,900
Uncertain	2,000	2,600	2,900	4,200
Total listings	25,488	32,318	41,865	59,900[b]

SOURCES: Derived from Boston directories for 1846, 1851–52, 1855–56, 1860–61.
a. Based on samples of one in every sixteen listings.
b. Estimate based on the size of the completed sample.

ers.[8] But even if the figures omit half the daily traffic, which is highly unlikely, the magnitude of commuting would not approach the level projected by the mayor in 1848.

Moreover, transportation costs channeled commuter settlement along narrow lines. For a decade, lowered rail fares and improved omnibus service pushed commuters ever farther into the suburbs. In 1846, Roxbury and Cambridge accounted for more than half of the suburban residences listed (table 5.3). By 1855 their share dropped to a quarter, while that of the more remote suburbs rose to nearly half. But at that point three changes stabilized and even reversed the trend. Railroads raised their rates in 1855. Street railways, offering the first truly cheap service but reaching only the nearest suburbs, opened in 1856. Two years later all the bridges to Cambridge finally became free. Consequently, new commuters of the late 1850s concentrated in the inner suburbs.

Even within the inner suburbs, commuter residences of the late 1840s and early 1850s were grouped in nodes about the thin skeleton of transportation (fig. 7). In Cambridge most commuters before 1855 lived in three areas: along the omnibus lines in Cambridgeport, along Brattle Street in Old Cam-

Table 5.3
Distribution of Suburban Residences,
1846–61

Suburb	1846[a]	1851	1855	1860
Chelsea	9%	10%	12%	15%
Charlestown	12	16	12	13
Cambridge	23	17	12	15
Other northern	9	15	23	21
Roxbury	28	20	13	15
Other southern	14	17	24	18
Total suburban listings in sample	96	222	445	674
Estimated suburban listings in entire directory	1,500	3,600	7,100	10,800

SOURCE: Derived from Boston directories.
a. Sample size for 1846 is too small for reliability.

bridge, and near the Fitchburg rail station in northern Cambridge. In Somerville, Boston workers clustered in knots at each of the depots and along the old road to the peninsula.

From the Boston viewpoint, the growth of commuting involved a spread to some new occupation groups, but not all. Wholesale merchants, the core of the transitional commuter population in the 1840s, were joined by bank workers and lawyers. Bankers, with short hours and relatively high incomes, were among the first to migrate. In 1846, roughly 30 percent of the 128 major staff members of the large Boston banks lived in the suburbs and 65 percent in the city (table 5.4). By 1851, bank personnel numbered 186, of whom 44 percent commuted and 50 percent were Boston residents.

Table 5.4
Suburban Residents among Bank Employees,
1846 and 1851
(as percent of total in each rank)

Position	1846	1851
President and cashier	11%	15%
Teller and bookkeeper	60	55
Clerk	10	55
Messenger and porter	—	5
Total number of employees	128	186

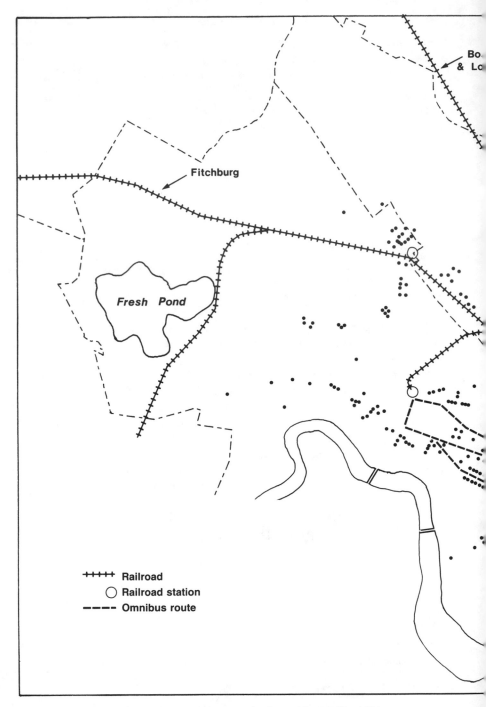

Figure 7　Residences of Boston Employees in Cambridge and Somerville, 1850

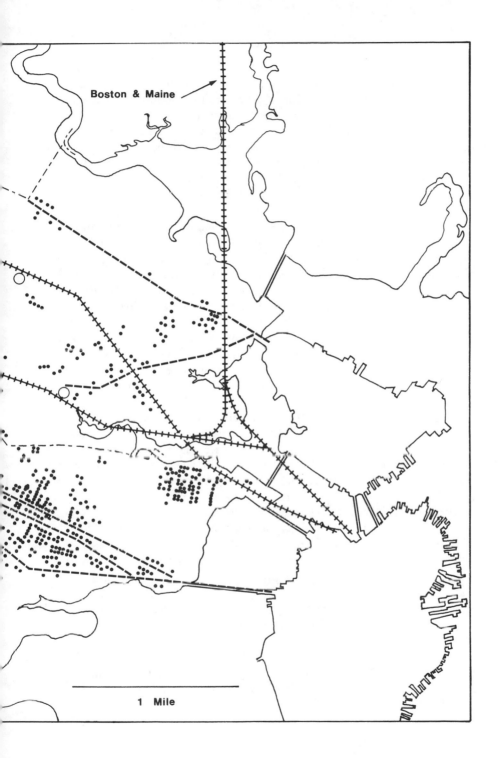

Boston & Maine

1 Mile

Even among bank workers, the expansion of commuting was a selective process. The presidents and cashiers had prestigious homes on Boston's crescents and squares. Few of them moved in this period. Neither did low-ranking messengers and porters, who could not afford high fares. Instead, commuting spread among the middle-ranking staff of Boston's banks—tellers, bookkeepers, and clerks. These men enjoyed stable, moderately high incomes, but could not pay for a fashionable address. In a period when available middle-class housing in Boston was shrinking, they sought suburban residence.

Boston Directory data also suggest that the habit of commuting may have spread through contacts at the bank. In 1846 Boston's largest bank had only one commuter employee, the first teller, who lived in Charlestown. By 1851 all but one of the tellers, plus one of the clerks, had also moved to Charlestown. Both of the bookkeepers and two other clerks had moved to Roxbury. The Washington Bank employed two Roxbury commuters in 1846. By 1851 all but one of its staff, including the president, were Roxbury citizens. Among lawyers, too, the late 1840s and early 1850s saw an extension of the journey to work. In 1846 roughly three hundred lawyers were listed in the Boston business directory. About 25 percent of these were suburban residents. In the early 1850s the number of listings rose to four hundred, and the commuter proportion to about 49 percent (table 5.5).

Some of the new commuters were children of previous suburban residents. Improved transportation allowed moving one's place of work just as it allowed changing residence. Suburban records contain numerous cases like that of the Saunders family in Cambridge. William A. Saunders, whose ancestors had lived there in the eighteenth century and whose father was a northern Cambridge carpenter, became the first member of his family to work in Boston. Around 1840, when he was twenty-two, he became a hardware dealer in the city. Three of his younger brothers soon followed; by 1850 all four were making a daily trip.[9]

On the other hand, many kinds of workers did *not* enter the commuting pattern before the late 1850s. The process evident within the banks—a sifting of workers by rank—reflected changes in the whole labor force. The financial-mercantile elite stayed in the city. So did those whose work involved long, strict hours and/or low wages. Physicians, for example, remained close to their patients and facilities in Boston, despite incomes that might allow commuting (table 5.5). Henry Ingersoll Bowditch, a staff member of Massachusetts General Hospital, exemplified the doctors' dilemma. He made a brief entry into commuting about 1850, buying a house in Weston

Table 5.5
Residences of Attorneys and Physicians
Listed in the Boston Business Directory, 1851–60

Place of Residence	1851	1855	1860
A. Attorneys			
Boston	194 (51%)	204 (49%)	236 (43%)
Suburbs	144 (38%)	174 (42%)	276 (51%)
Residence uncertain or not listed	46 (12%)	37 (9%)	32 (6%)
Total	384	415	544
B. Physicians[a]			
Boston	31	48	75
Suburbs	2	4	9
Residence uncertain or not listed[b]	18	23	21
Total	51	75	105

SOURCES: Derived from comparison of the business and main directory listings.
a. These tabulations do *not* include the members of the Suffolk District Medical Society, who were by definition resident in Boston, and who numbered more than 200 throughout this period.
b. Most of these were probably city residents whose homes were also their offices.

near the Worcester Railroad. But the journey became a strain on his finances and his schedule, and he sold the house in 1856.[10]

Most shopkeepers and artisans also remained city-bound. Among those listed in the Boston business directory as bakers, apothecaries, and mechanics, only a small percentage had suburban residences before the Civil War. The proportion was a bit higher for carpenters, masons, and painters (table 5.6). In this period of widespread construction, they could find work in both city and suburbs.[11] High wages and plentiful job openings allowed a few to move outside Boston—but not far outside; in 1855 almost all of the suburban-resident building tradesmen lived in the contiguous suburbs. They could be walking rather than riding "commuters." Furthermore, at least 80 percent of the workers in these trades still lived in Boston.

This selective expansion of the commuter habit produced a noticeable, class-based change in the Boston labor force. It did not measure up to the mayor's dreams, but it was enough to provoke a great deal of discussion. The

Table 5.6
Residences of Carpenters and Painters
Listed in the Boston Business Directory, 1851–60

Place of Residence	1851	1855	1860
A. Carpenters			
Boston	222 (80%)	216 (76%)	257 (80%)
Suburbs	32 (12%)	48 (17%)	54 (17%)
Residence uncertain or not listed	22 (8%)	20 (7%)	9 (3%)
Total	276	284	320
B. Painters			
Boston	118 (80%)	113 (75%)	91 (72%)
Suburbs	19 (13)	27 (18)	30 (24)
Residence uncertain or not listed	10 (7)	11 (7)	6 (5)
Total	147	151	172

city, it seemed, was losing an important segment of its young middle class: the specialized merchants, lawyers, and rising bank workers.

From the viewpoint of the suburban villages, this same expansion produced a revolutionary windfall—a change far more dramatic than the one in Boston. Between 1846 and 1850, known commuters rose from 6 percent to 11 percent of the *Boston Directory* listings. Between 1840 and 1850 they rose from 7 percent to 19 percent of the male household heads in Cambridge and Somerville (table 5.7). Samples from the later directories indicate that the proportion of commuters in the inner suburban population peaked at about one-quarter of the household heads in 1860.[12] Though there would later be many more commuters, they would never again make up so large a share of the suburban population. Since the suburban communities were far smaller than Boston, the new commuters also accounted for a significant share of the *increase* in population. New commuters made up 30 percent of the incremental rise in household heads for the two suburbs between 1840 and 1850, and almost half of the increase for the biggest community, Cambridgeport.

This new population of commuters was more diverse than the small group of transitional commuters had been. In both Cambridge and Somerville, the Boston-employed now included measurable percentages of skilled and semi-

Table 5.7

Estimates of Commuter Role in Suburban Population Growth, 1840–50

Suburban Population	Somerville	Old Cambridge	Cambridgeport	East Cambridge	Cambridge Total	Cambridge and Somerville Total
Male householders, 1840[a]	215	262	578	472	1,312	1,527
Known commuters, 1840	10	12	61	14	87	97
Males householders, 1850[b]	628	632	1,120	768	2,520	3,148
Known commuters, 1850	128	100	302	77	479	607
Increase in householders	413	370	542	296	1,208	1,621
Commuter increment as percent of householders increment	29%	24%	45%	21%	33%	32%

SOURCE: Linked population data.
a. Omits a few black householders, who could not be reliably traced into Boston records.
b. Estimates from sample data.

Table 5.8

Selected Occupations of Suburban Residents by Place of Work, 1850
(percent of those reporting occupations)

	Somerville Residents Employed in				Cambridge Residents Employed in			
Occupation	Boston	Somerville	Not Available	Total	Boston	Cambridge	Not Available	Total
Farming	2%	*	15%	12%	—	3%	1%	1%
Unskilled labor	—	*	12	10	1%	4	18	10
Semiskilled	13	*	19	19	9	18	26	20
Skilled	17	*	23	23	19	31	37	31
Clerical	13	*	1	5	15	5	4	7
Food dealers	6	*	4	6	7	7	2	5
Bankers, merchants, wholesalers	28	*	4	12	12	1	1	4
Professional	2	*	2	2	6	7	3	5
Number reporting occupation	125	20	232	377	435	743	955	2,133
Number linked from directories to census[a]	127	20	269	416	471	837	1,295	2,603

*Not significant.

a. Totals differ slightly from those for linked population in table 5.9, because table 5.8 omits a few suburban residents who worked in some location other than Boston or their home suburb.

skilled workers (table 5.8). On the whole, however, the commuter group was still dominated by mercantile, professional, and clerical workers, who were far more prominent among the commuters than in the suburban population at large. In the late 1840s and early 1850s Cambridge and Somerville gained young but prosperous Bostonians like Samuel Batchelder, a manufacturer and financier, and Enoch Robinson, owner of a large lock company.[13] These men and their commuter neighbors bought large houses and installed large families. Only 28 percent of the linked population had families of 5 or more, but 33 percent of the commuters did.

The impact of commuter migration on the suburban villages becomes still more apparent if we trace the 1850 residents backward and forward through local records (table 5.9). For this purpose, I have divided Cambridgeport into the two areas that would become separate wards in 1856. The results demonstrate the difference between those employed in Boston and those working in the suburbs. More than half of the known suburban employees in 1850 had been living in the same community five years earlier. Only 35 percent of the commuters had been. Naturally enough, there were more of these long-term suburban residents in the early areas of commuter settlement. In the Dana Hill section of Cambridgeport and in the "walking commuter" center of East Cambridge nearly half of the Boston-employed had been suburban residents since the mid-1840s (49 percent and 45 percent). Only about 10 percent of the commuters in these areas had been listed as Boston residents in the *Boston Directory* for 1846. In most other suburban areas, however, the commuters were recent arrivals. In Somerville, only 30 percent had been taxpayers in 1845; 34 percent had then been living and working in the city. In all areas, these true commuters were not only recent arrivals but transients. Unlike the transitional commuters of 1840, they would prove to be no more stable than the population as a whole. In Somerville especially, the new commuters flooded in after 1845, but many of them left by 1860.

Thus the commuter migration recruited people selectively from the Boston labor force and inserted them selectively into some areas and occupational levels in the suburbs. Commuting to work was still a practice open only to those with high income and flexible schedules, but there were now large blocs of such people in the inner suburbs. Moreover, the impact of commutation went far beyond the journey to work. The commuter migration went hand-in-hand with a still more intensified use of public transportation for other purposes. The same men who became commuters also rode mass carriers for business, social, or political errands. An example of this shift in behavior may be found in the career of Richard Henry Dana, Jr. On the surface, Dana seemed to be the prototypical new commuter. As a young, married

Table 5.9

Residence and Employment Histories of the Linked Population, 1844–60

Population Characteristics	Somerville	Old Cambridge	North Cambridgeport (Ward II)	South Cambridgeport (Ward IV)	East Cambridge	Cambridge Total	Cambridge and Somerville Total
Male householders, 1850	628	632	648	472	768	2,520	3,148
Linked population, 1850	419	678	711	575	680	2,637	3,056
Known commuters, 1850	128	100	209	93	77	479	607
Known suburban employees, 1850	*	236	180	142	247	805	—
Status of commuters, 1844–46 (as percent of 1850 commuters) Boston resident *and*							
Boston employed	34%	23%	13%	6%	8%	13%	21%
Boston employed	56%	55%	53%	32%	34%	46%	49%
Suburban resident	30%	38%	49%	39%	45%	43%	35%
No Data	30%	13%	31%	58%	45%	36%	34%
Status of suburban employees, 1844–46 Suburban resident	*	61%	52%	56%	53%	56%	—
Percent of all commuters still resident, 1860	41%					31%	
Percent of linked population still resident, 1860	45%					31%	

*Number too small for significant calculation.

lawyer, he lived and worked in Boston, spending occasional summer periods in Roxbury. As his career advanced, he bought land in his ancestral town of Cambridge, built a house near Harvard Square, and moved there in 1852.[14]

Dana remained a commuter for most of his life, but the commuter trip comprised only a small part of his customary daily travel. With a busy legal practice and political hopes, he moved throughout the Boston metropolitan area at extraordinary speed. In 1853 he journeyed one evening to give a lecture at North Bridgewater and spent the night there. His journal gives the following account of the next day:

> After an early breakfast, left for Boston, where I arrived soon after 9, argued *Rand v. Mather* before the full bench Sup. C't., closing at 2 o'ck., without dining took 2½ train for Dedham and began the trial of *Bigelow v Wood* immediately on my arrival—Immediately on adjournment of the Court took cars for Boston and thence coach to Charlestown, and lectured 1¼ on Burke, returned to Boston, had an interview with Dr. Townsend, who is a witness in *White v. Braintree*, and thence to Cambridge—all this time eating nothing but a few figs and a sandwich in the coach—a pretty good day's work![15]

Dana was an exceptionally energetic man and this was clearly an exceptional day, but many of his less crowded days included the same frenetic movement, beside which the simple trip to and from Cambridge must have seemed pale.

For women, public transportation brought another sort of revolution. In fact, the gradual conversion of suburbanites from walking to riding probably occurred more quickly among women than among men. Into the 1850s, people like Dana continued to save money by walking to work. Suburban wives and daughters had once done the same when visiting or shopping in the city. But in the 1850s such women seem to have used public carriers more often. Dana's wife Sarah, for example, sometimes accompanied him in the morning to Harvard Square, where she boarded an omnibus for a shopping trip, while he followed along the same route on foot.[16]

Contemporary accounts by suburbanites—not Bostonians—hinted at the varied pattern of public transportation usage. A description of Malden in 1846 noted the impact of the railroad on town society. Fifty years earlier, said the author,

> a Malden lady wishing to visit Boston by land, had to rise early, and travel by wagon, side-saddle, or pillion . . ., and when arrived, was so fatigued by her day's journey, that she had to rest a day or two before she was able to make her "calls."
>
> But now, how changed! Those cruel turnpike killers, and despisers of horse-flesh, the legislators of Massachusetts, have granted permission

to a number of men to set up a long, narrow building on trundles, a sort of travelling-meetinghouse, with a bell to it, and a row of pews on each side of the aisle . . . By this mode of travelling, a lady or gentleman at Malden may leave home at almost any hour, go down south to Boston, a distance of five miles, see their friends, do their errands, and return, in one short sunny hour.[17]

The railway worked this sort of revolution in many suburban towns, bringing them suddenly from the hinterland to within a few minutes' reach of the city. Many residents of these towns shared the reaction of their contemporary Thoreau: the train whistle of the 1840s remained a lifelong symbol of their shattered solitude.

By the mid-1850s the shift from walking to riding was far advanced. More commuters, and more use of public carriers for trips once accomplished on foot, had firmly established a pattern of travel that was to characterize suburban life for decades to come. A Medford observer of 1855 recorded the use of local trains for varied purposes by varied citizens:

The number of gentlemen who reside here, and do business in Boston, is very large, and they are multiplying every month. The cars on both railroads are filled every morning,—the earliest with laborers, the next with merchants, and the last with ladies.[18]

Though this description was too sweeping (very few true "laborers" could afford to ride the train), it nonetheless captured the way in which public transportation had penetrated the lives of suburbanites. As they became more habituated to trains and omnibuses, suburban residents stepped up their pressure for still more specialized service of local traveling needs.

Omnibus, Railroad, and Streetcar
The Mobility Revolution Completed

Between 1845 and 1855 a greatly enlarged constituency of riders once again provoked change in the means of transportation. Omnibus and local train routes multiplied and branched to become a true system rather than a patchy collection of lines. The limits of both kinds of conveyance became starkly obvious. In the early 1850s entrepreneurs throughout the region, led by suburbanites, turned swiftly to the streetcar as a means of advancing the suburban vision. By the Civil War, the technology, organization, and policies of urban mass carriers had taken forms that would not change substantially until the electrification movement of the 1880s.

For both omnibus and railroad proprietors, the riding explosion of the late 1840s meant a change in the scale and complexity of business. In the beginning, organization, more than technology, was the key to expansion. The omnibus of the 1840s, for example, had already reached limits of size and capacity. With a team of several horses it was longer than a modern tractor-trailer and more difficult to maneuver. Passengers sitting, standing, and perched on the roof made the vehicle unstable and strained the horses. To cope with more riders, the proprietors could only buy more coaches and run them more frequently.

In the suburbs served only by omnibuses this kind of expansion went on with a vengeance and changed the character of business. By the late 1840s the original small-scale innovators had retired, to be replaced by ever larger and more consolidated partnerships. The new owners, like the pioneers, had often started in the tavern or stable business, but no one innkeeper or stabler could now support an omnibus line. By the early 1850s five companies controlled the Cambridge, Charlestown, and Somerville service. The largest of these, in Cambridge, was capitalized at $50,000, and owned 16 omnibuses and 180 horses. Each of its vehicles made dozens of trips daily, and the company paid $11,000 per year in bridge tolls.[19] First in competition, then in collusion, these companies extended their reach into what had been railroad territory—northwestern Cambridge, Somerville, and the ring of suburbs farther west. By 1854 hourly service covered most of the two inner suburbs, and the three Cambridge villages had fifteen-minute service through most of the day.[20]

For railroads the task of expansion was in some ways easier. Since they controlled their rights of way, they did not need to insert vehicles into a traffic stream. They could also add capacity by adding cars or making them larger. Scheduling, however, was their primary tool of expansion. By 1850 each suburban station on the Lowell, the Maine, and the Fitchburg handled well over a dozen local trains daily. Both in the suburbs and in Boston the railroads were coordinated with special omnibus service to distribute passengers from the depots. Competitive fare reductions allowed rail commuters with yearly passes to reach Boston from the inner suburbs for about 10 cents a day.[21]

Just as the omnibus lines encroached on railroad territory, so the railroad came to serve some omnibus communities. This, too, was the work of suburban entrepreneurs, who besieged the legislature with requests to incorporate "branch" railways. These promoters sought to build links from various villages to the existing main lines and to obtain running rights into the city, thereby avoiding the impossible expense of carving out a new rail approach. Frequently the locals offered to construct and maintain a branch if the main line company would operate the trains. This branch strategy, first devised in the late 1830s, became a craze in the mid-1840s. Within inner Middlesex County alone, five branches were incorporated between 1844 and 1846.[22]

These movements presented the rail companies with a twofold challenge: on the one hand they promised new customers; on the other they sometimes threatened to construct spurs in inconvenient places or, worse, to link them with competing main line companies. To avoid such disasters the large companies usually came to terms with the suburban upstarts. Sometimes they headed off branch applications by building the lines themselves.[23] Trains on these branches carried commuter service to a new level of perfection. On the through routes, the needs of Boston and other large cities governed scheduling. Only a few "specials" catered to suburban wants. But on the branches all the trains were specials, and timetables were adjusted to suit commuters and shoppers.[24]

Old Cambridge entrepreneurs, bypassed by the first wave of railroad building, turned to the branch device in 1848, under the leadership of Gardiner G. Hubbard and Estes Howe. Hubbard and Howe were typical of the men who dominated suburban development in the late 1840s and 1850s. Neither was born in Cambridge, but both had lived there while attending Harvard. Hubbard, a product of the law school, practiced and lived in Boston until 1846, when he married and moved to Old Cambridge. Howe, a graduate of both the college and the medical school, went first to Ohio, where he practiced until the death of his wife. Returning east, he lived first in Boston and later with relatives in Cambridge, and in 1848 he remarried and settled in a house of his own near the Common [25]. Their five partners in the Harvard Branch Railway were all young suburbanites who had invested heavily in local business and real estate, not only in Cambridge but in Medford and Charlestown as well.[26]

The Harvard Branch opened in 1849 from a station near the college to a junction with the Fitchburg in Somerville. It was a typical branch promotion. The larger company provided trains; the suburbanites paid for upkeep. Yearly pass fares were cheap. Omnibuses provided service at both ends of the route. Despite such inducements the line failed in 1855. Most of the Cambridge commuters lived in Cambridgeport and followed a well-worn route over the bridge. Rail commuting via Old Cambridge was circuitous and expensive, and the western village simply could not generate enough traffic of its own.[27]

The failure of this spur symbolized the limits of the omnibus-rail system, limits that had become more visible with expansion. Railroads were fast and reached distant villages, but only the well-to-do could afford them. The cheapest fares were available only through yearly passes and therefore only to those who could be certain of yearly work schedules. Clerks and manual workers, whose employment might vary from month to month, had little use for commuter rail travel. Even for those with stable work, cheap fares were a temporary boon. Railroad managers found that commuters filled their trains but not their pockets. Long-distance passengers and freight produced more revenue. In 1855 the commuter bubble burst: local fares went up again.[28]

Suburbanites also discovered that railroads made troublesome neighbors. The trains had graduated from the stage of teakettle engines and tiny wooden carriages. Heavy locomotives and multiwheel coaches were now the rule even on branch lines. Scores of trains using such equipment passed through the suburbs each day, producing smoke and accidents. In 1849, at least 16 of the 29 serious accidents reported by the Maine, the Lowell, and the Fitchburg took place in the inner suburbs. The Maine felt obliged to defend rail travel against those who were "inclined to regard railroads as an infliction or encroachment."[29]

Omnibuses did not produce smoke and their proprietors did not have to juggle long- and short-distance fares. But omnibus travel had its own drawbacks. Some of them were old ones: limited range, bumpy rides, weather, and bridge tolls. Expansion added new problems of crowding, traffic jams, and accidents.[30] By the early 1850s some suburban residents were unhappy with both kinds of transportation. In January 1851, for example, the *Cambridge Chronicle* complained that the Harvard Branch Railroad was inadequate and called for more omnibuses. Only a few months later it accused the omnibus companies of crowding the streets and overtaxing their horses.[31]

All the inadequacies of public transportation were most sharply felt in Cambridge. For different reasons, residents of both Old Cambridge and Cambridgeport saw the situation of the early 1850s as one that threatened their most important interests. The men who promoted the Harvard Branch Railroad, some of them Boston-employed and all interested in Old Cambridge land values, watched the growth of new villages near distant railroad depots and lamented the failure of their spur. Meanwhile Cambridgeport businessmen, also investors in local land, saw the railroads divert the inland traffic that was the very foundation of their economy. The editor of the *Cambridge Directory* observed in 1849 that the opening of the Quincy Market in Boston, and the construction of the numerous railroads running from Boston, all of which by some fatality seem to avoid Cambridge, have almost annihilated the extensive trade which was formerly carried on between "the Port" and the country towns.[32]

In both Old Cambridge and Cambridgeport, the leading citizens felt deprived. But at the same time, the growth of the fringe economy and the expansion of commuting had provided these two communities with a large number of talented and wealthy residents—men experienced in many fields of business, finance, law, and even in railroad management. It was therefore not surprising that Cambridge became the first community in the Boston area to adopt an entirely new system of local passenger transportation: the streetcar.

The idea of using horses to pull tracked vehicles was older than the steam locomotive. Horsepower for railways had ample justification in theory, since animals were cheaper, easier to maintain, and more adaptable than steam engines. Thomas Tredgold, whose treatise of 1825 guided early railway builders in both England and America, gave equal consideration to both "species of power" and showed a slight bias in favor of horses.[33] The first railway in Massachusetts was a one-horse operation, and a state-commissioned report of 1829 recommended horsepower for the western hills. Well into the forties, horses were used in many ancillary railroad functions. They pulled test trains over new track, and real trains over at least one branch line. In New York and Philadelphia, public opposition to steam engines led some railroads to employ horses as "switch engines," bringing trains from the city limits to downtown terminals. In the case of New York's Harlem railroad, the final stretch of track ran through the city streets. The use of horses there produced a system resembling the streetcars of the future.[34]

It was only a short step from such practices to a horse-drawn railway designed exclusively for local city service. Horse railways promised to combine the low cost, flexibility, and safety of animal power with the efficiency, smoothness, and all-weather capability of an iron right-of-way. They were, in short, a blend of the virtues of omnibus and train. In 1852 several companies tried the innovation in New York. Their success was immediately noted and widely discussed in Boston and its suburbs.[35]

The first attempts to bring horse railroads to New England came from groups organized in Roxbury and Cambridge in the winter of 1852/53. Forty years of suburban enterprise came together in the promotion of the streetcar. In May 1853, the legislature chartered the Cambridge Railroad Company, the first horse railroad in New England. Heading the list of incorporators were names that joined the era of fringe enterprise with the era of branch railroads: Isaac Livermore, C. C. Little, G. G. Hubbard, and Estes Howe. Among the nine directors were a soapmaker, a Faneuil Hall marketman, a Boston wholesaler, a real estate speculator, and an omnibus proprietor. Six worked in Boston, three in Cambridge. The directors lived in Cambridgeport, Old Cambridge, northern Cambridge, and Somerville, but not in East Cambridge or Boston.[36]

Somerville had fewer people, a smaller tax base, a less diverse economy, and a shorter history of development than Cambridge. But these deficiencies were no obstacle to promotion, because the fever of suburb building had spread throughout the region. Just as they had launched a new town, Somerville entrepreneurs proposed a horse railroad and found supporters within and without their community. The leading figure was George Brastow, the land developer who had moved to Somerville just as the town was created. By 1850, when he was thirty-eight, he had amassed a fortune dealing in land near the Fitchburg but still had many lots to sell.[37]

In 1854, Brastow and six others formed the Middlesex Horse Railroad Company, a venture that reflected Somerville's difference from Cambridge. Whereas Cambridge men started and ran their own railroad, Somerville promoters drew heavily on outside backing. Only two of the seven incorporators lived in Somerville at the time. Of the other five, one was the Boston partner of a Somerville resident, one ran an omnibus line in Charlestown, one was a brickmaker with yards in Cambridge, and two were Bostonians who had no visible connection with the suburbs.[38]

Yet these two corporations, so different in composition and backing, also reflected an emerging similarity between Somerville and Cambridge—a movement of all the fringe villages toward a common pattern of suburban promotion. For many of the backers, the streetcar was an element in a larger vision of growth. John and Isaac Livermore, both directors of the Cambridge company, had a hand in nearly every phase of suburban development. Isaac ran the free bridge company and helped write the city charter. John joined with Hubbard and Howe to organize a gas company and a waterworks while they were promoting the streetcars. Brastow and two of the Cambridge promoters had spent years buying and subdividing land, building cottages, and touting suburban amenities. All three of these developers had been separatists in 1842, trying to create attractive residential corporations in western Cambridge and Charlestown.[39]

After assorted problems of finance and construction, both corporations opened rail service along the old omnibus routes, in Cambridge in 1856, in

Somerville in 1858. Extensions were planned even before the first cars ran. Rapid construction in the late 1850s linked East Cambridge with Cambridgeport and Boston, extended service through western Cambridge and northern Somerville, and stretched the end of the line into Malden, West Cambridge, and Watertown before the Civil War. By 1860 the realm of half-hourly streetcar service extended through all the main centers within five miles of the city.[40]

Very quickly, the street railway became a fixed part of suburban life. The scale of its operations soon surpassed even the biggest omnibus companies. By June 1857, a year after its opening, the Cambridge Railroad used 30 cars and 220 horses and carried an estimated five thousand passengers daily. Omnibuses disappeared from the commuter arteries, though they retained a role as "feeders" in the suburbs and distributors in Boston.[41]

The first few years of operation also brought signs of the streetcar's long-term impact. In the beginning, those who rode the horse railroads were similar to those who built them. The period after 1855 saw a dramatic increase in the number of commuting attorneys (table 5.5); by 1860 more than half the lawyers listed in the business directory lived outside Boston. The Panic of 1857 and the ensuing economic decline probably slowed the spread of riding to nonelite groups, but the trend was clear even in the late 1850s. With fares fixed by law at five cents, streetcars allowed many more workers to ride. The suburbs became accessible to doctors, skilled workers, clerks, and even some laborers. Along with the freeing of the bridges, streetcars also weakened the long-standing difference in conditions of access that separated Cambridge from Somerville and the various parts of Cambridge from each other.

"Commutation," considered in this larger sense, involved far more than a change in fares, apparatus, or the distance to work. The mobility revolution had outgrown its origins in the hustling enterprise of the fringe. While there was a direct connection between the coaches of the 1820s and the streetcars of the 1850s, the latter also symbolized a reorientation of goals and resources in the suburbs. Mass carriers, mass commuting, and residential promotion now ranked among the central engines of growth. Cheap riding by large numbers confirmed the transition from fringe society to a new kind of suburban community.

This reordering was no brief or simple process. The mobility revolution itself took thirty years, and it was not the only influence upon community development. Suburbanites found that mobility carried them ever more clearly into a metropolitan setting. They had to think and act not only as residents of their respective villages, but also as part-time or potential citizens of the metropolis. In these circumstances, how could they integrate what they valued from the fringe with what they wanted from the city? Put another way, how could they control the degree of their urbanization? The new suburbs that took form in the fifties were premised upon riding, but shaped by a lengthy and contentious period of suburban wrestling with these dilemmas which riding brought to them.

PART THREE

Settling Down

6

Suburban Society: Goals and Boundaries

Porter Square Cattle Market, northern Cambridge,
late 1850s. In the background are the Porter Hotel
and the spire of the Congregational Church, which also appears,
viewed from the other side, in the illustration on the cover.
Ballou's Pictorial Drawing Room Companion, 2 July 1859.
Courtesy of the Boston Athenaeum.

IN THE 1830s and early 1840s, people on the fringe encouraged and exploited the mobility revolution. In the late 1840s and 1850s, they had to assimilate that revolution and adjust to its implications. They could take pride in their achievements: New means of access to the city, remodeled governments in the suburbs, and dramatic growth were all evidence of success. Yet in their success they had started engines which took off in unexpected directions. Socially and politically, the suburbs in the 1850s became communities different from those envisioned before 1845. Exploding populations and greater access to Boston produced clashes of interest and anxiety about the future.

Until the late 1850s, middle-class suburbanites struggled to preserve the New Model ideal of the early 1840s. They had a vision of small enterprise and scattered residential settlement; of simple, cheap, municipal corporations; of leadership by the natural stewards of the community, whether they were deacons or tradesmen or commuters, old or new residents of the town. The New Model ideal had always been flawed by contradictions, and these were highlighted by the booming growth of the period 1843–57. Growth brought large-scale enterprise into small-town settings, sparked conflict between fringe entrepreneurs and commuters, and threatened the cooperative voluntarism that underlay the ideal.

As reality threatened the dream, influential suburbanites redefined their goals. To preserve even part of the vision, they had to narrow and sharpen their conception of suburban society: it was to be devoted primarily to middle-class, native-born commuter residence, not to industry or commerce. They had also to refine their conception of suburban government: it was to provide residential services and to promote the interests of each residential suburb vis-à-vis those of its neighbors or of the city. By the 1860s, residential growth seemed to suburbanites the single best hope for the future. All other interests, whether they were left over from the fringe or advanced from the city, were seen as threats. The last three chapters of this book outline this process of social and political redefinition, which accelerated to a crisis in the late 1850s and then stabilized in the decade of Civil War.

Industry, Residence, and the New Suburban Landscape

For suburbanites, the elevation of residential goals and the displacement of the fringe inheritance was a response to social strains that arose from both external and internal sources and appeared in a particular sequence. The shift to a residential definition of society was not simply thrust upon them from without. Commuters, the apparatus of commutation, and the more general shift from walking to riding were central ingredients. But there was no mere conquest of the suburbs by Bostonians, or extension of Boston's kind of urbanism. To look at it this way is to ignore the whole previous history of separate development and to misread the roles played by commuters and noncommuters alike. Suburbanites defined residential society because they were worried about change in the suburbs as well as in the city-suburban relationship.

From their viewpoint, the social transformation of the late forties and fifties presented two related challenges. One was a problem of social geography. The array of separate villages was disappearing as settlement filled the gaps and the life of the suburbs became more entangled with that of the city. Suburban society became less a collection of villages, more a mosaic of neighborhoods or zones, which did not always fit together harmoniously. The second problem involved social organization. Density and numbers eroded the small-town basis of cooperation and leadership. Institutions and norms inherited from the fringe could not easily accommodate big corporate enterprise, immigrant wage laborers, or masses of unrooted commuters. Both kinds of change caused elite suburbanites to worry about boundaries, not only between city and suburbs, but between areas, classes, and activities within the suburbs, between moral and immoral behavior, and between reliable and unreliable leaders. Their vision of a residential role for the suburbs within the metropolis was directly related to their quest for secure space within a troubling suburban landscape.

In this readjustment of their vision, the timing of the mobility revolution was crucial, since it made some areas and activities seem substantially "safer" than others. During a critical ten-year period from the mid-1840s to the mid-1850s, residential promotion seemed to be an unqualified blessing. In these years, suburbanites faced rapid growth, a flood of well-heeled commuters, and speculative promotion, but significant barriers remained between city and suburban society. Until the horsecars came, commuting was still an elite activity—open to a much larger elite, to be sure, but still closed to those who did not fit prevailing notions of respectability. City and suburban economic spheres were joined regularly only for the prosperous. In the late 1850s, the streetcars and the freeing of the bridges dropped most of the restrictions and began to merge those spheres—but this occurred only after residential promotion and mass commuting were thoroughly established elements of suburban society.

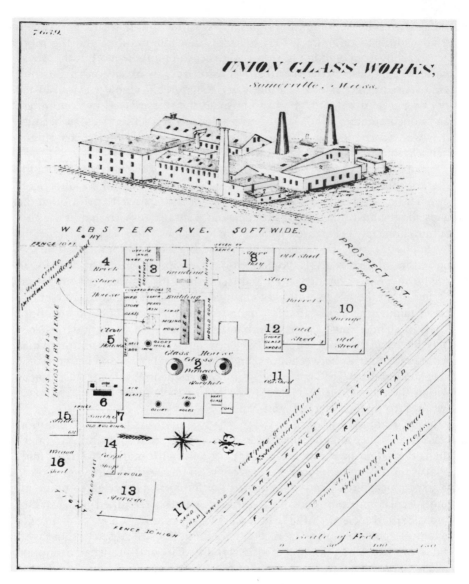

Union Glass Works, Somerville, showing the new scale of railroad-oriented industry in the 1850s. Courtesy of the Somerville Historical Society.

In the meantime, the suburban elite faced dramatic and often threatening changes from nonresidential growth. As they saw it, after 1845 the environment was marked by radically increasing economic diversity and contained many sources of prosperity and many surprises. Improved transportation, for example, stimulated not only the residential part of the suburban economy but the manufacturing and commercial parts as well. There was no simple replacement of fringe activities by residential promotion. Rather, the mobility revolution produced a change in the mixture of residential and nonresidential pursuits, a finer differentiation of land use, and sharp juxtapositions of different and neighboring activities. In some ways, residential development became important *by contrast* with other processes of suburban growth.

Before the mass-transportation era the suburban economy had two foundations: country traffic and city-oriented manufactures. After 1840, improved transportation undercut the former and changed the character of the latter. Railroads from distant places bypassed the brokerage points on the fringe. Farmers shipped by rail direct to the center, those who dealt in their products moved from the periphery inward, and Boston businessmen took over many of the functions once carried out in the towns nearby. Meanwhile, rail freight transportation opened bigger markets for manufactures and enhanced the value of empty tracts of land available in the suburbs. In East Cambridge, eastern Somerville, and Cambridgeport, rail spurs allowed an expansion of existing fringe pursuits and fostered new, factory-based heavy industry (fig. 8). Two new glass companies appeared in East Cambridge and Somerville. With the older New England Glass Company, they employed at least 631 people by 1855. Slaughterhouses in the same era evolved into huge rail-based packing plants. Brickyards in western Cambridge and Medford mushroomed, opening new clay beds, employing scores of unskilled workers, and shipping millions of bricks by rail to the city and beyond.[1]

In Cambridgeport and southern Somerville, heavy industry—a brass tube works, several foundries, and a railroad car factory—replaced some of the artisan shops. By 1855 the car factory had become a major supplier of rolling stock for the northeastern states, employing 250 men. At the same time, some of the older craft industries—soapworks, tanneries, smithies, wheelwrights—expanded in the prosperous years from 1843 to 1857.[2]

Along with expanding production appeared new agencies of finance. In the entire Charlestown-Somerville-Cambridge area in 1845 there were three banks and two savings institutions. No new bank of any kind had been established since 1834. By 1861 there were eight banks and five savings banks. Some of the new firms were offshoots of the old: The Cambridge Bank, for

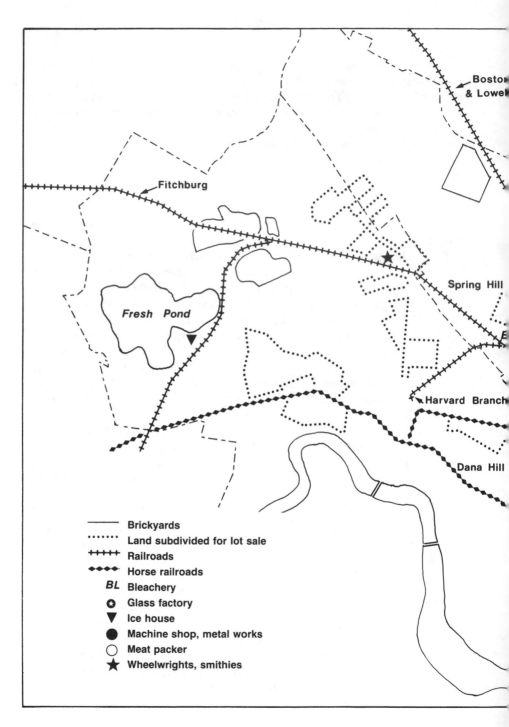

Figure 8   Locations of New Economic Activity, 1843–60

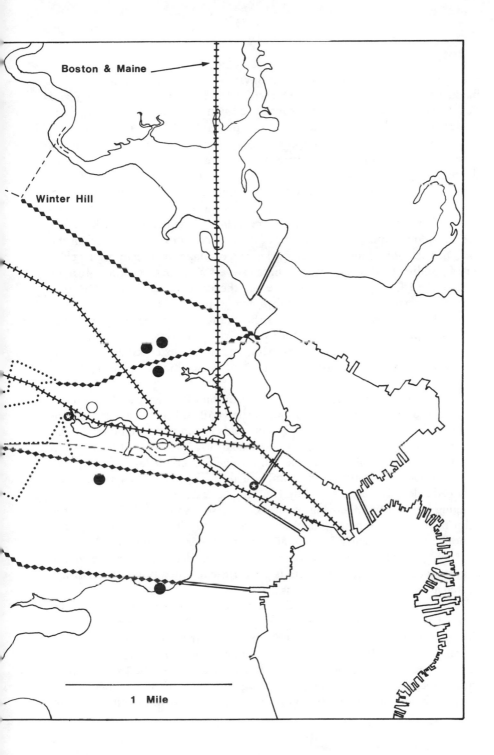

Boston & Maine

Winter Hill

1 Mile

example, spawned the Cambridgeport Savings Bank and the Cambridge City Bank, a short distance down Main Street, in 1853. Northern Cambridge and East Cambridge both produced specialized banks serving the needs of the cattle market and factory communities, respectively.[3]

The new pattern of growth also changed the composition of the suburban labor force. Each suburb experienced a few overall changes: an increase in the number of unskilled workers in Cambridge (from 14 percent to 20 percent of those reporting occupations in a sample of census household heads), of clerical workers in Somerville (from 2 percent to 12 percent), and of certain skilled occupations (metalsmiths, machinists, engineers) in both places. Perhaps more important to contemporary suburbanites were changes in the local distribution of jobs. In each of the fringe villages there had been a cluster of building tradesmen, two or three lawyers and doctors, and a store or two. In the 1850s such people who served the local residents spread beyond the old centers. Listings in the Cambridge business directory provide an imperfect but unmistakable measure of the change. Each year they included more specialized and urban categories of work (architects, surveyors, sellers of stationery and notions, confectioners, and half a dozen kinds of masons and woodworking specialists), and gave addresses more remote from the original foci.[4]

These changes in the types, scale, and location of industry and commerce had roots in the fringe, but the boom of the 1850s substantially altered that earlier pattern of growth, sifting out some old elements and changing the importance of others. One change was the near disappearance of farming. In 1840, the agricultural share of the Cambridge-Somerville labor force probably approached one-fifth of the total (see above, pp. 30 ff.). By 1850 it had dropped below 10 percent, and by 1860 to about 2 percent.[5] Only a handful of aging farmers and a few big commercial nurseries survived to connect the suburbs to the rural past. The new economy also offered less to the young opportunists of the early Jacksonian era—the tavernkeepers, omnibus proprietors, peripatetic small speculators. Taverns declined along with the country wagon traffic, and omnibus concerns expanded briefly, then disappeared as the streetcar corporations grew.

There were individuals who made a successful transition from the speculations of the fringe to the new economy of the 1850s, but they did so by changing the scope of their activities, absorbing small concerns, and reaching out to new markets. Peter Hubbell, for example, began a long and prosperous career in this region as a small-time brickmaker. In the 1840s he tried various locations in Somerville, Cambridgeport, and finally northern Cambridge. There, with the aid of a partner, he struck it rich. For fifteen years, through lease and purchase, he assembled clay land along the railroad. In the fifties he bought out his partner and introduced steam-powered brickmaking machinery. By the end of the decade he had established a sprawling complex of pits, yards, sheds, and rail sidings, worked by scores of Irish laborers, which he managed from a mansion in Charlestown. Soon after, he incorporated the whole as the Bay State Brick Company, an enterprise that would dominate northern Cambridge well into the twentieth century.[6]

Hubbell's story was not typical of individual careers; only a few had his shrewdness and luck. But his successful adaptation did illustrate the general change in the economy. Farmers and fringe hustlers were in decline. The hallmarks of the new economy were an increased scale of operations, the consolidation of small units, close connections with city and regional demand, and large numbers of low-skilled wageworkers. The shift to the new pattern of the 1850s also involved several dramatic changes in social geography. In the old fringe era, nonfarm activity clustered heavily in the village centers. Now railroad lines, plus a need for big tracts of land, carried industry into new areas. Instead of three or four village centers, one could distinguish a variety of economic zones. A comparison of figure 6 with figure 2 suggests the magnitude of the industrial diaspora. East Cambridge and the Lower Port area of eastern Cambridgeport remained the dominant locales, but in the fifties there were manufacturing establishments all along the railroad through eastern Somerville and northern Cambridge. Big chunks of farmland in the western areas were taken over for brickyards, tanneries, and the barracks and boardinghouses that sheltered their workers. More big parcels were taken by the new rail and streetcar corporations for sidings, switchyards, and stables.[7]

These establishments brought machinery, smoke, noise, and odors to areas that had recently been rural. They dumped their waste products in the back lots and streams of the region. They deepened the industrial mark on the landscape. Most important, from the viewpoint of the middle-class, native-born suburbanites, they created concentrations of unskilled workers, many of them foreigners.

In 1840 the suburban population had been overwhelmingly native-born. Only near the East Cambridge glass factories was there a noticeable community of foreign-born workers, and these were highly skilled, proud, and prosperous craftsmen, living in single-family houses which many of them owned. The opportunities of the fringe also attracted newcomers from the New England interior, but few from overseas. After 1845, the great Irish famine migration changed that pattern for the nearby suburbs as it did for Boston, and the geography of industrial growth heightened the impact of migration. By

1850 more than a fourth of the household heads in both Cambridge and Somerville were foreign born, and by 1860 that proportion rose to two-fifths (see table 6.1). In northern Cambridge and East Cambridge the foreign-born were in the majority; in Somerville and the most industrialized parts of Cambridgeport, nearly so. The flow of immigrants into these areas was all the more visible because it contrasted with migration streams into other areas nearby. Where the Irish settled most heavily, the proportion of native-born newcomers (born in the U.S. outside Massachusetts) shrank. But in Old Cambridge, the old center of Cambridgeport, and some parts of eastern Somerville, the boom of the 1850s enlarged the receiving areas of native-born migrants, and the foreign-born remained a distinct minority.

At the neighborhood level, these variations in nativity were even more striking. Households in the oldest areas—along the arterial roads and in the village centers of Old Cambridge and Cambridgeport—remained mostly native-born. But startling things occurred very close by, in previously empty areas. In 1840, even in 1850, the census takers found relatively few people in the flatlands separating East Cambridge from Sandpit Square in Somerville or in the great fields north and west of Porter Square in Cambridge. By 1860 the enumerators who probed these areas recorded page after page of propertyless Irish households. In northern Cambridge they found families like that of John Dalton, laborer and boardinghouse keeper, whose "household" included wife, children, two domestics, and seventy-three foreign-born brickmakers. Along the railroad in southeastern Somerville the enumerator visited several stretches of 60–100 households in which only the youngest children had been born in America and in which nearly everyone was employed in the bleachery or the tube works.[8]

Middle-class suburbanites could see the effects of economic transformation not only in their surroundings and among their neighbors but in the tax rolls compiled yearly by the assessors (and published from the mid-1840s on).[9] Commercial and industrial firms and their leaders gained new prominence among the wealthy. In the 1840s the biggest taxpayers in Cambridge and Somerville were the large estate owners and farmers of the western areas, followed by the glass company and a variety of fringe enterprises—nurseries, lumber wharves, ice and brick producers. By 1860 there were fewer big landowners, and they had slipped down the list of ranking taxpayers, displaced by the glassworks, bleachery, meat packing and other big businesses. The new economy also provided a basis for several new individual fortunes. In 1860, Cambridge and Somerville contained 132 male individuals assessed for $20,000 or more.[10] Of these, 72 represented new wealth—people who

Table 6.1

Nativity of the Suburban Population, 1850 and 1860

A. Total Population

Place of Birth	Somerville		Cambridge	
	1850	1860	1850	1860
Foreign	29%	43%	33%	46%
Massachusetts	35	29	44	34
Other U.S.	38	28	24	20
N	145	157	351	505

B. Cambridge by Wards

Place of Birth	North Cambridge		Old Cambridge		North Cambridgeport		South Cambridgeport		East Cambridge	
	1850	1860	1850	1860	1850	1860	1850	1860	1850	1860
Foreign	39%	58%	23%	29%	27%	47%	21%	32%	50%	58%
Massachusetts	38	30	67	50	44	29	58	41	23	26
Other U.S.	22	11	10	19	29	22	22	26	28	17
N	28	43	58	76	91	138	71	116	103	132

SOURCE: Interval sample of census households. Cambridge had only three wards in 1850. Sample households have been reallocated into the five wards of 1860 through use of directories, maps, and tax records.

were not present ten years earlier or had doubled their assessed value over the decade. About a third of these arrivés gained wealth in occupations connected with the suburban industrial-commercial boom of the 1850s: builders, masons, grocers, shoe dealers, agents and owners of manufacturing firms, and a few dealers in land.[11]

The promotion and settlement of commuter residential areas took place within this booming industrial and commercial context. In this realm, too, growth brought departures and surprises, and some of these were analogous to the changes in other areas—matters of scale and specialization. But residential development took on special prominence for two reasons. First, it changed the landscape in ways that contrasted sharply and favorably with the changes wrought by industry. Second, the sequence of change was different: until the mid-1850s residential promotion did not involve many innovations in procedure or new institutions.

In the beginning, residential and nonresidential growth seemed to flow from the same sources. Both were parts of a general entrepreneurial surge that brought prosperity. The same railroad that carried bricks, butchered meat, and metal tubing from the suburbs brought the elite commuters of the late 1840s and early 1850s to new homes. While industry transformed the flats south of the Fitchburg in Somerville and northwest of Porter Square in Cambridge, small lot promoters were at work literally on the other side of the tracks—in the hills north of the Fitchburg railroad and in the fields east of Porter Square (see fig. 6). The omnibus lines encouraged similar promotion in the Dana Hill area, just north and west of the factory-foundry area of Cambridgeport. Like the expansion of industry, this expansion of residence took place in previously undeveloped space, outside the old village centers, between the old road-centered strips of enterprise.

Like nonresidential growth, the initial pattern of residential growth had roots in the dreams and goals of the thirties, altered by new features of scale and proliferation. The general idea of lot subdivision, after all, went back to the schemes of Craigie and the Cambridgeport proprietors at the turn of the century. New Model reformers had connected such ideas to the notion of commuter residence, and the railroad spread the vision throughout the Middlesex region. Not only in Cambridge and Somerville, but for miles beyond, railroad villages sprang from the fields between the mid-1840s and the big hike of railroad fares in 1855.[12]

In the inner suburbs the successful development of the 1850s sometimes had direct links to the experiments of the 1830s. When Hayward, Whittemore, and the other New Model reformers projected their residential vision, they expected individuals and informal groups of neighbors to do much of the work. The railroad companies, then just beginning to discover commuting, were the only large, chartered, heavily capitalized elements involved in the suburban dream. By and large, omnibuses and walking took care of transportation. Water, drainage, and amenities, if any, were the concerns of the builder and the homeowner. Even the biggest and most novel improvements—public space, graded schools, regular streets, the reform of local government itself—were to be projects of the most eminent citizens in town meeting.

In the 1840s and early 1850s, residential development—much more than industrial or commercial—still seemed to be an expansion on this earlier model. Among the main promoters of the fifties were people who began their careers in the fringe period: entrepreneurs like George Brastow in Somerville, the Dana family in Cambridgeport, and George Meacham in North Cambridge. Like Peter Hubbell, the brickmaker, these promoters made the shift from the erratic speculations of the fringe to the booming development of the economy after 1845, but unlike Hubbell, they did so without immediate innovations in organization or technique.

Even the horse railroads, which would grow into the largest, most visible, and most controversial corporations in the suburbs, seemed at first like the banks and bridge companies of the past—efforts by the civic-minded "best men," suited to the needs of the suburbs.

In the spring of 1853, when Cambridge promoters organized the first horse railroad company, the *Cambridge Chronicle* hailed the enterprise: "The grand object for the people of Cambridge, in which also Bostonians and the community generally have a common interest, is to secure a commodious, cheap, and expeditious means of conveyance to and from the metropolis." The railroad would enhance property values, reduce paving expenses, and provide better accommodation than steam. What could be better than to "be whirled into Boston, *a la* steam, on iron rails by horse power." Later, when steam railroads hiked their fares, the horsecar promoters seemed even more truly stewards and benefactors of the community. "It is a great relief and pleasure," said a North Cambridge resident, "after having travelled . . . in the heat and dust and I may say smoke of the steam cars, and being thrown off . . . at Porter's Station, to enter the Cambridge cars and find those connected with them kind and obliging."[13]

Only in the mid-fifties did suburbanites begin to qualify this conception of the streetcar companies as neighborly and humane institutions. When the lines were open and running, it became clear that these corporations were not like the village-based organizations of the fringe. With the permission of local governments, but without much detailed supervision, the corporate directors made decisions that had sweeping consequences. Within months they had bought out or destroyed the omnibus proprietors. Each year they permanently altered more miles of public streets by laying track and regrading the surface. (Industrial promoters, by contrast, left their imprint largely on private land.) Scores of cars, horses, drivers, and conductors made the corporate presence obvious and underlined the new relationship between residential development and company enterprise.[14]

In the same way the activities of the gas and water companies were at first welcomed, and only later seemed questionable. Beginning in 1853, local corporations undertook to supply such residential amenities to old Cambridge and parts of Cambridgeport. By the mid-fifties they too were engaged in the seemingly endless process of ripping up streets—to lay mains and then soon after to enlarge or extend them. Somerville promoter George Brastow persuaded the Cambridge water company to supply Fresh Pond water to his Spring Hill subdivision and lobbied the Somerville selectmen to give their blessing to the deal. In the name of residential promotion, both gas and water companies blurred all the old town and village distinctions, pushing through service to those areas where lot sales prospered—Spring Hill, northern Cambridge, and Dana Hill—while largely ignoring the old industrial and commercial centers in Cambridgeport and East Cambridge.[15]

In the late 1850s, corporate enterprise and steam railroad fare increases combined to add intensity and visibility to residential promotion in the inner suburbs. Cambridge and Somerville now had cheap transportation and city amenities. The outer suburbs were suddenly more expensive. Consequently, the boom focused on a few small areas of the inner suburbs, which quickly took on all the attributes of the streetcar suburbs that would become dominant in the 1870s: large corporations provided transportation and services, a few leading speculators and many small investors did the work of subdivision and sale. As individuals or in small collaborations, they laid out streets and built clusters of houses—two, five, perhaps ten structures at a time.[16]

In Cambridge and Somerville, such efforts were keyed to every form of transportation and designed to carve out and protect areas for residence in the context of the fringe. The Dana family in Cambridge, the Brastow-led group on Spring Hill in Somerville, and other groups in northern Cambridge all made careful use of deed restrictions. Titles to new lots contained covenants against using the property for any major commercial or industrial purpose.[17]

These developments, however, reached a peak only in the late fifties. For most of the decade before that, residential development remained popular, noncontroversial, and surrounded by a powerful glow of rural nostalgia. The rhetoric employed by promoters and journalists stressed the dream of "country residences" (see chap. 5), and some buyers of suburban homes seem to have purchased the vision along with the property. Thus, among the new rail commuters in Somerville, perched on their hillside lots overlooking the bleachery and the tube works, were a number who identified themselves to the census taker as "farmer" or "yeoman." Twenty years before, there had been true farmers in that location. But in the 1850s most of the inhabitants were in fact Bostonian migrants—who may have had vegetable plots and gentleman farmer pretensions, but whose feet were mired in the paper of their city offices.

Residential promotion was also popular because of its ties to wealth. Throughout the forties and fifties, in both the small-scale period and, after 1855, the state of intense, corporate-backed activity, residential development contributed heavily to the change in suburban tax rolls—and in ways more extensive and seemingly more healthy than the changes caused by commerce and industry. Lot promotion brought the suburbs a different kind of wealth: not only prosperous firms and rich individuals but a large and expanding class of respectable homeowners. In further contrast with industry, which attracted poor immigrants, residential promotion pulled in gentlemen of property. Indeed, despite the rise in industry and the rapid growth of population in general, the residential boom sustained a strong upper middle class in the suburbs. During the 1850s the proportion of male taxpayers who were assessed for any substantial amount of property (here defined as $4,000 or more) remained relatively constant in each of the suburban communities (see table 6.2). New commuters played the major role in preserving the numerical strength of this property-owning class. In 1850 there were 561 men in the $4,000+ bracket, 27 percent of whom worked in Boston. By 1860 the group had expanded to 909; 39 percent of this total and 58 percent of the new additions were commuters. (See also table 5.7 above, and accompanying discussion.)

On top of this broad-based prosperity, residential growth also produced the same kinds of highly visible corporate and individual wealth generated by industry. The horse railroads and utilities, of course, were among the suburbs' very largest taxpayers by 1860. Some spectacular success stories, too, were based on shrewd lot promotion. North Cambridge resident Henry Potter, for example, began his career in the 1840s as a Faneuil Hall dealer in meat and set up a meat-packing plant near the Porter Square cattle market. This business made him a moderately prosperous man by 1850, but in the

Table 6.2

Male Taxpayers, Cambridge and Somerville, 1850 and 1860

Taxpayer Characteristics	Somerville	Old Cambridge	Cambridgeport	East Cambridge	Total
A. 1850					
Total paying poll tax	815	915	1,538	983	4,251
Males assessed for $4,000 or more	126	161	199	75	561
$4,000 assessments as percent of polls	16%	18%	13%	8%	13%
Known Boston workers as percent of $4,000 assessments	29%	21%	36%	13%	27%
B. 1860					
Total paying poll tax	1,800	1,290	2,739	1,600	7,432
Males assessed for $4,000 or more	251	249	314	95	909
$4,000 assessments as percent of polls	14%	20%	12%	6%	12%
Known Boston workers as percent of $4,000 assessments	46%	35%	43%	16%	39%

SOURCE: Compiled from Cambridge tax rolls, 1850 and 1860 (microfilm, Cambridge Public Library), and Somerville tax lists published in the annual reports. Workplaces were obtained through linkage of tax entries to Boston and Cambridge directories.

following decade he began promoting lots near Porter Square and became a truly wealthy one. By 1860 he was the eighth biggest taxpayer in Cambridge. A few years later he would close down the packinghouse and sell that property too for building lots.[18]

When contemporary suburbanites looked for evidence of prosperity, this residential boom counted heavily in the balance. By the late fifties, the editor of the *Cambridge Chronicle* compiled long lists of houses under construction, emphasizing the value of each. Somerville's selectmen, while worrying about the strains of rapid growth, welcomed commuter residents because they "add largely to the value" of land.[19] Wealth represented by respectable families in houses was now at least as important as any other kind in the community inventory. In the long shift away from a fringe economy toward one that assimilated the mobility revolution, activities linked to residence assumed a new and powerful position. The suburban communities no longer focused on trading and shipping country goods or making small products for the city. The new foundations of the peripheral economy were heavy manufactures for a regional market and providing housing, transport, and services for Bostonians.

Taken all together, the varied kinds of enterprise and growth occurring in the suburbs placed the inhabitants in a new, rapidly changing, unpredictable environment. For middle-class suburbanites, the situation was both exciting and confusing. Prosperity of all kinds was desirable, but the new economy of the 1850s brought sharper contrasts between the different forms. Within the industrial sphere, there was a contrast between the old centers of shop manufacturing—which continued to attract native-born workingmen to Cambridgeport, eastern Somerville, and the cattle market vicinity of northern Cambridge—and the new zones of heavy industry and extraction—which created foreign-born concentrations in newly opened areas. There was also a more general contrast between nonresidential growth—with its new scale, machinery, and immigrant work force—and residential expansion—with its attraction of genteel taxpayers.

These contrasts were all the more striking because increasing population density brought everything closer together. Native-born soap-factory workers in eastern Cambridgeport lived but a few hundred yards from an Irish settlement on previously empty flats in East Cambridge. Elite residential communities were check-by-jowl with other land uses: Brastow's Spring Hill was across the road from the old bleachery; the northern Cambridge railroad village was next to the cattle market. The New Model vision had presumed a diverse economy, but in this new landscape diverse elements seemed to clash rather than blend harmoniously.

Domestic Space and the City Threat

In response to these shifting circumstances, suburban leaders both refined their thinking about what suburbs should be and became steadily more anxious about what they were. As the economy departed from its fringe inheritance, becoming more diverse and specialized, so influential suburbanites moved beyond the fuzzy, informal program of the New Model reformers. In their response, evolving between 1845 and 1860, three goals may be distinguished: an attempt to ensure the absolute moral purity of small residential neighborhoods, an effort to defend entire suburban municipalities against undesirable influences from the city, and an effort to combat generalized urban evils within the suburb itself.

The sequence of economic change strongly influenced the sequence of response. From the early forties to the mid-fifties, the suburbs experienced a stage of growth in which industry grew more obtrusive and residential promotion seemed an unmixed blessing. Only in the late fifties did commuters and residential institutions become problematic. In parallel fashion, suburban spokesmen spent a decade glorifying residential interests and domesticity, heightening residential-industrial contrasts, and raising anxiety over threats. But in the late fifties, suburbanites had to confront conflicts between residential goals and other interests and doubts about some of the means they employed to promote a wholesome domestic environment.

Central to the whole pattern of defensive response was the definition and protection of residential neighborhoods. In a later era, Americans would pursue this goal through zoning—classifying broad and precisely defined tracts of land for residential or other use and enforcing the boundaries through legal procedures. In the forties and fifties, the concept of land-use classification was sixty years in the future. Antebellum suburbanites did not think in these terms. The steps they took in the 1850s were based on a different conception of neighborhood.[20]

Investigators of the twentieth-century city sometimes ask its residents to draw "cognitive maps," which indicate the boundaries and focal points of their personal communities.[21] Modern city dwellers commonly define these communities in terms of perceived limits—streets, railroads, waterways, or adjacent areas of very different population or economic usage. Although they may differ on the exact location of boundaries, they agree in stressing the borders as essential to the notion of neighborhood.

When suburbanites of the 1830s and 1840s spoke of their communities, they rarely mentioned boundaries. The social geography of the fringe, centered on the villages and the wandering roads that linked them, emphasized focal points instead. Striking evidence of this orientation survives in the recollections of a few of Somerville's pioneers. Late in the nineteenth century, the town's oldest inhabitants were asked to describe the "neighborhoods" of their youth.[22] Invariably the request triggered a detailed and geographically ordered list of buildings, parcels of property, ponds, woods, and other landmarks. These elderly suburbanites spoke as if they were walking through the old town, gossiping about neighbors and noting what could be seen from various vantages. Although their memories were remarkably accurate about details, they were notably vague about limits. When used to produce cognitive maps of a sort (fig. 9), they clearly indicate an orientation to clumps of houses and other landmarks and only a vague sense of what lay beyond; their neighborhoods shade off into ill-defined space.

Residentially oriented suburbanites of the 1840s and 1850s inherited and subtly modified this older conception of neighborhood. Throughout this period they continued to emphasize the ingredients of community more than the borders. They did not simply shift from a fringe notion of neighborhood to a city district conception. But as they clarified the goals of residential development, they gave more stress to those neighborhood ingredients that were connected with domesticity. And as the ill-defined spaces began to fill up, they paid more attention to the relationships between their residential areas and the sharply divergent areas nearby.

This shift toward the residential neighborhood gained strength from a new emphasis on domesticity in middle-class culture at large. Since the fringe era, the most important ingredients of community had been neighbors and their homes. In the Victorian era "home" took on powerful added connotations. Writers on religion, like Horace Bushnell, argued that good family relations in the home were essential to the nurture of children and the moral health of the Republic. Writers on architecture and building, like Andrew Jackson Downing, insisted that the style and internal arrangement of houses—especially new houses in the suburbs—were crucial in fostering strong family bonds and humane sentiments. Writers on homemaking and the role of women, like Catherine Beecher, emphasized the sanctity of the domestic sphere and elevated the responsibility of women in safeguarding it. Home and family, in general, were among the chief bulwarks against moral corrosion in a commercialized and industrializing world.[23]

The new ideology found ready expression in Boston's inner suburbs. John Ford, editor of the *Cambridge Chronicle*, happily dispensed home ideals in editorials, homilies, and book reviews. He lectured his readers on the importance of "sociability" in the home, lest children seek it abroad and fall in with bad company. With a nod toward Beecher and the building journals, he advocated standard plans for houses, designed for the convenience of the homemaker.[24]

In such statements Ford merely echoed the popular writers on domesticity, who focused on individual dwellings and social relations within them. But Ford and other suburbanites went further. Infected with residential boosterism, they combined the new ideas about home with the established, focal-

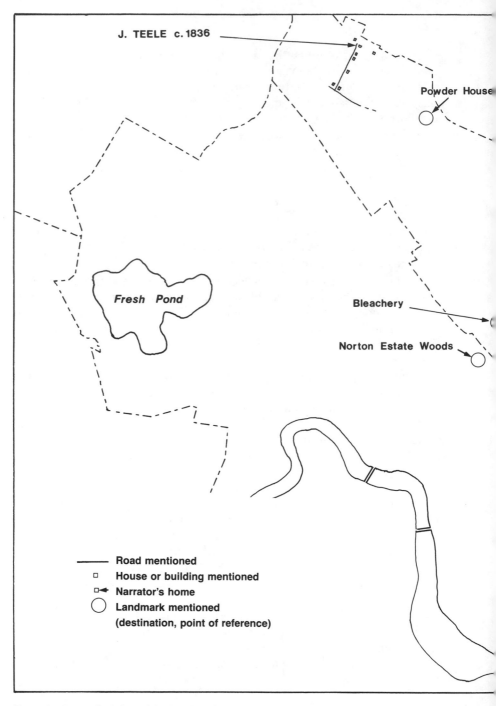

Figure 9 Remembered Neighborhoods, 1836–50

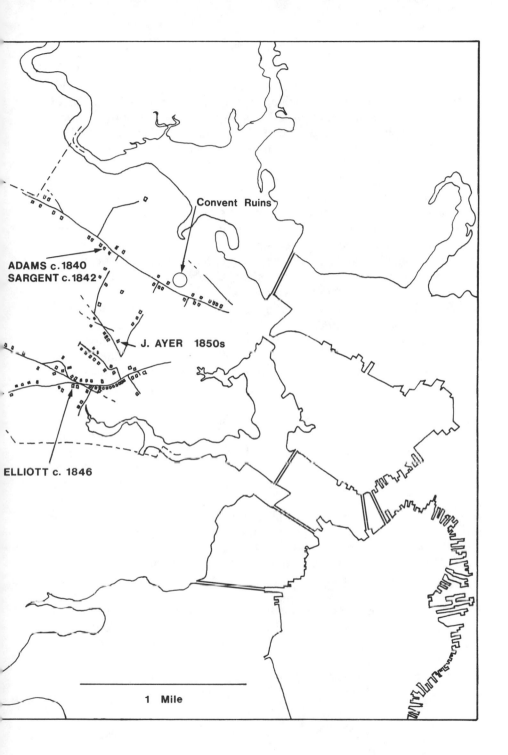

Convent Ruins

ADAMS c. 1840
SARGENT c. 1842

J. AYER   1850s

ELLIOTT c. 1846

1   Mile

point-centered notions of neighborhood. They extended the concept of domesticity beyond the house, attaching it to groups of houses and areas of respectable, middle-class residence. A domestic environment for the home was just as desirable as domesticity in the home. Thus, when Ford and others spoke of Cambridge or Somerville as "desirable as a place for residence," they frequently linked that phrase explicitly with the moral, aesthetic, and practical aspects of domesticity. They wanted their communities to inculcate the habits and sentiments and in general to maximize the advantages of home. By the late 1850s, some felt that the domestic sphere included the whole suburban residential sector: a newspaper correspondent defended that sphere against the threat of Sunday streetcars. Cambridge citizens, he said, already had business interests in Boston. If they moved their "religious, educational, moral, and social" interests there, too, then "Cambridge cannot be a home, according to the New England idea of home."[25]

When residentially oriented suburbanites felt threatened by the increasingly sharp contrasts in the landscape around them, their response drew upon this ideologically charged, home-centered conception of neighborhood and community. They paid more attention to the borders between middle-class residential settlements and other economic areas, but they did not—could not—simply draw lines around tracts of land in a categorical fashion. Rather, they tried to strengthen the ingredients of community and to assert the influence of domesticity more aggressively against neighboring threats.

In promoting and protecting their neighborhoods, these suburbanites made two important changes in their thinking about space. On the one hand they devoted more energy to the particular features of small areas; on the other they generalized the goals of domesticity, making them a duty and a priority for the whole suburban community. They shrank and strengthened their neighborhoods; they tried to make their neighborhoods the most important in town, and the touchstones of its collective pride and policy.

In clarifying domestic space at the local level, the deed restrictions that some promoters had attached to individual plots were but a first step. As they built homes on these lots, promoters and residents also founded new institutions, meant to serve small neighborhoods and to promote respectable behavior in the vicinity. At the same time, they turned the influence of these institutions against nearby centers of "immorality"—which coincided, mirabile dictu, with the taverns, shops, factories, and trading centers of the fringe economy.

The change in suburban thinking was evident in a new wave of church founding after 1840 (see fig. 5), which spread into new territory. Meetinghouses appeared in northern Cambridge, on the hills of Somerville, near Sandpit Square and Neck Village. Some of these simply reflected still more sectoring and shrinkage of the old church attendance fields (see chap. 2). The Somerville First Methodist Church, for example, gathered when Methodists in southern Somerville, formerly members of the East Cambridge church, became numerous and wealthy enough to support their own. The same kind of subdivision split Old Cambridge Baptists from Cambridgeport, Cambridgeport Episcopalians from Old Cambridge, and northern Cambridge Congregationalists from the First Church.[26]

But there were also new motives for church founding after the mid-1840s. Residential promoters like Brastow sought churches to ornament their little communities. More important, middle-class residents founded new churches to safeguard their areas against perceived moral threats. Thus the Perkins Street Baptist Church, founded in 1845, was a Somerville weapon against the "ungodliness and moral destitution" of Neck Village, with its tanneries, taverns, and wharves.[27] At an 1851 church dedication in northern Cambridge, the speaker compared the church to the common school and the household. The new edifice was not "consecrated to the affections which cluster around a New England home," but it was "a *House of God*: a *home* for the religious affections of His children." A Congregational newspaper, commenting on his address, welcomed the new church as a defense against "flagrant violations of order and morality" in North Cambridge: "The presence of a church, the labors of a pastor, added facilities of intercourse among families, and mutual acquaintance will do much toward removing the evil." The editor suggested, with poignant anachronism, that "the city of Cambridge could well afford to pay something toward the enterprise."[28]

Schools, like churches, were to be rallying points for domestic moral influences. Horace Mann's statewide campaigns for school reform provided a rhetorical basis for local action. He and his associates believed city growth led to family collapse, making public schools all the more necessary to ensure the moral upbringing of future citizens.[29] Suburban advocates of school reform turned such arguments into weapons of warfare in specific localities. After the mid-forties, school committees in Cambridge produced a school-by-school evaluation in print, assessing the physical condition of buildings and the intellectual and moral achievements of the schools. They called for citizens in each area to form alliances of parents, the clergy, and local officials aimed at making the schools "sanctuaries of purity" and "public nurseries of virtue." They worried about particular schools—in the industrial Lower Port, East Cambridge, and later northern Cambridge—which catered to children of varied class and ethnic backgrounds. Vandalism, bad behavior, and erratic attendance in these schools reflected the "depravity" and "want of family government" in the vicinity.[30]

The arrival of the Irish and the rapid expansion of industry heightened such fears. The Reverend James D. Green, who served ten years as a Congregational minister in East Cambridge and many years as state representative and school committeeman and then became first mayor of the city, saw the schools as bastions against rising danger. As ex officio chairman of the school committee, he turned the annual reports into long sermons on the need to expand the umbrella of domesticity. With so many diverse children arriving so fast, some of the schools might become demoralizing, so that "the child, who had been trained at home in innocence and loveliness, no sooner enters them, than he is exposed to be corrupted by vicious associates." The community, through its schools, had to supply missing parental influences, had "to say . . . to all neglected and abandoned children,—'I will be to you instead of a parent. The control, that your natural parent is unable or indisposed to exercise, I will assume. You cannot be permitted to follow your idle, roaming, and vicious propensities.'" As allies of the home, the schools had to bring all children into the sphere of nurture because that sphere was severely threatened by "the moral dangers that are thickening around our youth, the total want of all moral and religious instruction for many at home, the exposure of others from day to day to the most corrupting examples, . . . the thousand agencies at work to corrupt the public morals, the licentious publications of the day designed to lure the young to ruin, . . . the tide of immigration pouring in upon our land, bringing with it the ignorance and vice of older countries, and lastly, the fearful increase of crime, especially of juvenile depravity."[31]

Green and others invested the schools with a twofold moral purpose: they were to buttress home influences where they existed and to extend such influences to children who lacked them. As suburbanites carried such ideas into practice, they changed the schools into a different kind of neighborhood institution. They did so because they had to reconcile several pressures implicit in the new goals for schooling. First, both reformers and speculative promoters wanted schools very close to residential areas. In earlier decades, it was assumed that children who lived outside the village centers would walk the necessary miles. Now Cambridge and Somerville were convulsed by long disputes over locating schools, as each residential cluster pressed for its own accommodation. Some Somerville citizens, led by the brickmaker and land speculator Clark Bennett, found it unacceptable for children to walk more than half a mile and complained of the necessity of driving them to school on the way to work. Moreover, Cambridge and Somerville school reformers insisted that the schools be moved away from their old sites on the main roads because these were contaminated by the proximity of stables and shops and "unsuited by location on a complete thoroughfare" for children.[32] On the other hand, many of the same people wanted comprehensive schooling—a network of schools that would take in the children of immigrants and factory workers as well as prosperous homeowners. For some, efficient fulfillment of this goal required large, centralized schools like those advocated by Mann and Henry Barnard for the big cities.

The result, emerging in the early fifties, was a new, specialized distribution of schools. Both Cambridge and Somerville responded to residential pressure by embedding primary schools within the neighborhoods. As some critics noted, they were liberal in providing such schools for the residents of Dana Hill and sluggish about building them for the children of "New Dublin" near the brickyards.[33] But the general goal was to sweep all children into schools near their homes and to make schools the provider of home influences. At the same time, both communities tried to centralize the grammar and high schools, building larger structures at points that served several areas of residence. Suburbanites did not plan such a system; they assembled it piecemeal. Politics, speculative interests, and shifting population all encouraged constant tinkering. But by 1855 both suburbs had made a clean break with the little schoolhouse by the roadside. Even as they argued about sizes, locations, and arrangements, they adapted the schools to the pattern of residence and justified all schools as neighborhood institutions and props of domesticity.

In a less dramatic way, some suburbanites tried to apply the same philosophy to public parks. Neither Cambridge nor Somerville created any new public parks until after the Civil War, but residential promoters landscaped some areas, citizens of both places agitated for "public squares," and committees deliberated about sites, all with the enthusiastic support of *Chronicle* editor Ford. Parks, too, were to be adjuncts of the domestic sphere. Children, especially those who lacked a suitable home environment, needed places for recreation. Without parks, middle-class children might become mere stunted bookworms, while those from crowded districts would wander the streets, idle and prone to mischief. For adults too, trees, greenery, and "reservoirs of pure air" were essential to a healthy home environment. As in the case of schools, park advocates wanted both neighborhood institutions—"small squares scattered over the city"—and agencies of uplift for the whole population.[34]

All these promotional activities worked together to shrink the suburban concept of neighborhood. Instead of the big, fuzzily defined communities described by the older Somervilleans, neighborhoods became small residential districts fortified by their institutions: churches, schools, and perhaps parks. The promotion of domestic space also elevated the middle-class residential neighborhood to a position of paramount virtue. It was the epitome of suburban achievements. In 1857 a Cambridge citizen rejoiced that certain streets in the Dana Hill vicinity had become "an earthly paradise" because of the combination of dwellings, schools, trees, and proximity to Boston via the "horse railroad institution." *Chronicle* editor Ford, who tried hard to represent industrial and commercial interests as well as residential, ultimately bent to the power of the residential ideal. In the early fifties he had argued for a new wholesale marketplace, for landfill to provide industrial sites, and for measures to bring water to factories. By the mid-fifties he was convinced of residential primacy. Cambridge, he said, "will not be likely to have very great facilities for business." Its future growth would depend almost entirely on "its attractions as a place of residence."[35]

This celebration of neighborhoods was, however, only one component of the suburban response to changing social geography. Because neighborhood promotion depended on recruitment from Boston and competition with other communities, suburbanites became more sensitive to relations between their suburbs, other suburbs, and Boston. A particularization of interest at the neighborhood level went hand-in-hand with a more vivid conception of the suburban town or city as a competitive entity—a unit in the metropolitan complex. From the mid-forties on, promoters, newspaper correspondents, and municipal officials all argued that Somerville and Cambridge had to keep steady pace with their municipal neighbors. This was a line of reasoning never heard in the fringe period, when there was plenty of competition between villages but only occasional rivalry between municipalities. Now, school committes worried about loss of teachers to higher-paying rival suburbs and began to make regular reports on the comparative advantages of their communities versus the competition.[36]

With regard to Boston, the goal of suburban spokesmen was to import desirable people and institutions but to screen the imports carefully. The *Chronicle* rather haughtily suggested that two kinds of people were "mistaken in being suburban at all": those who worked for others and could not control their schedules, and those who gave too much time to work, leaving none for relaxation. Instead, Ford sought to attract people who could strike a balance between worldly and domestic affairs: "It is the ever apparent desire of the denizen of the crowded city across the river, if he has a soul not dead to everything but gain, to find a place in the country convenient to his business, where his family can escape the moral and physical miasma of the metropolis."[37]

In the competition for such people, some city institutions were welcome tools. Advocates of water, gas, streetlights, and sidewalks insisted they were essential to the community's success—ornaments of the residential neighborhood, aids in selling lots, lures for city migrants. By 1850 Cambridge had a newspaper and an annual directory, and a Somerville printer was preparing to experiment with a directory too. Boston newspapers, once a rarity, were now available for daily delivery through local newsdealers. Such improvements were all to the good, but the city should be kept at bay. The *Chronicle* and the directories continually stressed the differences between urban and suburban needs. Even as they aped city practices, they chastised their neighbors for shopping or amusing themselves in Boston, urging instead the patronage of local facilities.[38]

The underside of this boosterism was a growing fear that city people and city habits would invade the suburbs. It was obvious to suburbanites that they lived in a refuge. Newspapers told them of racial and nativist riots in Philadelphia, of immigrant poverty, epidemics, and crime in all the big cities. Yet until the late fifties Cambridge and Somerville remained almost entirely free of such city troubles. There were no riots or strikes. Cholera, which ravaged Boston and other centers in 1849 and 1854, touched only one family in East Cambridge. Near the suburban industrial centers there were ragtag settlements of the poor, but none of the dense tenement zones that contemporaries associated with the word "slum."[39]

Nevertheless, the situation was changing. The suburban elite worried constantly about possible troubles and shaped its actions to cope with a half-imagined underclass threat. What they saw in Boston and heard of other places convinced them all the more of the need to promote domestic institutions and defend their borders. In 1847 the *Chronicle* editor asked why crime was on the increase in Boston and offered three answers: too many ignorant foreigners, the neglect of parents in sending children to school, and the "idle habits of young men." It was fortunate, he noted, that Mayor Green and the school committee were on guard against such evils in Cambridge. Throughout the late forties and early fifties, Ford and his correspondents provided condemnations and warnings of suspicious intruders from the city: well-dressed burglars, con men, and joyriding adolescents. They blamed the "B'hoys" of Boston for bad manners, reckless driving, petty theft, vandalism and every other offense against decorum.[40]

Like the emphasis on domesticity in the neighborhoods, this heightened concern with the Boston-suburban border reflected broader cultural trends. Well-to-do suburbanites shared the fears and opinions of elite citizens in other urban communities. In big cities and industrial centers, prosperous residents of this period worried that urban growth was dissolving the moral order—destroying the authority of employers, religious leaders, and respectable politicians; crowding the cities with immigrants who overwhelmed city institutions. In part because of this fearful vision, city elites also hardened the standards of public morality, so that behavior once taken for granted—idleness, rowdyism, casual drinking—became unacceptable and subject to strenuous corrective action.[41]

In the suburbs of the late 1840s and early 1850s, such fears took on a special intensity and focus. Residentially oriented suburbanites occupied a peculiar position in the urban growth process. They lived in small neighborhoods devoted to the aggressive promotion of pure domesticity. They were citizens of municipalities engaged in continuous rivalry with each other and anxious to distinguish themselves from Boston. Yet they were free from most of the major problems that actually confronted residents of the big cities. Indeed, in the time before streetcars and free bridges, they still lived in a world of privileged access. What worried them was not just the immediate and limited reality of specific city intrusions, but the possibility that urban growth would undermine society in the suburbs as well as in the city. Thus the third component of their response to changing social geography, in addition to purifying neighborhoods and enhancing the competitive position of their municipalities, was an effort to keep the suburbs from becoming too citified in a moral sense, to prevent growth in the suburbs from bringing on the disastrous results they believed it produced in the city.

In such an atmosphere, it was easy to overreact. Suburbanites were quick to identify and exaggerate any sign of city evils cropping up within the suburbs. Mayor Green, delivering his inaugural address to the Cambridge city council, slipped into emotional language for which he then apologized. His subject was the fire department, which he praised for efficiency but warned against misbehavior:

If, however, . . . leaving their proper sphere, and their usual party connections, they combine in measures to influence elections, . . . it becomes a serious question, whether we are not fostering the growth of a power in our midst, which will one day lead, if unrestrained, to the enactment among us of the scenes which have rendered the same department in Philadelphia so notorious.[42]

Green's emotion was oddly misplaced. Nowhere in the Cambridge town or city records, local newspapers, or contemporary memoirs, is there any evidence that the Cambridge firemen had committed any misdeeds—apart from the outbursts of competitive high spirits that had always been customary for fire companies. It was Green's fear of city behavior, rather than the fire department's sins, that provoked his lecture. A similar paranoia appeared in 1850–51, when Cambridge built a new almshouse, which then became an issue in the 1851 city elections. Critics distributed handbills condemning the structure as a luxurious "pauper hotel," which would attract undesirables. "I sincerely believe," said a writer to the paper, "that the reputation of this house has already extended to the poor in foreign lands."[43]

Despite their fears, suburbanites tried, as late as the 1850s, to sustain confidence in their traditional defenses: their relative isolation from the city, the radiant power of their domestic institutions, and most of all the moral authority of elite citizens. The *Chronicle* took the occasion of an 1851 gambling raid in Boston to warn the young men of Cambridge. "In a community like ours," such immoral behavior would be disastrous. Secrecy and disguise were useless; escaping detection "is almost morally impossible. The gambler, the young man of irregular habits, must be known; the eye of the community is upon him." Persons of any "standing or position" were deceived "if they suppose they can visit the bar room or the gambling saloon, unobserved. . . . no pretention, no position can save their fair fame from blasting and mildew, and damning reproach."[44]

Those who put their faith in "the eye of the community" could take heart from several incidents that seemed to confirm the unity and moral influence of respectable citizens. Late one summer night in 1852, an arsonist tried to burn the shop of a carpenter and master builder in Cambridge. Neighbors alerted the owner, a prosperous man and a large property owner. He extinguished the blaze and then spotted a young man walking nearby. The stranger stopped immediately when hailed and allowed himself to be escorted, unrestrained, more than a mile to the watch house—even though his pockets contained matches, wicking, and a "murderous instrument." In 1856 a disputed footrace in East Cambridge produced an unruly crowd which assaulted a watchman—but dissolved completely when the mayor arrived and spoke a few words. In the same year vandals burned a load of hay left overnight in Harvard Square by a Framingham farmer. Local residents, ashamed of this disgrace to the city, contributed enough to reimburse the owner on the spot.[45]

By the mid-fifties, this kind of confidence had an increasingly shaky basis; there was too much evidence that the traditional defenses were unreliable. Promotion of domestic influences, campaigns against city invaders, and efforts to sustain respectable unity did not prevent corrosion within. The *Chronicle*, for example, provided more stories of hard core crime in suburban industrial areas: domestic quarrels that ended in murder, armed robbery on the bridge approaches, "savage attacks" on watchmen and streetcar conductors.[46] Most disturbing of all were signals that the moral authority of the elite, and perhaps even the unity of the elite, was eroding. Nothing frightened suburban property owners more in this regard than the mixed success of their attempts to deal with arson and drunkenness.

Arson, for suburbanites, was the most mysterious of urban evils. From the late 1830s to the Civil War, Cambridge and Somerville were plagued by incendiary fires. Suburbanites at first blamed them on Boston invaders—"juvenile 'outsiders'" who were "fiends in human shape"—but their accusations betrayed a nagging worry that the criminals might be in their midst. Fires in the suburbs, for one thing, were not like those in the city. As far back as the 1820s, Mayor Quincy of Boston had noted that the urban poor regarded fires as "harvests" from which they might furnish their homes. But in Cambridge and Somerville, incendiaries struck barns, schools, and unfinished buildings, which might make a pretty blaze but would offer little reward.[47]

Since they rarely caught the offenders, suburbanites had little firm knowledge about the reasons for their affliction. But what they did discover was not comforting. In the 1850s it became plain that some of the culprits were not Bostonians bent on looting but local delinquents engaged in malicious mischief and perhaps revenge. Many youthful suburbanites clearly enjoyed the tumultuous atmosphere prevailing at fires and the camaraderie of fire company activities. The firemen, disciplined by the New Model reforms of the 1830s and overworked by the rising tide of fires, were beyond any serious accusation of arson.[48] But watchmen arrested boys too young to be firemen and hangers-on at the engine houses, some of whom were caught in the act of setting fires. Worse still were the nocturnal assaults by vengeful individuals, like that of a young Somerville brickyard worker who burned the barn of Deacon Robert Vinal, one of the town's most prominent men. Such firebugs were not only criminals, they were severe threats to the new, residentially oriented conception of the suburb that elite residents wanted to believe in and project to others. The *Chronicle* noted with alarm that a Boston newspaper was reporting "the usual Saturday night fire in Cambridge." The Somerville School Committee denounced an arson attack as bad suburban citizenship; "it indicates a disregard for the good name of the town not even second in social perversity to the disregard of the rights of property." Even after the fires, suburbanites hustled their neighbors to clear away the debris, lest the sight of it discourage lot sales.[49]

Against this threat, suburbanites mobilized their traditional moral weapons in vain. They sermonized. They offered rewards and advertised them in city and suburban newspapers. They called indignation meetings. They tried to rouse the stewards of the community to exert their personal influence in restraining behavior at fires. They retained attorneys to seek evidence for exemplary prosecutions. They hired private police and had them deputized by local authorities. On one occasion 28 Somerville property owners became "special police" themselves. Still the fires continued, in waves that ebbed and flowed with no clear-cut relationship to cause or the means taken against them.[50]

Less mysterious, but just as disturbing, was the upheaval surrounding battles against intemperance. Temperance reformers gained a strong foothold among the Whig leaders of the New Model communities in the 1840s. Cambridgeport, in particular, was a hotbed of agitation for temperance along with other reforms. In 1846 the municipal Fourth of July celebration, devoted to liberty and temperance, featured lemonade, cold water, and a speech against the Mexican War delivered by a freed slave. In Somerville, the brickmaker land speculator school reformer Clark Bennett led the small but vocal Washingtonian Society. He and his associates persuaded the town meeting to go dry. Armed with town sanction, they fought neighborhood drinking throughout the forties and into the fifties, nagging the selectmen to crack down on illicit grog shops near the bleachery and tube works. Bennett, who was also an officer of the fire company, was clearly stung to the quick when neighbors accused him of allowing disorderly conduct in the firehouse. His response was to demand community action against demon rum.[51]

In this period temperance enjoyed the support of a coalition of suburban interests: commuters like John Barbour of Cambridgeport, native-born fringe entrepreneurs like carriagemaker Walter Allen of northern Cambridge, ministers and civic officials in all parts of Somerville and Cambridge were active backers. Even some liquor sellers tried to cooperate in what seemed a broad-based movement for civic betterment. Zachariah Porter, whose hotel and cattle market fixed the original center of northern Cambridge, agreed to close his bar on Sundays to discourage drunken excursions by Boston undesirables. In 1852, when Walter Allen and others promoted a new church in the area, Porter hosted a cold water levee to welcome the new congregation. John Ford, who had great faith in the unity of respectable opinion, rejoiced in his paper in 1851 that "Cambridge will be redeemed" from alcohol.[52]

By the mid-fifties, however, temperance ceased to be a unifying cause. Instead, it was the issue of drinking that first brought into the open the latent conflicts between fringe-based economic growth and residential promotion. Temperance provoked the nearest thing to a riot since the convent burning in 1834. Temperance produced fragmentation, open disputes, and mistrust among influential suburbanites.

The process of erosion began in the spring of 1852, in response to an external stimulus. In the preceding year the Maine legislature had passed a statute banning the manufacture and sale of alcoholic beverages. Between 1851 and 1855 temperance groups secured passage of similar "Maine laws" throughout New England and in some states of the Middle Atlantic and the Middle West. The Massachusetts legislature was one of the first to act, passing a prohibition statute in the spring of 1852. In July, when the law took effect, suburban temperance advocates organized to promote enforcement. Volunteers agreed to enter saloons, buy drinks, and then file complaints against the vendors. They retained attorney Richard Henry Dana, Cambridge commuter and temperance man, to aid in prosecution.[53]

Predictably, this campaign encountered strong opposition. Anonymous authors circulated handbills listing the names of the first three complainants and urging citizens to spit on them in the streets. When the drys targeted and indicted Zachariah Porter, he and other innkeepers began a countercampaign for repeal of the law. In September, when they came to trial in Watertown for selling liquor, a mob from Cambridge descended on the courthouse, "hooting, shouting, and drinking," and threw tobacco at the judge. Spotting one of the three complainants named in the handbills, someone in the crowd yelled "there is Christopher Columbus Richardson, the first informer in Massachusetts—mark him." Assaulted by the crowd, Richardson drew a pistol. Someone took it, beat him with it, and then filed a complaint in court charging him with carrying a concealed weapon.[54]

From the prohibition viewpoint, such outrages only confirmed the evils of selling rum and elevated that offense to a level with arson. There was nothing wrong, said a letter to the *Chronicle*, with informing on liquor sellers. "If I can discover any incendiary firing my own or my neighbor's building, am I mean for informing of him? Now the chief difference between the evil of firing a man's building, and firing his brain and body, is that the law against one is of older standing than that against the other." The drys redoubled their efforts. They lost the case against Porter on a technicality but continued the crusade of entrapment. Porter now found himself attacked by the very neighbors to whom he had opened his hotel a few months before. He renewed the repeal drive and fought litigation against him all the way to the Supreme Court. For three years the struggle continued, until he lost his final appeal in 1855.[55]

Prohibitionists cheered this and other victories and also found some evidence of success in persuasion through moral force. By 1857 Samuel Knight of Cambridge, whose bar had been one of those first targeted in 1852, had undergone a conversion to total abstinence. Now he was elected president of the Temperance Association and led evangelical prohibition meetings on into the late 1850s.[56]

Yet such successes were dearly bought. The prohibition campaign not only opened class cleavages and made enemies of such former community pillars as Porter, it alienated some of the suburbs' most eminent leaders. Some of these were initial supporters of the Maine law but defected because they wanted no part of the informer campaign. Some, like John Ford and the Livermore family, had always been skeptical of a "moral reform effected by compulsory means" and recognized early that the Maine law would ultimately prove a dead letter. Even Mayor James Green, whose credentials as an evangelical reformer were unimpeachable, doubted the constitutionality of the Maine law, feared its divisive impact, and responded angrily to a petition from drys accusing him of lax enforcement.[57]

Drinking, like arson, could not be eliminated by traditional means. In the growing, diversifying suburbs, it was impossible to keep track of proliferating deviant behavior, let alone track the offenses to a source. Suburbanites bolstered their generalized defenses and directed them against the most likely sources they could see: the city across the river and the pockets of working-class settlement and culture in their midst. They enjoyed just enough success to sustain their faith into the early 1850s. But the effort only cast a spotlight on the widening fissures in suburban society: between the residential clusters and the immigrant areas, between those who believed in the power of moral institutions and those who were clearly beyond their influence, even between members of the prosperous and respectable elite.

By the mid-fifties it was clear that the New Model synthesis would not guarantee social harmony, that some urban evils were already present in the suburbs, and that further growth along the same lines would likely aggravate them. Residentially oriented suburbanites had a more explicit sense of their goals and a sharper conception of the boundaries between areas and interests around them. But they were uneasy about the future. What means should they adopt when traditional institutions proved inadequate? Who would lead them when some of the property-owning stewards now seemed part of the problem? In 1854, "A Citizen" captured some of their distress when he wrote to the *Chronicle*. He complained of poor relief wasted on "improvident foreigners," but the bulk of his attack was aimed at Cambridge slumlords, "people of ample means, who build or fit up wretched abodes, destitute of nearly every comfort and convenience," thereby attracting "a miserable class, . . . *who would not come but for such accommodations being provided*. Good neighborhoods are disturbed, and property depreciated by such unwarrantable conduct."[58]

This citizen's lament, mingling xenophobia, humanitarianism, and a distorted notion of social and economic change, would be echoed through the decades in communities across the land. It reflected both a sharpened idea of neighborhood and a confused apprehension of suburban growth. It also suggested the outlines of the two mounting conflicts of interest in the suburbs of the late 1850s: between the promotion of residences and the factory- and immigrant-based industry of the fringe and between discontented citizens and the elite leaders they felt had failed them.

According to the New Model ideal, such problems should be resolved through the agencies of local government. There the stewards of the community would join in promoting enterprise and settling conflict. But the same conflicts of interest that roused social anxiety were also altering local government. On that front, too, suburbanites faced a shifting landscape and found it impossible, as citizens or officials, to behave as they once had. By the Civil War they surrendered some parts of the New Model ideal of government, though the process was painful and marked by crises of which the temperance battle proved merely a harbinger.

7

Suburban Government: Setting, Roles, and Structure

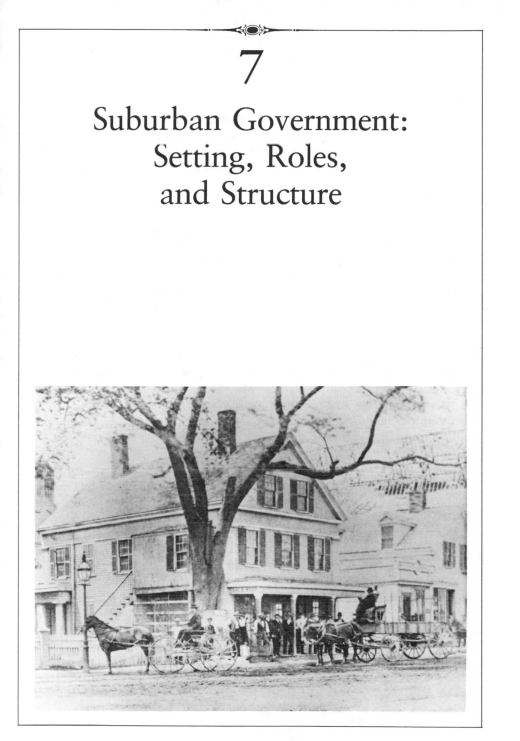

Stores in Sandpit Square, Somerville, a center of
political discussion in the mid-nineteenth century.
Courtesy of the Somerville Historical Society.

I N THE middle to late 1850s, the suburban attempt to clarify social goals and the anxiety surrounding that attempt lent a peculiar intensity to local politics. Municipal government in that period became an arena of dispute, confusion, and uncertainty, where mundane questions of appointment and budgeting called forth mass organization and passionate rhetoric and where even the most popular administrator of the decade was vilified and swept from office a few months after his election.

It is tempting to see this period of crisis as merely a local illustration of national and state developments. For suburban residents as for other Americans, the 1850s were years of political turmoil, party collapse, and mistrust of old leadership.[1] These larger changes did indeed have local effects. Yet suburbanites of this era were also engaged in a separate redefinition of local politics and government, and the most important issues, events, and changes at that level were different from those that occupied the state and national stages. Local circumstances raised difficult questions for suburbanites: in the face of unprecedented growth and diversity, how could they finance public services and allocate resources fairly? How could they alter the simple, cheap, voluntaristic governments they had set up in the 1840s without losing their essential virtues? In the face of obvious conflicts between residential promotion and other pursuits, how could government continue to be a tool of enterprise? In the face of mistrust between members of the elite, how could suburbanites be sure their leaders were responsible? How could they recognize the natural stewards of the community?

Not until the 1860s would suburbanites answer such questions in ways that would make them comfortable. Then, they would readily accept certain features of big city administration: a salaried bureaucracy, an ongoing debt. Then, they would openly accept the primacy of residential interests, confining and restricting industry and fringe pursuits. Then, they would give up much of the stewardship ideal, accepting a split between the roles of citizen and official. Meanwhile, in the 1850s, they moved toward these changes in a quarrelsome and experimental way. Beneath the rhetoric, they were continuing a long process begun in the New Model era—the adaptation of city institutions and practices to serve residential society and to promote suburban independence. This penultimate step in the creation of distinctively suburban governments involved several threads of development. This chapter will pick them apart, analyzing the demands of local evolution, the impact of large political changes, and the influence of particular local clashes in the late 1850s.

The Local Balance and the Larger Setting

In reconstructing suburban governments, the New Model reformers took certain conditions for granted. They assumed, fundamentally, that their communities would be run by propertied gentlemen—a reasonable belief, since their whole package of constitutional changes was aimed at shrinking and stabilizing the ruling bodies. Government by gentlemen had three important corollaries: first, the reformers assumed that good citizens, whatever their ties to particular interests or areas, would ultimately be able to agree about municipal affairs. If they came together in small numbers, made an effort to include all important interests, and shared a basic level of trust, they would hammer out balanced settlements just as the old town meetings had.

Second, they assumed that party allegiance and party apparatus would be of little consequence in local affairs. After all, most of the founders of new communities were Whigs, and the few Democrats involved were men like Samuel Parmenter and Ephraim Buttrick of East Cambridge—local entrepreneurs and community stewards like their neighbors of the opposite party. Finally, they assumed that voluntarism would sustain local government. Like the deacons and selectmen of the old villages, gentlemen of the new suburbs would actively participate in meetings and caucuses and would shoulder the burdens of local office when asked.

Through the forties and into the early fifties these assumptions remained largely intact, although the pressures of growth strained them severely and prompted a good deal of public exhortation.[2] Especially in Cambridge, arguments about geographical representation tested the ability of gentlemen to agree. James D. Green, the Old Cambridge conservative who served as first mayor, retired after two terms. The Whig slate-making caucus then put forward a Cambridgeport man, who also served two terms and sought to retire. In 1850, logic suggested a mayor from East Cambridge, but the caucus, dominated by Old Cambridge Whigs, tried to renominate Green. Voters in the other two areas revolted, held a rival caucus, nominated and reelected the Cambridgeport incumbent. The *Chronicle* denounced "sectional feeling" in local politics, but similar disputes occurred in 1851 and 1852, when some citizens refused to cooperate in the process of balancing offices among the wards.[3]

These disputes also raised fears about the nonpartisan, voluntaristic organization of local politics. The problem was not one of straightforward party divisions: until the end of 1853, the city caucus sponsored by the Whigs was open to all; Free-Soilers and Democrats attended and were nominated for office. On one occasion a prominent Democrat, put forward by an East Cambridge group, withdrew so that the Whig nominee would gain a clear victory.[4] Nevertheless, when suburbanites divided along geographical lines, they employed organization and tactics they had learned in partisan conflicts: rallying committees, torchlight processions, brass bands, and campaigns of rumor and innuendo. In 1850, opponents of Green's reelection distributed an anonymous handbill that asked:

> Will you permit the clique of Harvard College and Old Cambridge, after their attempts to be set off from the town, to elect all the officers of the city from their own section, and rule with aristocratic sway the municipal affairs of the people?[5]

The following year Old Cambridge residents tried to subvert the caucus by circulating false reports that drunks had swayed the meeting and by passing out fraudulent ballots which changed the list of nominees. Such things were common enough in party conflicts, but clearly outside the New Model rules. Angry writers to the newspaper reminded their neighbors that the system of caucuses relied on "each man's sense of propriety and decorum," and that "all honorable men are bound by the action of a Convention in which they act and vote."[6]

The worst result of such conflicts, according to *Chronicle* editor John Ford, would be to undermine voluntarism. "What we want is the best men for municipal officers, independent of party ties, or personal or sectional biases." But why should a gentleman serve if "he becomes the mark of every malcontent." Too much local recrimination would destroy the foundations of stewardship. "How many of those who have been called to responsible stations in our City government, have learned that the sure way to lose the esteem of . . . their fellow citizens, is to attend faithfully, assiduously, energetically to the duties of their station."[7]

As yet suburbanites had not questioned the New Model assumptions themselves. Until 1852 it still seemed reasonable to hope that genteel gatherings, nonpartisanship, and voluntarism would prevail. Despite the strains, there was evidence of success: East Cambridge did eventually provide a mayor, party loyalties were in fact set aside in the caucuses, and the voices of eminent men could still swing a meeting. As late as February 1852, John Ford could rejoice that the caucuses were promoting "unanimity of feeling" and supplying "prompt and active men." "Within our own municipality we are all friends and neighbors."[8]

Events of the mid-1850s made such assumptions untenable and opened the way for a crisis at the end of the decade. In the summer of 1852, the Maine law prohibition controversy sharpened divisions within the suburbs. Very soon after, the tides of state and national politics washed into the local arena and overwhelmed old arrangements. Then, in the backwash of that mid-fifties political jolt, suburbanites had to confront questions raised by long-term local change—especially pressing in the period of explosive, street-car-fostered growth after 1856. In the political sphere as in the social, a combination of shocks from the outside and steady pressure within produced intense anxiety in the late 1850s.

The intrusion of larger politics in 1852–53 began the erosion of confidence. This was all the more distressing because suburbanites thought they had successfully prevented it. Despite their participation as individuals in the mounting state and national strife of the late forties, their circumstances and their self-restraint had kept the local government more or less isolated from partisan affairs. Indeed, the direct spillover of party conflict into the suburbs must be seen as a late and relatively brief episode in a long history of state and national tumult.

Between November 1848 and the winter of 1857/58, Massachusetts experienced a decade of political instability.[9] For many years before 1848, the Whigs had been the usual victors in state elections, with only occasional losses to the Democrats and small defections to nativist and Liberty party candidates. After the fall of 1857, the Republicans controlled the state and restored predictability. In between, voters and politicians faced a confusing array of issues and appeals; no election could be forecast; no officeholder could feel secure.

For Bay Staters, this era of crisis fell into three distinct periods.[10] Dramatic Free-Soil gains in 1848 proved the Whigs were vulnerable. From 1849 through 1853, an uneasy coalition of Free-Soilers and Democrats gained a tenuous hold on power by exploiting Whig divisions. But the Whigs remained strong in the cities, and the coalition included too many strange bedfellows: nativists, temperance men, and Irish Catholics, not to mention Free-Soilers and pro-South Democrats. It fell apart during 1852–53, amid bitter quarreling that showed the cleavages in all the old parties. In the second stage, from December 1853 through 1855, Know-Nothing nativism took over, winning a series of local elections and then sweeping the state. But this, too, was an unstable rule: Know-Nothingism attracted neophyte voters who would not be a reliable, long-term constituency; most Free-Soilers and many old Whigs simply stayed home. The third and final period began in the summer of 1855, when non-Know-Nothing antislavery men became the core of the fledgling Republican party. Their movement lured old voters back to the polls, gathered strength in the Fremont enthusiasm of 1856, and culminated in state victory the following year.

In this decade of turmoil, the height of confusion, the most bitter conflicts, and the time of maximum spillover into local politics came between the summer of 1852 and the fall of 1854. In those two years, the Free-Soil–Democratic coalition came unstuck. The dying Whigs, whose last strongholds were in Boston and the other big cities, rallied just enough to defeat a reform-oriented, coalition-backed state constitution in November 1853. A month later, a Know-Nothing backlash swept the Whigs from power in five city governments. In some communities the struggle continued for months, as shriveled and desperate Whig committees pulled out all stops in a losing effort to build up their local bases.

In Cambridge and Somerville, which had been among the strongest bastions of Whiggery since the New Model reforms, the death throes of the coalition and the Whigs had serious repercussions. Apart from pitting neighbors against each other, arguments over state politics raised the level of anxiety about social change and widened three important local divisions.

First, the intrusions of party hostility thoroughly destroyed trust among many of the influential men who made up the old elite. Until late 1853, Free-Soilers, Democrats, and temperance men continued to caucus with the dominant Whigs in the ongoing effort to find the "best men" for local office. But the struggles of that fall and winter left no room for cooperation. When the Cambridge city elections came up in March, a group calling itself the citizens caucus nominated a slate dominated by temperance and Free-Soil advocates. The old Whigs would have none of it. Fresh from their November victory over the proposed state constitution and frightened by the nativist wins in other cities, they held their own caucus and rejected most of the nominees for mayor and aldermen. Moreover, they purged the caucus itself of those who supported the citizens ticket, and in a slap at John Ford (a Whig turned Free-Soiler), they resolved to start "a Whig paper" in Cambridge.[11]

Although the Whigs carried this election, they could never again claim to speak for the local elite. In the next city election, Know-Nothings defeated Whigs by a margin of almost two to one, with their ticket headed by a Free-Soiler who had been one of the rejected citizens nominees for alderman.[12] Others rebuffed by the closure of the Whig caucus would never return. The most important of these was John Sargent, a prosperous Cambridgeport commuter, city councilman, and active Whig, who had often been suggested as a mayoral candidate. At the Whig caucus he engaged in heated debate over the motion to purge the meeting and walked out of the gathering. As it developed, he was also walking out of the council of local stewards the Whig caucus had once represented. When he returned to Cambridge politics as the most important mayor of the late fifties, he would bring to that office a very different conception of leadership.

In addition to widening the fissures within the local elite, the spillover of state politics also reinforced existing geographic and social cleavages in the suburbs. The open Whig caucus had once been a meeting ground for diverse interests. When it collapsed, there was no comparable organization at the local level. The Know-Nothings deliberately avoided public meetings, and their goal in any case was to break with the established pattern of leadership. Their success was reflected in the makeup of the Cambridge Common Council during the year of Know-Nothing rule (1855). Of twenty city councilmen in office that year, fifteen had never served in office before and ten would never serve again. By contrast the 1854 council had contained fourteen veterans and only two one-timers.[13] After this disruption, no new mechanism of local consensus emerged until 1857. Instead, partisan ties defined the slate-making meetings, and the magnetism of state politics pulled suburban citizens into new groupings that reflected local divisions—geographic, ethnic, and occupational.

Most obvious was an overall geographic split between the diehard Whigs, whose strength lay in Old Cambridge, and former Whigs in Cambridgeport and East Cambridge. Voting returns in state elections show that the Whigs retained a plurality in Old Cambridge through 1855, while Know-Nothingism destroyed the Whigs elsewhere in 1854 (table 7.1). It was therefore no surprise when, early in 1855, conservative Whigs and Old Cambridge entrepreneurs tried once again to split off the western part of Cambridge as a separate town. Citing Somerville's precedent, they went to the legislature in February. Once again they met overpowering resistance from the eastern communities. Commuters and fringe industrialists united in opposition, and John Sargent, so recently disgusted by the closed Whig caucus, delivered a "stirring speech," which galvanized a large meeting of remonstrants.[14]

Yet the collapse of Whiggery also had an impact within Cambridgeport and East Cambridge. Here the emerging cleavage was partly geographic, partly a matter of ethnicity and class. It lay between those oriented to reform (especially temperance), many of whom were commuters in the Dana Hill region and in the North Cambridge railroad corridor; and those for whom nativism was the primary political magnet, many of whom were anti-Irish

Table 7.1

Cambridge Votes in Gubernatorial Elections
(party vote as percent of all votes cast in ward)

Party	1850	1851	1852	1853	1854	1855	1856	1857	1858
Old Cambridge (including North Cambridge)									
Whig	75	70	69	73	57	33	16		
Democratic	11	15	12	12	8	23	22	18	35
Free-Soil/ Republican	15	15	18	10			55	46	54
Know-Nothing/ American					34	25		36	12
Cambridgeport									
Whig	53	53	59	55	29	15	8		
Democratic	28	30	18	25	6	35	31	23	37
Free-Soil/ Republican	19	18	23	16			53	45	55
Know-Nothing/ American					63	29		32	8
East Cambridge									
Whig	60	57	59	61	31	11	12		
Democratic	25	30	26	27	6	45	43	41	46
Free-Soil/ Republican	15	13	15	11			43	23	44
Know-Nothing/ American					62	37		46	10

SOURCE: Calculated from election return data printed in the *Cambridge Chronicle*.

workingmen in the Lower Port, East Cambridge, and northern Cambridge. This division became evident in the unraveling of the Cambridgeport Whig organization. In 1855 the Whigs of that ward chose their last rallying committee for a state election. It contained eighteen young men, nine of whom were clerical and mercantile workers in Boston, nine of whom were tradesmen in the Port. Within eighteen months, at least six of the nine commuters were active Republicans, while six of the nine locals had gone nativist.[15] The split became still more obvious as new party organizations pulled in large numbers of workers. A map of the convention delegates and local committee members who supported Fremont-Republican or nativist candidates in 1856 and 1857 shows that the former included many commuters from Dana Hill and North Cambridge, while the latter included craftsmen and small manufacturers who lived near the immigrant-industrial areas (fig. 10).

Finally, the spillover of larger politics roused new concern about the city-suburban boundary by inflaming an ongoing debate about the annexation of the suburbs. The idea itself was not new and many of the rationales would be heard again. Some residents of Charlestown had proposed a merger with Boston since the 1820s, and new advocates appeared there as well as in Boston and Roxbury in the 1840s and 1850s. Philadelphia's successful campaign for consolidation of the city with all its contiguous suburbs encouraged such proposals. After the Civil War, a revived annexation movement would eventually bring in four of Boston's neighbors before dying away in the late nineteenth century.[16]

Between 1852 and 1854, Bostonians and suburbanites engaged in strenuous arguments about annexing Roxbury, Charlestown, and Cambridge. These discussions were a direct and vivid manifestation of the problems and anxieties raised by suburban growth. Much of the pressure came from Boston, where merchants and civic leaders fidgeted over the exodus of the well-to-do, the growing political power of the Irish, and the decline of trade. In the eyes of these people annexation would expand the tax base, counterbalance the immigrant influence, and improve Boston's competitive standing vis-à-vis New York and Philadelphia. But the suburbs had the decisive voice, because annexation required a referendum in each affected community. In Roxbury and Charlestown some citizens argued for union because a merger with Boston would provide greater financial resources and better administration. In Cambridge some felt that annexation would give access to Boston's new water system and open the way to "one grand New England metropolis."[17]

Prevailing opinion in Roxbury and Cambridge, however, ran strongly against annexation. John Ford carried numerous editorials opposing the city threat. "The public affairs of Charlestown, Cambridge, and Roxbury," he said, "can be better administered in their present form of separate independencies than by union with the scheming city of notions." Lest his readers miss the point, he ran an article on the same page headlined "Increase of Drunkenness and Crime in the City of Boston."[18]

The public content of such annexation discussions arose from local concerns—issues that had been there before and would be there after. But the timing and intensity of the early fifties debates was determined by the spillover of external politics. Especially in Charlestown, where annexation had a serious chance, the large-scale maneuvers of Whigs and coalition completely

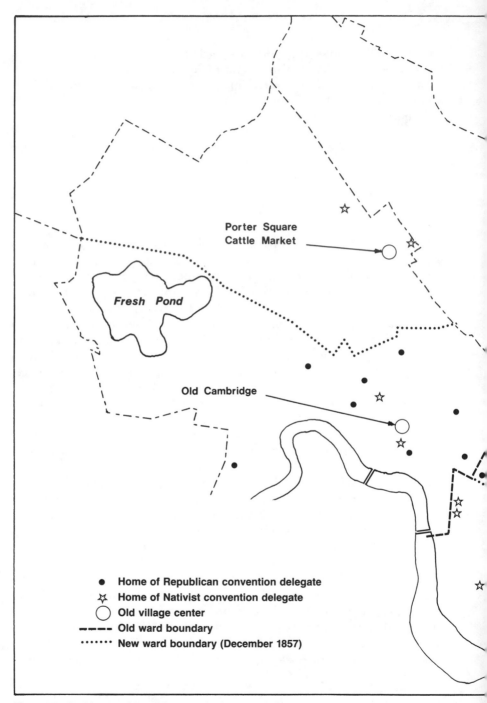

Figure 10   Residences of Republicans and Nativists, 1856–57

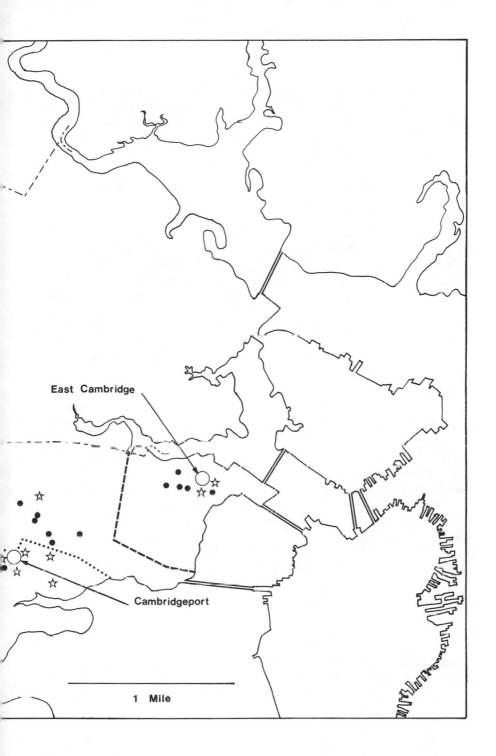

East Cambridge

Cambridgeport

1 Mile

overwhelmed local politics. In Charlestown the leaders of the 1853–54 annexation movement were W. W. Wheildon and George W. Warren, both old-line Whigs with strong ties to the Cotton Whig organization in Boston. In Charlestown as in Boston men like these were frantically trying to profit from the coalition's troubles. They hoped to rebuild Whiggery by courting discontented Irish voters, who disliked the Democratic alliance with nativist Free-Soilers. For Wheildon, Warren, and other Whigs, annexation was a path to increased political power. It would join the Whig-Irish alliance of Boston with that of Charlestown and undercut the coalition's representation in the legislature. As might be expected, opposition to annexing Charlestown came from Democrats and Free-Soilers all over the state. The leader of the antiannexation forces in the city was J. Q. A. Griffin, a Whig turned radical in 1848 and a strong Free-Soiler. In the legislature the bill was opposed by William S. Robinson, Free-Soil representative from Springfield, elected on a coalition ticket. And when the measure was approved, the opposition forces brought in Benjamin F. Butler, one of the Democratic architects of the coalition, who successfully argued against it before the Supreme Court.[19]

Such machinations probably lay behind Ford's fear of "scheming." They certainly helped to destroy suburban confidence in the old ways of doing local business. Embittered relations among leaders, the collapse of the caucus system, the attempt to manipulate local boundaries for partisan purposes—all left a legacy of mistrust that lingered after the period of direct spillover ended.

Still, it became plain in the late fifties that political turmoil at the local level was different from the process of statewide realignment. The period of maximum conflict and bitterness in the suburbs came in 1858–59—long after the intrusion of party struggles and more than a year after the Republicans restored stability to state politics. The issues that provoked this crisis were specifically local, arising from long-term changes in the suburbs and in the relationship between suburbs and city. When they emerged from the furor of the 1852–54 period, suburbanites found that they could not restore old balances but had to adjust to changes in their roles as citizens and leaders and in the mechanisms necessary for government.

The Citizen as Petitioner

As the suburbs grew and diversified, and as the New Model assumptions crumbled, influential suburbanites reacted with piecemeal, half-acknowledged adjustment which cumulated into major change. As citizens, they acted less often as bargainers in a forum, more often as applicants to an establishment. As officials, they could no longer be generalized stewards; more and more they became managers with an organized constituency. In both roles they slipped steadily away from their ideal of a debt-free, volunteer-based, democratically malleable government.

These changes in roles and structure occurred gradually, without obvious benchmarks. The alteration of the citizen's role, for example, happened in the course of disputes about the provision of services. Suburbanites had always sought favors from their governments—schools, road maintenance, backing for public-spirited enterprise—and they continued to seek the same things through similar channels in the 1850s. But by the mid-fifties there were many more citizens asking for new kinds of favors, and they found it harder to agree on an equitable division of the pie. Moreover, those who asked were less often the same people as those who decided: the pool of petitioners grew; the governing bodies grew more distant and formal.

Many details of this subtle transformation are obscure. Suburban residents did much of the business of governing orally. The minutes of their meetings noted results, with little account of initiatives or negotiations. The public statements of their leaders combined stirring phrases with cryptic innuendoes, alluding to matters they understood but later readers cannot. Yet one remarkable source survives in Somerville. Late in the nineteenth century, some dedicated civil servant collected and stored nearly all the working documents of the Somerville selectmen and aldermen—petitions and letters from the public, notes for oral reports in town meeting, communications from other local officials. These documents, when combined with the minutes of selectmen and town meetings, provide a continuous record of interaction between government and people. In the nineteen years between Somerville's founding and the war, 810 people signed 136 petitions to the selectmen. These applications, containing more than 1,800 signatures, provide clues to citizen wants and attitudes. They reflect an important change in the array and kind of pressures on government. They not only illuminate Somerville affairs but offer a guide to the interpretation of thinner records in Cambridge.[20]

In Somerville and Cambridge, throughout the period 1845–60, the strongest pressure for change in government arose from the promotion of residential neighborhoods and the domestic suburb. In the forties this pressure did not produce conflict. All influential citizens supported key goals such as education, low taxes, and a strong municipal reputation. The demands of residential promoters were the same as those of their neighbors. Gradually, however, residential requests diverged from the old pattern, and residential promoters began to use political means to bolster the primacy of domestic interests.

These shifts toward a petitioning citizenry and residential aggressiveness began almost imperceptibly in municipal actions concerning schools and roads. Traditionally these had been the most important items of public business and the major categories of expenditure. No one was surprised, in the late forties and early fifties, when population growth produced more petitions for schoolhouses and road maintenance, and few questioned the expense. Enthusiasm for the common schools and competition with other suburbs led to lavish expenditure for education. Yet there were changes in the content and tone of citizen requests. As we saw above, the domestic ideal prompted demands for numerous small primary schools embedded in the neighborhoods. In the forties, school committees praised citizens for helping in the work of locating and landscaping these schools and for attending meetings and examinations. But in the fifties citizens increasingly treated school committeemen and teachers as public employees, from whom they demanded ever higher levels of service. In 1855 "A Friend to Little Children and to the Free Schools" wrote a huffy letter to the *Chronicle*, insisting that teachers should get to work earlier on stormy days, so that children would not have to wait outside. The writer also thought that teachers, or some other city employee, should be required to shovel snow from the walks. At about the same time, commuter residents of Dana Hill threatened to put their children in private school if they did not get the new school they wanted. By 1858, parents complained regularly that teachers were "overtaxing" their children, and those in one neighborhood supported their offspring in boycotting an unpopular master hired by the school committee to fill a vacancy.[21]

In a similar fashion, general enthusiasm for good roads masked a shift in demand. Citizens rarely complained when their leaders hiked road budgets, experimented with new pavements, or acquired new sources of gravel and stone. As with schools, population growth and residential promotion led first to an expansion of old activities and then in the fifties to a change. In Somerville, neighborhood promoters began to ask for public maintenance of side streets as well as arteries. Between 1842 and 1860, more than a third of the petitions submitted in Somerville sought grading or acceptance of residential streets. Many of these roads, built on steep inclines by developers of scenic hillside lots, presented maintenance problems of the worst variety. The formula for action in these cases was the same as it had been in the fringe era—private construction, public maintenance—but there was a significant shift in the type of streets discussed and in the rationale for their acceptance.

These new petitioners made no pretense of benefiting the public at large; the interests of neighborhood and local property were paramount. They sought streets "for the accommodation of the inhabitants of Spring Hill" or because they had spent "about twenty thousand dollars . . . on dwelling houses and buildings."[22]

Along with demands for schools and roads, residentially oriented suburbanites began to ask for new favors in the 1850s: public water supplies, sewers, gas lights, and parks. Here, too, the first initiatives resembled the public-private partnerships of the past but expanded the public role. Private corporations supplied gas and water, but Cambridge and Somerville granted liberal terms for the use of the streets, and Cambridge loaned the water company $50,000. It took only a short step to request full-scale public utilities, requiring huge outlays and long-term debts. Boston itself acquired a public water supply only after twenty years of controversy, in 1848. Two years later, residents of Cambridgeport asked their city to buy into Boston's supply.[23]

The Somerville petitions reflect all of these overall changes in public pressure and also the increasing accuracy of the term "pressure." In the 1850s the selectmen received many more petitions than they had in the 1840s and more people had signed them (table 7.2). More than 90 percent of the petitioners

Table 7.2
Somerville Petitioners, 1842–60

	1842–50	1851–60	Total
Total number of petitioners	48	88	136
Total number of signatures	540	1,295	1,835
Total number of signers	244	566	810
Petitioners who served as selectman or alderman, 1842–85 (by date of first petition)	35	20	45
Petitioners who signed various numbers of petitions, by date of first	first signature 1842–50		first signature 1851–60
	signed 1842–60	signed 1842–50	signed 1851–60
1 petition	92	147	355
2–3	68	61	173
4 +	84	36	38
Total	244	244	566

Table 7.3

Place of Work of Most Active Petitioners, 1842–60
(more than four in four years)

Place of Work	Date of First Signature		Total
	1842–50	1851–60	
Boston	17	25	42
Suburb or uncertain	19	15	34
Total	36	40	76

in the latter decade signed only one request in ten years. In Somerville's early years there had been more people who signed a large number of petitions. The shift was even larger than these summary statistics indicate: in the 1840s six men signed more than nine petitions apiece; in the 1850s only one citizen was so energetic.

Along with the change in volume came a change in the petitioners. Throughout this period those who signed such requests were a small part of the adult male population.[24] In the beginning one could not easily distinguish the most active petitioners from the governing elite. Many of those who first signed in the 1840s eventually served in town office themselves. Among these veteran petitioners were men like George Brastow and Charles Forster, who promoted their own neighborhoods, paid for amenities from their own resources, petitioned for government favors, and also served without pay in town office. In the 1850s the most active petitioners were more often true Boston commuters who never served in office (table 7.3).

Still more striking was a change in the pattern of *success* of petitioning. The signers represented many suburban interest groups—old farmers, fringe entrepreneurs, and Bostonian migrants. Because petitions often led to confused town meetings, peculiar alliances, and obscure compromises, it is impossible to measure exactly the relative success of any particular group. Yet there was a clear shift of town priorities visible in the debates over acceptance of roads. Over the whole period, the most successful petitions were those seeking acceptance of residential streets on Spring Hill and Winter Hill, the two major areas of commuter settlement. The least successful petitioners were northern brickmakers seeking acceptance of crosstown roads for their teams and a cluster of artisans, brickmakers, and old landowners near Sandpit Square who fought for ten years to gain acceptance of a road linking their area to the north side. In short, new residential promoters became more successful than the representatives of old fringe enterprise.

The mid-fifties disruption of politics accelerated this shift toward residential power. Until then, residential promoters and representatives of the old industrial fringe managed to find common ground and mechanisms of cooperation. Clark Bennett, the brickmaker-speculator-reformer of Sandpit Square, enjoyed cordial if argumentative relations with the commuter-developers on the hills. His petitions (he signed sixteen) generally failed, but the commuters shared his temperance views and he joined them on town committees to promote schools. In Cambridge in early 1852, soapmakers, stablers, and other fringe entrepreneurs of the Bennett variety joined with commuting Boston merchants and *Chronicle* editor Ford to solicit subscriptions and petition the city for lights on Main Street. Their committee was politically as well as economically diverse, including Democrats, conservative Whigs, Free-Soilers, and temperance men—some of whom, a short time later, would not gather in the same room.[25]

Such cooperation declined in the political climate of the late fifties. Instead, residential interests began a long-term process of confining and purging the inheritance of the fringe. There would be brickyards and other remnants in Cambridge and Somerville for many years, and some of their proprietors would continue to speak with authority in town councils. But the more objectionable aspects of fringe society came under open attack. Just as they directed the power of moral institutions against fringe vices, so residentially oriented citizens now sought to turn governmental authority against some parts of the fringe economy. First in Cambridge, then in Somerville, there were campaigns for bylaws and ordinances that would eliminate noxious manufactures, manure piles, pig keeping, and the "swill boys" who collected night soil.[26] In 1857 Cambridgeport residents launched an attack against a new chemical plant on the Cambridge-Somerville border. John Ford, who knew that some industry was important to the tax base, tried to come to its defense. Granting that "the neighborhood has always been unsavory," he insisted that the chemical factory should not be confused with "a distillery of quite another character just over the Somerville line," nor should it be blamed for the smell of the soapworks nearby. His words were to no avail. Within a month the pressure of petitions led the Board of Health to order removal of the "nuisance known as the Boston Chemical Works" forthwith.[27]

That same fall, a long controversy over the Cambridge Water Works showed the declining power of the fringe. A few years before, when the residential promoters of Dana Hill, Old Cambridge, and Somerville sought running water, Cambridge loaned the water company enough to allow laying pipes to those areas. Now the company was again short of funds, while the industrial areas of East Cambridge and the Lower Port still lacked water. Seventy small manufacturers and tradesmen, including some of the oldest and most established entrepreneurs in the area, petitioned the city to buy the Water Works outright. The mayor and a city council committee supported the proposal. But commuters joined with Old Cambridge fiscal conservatives to defeat the measure in the Board of Aldermen and then to block a movement for a popular referendum.[28] In the campaigns against nuisances and in this denial of water to industry, there were signs of things to come. Not yet, but soon, the forces of residence would consider the whole fringe pattern a "nuisance" to be abated.

The Official as Manager

These changes in the volume and character of citizen demand produced governmental changes in response. Here, too, the word "response" became more accurate over time. Stewardly officials of the 1840s did not simply react to citizen pressure. Often they embodied it and moved in sympathy with their neighbors toward modern goals. School authorities, for example, treated pressure for more accommodation as both a problem and an opportunity. In 1845 the beleaguered Cambridge school committee complained that the population of new areas like Dana Hill, "spreading off in unexpected directions," made it impossible to choose proper locations for many small schools. But growth provided an ideal chance to experiment. In both Cambridge and Somerville, school authorities gave primary schools to the neighborhoods but also did what Horace Mann and the New Model reformers had suggested years before: they channeled many local requests into a movement for large centralized grammar schools, holding hundreds of pupils. By 1859 the Cambridge school committee spoke proudly of its achievements. In the preceding years, said its report, "every part of the machinery of our school system has moved with little, if any, friction."[29]

In coping with pressure for neighborhood amenities and residential streets, officials followed a similar line of evolution and justification. Petitioners wanted public action to benefit small areas and private property. Officials, who had often been petitioners themselves, were generally sympathetic. They saw neighborhood promotions, however narrow, as a public benefit. They stretched their responsibility as stewards, once confined to maintaining major arteries and paying a teacher or two, to a whole new class of actions that served the community as competitive domestic suburb. "Within five years," said the Somerville selectment in 1856:

the inhabitants of our town have increased nearly 75 per centum. This ratio of increase is not likely to be lessened, since, while the cities are crowding and forcing the people beyond their limits, the present policy of railroad managers will tend to prevent their locating at any great distance from the centres of business. The class of people thus making up our population, requires conveniences such as have been enjoyed in larger places,—ornamental and comfortable public buildings, good roads, proper sidewalks, light streets, and efficient police regulations. Locating among us, they add largely to the worth of vacant land in their neighborhood.[30]

Citizens encouraged their officials in these first steps toward a service-oriented government. But such a government required, as the Cambridge school committee put it, "machinery." In 1845, Cambridge and Somerville together had 18 small schoolhouses and employed 39 teachers. By 1860 they had more than 30 large school buildings and a teaching staff of 133. They also paid more than two dozen people to maintain the buildings. In fifteen years, school budgets rose from $18,000 to $58,000. Road maintenance costs rose from $11,000 to $28,000 and by 1860 the two suburbs paid well over a hundred men to keep up the streets. Other expenditures kept pace with these, and outran population growth, so that per capita outlays rose as well (table 4.1).[31]

The financial burden of expansion fell more heavily on Cambridge than on Somerville. The newer community, blessed with a smaller, wealthier population, escaped increases in taxes or debts. While assessment rates rose past $9.00 per thousand in Cambridge and Charlestown, Somerville *reduced* its tax rate from a high of $6.40 (1855) to $5.70 in 1860. Cambridge and Charlestown became heavily indebted, not only to their local banks but to some in Boston and Lowell as well. Somerville, by contrast, borrowed sometimes from its own wealthy citizens, occasionally from banks, but never in this period resorted to the short-term loans that Cambridge and Charlestown took out every month.[32] Measured by the simple outward signs so dear to antebellum accountants, the Somerville corporation was healthier than its neighbors.

In Cambridge, too, the pressures of growth produced distance and formality in government more quickly than in Somerville. Under the terms of the city charter, the aldermen were supposed to be direct equivalents of the old

Table 7.4

Continuity of Leadership in Cambridge

Selectmen and aldermen	Elected in				
	1826–35	1836–45	1846–55	1856–65	1866–75
Total	18	32	41	52	68
Served earlier as selectmen	4	7	6	1	
Served earlier as aldermen				3	10
Total with prior experience	4	7	6	4	10

SOURCE: Calculated from lists of civil office holders in Paige, *History of Cambridge.*

board of selectmen—nominated to ensure geographical representation but elected at large. Yet the aldermen proved not to be the long-term stewards of old. Even before the city charter, the selectmen were moving away from the traditional ideal. Fewer and fewer of them were the multipurpose economic, moral, and political leaders of the past (see fig. 6, above). The aldermen continued the trend. As time passed, more of those chosen were newcomers to public office, and they also tended to serve shorter terms (table 7.4).

There were also changes in the roles and attitudes of city executives. School committeemen, trying to keep track of thousands of children, moved toward stricter rules and a more defined hierarchy. They strengthened principals and campaigned for a salaried superintendent ("a school, like an army, must be under one head," said the 1854 report). They tried to deemphasize the role of parents, who should "let the teachers and the committee . . . be the judges of the proper classes the children should be placed and kept in." Only the committee, they insisted, could decide on teacher qualifications, and it was a serious question "whether the commitee shall act independently . . . or whether they shall be governed by the opinions or prejudices of persons who have no official responsibility in the matter."[33]

The most important change, however, occurred in the role of mayor. James Green, the first mayor, had cast himself in a role of moral leadership similar to that played by the chairmen of the old board of selectmen. When he completed his first stint in the office, an appreciative editorial in the *Chronicle* said nothing about his abilities as head of the city administration but praised him for his crusade against horse racing, Sabbath desecration, and drinking and for his efforts "to restore fathers to an *honorable* supremacy in the domestic circle and usefulness in the busy world" and "in short, to make peace and order take the place of rowdyism and disgrace."[34]

As the city grew, Green's successors had to devote more time and words to matters of finance and staffing than to exhortation, but until the mid-fifties they did little to expand the administrative side of the mayor's office or to exploit the bureaucratic powers latent in the city charter. Then, in 1855, after the Know-Nothing revolt, the city elected a new kind of mayor. John Sargent, who had walked out of the Whig caucus to protest its closure, who had rallied the opposition to Old Cambridge separation, defeated the Know-Nothing incumbent and took office at the start of 1856.

Sargent had some of the background that suburbanites expected in a steward. He had been a successful Boston businessman, state representative, moderator of local meetings, and chairman of the Whig city committee. Although he was popular with his fellow Cambridgeport commuters, he also won majorities in every ward of the city and stayed in office for an unprecedented four terms. The *Chronicle*, hailing his third victory, expressed pity for whoever would someday succeed him.[35]

In office, Sargent strengthened and expanded the city establishment. He pressed the city council to hire more supervisory and clerical personnel, explored new sources of revenue, and shortened the timetable for tax payments. Whereas Green had employed the rhetoric of domesticity, Sargent deployed the apparatus of residential services. He was all for streetlights, sidewalks, sewers, and parks. He dispatched city crews to prune back or cut down trees that obstructed traffic. He encouraged the horse railroad, and he thought the city should buy the water works. In 1857, after Republicans gained a clear hold on state government, Sargent also spurred an effort to reconstruct the nonpartisan balancing mechanism of local politics. First, he and his associates reorganized the city wards. They divided Cambridgeport in half, separating the industrial Lower Port from the Dana Hill commuter area. They also placed the Irish-and-commuter community of northern Cambridge in a ward separate from the Old Cambridge center. There were now five "communities" in Cambridge, imposed from above in an effort to preserve a rough balance of political interests. The same reformers then tackled the problem of nomination. The caucuses were gone, but Sargent and the leaders of all three major parties organized the Municipal Nominating Convention, in which delegates from meetings in each ward joined to put together a citywide slate.[36]

In his actions and his public statements, Sargent stressed the independent powers of municipal government—those that did not require state sanction or appeal to the public. Although he eagerly and successfully sought support for his projects, he could not conceal his annoyance at the importunities of some citizens. He urged the city council to join him in displaying "manly independence" in their "daily intercourse with the people, which affords to every citizen an opportunity to press upon our attention his own peculiar views, and personal wishes, and which are not unfrequently urged in a manner which seems to say, I must be obeyed." This was the voice of an administrator addressing the public, not that of a gentleman steward speaking to his neighbors.[37]

In Somerville, there was no city administration, the late fifties did not produce a Sargent, and the selectmen clung to the language of stewardship. But in Somerville as in Cambridge government was becoming big business, and the selectmen found themselves thrust into the executive role. In 1857 they scolded new commuter residents, who "migrating from cities, accustomed to a different administration of affairs . . . forget that on them personally rests the responsibility and the consequences of the acceptance or defeat of the various measures proposed for their consideration."[38]

Whatever their opinions, officials had to adopt more formal procedures simply to cope with the volume of work. Even when it was a town, Cambridge had issued printed reports, set up a finance committee, and improved its accounts. The city government institutionalized and extended these steps. By the late fifties Cambridge residents received a thick volume of annual reports, with detailed breakdowns of the budget, certified audits, and pages of statistics recording children educated, fires fought, paupers fed, and the like. Somerville, dedicated to small-town government, tried to get by with old-fashioned and informal procedures. Its first financial reports, though printed, were little more than ledger-sheets set in type. The officers made oral reports in town meeting. The selectmen handled town business in irregular meetings—frequent in winter, rare in summer.

It could not work. Citizens demanded written reports. The selectmen, under pressure of petitions, legal documents, and ever more complex accounts, met more often. They set a weekly schedule throughout the year, and still the business grew, spilling over into scores of adjourned meetings and evening sessions. They farmed out work to standing committees and salaried employees. By the late 1850s the annual record of the town officers' work—printed, tabulated, and audited—was little different from the Cambridge reports.[39]

In Cambridge and Somerville, the effect of these shifts toward managerial officials and a bureaucratic system was to strengthen government and to commit it strongly to the expensive services desired by commuter residents. Not surprisingly, such changes alienated several categories of suburbanites. In Old Cambridge, the Sargent government's tree cutting incensed conservative residents; they preferred the irregularity of travel and the low rates of taxation that had formerly prevailed. In East Cambridge and the Lower Port there was strong resistance to centralized administration. On four occasions between 1846 and 1860, city authorities tried to establish a single city marshal or police chief. For John Sargent the administrator, police decentralization was chaos: "You might as well attempt to conduct the affairs of an important railroad or manufacturing corporation without a proper system or a responsible head, as that of a police department." Yet three times the city backed down, abolishing the office in the face of local demands for three independent constables. In 1857, when Sargent reinstituted the marshal's job, vandals ransacked the home of the man appointed to the post. These protests did not by themselves upset the trend toward bureaucratic government, but they were elements in a wider discontent that would soon erupt.[40]

The Crisis of Stewardship

By the late fifties, the several streams of political and governmental change in the suburbs had produced a wide variety of disgruntled citizens. There were diehard Whigs and other conservatives in Old Cambridge for whom James D. Green (still a Whig at the end of 1856) was a symbolic figure. There were nativist workingmen in East Cambridge and the Lower Port who resented the commuter-Republican domination of local affairs. There were small manufacturers disappointed in their quest for water. Between 1856 and 1859 these various discontents exploded in a series of emotional revolts. The outbursts were disconnected, but the common denominator was a fear of irresponsible power, a fear that the management of the community was slipping out of control. The first targets were the institutions that served residential growth, but the ultimate target was John Sargent.

Sargent's loss of stature was as much symbolic as personal. In moving away from stewardship and embracing residential primacy, the horse railroad, and a service-oriented government, he confronted local problems and tensions left in the aftermath of statewide political upheaval. Clearly the Republican synthesis that produced statewide stability did not resolve local difficulties. Tensions in the suburbs arose from economic diversity, the changing relationships between citizens and officials, and the rising power of domestic interests. As state politics settled into new grooves, these local tensions became more important. Sargent, in addressing them, had enlisted broad support but had also invited the mistrust of those who were discontented—either because they wanted to preserve small-town elitism or because they felt cheated by the commuter path of progress.

The chain of events leading to Sargent's fall began with complaints about the horse railroads. As suburbanites realized the magnitude of the streetcars' impact, the companies lay open to attack on several grounds. Their schedules determined the movements of increasing numbers of suburbanites; their tracks and equipment appeared ubiquitous; and their charters allowed them to exert significant power without being elected. It did not matter that suburban residents had fostered the mobility revolution, had encouraged commuter railroads, had founded the streetcar, water, and gas companies. In the fifties many suburbanites feared their communities were being "governed" by irresponsible corporations with long-term charters, vast wealth, and privileged rights to run over and dig under the public roads.[41]

The revolt against transportation drew upon a sense of betrayal and a fear of corporate power that went back to the forties. When the railroads came, suburbanites expected easy travel but found that smoke, accidents, and damage to the roads were part of the package. In 1848 Somerville's town meeting drafted a "memorial" against "Rail Roads, which have been thrust upon them." They complained of "the futility of any struggle against combined legislative and corporate influence" and demanded more restrictions in future charters. When the railroads raised their passenger fares in 1855, another storm of rebellion swept through the suburbs. Near Porter Square, dozens of northern Cambridge and Somerville commuters held protest meetings and pledged themselves to a boycott of the Fitchburg. In railroad-dependent Somerville the town meeting passed resolutions condemning the Fitchburg as a "nuisance," since it "has ceased to be a benefit to the town." They sent a committee to the legislature to demand the use of horses instead of steam within Somerville limits and to insist that gates at grade crossings "swing against the railroad instead of across the highway."[42]

It was one thing, however, to attack big companies based in Boston, quite another to attack those started by suburban neighbors. John Ford, who sympathized with the revolt against the steam railroads, nevertheless tried to convince suburbanites that their own, locally sponsored corporations were different. One of his headlines of December 1855 asked, "Have We a Corporation with a Soul among Us?" Yes, he replied: the Hancock Free Bridge Corporation, which was nearing its long-term goal of freeing the West Boston Bridge and in the meantime spent large amounts in cooperative grading and filling projects with the city. Ford was even more enthusiastic about the horse railroad, praised its promoters, disallowing any doubts, and pronouncing it a complete and unqualified success three days after it opened in 1856.[43] Yet for some residents, the corporations within the suburbs became more troubling than those outside, in part because their actions seemed to reflect a betrayal of stewardship. Conservative residents feared the horsecars would break down the city-suburban border. A week after the first line opened, "John Smith" noted that Cambridge had 14,000 residents, "and anything that can entice six thousand of them to spend their time in the cars, is a domestic calamity, and if they do not belong to Cambridge, why should Cambridge spoil her beautiful avenue to accomode [sic] strangers and incommode her own citizens." When the corporation tried to build a stable in the Old Cambridge center, critics denounced "this rich and powerful company" in the same language they had used against the steam railroads.[44]

Some commuters—especially those who did not live near the horsecar route—even resented the change in the conditions of travel. After six weeks of streetcar operation, a commuter meeting called for a restoration of omnibuses. Speakers denounced the corporation and John Ford alike, insisting that the streetcars were a fad; traffic would soon return to its "natural channels."[45]

In these protests some of the loudest voices were those of people who already had complaints about other changes evident in the suburbs. Old Cambridge residents annoyed by tree cutting also denounced the streetcar stables. Militant temperance men, rebuffed since 1853 in their efforts to use city power for prohibition, now condemned the railroad and the city establishment. As the railroad grew, experience gave ammunition to its critics. In the beginning the city fathers naively expected the streetcar company to lighten the municipal burden, since the city's agreement with the company called for the railroad to pave and maintain that part of the street adjacent to its track. But it soon appeared that the cost of widening bottlenecks caused by the railroad's preemption of space would far outweigh the savings. And since traffic shifted toward the shoulders of the road, where the pavement was softer, repairs became more onerous, not less.[46]

The cost of changing the city fabric, however, was a less important issue than the manner of deciding about changes. From 1856 through 1859 the city, the citizens, and the streetcar company became embroiled in almost constant arguments about new routes. Disappointed residents suspected connivance between government and corporation, and these fears broke into the open in 1859. Riders who were bypassed by existing service sought a franchise to build their own railroad north of and parallel to the first one. The Cambridge railroad countered with an application to build the line itself. Caught in the center, Mayor Sargent and the aldermen temporized, investigated, and then, in a closed session, gave the line to the existing company.[47]

This decision stirred resentment against Sargent's whole administration. In the name of efficient management, he had removed a vital decision from the realm of public discussion and influence. The promoters of the new railroad were, as the *Chronicle* noted, "men of property and standing" who were accustomed to participating in decisions of this sort. Sargent shut them out. He was also guilty, some felt, of sacrificing neighborhood interest to the will of a corporation, if not of outright corruption.[48]

A crowded indignation meeting revealed the depth of mistrust and conflict. As soon as the gathering was called to order, an observer noted, "it was evident that a great many friends of the company were there and endeavoring to control the meeting." Angry citizens named a committee to draft resolutions, headed by one John Barbour. Barbour was a prosperous commuter, a prominent Baptist, and among the most militant temperance men, but he had never held public office and he clearly mistrusted Sargent's style of leadership. He reported resolutions, passed decisively, which condemned the aldermen's decision "as an act not becoming the dignity of a deliberative body," and "as tending to destroy all confidence in the firmness of the men whom we have placed over us." In rhetoric worthy of larger causes—and reminiscent of the days of stewardship—he and his colleagues vowed to pursue the idea of an independent railroad and to work "in the great enterprise until . . . the people shall be released from the grinding weight of the iron heel . . . with which a few speculators have endeavored . . . to trample upon their rights."[49]

In addition to these escalating fears of centralized management and corporate influence, one other element fueled the rising discontent and focused complaints on Sargent. This was the old and emotion-laden problem of debt, exacerbated by the nationwide economic crisis of 1857. Once again in the late fifties suburbanites faced the dilemma first seen in the 1830s, when Cambridge residents found that improvement enterprise could be expensive. Clark Bennett, brickmaker, school improver, petitioner for fire engines, and temperance man, embodied the conflict. Almost every year he joined his neighbors in asking for more from their government. Just as constantly he urged fiscal restraint, speaking proudly of the way Somerville, "from the day of its incorporation has ever adhered to this motto—tax modestly; pay promptly; keep free from debts."[50]

Many of Bennett's peers displayed the same mixture of conflicting desires, but in the long period of prosperity from 1843 through the first years of Sargent's administration, they could live with the conflict. An atmosphere of economic crisis took away the luxury. The winter of 1857/58 brought unemployment and hardship for suburban workers. Both Somerville and Cambridge authorized special appropriations to put the needy to work on the highways. In Cambridge, tight money exacerbated city debt, as interest paid for temporary borrowing reached record levels.[51] The Panic of October 1857 caught Mayor Sargent at the worst moment—only a few months after the tree-cutting controversy, only two months after a major dispute over streetcar routes, and in the midst of his effort to obtain city purchase of an insolvent water works.

In such a climate Sargent became a villain. Once he had enjoyed citywide support, but in 1858 conservative citizens based largely in Old Cambridge began a movement to oust him, choosing "Temperance and Retrenchment" as their slogan and directing most of their attack against improvements under his regime. Sargent rode out this assault, but he was a marked man. By the following autumn, he was not only blamed for extravagance but suspected of making a secret deal with the streetcar company.[52]

To head their challenge, discontented citizens called once again on James D. Green, the city's first mayor. Green was a logical choice for people who struggled to reconcile their own contradictory attitudes. He had no fear of the city form of government and believed in strong municipal action to provide schools and main roads and above all to defend suburban homes against invading Bostonians and local undesirables. As mayor he had used the limited powers of the office with evangelical vigor. In the small arena of Cambridge, his administration resembled the more famous regime of Josiah Quincy in Boston. Like Quincy, Green was both a sensitive politician and an eloquent spokesman for integrity, caution, and limited government. An old Whig, a former minister, an old-fashioned steward, Green was a strong symbol in bewildering times.

The pattern of voting in his narrow victory over Sargent reflected the salient issues of the late 1850s—centralization, corporate influence, and town finance. Sargent won in Cambridgeport, his home and the main source of commuter pressure for residential improvements. He lost East Cambridge, Old Cambridge, and northern Cambridge. In the preceding three years, East Cambridge citizens had been the most outspoken opponents of a city marshal; East Cambridge and northern Cambridge residents had been the promoters and potential customers of the defeated streetcar line; Old Cambridge had been the center of fiscal conservatism.[53]

In a ringing inaugural address, Green voiced all the sentiments his followers wished to hear. "In the onward progress of the world," he intoned, "a principle of conservatism is as necessary for our well-being as . . . the governor for the safety of the steam engine." Without mentioning any specific individuals or acts ("I judge of no man's motives"), he accused the preceding administration of promoting "agitation and change without any real progress" and of allowing their behavior to become suspect. Public servants should be beyond reproach, especially when "in the government of some of our largest cities, official corruption has become glaring and notorious." He reassured the public of his own humility, his determination to be merely a "chosen agent," incorruptible and fully accountable. Item by item, he reviewed the budget, opposing public expenditures for grading residential streets or building parks—things that should be done "by private subscription."[54] But the longest part of his speech was reserved for a sweeping and emotional attack on corporations that made fortunes from their privileged position and took advantage of the suburban need to ride:

> Consider how the case stands. Here are two Corporations, under virtually the same direction, wielding a joint capital of half a million dollars, exerting a certain control over our principal streets, possessing a monopoly of the transportation of passengers to and from the metropolis,—and all this within the jurisdiction of our City. It is a new and anomalous condition of things.[55]

Yet behind this defiant conservatism, Green's speech acknowledged many changes that could not be undone. Cambridge could not reduce its expenditure for schools, lest it lose good teachers and the system's good repute. Nor could it cut the cost of the fire department, given the pace of growth. The police, too, were essential, because Cambridge was next to Boston and "so much exposed to having crowded out upon us a population requiring unceasing vigilance, for the protection of person and property." Even the huge expense on roads and streets could not be speedily reduced, given contracts already let and repairs clearly needed.[56] Green promised to reduce taxes and city expenditures and to eliminate the city debt but did not say how. However reassuring his words, many citizens must have suspected they were an illusion—a balm, not a cure, for the pains of growth.

The fact was that both Cambridge and Somerville were already in many ways mature suburbs. Though many citizens grumbled and balked at recognizing the changes, both communities had elevated residential interests to a primary level in policymaking, had committed their resources to providing residential services, and had established their positions as independent and competitive units in the metropolitan complex. The Green uprising changed none of this; it merely allowed suburbanites to postpone recognition and to persuade themselves that stewardship still worked.

Green's political resurrection, which symbolized the frustrations of the late 1850s, proved relatively brief. Reelected one more time in December of 1860, he resigned, exhausted, after a few months of running the city under the pressures of a war for which he had little enthusiasm. In 1848, when he first retired from the mayoralty, the *Chronicle* lavished praise on his moral leadership. In 1861, the news of his resignation appeared without editorial comment, buried amid stories of recruiting and reports from Bull Run.[57] Although he lived until 1882, Green played no further role in public affairs.

The last crusade of James D. Green reflected the growing pains associated with the transition from fringe villages to residential suburbs. His departure from office was one of many indicators of a change in the makeup and goals of suburban leadership in the late 1850s and 1860s. Although suburban leaders had in fact been modifying the stewardly role since the early nineteenth century, people like Green or even Sargent in his early career were close enough approximations to make the illusion of stewardship plausible. The crises of the 1850s revealed its implausibility.

Moreover, even the quasi stewards of the fringe era were now fading away. Through death or retirement many of those prominent in developing the fringe dropped from view. Royal Makepeace, the only surviving member of the Cambridgeport Proprietors, died in 1855. Zachariah Porter, founder of the northern Cambridge village, followed in 1868. While Cambridge and Somerville still contained many descendants of the big entrepreneurial families of the fringe—the Hoveys, Masons, Tuftses, and Sanborns—the founding generation was gone before the Civil War. So too, by 1870, were many of the transitional commuters and New Model reformers of the 1830s. Three of the four Cambridge government innovators—Hayward, Parmenter, Whittemore, Buttrick—died between 1861 and 1866, and the fourth was in secluded retirement. Francis Bowman, the peripatetic land speculator who helped to found Somerville, disappeared during the 1860s. John Edgerly, his colleague in town making, lived until 1872 but dropped out of public life in the late 1850s.

Those few local leaders who survived the turmoil of the 1850s and remained active in later years revealed a new attitude toward government and the suburban role in the metropolitan area. John Sargent, though he never again ran for mayor, completed his transition from local Whig leader through Free-Soil activism to become a prominent Massachusetts Republican and a bureaucratic official. In the 1850s and 1860s he became state senator and federal tax collector. He also served Cambridge as head of the Water Board, a large agency set up to provide a uniform public water supply to all parts of the city. George Brastow, the Somerville speculator and horse railroad promoter, also became an active participant in statewide politics and an officer in the Union army. In the late 1860s, as selectman, he led a campaign to prevent Somerville's annexation to Boston and then another campaign to obtain a city charter. In 1871 he became first mayor of the city of Somerville.

Perhaps the most dramatic indication of change came in the career of Clark Bennett, brickmaker, speculator, and temperance man. In the 1840s and 1850s, Bennett tried to pursue contradictory goals: residential services and low-cost government. In the late 1860s he came down squarely for a service-oriented, high-budget, activist local government in Somerville. He led a successful campaign for public water supplies and then became a promoter and manager of the Miller's River Abatement Project—a large, cooperative, regional effort to control pollution and flooding in the area between Cambridge and Somerville.

The disappearance of old stewards and the new prominence of bureaucratic leadership, however, were only signals of a larger process of maturation in the suburbs. Suburban growing pains did not really end until the initial growth cycle was complete—that is, until residents and leaders both acknowledged their unique suburban status. In the 1860s they would reach this level of maturity. After the Civil War, no suburbanite could pretend that the suburbs were still villages. At the same time, many suburbanites realized that they could defend their communities against the worst evils of the city.

In dispassionate moments, some suburban residents of the late 1850s already saw and acknowledged the new role of suburbs in the metropolitan community. When, in 1858, all the bridges finally became free, a few noted that the event marked the end of a chapter as well as the beginning of a new one. Appropriately, the calmest and most astute analyst of the change was a man who had done much to bring it about. Isaac Livermore—entrepreneur, free-bridge promoter, speculator, commuter, loyal citizen—happily reviewed the new basis of suburban prosperity:

> The principal portion of the trade which was formerly carried on in Cambridge, has been transferred to the city of Boston, yet Cambridge retains as citizens many of those who were formerly her traders, and the narrow limits of Boston being filled by an increasing trade, numbers of its worthiest citizens were driven to the country for residences, and Cambridge has received its full share of the benefits.[58]

Livermore presided over Cambridgeport as an éminence grise until his death in 1880. For him, the change from fringe to suburb was a comfortable transition, already largely accomplished by the late 1850s. But for many other suburbanites both the extent of the change and it merits were unclear when the war came. The crises of the 1850s left a painful residue. Ironically, the crisis of war would help to resolve some suburban frustrations.

Epilogue:
Civil War and
Suburban Identity

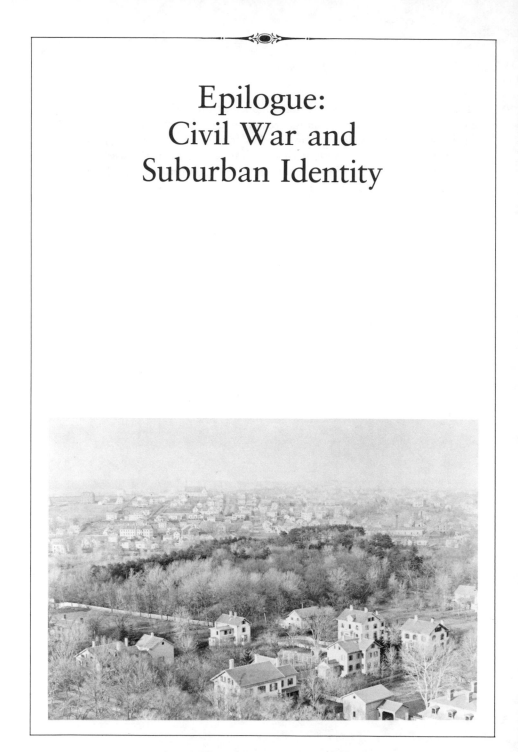

View of Cambridge and the Spring Hill area of Somerville,
as seen from Old Cambridge looking northeast, 1875.
In the center distance is George Brastow's speculative development.
On the right center are structures of the bleachery and the tube works.
Courtesy of the Harvard University Archives.

W ARS, especially long wars, bring home harsh realities. For American cities and suburbs, the experience of the Civil War was not confined to wartime itself. The dislocations and readjustments brought on by war stretched through the 1860s, reshaping urban demography, economics, and government. A decade of war and readjustment clarified the future of Cambridge and Somerville and induced their leaders to accept their new status—neither village nor city, but suburban.

In the 1850s, the pattern of suburban growth had been ambiguous and confusing, full of unresolved contradictions. Heavy industry, intensive residential development, and lingering fringe activities flourished next to each other. Juxtaposition made uneasy neighbors. Residential promoters, gaining more influence, seemed uncertain about their sphere of action: on the one hand they carved out and defended little enclaves of domesticity; on the other, they sought to command the resources and shape the policies of the whole community. In their arguments about municipal finance and leadership, suburbanites glossed over contradictory desires: for village government and city amenities, for thrift and modernity, for voluntarism and efficiency. By the 1870s, both the direction of future growth and the goals of suburbanites were more sharply defined. Cambridge, Somerville, and even more remote suburbs had come to grips with a new identity as commuter-based, residentially dominated, politically independent suburbs.

The essential ingredients of such communities were all there in the 1850s. The experiences of the war decade were catalytic, fusing the inherited elements and making the new synthesis—the residential suburb—plainly visible to all. Of course, not every change was a result of the war. Some developments were already underway; some would have occurred regardless. But in terms of suburban identity—the suburban residents' explicit recognition and pursuit of an independent, residential role in the metropolis—the war was a watershed.

In Cambridge and Somerville, the suburban pattern crystallized during the 1860s in three ways: first, war and Reconstruction clarified the lines of economic growth, encouraging rail-based heavy industry, hastening the decline of small fringe enterprises. Second, residential promoters went on the offensive, driving fringe activities from the path of commuter settlement. Third, local governments emerged from the war with new vigor and expertise, ready to manage and defend a suburban kind of growth.

The Economy Winnowed

In the suburbs, as in every northern community, the most visible sign of war was the departure of men. In 1861, Somerville's Sandpit Square became

219

Union Square, the site of a major recruiting office. In the ensuing months and years, hundreds of suburbanites marched past its flagpole and into service. Local historians, sifting state and federal rosters, estimated that the 17 inner Middlesex suburbs, which together contained about 40,000 adult males in 1860, furnished about 15,000 enlistments. While this number included many reenlistments, it is plain that military service removed a large part of the suburban labor force.[1]

The loss of such numbers, temporarily or permanently, clamped the brakes on suburban expansion. During the 1850s, the average rate of increase in population in the fan-shaped area of 17 suburbs northwest of Boston had been about 5 percent, and the fastest-growing communities had more than doubled their population. But in the five-year period 1860–65, the average rate dropped below 2 percent a year, and none of the communities grew by more than 20 percent. In several suburbs, shops closed and commerce stagnated, especially during the nationwide recession of the first two years of war.[2]

In every community war twisted the economy in new directions. But the long-term impact was different in each place. Some centers of fringe industry did not survive. War brought disaster to the Medford shipyards, when mercantile orders dried up and the navy expanded its shipyards in Charlestown. Of the ten Medford yards only one remained in operation in 1865, and its output for that year consisted of one vessel. The Cambridge glass, soap, and oil factories lasted longer, but after the war they slowly fell prey to competitors in New York and Pennsylvania. New, coal-fired glassworks sought locations close to the sources of fuel, and petroleum products displaced those made from animal fat.[3]

Yet even during the war and especially afterward, national demands brought propsperity to some industries, encouraged growth and centralization, and fostered regional integration. During the 1860s, some inner Middlesex producers shared in the growth of a huge rail-integrated complex centering on Boston—a metropolitan rather than suburban economy. The boot and shoe industry, for example, continued its shift toward factory production, while growing fat off military contracts. In the area north and east of Somerville, giant shoe plants appeared near rail lines. Using recently perfected processes, new entrepreneurs like Elisha Converse began making rubber shoes in the same era. By the 1870s, Stoneham, Woburn, and Malden, remote villages in the 1850s, had acquired busy railyards, smoky skies, and a pervasive smell of leather and rubber.[4]

In Cambridge and Somerville, the war-fed economy of the 1860s also transformed the industrial landscape. Rail shipment gradually undercut the function of the cattle markets in Brighton and northern Cambridge. These centers—with their complexes of tanneries, stockyards, slaughterhouses, and taverns—declined in the late 1860s. At the same time, the rail network fostered the huge slaughtering and packing plants on the Somerville–East Cambridge border. Refrigeration furthered the process in the 1870s. By the end of that decade a single plant in Somerville contained more than a dozen buildings, including a power plant, refrigeration equipment, and rail sidings that could handle two hundred cars at once. The Fresh Pond brickyards in western Cambridge also took advantage of better rail connections. Opening new clay beds and adopting steam-powered machinery, these yards grew far larger than the old ones near Sandpit Square.[5]

Taken all together, these changes spelled the demise of the original fringe economy—a decline foreshadowed in the 1850s but accelerated in the decade of war. As industry centralized, carving out larger blocks of territory near the railroads, the scattered centers of crafts and processing went into eclipse. In their place, the realm of domesticity grew.

The Victory of Residential Society

The first commuters, pioneering new habits of travel in the 1840s and 1850s, had been especially influential because they were an elite and because they made up a large proportion of the suburban work force. High rail fares and inefficient transportation had concentrated commuters in the inner suburbs. These conditions were changing in the late 1850s and changed more quickly in the following decade. By the 1870s there were many thousands of commuters, and there was nothing special about commuting.

Horsecars and heavy industry both helped to reduce the commuter presence in Cambridge and Somerville. Boston workers rode streetcars to more distant residences, and industrial employees bulked larger in the inner suburban labor force. Street railways were among those businesses that prospered even during the war. After the initial recession, companies in the Boston area resumed new construction in 1862. In Cambridge and Somerville, new links and branches, new rolling stock, and new lines running farther from the city appeared continuously through the 1860s. At the same time, large factories attracted noncommuting workers to eastern Somerville, East Cambridge, and Cambridgeport.[6]

Of course the total number of commuters continued to rise, even in places where they made up a declining share of the work force. Directory listings and streetcar timetables both reflected the ongoing expansion of the commuter habit. A sample of directories indicates that in Cambridge there were almost twice as many commuters in 1880 as there had been twenty years earlier. Working-class commuting encouraged the expansion of schedules, so that on the busiest routes in Cambridge, the horsecars of the late 1870s ran continuously, twenty-four hours a day.[7]

Moreover, the overall pattern of journeys to work became more complex, no longer limited to a few routes between Boston and the commuter enclaves on Dana Hill and Spring Hill. A small number of workers were beginning to commute *within* and *between* the suburbs. Some of those employed in the inner suburbs now lived in the outer ones. Workers in East Cambridge sometimes found homes in the western parts of the city. Cheap fares to Boston and intrasuburban commuting both worked to increase the diversity of the commuter population. Given a more sophisticated streetcar system, small steps of job mobility might lead to changes in residence. The career of William Mason provides an example. He began as a surveyor in Cambridgeport and boarded during the 1850s within two blocks of his office. In the next twenty years he achieved some success laying out lots and making plats. By the 1870s he bought land in northern Cambridge and commenced commuting to his established business address in Cambridgeport.

As commuting became routine, the areas of commuter residence spread beyond the early enclaves. Residential promoters turned public authority against noxious neighbors. In Somerville and Cambridge, petitioning citizens prodded health officials to close down backyard fringe enterprises—rendering vats, piggeries, soapboiling works. The long-developing battle between the Porter Square cattle market in northern Cambridge and the neighboring areas of residence ended in 1868–69, when public protest and economic change closed the market and the adjoining slaughterhouses. Purchasers of the vacated land split it into house lots.[8]

Near Sandpit Square, an era also ended in the late 1860s, when owners of several brickyards finally decided to seek a new role in the metropolitan economy—filling in their clay pits and dividing the land into small lots. All through the lowlands around the rechristened Union Square, the old owners and their children built frame cottages, homes for workers in the nearby factories. Clark Bennett, Somerville brickmaker, temperance man, and heavy petitioner for roads and schools, sold his brickyard and began a new career—selling insurance to homeowners.[9]

City Hall in the Suburbs

In the 1850s, suburban politics had reflected the divided and confused state of suburban thinking and especially the anxieties generated by the modernization of government. In the Civil War and its aftermath, some of the things that troubled suburbanites became less troubling, because they could no longer be changed. Prewar experience had already produced bureaucratic management and substantial deficit spending. But it took the experience of war to nullify complaints about big government and debt. In raising and equipping troops and supporting families at home, Cambridge and Somerville spent far more money and went further into debt than they had ever dreamed possible (see table 4.1). To meet recruiting quotas, the suburban towns resorted to ever higher bounties. Some of the money for such premiums came from private subscription, and some was reimbursed by the state, but as the war dragged on municipal governments shouldered more of the burden. Nonreimbursed expenditures grew larger. For all 17 inner Middlesex suburbs, such outlays totaled more than $1.2 million for the period 1860–65, or about $3.00 per capita per year. These local government expenditures, solely for recruiting, were equal to the total annual budgets of the 1850s.[10]

Spending at this level inevitably created huge deficits, nullifying the whole prewar argument about the danger of "permanent debt." By 1865 Cambridge and Somerville together were almost $650,000 in the red. The figures for indebtedness, like those for recruiting expenditures, dwarfed the budgets of prewar years. Paying for the Civil War led to a permanent change in thinking about local finance. During the war, many of the inner suburbs set up sinking funds designed to systematize the payment of debts. To improve matters on the revenue side, local governments obtained state authorization to charge interest on overdue taxes.[11]

Once they had learned to handle large sums and large debts, the suburbs continued to do so, turning the apparatus of war support to peacetime local improvements. In 1862 the mayor of Cambridge used his annual address to warn the city council about the dangers of debt. In 1865 a new mayor, in *his* annual address, was completely sanguine in reporting a half-million-dollar debt and suggesting that the city borrow more. Cambridge credit, he said, "could command the funds needed for the purposes of war or peace."[12]

Newly confident suburban authorities undertook major programs of public works after Appomattox. In 1865 Cambridge bought out the private water company and began expanding its system of supply. In 1866 Somerville took over from private suppliers the contracts for providing water there. By 1871 public water systems were also operating in more remote suburbs: Malden, Melrose, Medford, and West Cambridge. Of the 17 inner Middlesex suburbs, only Lexington, the most remote, had no municipal waterworks by 1885. In all cases, the municipalities applied lessons learned from the war. Debts for capital improvements were funded from the beginning and special authorities were created to build and operate the systems. By the 1880s, even small towns had the rudiments of bureaucracy.[13]

Local governments also took the initiative in programs of nuisance abatement. Public water supplies and heavy industry generated unprecedented problems of waste disposal. By 1865 the meat-packing plants in Somerville and East Cambridge had completely polluted Miller's River. In the late 1860s the two communities began a joint project of sanitary improvement, draining some areas and building an eight-foot trunk sewer. This was the first such program undertaken jointly by two local governments in Massachusetts and foreshadowed the famous metropolitan district commissions of the 1880s and 1890s. Somerville and Cambridge also petitioned the legislature for more powers to police the packing industry. Together with other suburbs, they won laws prohibiting slaughterhouses in any community of more than four thousand people, except under terms to be laid down by the affected local governments.[14]

These new government initiatives of the late 1860s did not provoke the controversies of the preceding decade. In city council and town meeting, there were arguments about priorities and about distribution of funds, but no serious challenge to deficit spending or to government enterprise in public works. The desirability of such amenities was taken for granted, the role of government as entrepreneur was unchallenged, and citizens were apparently more willing to accept a "funded" than a "permanent" debt.

It was obvious before the war that strong local governments would resist attempts to split off new towns from their territory or to annex land to Boston. In the late 1860s malcontents and speculators tried some of these old options without major success. After 1865 the trend of reorganization in the suburbs was toward city incorporation, not division or annexation. Cambridge, not Somerville, became the model for suburban government. Discontented citizens in western Somerville made attempts to divide the town in 1865 and again in 1868. But their efforts could not overcome powerful resistance from the selectmen, who insisted that "no private schemes or sectional ideas of change of boundary, will be permitted to check us in the proud and prosperous condition in which we now stand."[15]

During the same period suburban annexation did occur to the south and east. Between 1868 and 1873 Boston absorbed Dorchester, Roxbury, West Roxbury, Brighton, and Charlestown. The last two lay in Middlesex County, but both differed significantly from the other suburbs. In each case, the union with Boston was a kind of last resort. Charlestown and Brighton had both attempted to urbanize independently but were handicapped by small tax bases and land area too confined to allow much residential expansion. In both cases mounting financial problems helped to convince a majority of the voters to accept Boston's overtures. But the result of their annexation, and of the annexation movement as a whole, was to harden the remaining suburbs against the prospect of being absorbed. Observing the fate of those communities that joined the city, the holdouts concluded that property values declined, city services were slow to arrive, and local political influence was lost.[16]

By the mid-1870s, the suburbs of Middlesex County had effectively rejected both division and annexation. Instead, they turned enthusiastically to city incorporation. Any town of more than twelve thousand people could legally apply for a city charter. Somerville and Newton had nearly reached that level in the late 1860s. The Somerville selectmen responded to the 1868 division attempt by ordering a special census to prove the fact. The federal census of 1870 confirmed more than the requisite number for both towns, and each moved quickly to secure city organization, in Somerville in 1872 and Newton in 1873. The outer suburbs required time to reach the needed number, but long before city incorporation was legally possible, the direction of opinion in each community became clear. Malden and Waltham both seized upon city charters as soon as possible, in 1881 and 1884, respectively. And as early as 1880 citizens of South Reading and Woburn expressed confidence that they would take the same step, although both communities were at that point a few thousand inhabitants short of the target.[17]

The Suburban Response to the Challenge of Urban Growth

Aspiring to independent cityhood, these distant suburbs completed a long cycle of suburban evolution. They sought and planned for the status that Cambridge had assumed so gingerly three decades before. To be a suburb now meant to be a community shaped by commuters, a community serving residential needs, and a separate municipality.

Cambridge and Somerville had become such communities gradually, hesitantly. In the late 1860s, as they became models for others to emulate, they closed a long period in their own development, beginning with the fringe explosion of the early nineteenth century. Through most of this period, the leaders of these communities had not intended that they would be what they were in the 1860s. Even those who tried to plan for their communities often could not anticipate the results. The unifying theme in the suburban experience from the Federalist era to the Civil War was not a consistent attempt to create independent residential suburbs but a recurrent process of coping with the unique circumstances of urban growth on the city's edge and a continuous redefinition of community in those circumstances.

Thus the three phases of peripheral growth outlined in the introduction to this study may also be seen as stages in the evolution of suburban self-consciousness. Much of what happened in the first phase, between the beginning of the century and the depression of 1837–43, was unplanned and unrecognized. Peripheral entrepreneurs took actions that changed the suburban communities dramatically—extending transportation, intensifying and reorganizing the patterns of interaction between city and periphery, establishing new villages, and strengthening suburban institutions—but they had few comprehensive or long-term notions about what they were doing. In the second phase, beginning in the late 1830s, a few suburban leaders of the New Model generation did begin to perceive and promote a new role for the suburban villages in the metropolitan area. Recognizing the implications of the mobility revolution, men like Hayward, Whittemore, Parmenter, and Buttrick put their money into transportation and residential speculation, and their political energy into reconstructing governments. But the New Model ideal was controversial and riddled with contradictions. Many suburban leaders resisted expensive reforms and feared city involvement. The reformers themselves still thought in terms of suburban villages, governed cheaply and catering to small industry and elite commuters. Only in the third phase, from the late 1840s through the war, did large numbers of suburban leaders come to grips with the new conditions and problems of suburban community life. The big factory, the railroad, the flood of streetcar commuters, and the intrusion of party politics revealed the flaws of the New Model ideal. Those who weathered the storms of the 1850s narrowed and clarified the visions of their predecessors, finally arriving at a stable conception of the independent residential suburb. From the 1860s onward, they were comfortable with a level of citification that had caused them great anxiety only a decade before and confident that they could preserve their independence and their selective participation in metropolitan growth.

Seen in this long-term context, the leaders of the first suburbs were neither passive rural victims of the city's expansion nor urban colonizers of the periphery. Rather they inherited, elaborated, and extended a process of community building on the city's edge. They were accustomed to think of their communities as independent entities, and this way of thinking persisted throughout the early nineteenth century, despite massive changes in the nature of the communities and in the makeup of suburban leadership. From the Federalist era to the 1850s, suburban leaders shared a common allegiance to locality, whether they lived in a fringe village or in a speculative residential enclave, whether they were members of an old peripheral family or young newcomers from the city. Over the same period, suburban leaders lived with and wrestled with the ongoing problem of community autonomy unique to the city periphery. A fundamental localism linked Royal Makepeace, the Cambridgeport promoter, and John Sargent, the bureaucratic mayor, though they differed in almost every other way.

This inheritance played a large role in the suburban experience of urban growth and community development. Responding not only to those pressures and opportunities felt in many locales but also to locally specific challenges of the periphery, suburbanites created a distinctive kind of community and a distinctive approach to the urban challenge.

It is beyond the scope of this book to trace the history of suburban community development in the late nineteenth century. But it is not inappropriate to note how discussions of later suburbs have distorted our view of suburban origins and, I think, our understanding of how the the nineteenth-century city fragmented as it grew. From the 1850s onward, city dwellers and detached observers portrayed residential suburbs as exclusive and defensive enclaves for affluent escapees from the city. Already in the 1840s, the separatist and anticity statements of some vocal suburbanites like editor John Ford provided ample evidence for this judgment. In the late nineteenth century, as more commuters fled the city and more immigrants arrived there, suburban chauvinism hardened. By the end of the century, the independence of the many suburban communities had become a disaster for the metropolitan community, blocking the efficient delivery of services, depriving the cities of revenue, confining the poor to a deteriorating core, and allowing well-to-do city workers to avoid the burdens and responsibilities of city living. To those outside the suburbs, political boundaries seemed arbitrary, given the social and economic integration of the metropolis. After all, the spreading carpet of houses and the tangle of streetcar lines often made it difficult to recognize where the city limits were. In such circumstances, political localism was at best anachronistic and at worst malevolent. Every sensitive observer noted these problems and lamented their consequences for the core cities and the metropolis.

Much of what we know about suburbs is grounded in this later body of experience and discussion, in which the city is the focus, the main ingredients of suburban growth are economic and social rather than political, and the long-term negative consequences of elite suburban separation are so obvious as to be assumed. Such assumptions color even the best works of those who study early suburbs and the process of spatial differentiation. They are implicit, for example, in Sam Warner's otherwise sensitive account of Roxbury, West

Roxbury, and Dorchester, three early suburbs of Boston which were an-nexed. Streetcars and long-term socioeconomic growth are central to his study. Politics and community identity play almost no role, even in his dis-cussion of the annexation issue. He sees the struggle between suburban an-nexationists and their opponents as a straightforward conflict between new, middle-class, streetcar commuters who wanted better services and a share in governing the metropolis and older residents who were loyal to a nostalgic conception of the town and fearful of immigrants. In the 1860s and 1870s the service-oriented commuters carried the day, but in the 1880s, when met-ropolitan commissions provided services efficiently to city and suburbs alike, the commuters became ethnocentric and jealous of their independence. Thus, middle-class city refugees first encouraged and then rejected the move-ment for annexation.[18]

In a similar fashion, those historians and historical geographers who are concerned with the overall pattern of the nineteenth-century metropolis usu-ally presume that all change flows from the center. Thus Richard Walker, in a provocative synthetic essay on the beginnings of suburbanization, still insists that "the suburban movement represented the 'solution' of the dominant classes to the emergent contradictions of capitalist production as it took root firmly in the urban landscape, manifest in the areas known as the central business district and the slums."[19]

Such views unintentionally trivialize suburban history. There can be no question that independent residential suburbs were and are self-interested and often selfish entities. But the history of suburban particularism must be explored and explained, not taken for granted or passed off as a function of middle-class chauvinism. If one thinks of suburbs solely as residential ad-juncts to the city or as solutions to problems arising in the city or the larger economy, one overlooks the complex process of community building that created suburbs in the first place. Such a conception overstates the residential homogeneity of the suburbs, oversimplifies the outlook of suburban leaders on the metropolis, and ignores many of the forces that shaped suburban poli-tics. In the end, city-centered views provide a flimsy and partial basis for un-derstanding suburban history and suburban separatism.

This work provides a corrective to such an outlook, for the early stages of suburban growth. Many of the features that made Cambridge and Somer-ville distinctive in the early nineteenth century were present in other suburbs and would be present later. Suburban community growth usually involved older institutions and traditions as well as those imported from the city. Sub-urban communities were always diverse, and commuters were never the only group or even the most numerous group in the labor force (indeed, the statistics suggest that they were proportionally stronger in the 1840s and 1850s than ever again). Industry, though its form and significance changed, was a common and continuous part of the suburban landscape. What happened as the suburbs matured was not the wholesale displacement of old by new, locals by commuters, or industry by residence, but rather a reorientation—a change in the leadership and priorities of the community. For residentially oriented citizens, who could be old or new, locals or commuters, the creation of independent suburban municipalities was not just an act of flight from and defense against the city but an act of local redefinition. It was not just a solution to the contradictions of capitalist urban development, but a solution to the challenges of living on the periphery in the first half of the nineteenth century. Most of all, it was an effort to resolve the peculiar, intense suburban version of the problem of autonomy. Thus the annexation crises, which brought that problem to center stage, were not just struggles over services or between locals and commuters. They were highly visible manifestations of larger and less visible debates about the appropriate purposes and organization of the suburban community. The issue raised and was not merely how the suburbs should relate to the city but how citified the suburbs themselves should be.

In the first suburbs those debates were largely over by the 1860s. Moreover, the issues and the lines of argument had been set in a pattern that would not significantly change in the future. Of course there would be many variations on the suburban growth process and many repetitions of the debate about suburban community purpose. Time and local differences would alter the technology of transportation, the balance of residential and other uses, and the policies and structures of government. The issues surrounding suburban growth would rise again in other locales. To this day, in a thousand settings, American suburbanites argue about private land development, public responsibility, economy, amenities, citizen involvement, efficiency, and debt. But by the Civil War, suburban residents had already determined that the suburban *approach* to those issues would be different from the approaches of village or city. Independent, residential suburbs stand as monuments to their enterprise and reflections of their outlook on the world: innovative, competitive, localized, stubborn, at once parochial and urbane.

Appendix: Statistical,
Social, and
Biographical Data

Village Populations

When we visit a twentieth-century community, our first questions are likely to have statistical answers: How many people live there? What proportion are black, white, Latin, or what-have-you? How many are in the labor force, own property, have children? At the outskirts, signs tell us the population along with the name. A trip to the local library will soon provide answers to the rest of our queries. If we are sufficiently interested, we can obtain comparable answers for the same town for most of the last hundred years—and for other towns without even going there.

We have such data because we need them. The fundamental units of our society include hundreds and thousands of people. Governmental, business, and social transactions involve large amounts of discrete and precise information. We cannot understand or manage our world without resort to quantitative techniques.

Early nineteenth-century communities are less easily entered by avenues of statistics. By the end of the period studied in this book, Americans in large cities gathered statistics of many kinds. But in the earlier stages of "modern" urban growth, and in small places, residents had little need for statistics. When they did enumerate themselves, to satisfy the federal authorities at census time or the state's curiosity about militia strength, they did so slowly and inaccurately, with an eye to rough totals rather than individual or social data.

From the viewpoint of these early nineteenth-century Americans, certain kinds of "career data" (they would never have used the phrase) were more important than the statistical-social data we crave in the twentieth century. In understanding and managing their world—where we use quantitative information—they relied upon information about individual reputations, customary behavior, and all the ingredients of personal and social "standing." They did not measure people and their communities against numerical yardsticks. Instead, they looked for visible signs of wealth, demeanor, and authority. It is interesting to note, for example, that Samuel S. Green, Cambridge storekeeper and census taker in 1820, began his "data gathering" in each of the Cambridge villages with the households of the most eminent people: William Parmenter, manager of the East Cambridge glassworks; Bela Jacobs, pastor of the First Baptist Church in Cambridgeport; and Abiel Holmes, minister of the First Church in Old Cambridge. Green was an assessor, and therefore responsible for full and accurate records of every householder's property, but apparently he did not feel the same responsibility about census information: several of the East Cambridge and Cambridgeport entries provide name of the head and total number but leave all the other categories blank. For Green, the rows of household listings meant something quite different from our idea of enumeration.

In approaching early nineteenth-century communities, therefore, we need data that will not only satisfy our tastes but allow some knowledge of the contemporary viewpoint on the same places. To answer both needs, the available records cannot be used "as is." But scrutiny and comparison of several kinds of local records can make all of them more useful.

Concerning my two communities, it is difficult to answer even the most basic of our statistical questions: how many people lived there? The printed returns of the census provide a crude answer, but they embody many errors. Moreover, if we wish to answer detailed social, economic, and demographic questions about very small communities, we must be sure that our data match the social and geographical units important to contemporaries. To provide a realistic basis for that assessment, I have inspected, entry by entry, all the manuscript data from censuses of Cambridge and Somerville for 1820, 1830, and 1840. My goals were to detect errors, to lay a foundation for biographies of obscure suburbanites, to omit institutional populations which would distort the totals, and to reallocate people according to the village units they lived in, not the town units for which the federal government wanted data. This process yielded three of the main data files for this study (table A.1).

After noting (and where possible correcting) errors in the entries, my first step was to eliminate the institutional population. In this area the most significant institutions were the McLean Asylum on the Charlestown mainland, the Cambridge Jail, the Cambridge Almshouse, and Harvard College. Together, these contained more than 200 people throughout the period of study. Since each of the villages contained from a few hundred to a few thousand people, the institutional population, if counted, could seriously warp

Table A.1

Principal Data Files Used in This Work

Source	Number of cases	Universe or sample	Processing (manual or computer)	Cross-referenced with other files
1. 1820 census	531	U	M	2,3,5
2. 1830 census	1,149	U	M	1,3,5,7
3. 1840 census	1,763	U	M	1,2,5,7
4. 1850 census	502	S: ¼ Som. S: ⅛ Cam.	C	6
5. 1850 census index	c.11,000	U: adults	M	—
6. 1851 directory	4,434	U	C	9
7. 1850 linked	3,057	S: 1/10 Som.	C	1,2,3,9,11
8. 1860 census	431	S: 1/20 Cam.	C	—
9. *Boston Directory,* 1846, 1851, 1855, 1860	(varies)	S: 1/10	M	6,7
10. Cambridge tax rolls	100	S: ¼	M	—
11. Somerville petitions	810	U	M	7

Other alphabetized files:

Cambridge: All selectmen, aldermen, church deacons, bank officers, 1705–1877; all members of school committees, finance committees, 1833–55; members of fire companies, 1835, 1855; voters, 1822, 1836, 1839, 1844, 1851.

Somerville: All selectmen, aldermen, school committee members, 1841–85; taxpayers, 1845, 1850, 1855.

calculations based on village data. In the early censuses, when data was re-corded for entire households, not individuals, institutional inmates were not easily identified. Prisoners and college students, for example, were counted as members of the households of the jailor and the Harvard steward. No cen-sus before 1880 recorded family and household relationships, so there was no way to distinguish the kept from their keepers. To eliminate people in in-stitutions, I therefore had to omit everyone in the relevant households, in-cluding the officials and their families. The loss of a few was preferable to the inclusion of too many.

The next step in recompilation was to allocate data according to the geo-graphically distinct villages so important to contemporaries. These areas were not specified in the census. The federal government sought the popula-tion of towns and counties in order to determine congressional representa-tion. It did not call for data about smaller entities or for addresses of house-holds. Indeed, in an era when the roads themselves had shifting boundaries, and house numbers were years in the future, our notion of an "address" did not apply. To circumvent these limitations, I employed the following proce-dures: I assumed that the census taker recorded data in the order of house-holds visited. I then compared all the names in the census listings with rec-ords of known geographical locations for the same period—maps, property titles from the Middlesex County Registry of Deeds, and memoirs of inhabi-tants. This comparison provided locations for certain households, which I then used as landmarks in reconstructing the routes of the census takers. These routes, once established, allowed me to assign locations to the other census entries and to group all by areas.

This procedure embodies two weaknesses: a few listings (less than five in each case) for people living between villages remained ambiguous. More im-portant, the procedure entails a danger of circular reasoning when the data are used to trace migrations. The records used for assigning addresses were never compiled at exactly the same time as the census. Since people moved frequently, a location used to fix the enumerator's route might be incorrect, and therefore lead to fixing an incorrect route. If the households located ac-cording to this incorrect route were then found at different locations later, one might wrongly conclude they had moved.

For several reasons I believe errors of this sort were few if they occurred at all. Most of the households used as landmarks proved to be very stable when checked against all known records. The reconstructed enumerators' routes were plausibly consistent—not erratic as they would be if household mobil-ity produced false landmarks. Finally, my analysis of the richer data for 1850 and 1860 gave me added confidence in the procedure for earlier decades.

1850 Coding and Linkage and 1860 Sample

The data for 1820 through 1840 were all processed manually. I transcribed entries from microfilm to coding sheets and then to index cards. The coding sheets, which preserved the order of entries, were used in tracing enumerators' routes and in seeking clusters of population traits. The index cards were alphabetized for use in tracing heads of households (see the persistence tables in chap. 2) and manipulated to provide aggregate data for the villages.

The volume and types of data available for 1850 and 1860 made computer processing desirable. In that year the census takers began to record data for individuals, not households. They also collected new kinds of information: specific occupations, birthplaces, and value of real estate for each respondent. In addition, Cambridge and Somerville residents compiled directories for 1851 during the fall of 1850, a few months after the census. Each of these sources provides far richer data than was available for earlier years. By linking the census and directories, I assembled a computer-accessible file of information on 3,057 residents (file 7, table A.1).

For each individual, the linked population file contains information on age, occupation, sex, marital status, race, value of real estate, birthplace, place of work, place of residence, and various characteristics of family and household. Through cross-referencing this file with others, I added information on persistence and on changes in job, family, or taxation status. With the aid of three dedicated assistants, I traced every name in the linked population file through the more than 34,000 entries in the 1860 census and added data for those found.

The strengths and weaknesses of this file reflect not only the quality of the data but the procedures employed in coding, linking, and assembling records. The steps were as follows: I first coded all information given for the 4,434 people listed in both directories. My assistants then traced these individuals through the 1850 census and coded information for those found. We then did the work of tracing this initially linked population backward, forward, and laterally into other sources. To ensure uniformity in coding, my assistants spot-checked their work, coding the same data separately and then comparing the results. To allow tracing of persons not in the linked population, my assistants compiled a card index of the names of everyone aged fifteen or above in Cambridge and Somerville in 1850 (some 11,000 people).

This sequence of steps reflects a conscious choice between two possible procedures. I might have started with a systematic sample of the census instead of a complete coding of the directories. A census-based file would have ensured an accurate representation of the whole population but would have included fewer traceable members of the labor force and especially fewer of the commuters whose careers I wished to study. By starting with the directories, I created a file that includes a large proportion of the labor force and most of the traceable commuters but is inherently biased in favor of wealth and stability.

To assess these biases and to measure traits of the population as a whole, yet another file was necessary. Systematic interval sampling of the census schedules for both Cambridge and Somerville produced a computer-accessible file of information on 502 households, containing 2,017 people (file 4, table A.1). Table A.2 compares the sample and linked populations and indicates

Table A.2
Comparison of Sample and Linked
Populations, 1850

I. Age Distribution

	Somerville			Cambridge		
	Sample All Adults	Household Heads	Linked	Sample All Adults	Household Heads	Linked
60+	5.7%	9.0	10.5	9.4	10.9	10.6
50–59	8.5	11.0	12.2	9.9	15.4	11.0
40–49	13.9	20.7	19.8	16.8	23.3	22.0
30–39	27.7	38.6	38.2	27.2	33.9	33.0
20–29	44.3	20.7	19.3	36.7	16.5	23.3
N	459	145	419	1057	357	2635

II. Birthplace

	Sample Household Heads	Linked		Sample Household Heads	Linked
Ireland	20.7	7.6		23.0	12.2
Other Foreign	6.9	4.5		10.4	8.2
U.S. outside Mass.	37.2	40.8		22.7	27.5
Massachusetts	35.2	47.0		44.0	52.0
N	145	419		357	2649

III. Occupation

Unskilled	20.0	8.6		12.6	7.6
Professional	.7	2.1		3.4	3.9
Banker, Merchant	6.2	8.4		1.4	1.5
Skilled	20.7	20.5		24.2	24.9
N	145	419		357	2649

the nature of biases. As expected, the linked population provides an accurate representation of the heads of households by age groups, but underrepresents the foreign-born and workers in low-status occupations. These biases do not affect most of the conclusions drawn in this study. My argument has been based in part on a comparison of Boston-employed persons with the whole linked population. If the persons left out of the linked population could be added, the contrasts between commuters and the whole would almost certainly become *more* striking, since the whole linked population would then contain more manual workers and immigrants.

One additional file of data provided a basis for evaluating changes in the suburban population during the decade of the 1850s, when heavy industry and large-scale commuting became important factors in development. File 8 includes data from interval samples of the 1860 census manuscripts. These samples were stratified according to size of community, so that lightly settled Somerville and northern Cambridge were sampled more heavily than the denser parts of Cambridge. Computer processing allowed weighting the individual cases to compensate for the differentials in sampling intervals. Like the 1850 census files, the 1860 data were linked to directory listings and other sources of information.

Study Zones

The 1850 data allowed a more refined version of the village-recompilation procedure employed in analyzing the 1820–40 information. Here I began with two assumptions: first, that the addresses in the 1851 directories were accurate at the time of the 1850 census; second, that the census takers listed data in the order of places visited. Linkage of census and directory provided thousands of landmarks instead of the handful available for earlier decades. I could therefore reconstruct enumeration routes block by block, in far more detail than I could for previous years. The results confirmed both my assumptions. With many more reference points, it became quite clear that a few individuals had indeed moved between census and directory compilation dates—the initially plotted enumerations included some dramatic "excursions" from a consistent path. But because they were both obvious and rare, these erroneous reference points could easily be excluded. The resulting, corrected paths were clear and regular—moving steadily through the towns, circling clockwise around a block before moving on to the next one. They were so clear that they held up when checked against maps for 1851 and 1854 and detailed reminiscences by some residents of Somerville.

These detailed routes in turn allowed me to assign relatively precise addresses to the rest of the population. Using the computer, I then distributed the linked and sample populations according to a variety of geographical areas. Partly through trial and error, partly using landmarks that I knew were important to contemporaries, I arrived at 21 study zones for the two suburbs. These zones were defined to reflect political and economic circumstances, *not* for the sake of statistical convenience. As a result, they contain widely varying numbers of people and areas of land. In defining these zones, I began with municipal boundaries—between Cambridge, Somerville, and their neighbors, and between the wards of Cambridge. (Fortunately the five Cambridge wards of 1857 were created without altering the lines of the three older wards.) I then examined economic subareas: the commercial districts near Main Street in Cambridgeport and Sandpit Square in Somerville; the commuter residential areas on Dana Hill, Spring Hill, Winter Hill, and near the northern Cambridge railroad station; the brickmaking-industrial zone south of the Fitchburg railroad; and certain large properties divided en bloc into lots. In drawing these fine boundaries I employed the five volumes of the Cambridge Historical Commission survey; the Hales maps of Charlestown and Cambridge (1830), the Walling map of Cambridge (1854), the Draper map of Somerville (1852), and numerous other maps on file in the Harvard University Library, the Somerville Historical Society, and the Middlesex County Registry of Deeds; and the various local histories and genealogies cited in the Notes and Bibliography. Much of the discussion in chaps. 5–7 is based on analysis of these 21 zones, sometimes singly and sometimes collapsed into larger units.

Biographical Files

Taken together, the various files described above allow rough answers to some of our questions about communities: how many people were there, and of what kinds? They also provide a skeleton for files of biographies. In varying degrees of completeness, these files contain information about the careers of more than 10,000 individuals who lived in Cambridge and Somerville at some time between 1820 and 1860. They contain less precise information about another 10,000 to 20,000 dependents of these principals.

Through cross-referencing, these files allow an analysis of the membership of various local organizations: fire companies, churches, corporations. All the known members and officers of such organizations have been traced through the statistical files to determine the makeup of the organizations, the ages of their members, the overlap between various groups and careers,and the degrees of transience or persistence of the villagers.

For about 1,000 residents of the two communities, I have carried the process further, compiling a separate "elite" file, which draws together information from all the statistical files and adds genealogical, political, taxation, and other information. Such concentrated biographies were prepared for all holders of major public offices; all organizers and directors of bridge and turnpike companies, banks, land development partnerships, transportation firms, and other economic endeavors; and for a variety of people whose names crop up frequently in local records.

Two examples will illustrate the contents of these elite biographies. One is the record for Isaac Livermore, whose name has appeared often in the preceding chapters; the other is for Amos Hazeltine, who was never mentioned but exemplifies an important entrepreneurial type. For both men, census, voting, officeholding, and taxation data provide a career outline. But the "flesh" of these biographies—the bits of information that gave each person his place and influence in the early nineteenth-century community—comes from other records as well.

Livermore was almost a famous man. We do not have a published biography, a cache of papers, or a sketch in the *DAB*. But we do have information about him from published works about railroads, Boston commerce, and the biographies of other men. He was related to Congressman Anson Burlingame, and fragmentary information about Livermore apears in the Burlingame papers in the Library of Congress. The mark of his presence also appears in many local records—the standard history of Cambridge, the newspapers of Boston and the suburbs, the membership lists and petitions associated with half a dozen causes and promotions. He was clearly a man of stature and reputation.

Amos Hazeltine, by contrast, was a prosperous but obscure man. We have no obituary; we do not even know the date of his death. From the linked population data, we learn that he was born in New Hampshire in 1787, that he lived on the Somerville-Cambridge border, that he owned, by 1850, $12,000 worth of real estate. But Hazeltine almost slipped past the linked population net. He was listed in the Cambridge directory but counted in the Somerville census. Moreover, the summary of previous records indicates his citizenship in both places. His name appeared on land records and petitions relating to mainland Charlestown, and he served at least one term as a Charlestown assessor. But he also bought and sold land in Cambridge, and he seems to have been living there by the mid-1840s. In Hazeltine's career we have a record of successful opportunism, not the record of standing so evident for Livermore.

It is, of course, possible that all these records on Hazeltine do not pertain to the same individual. His name, after all, is spelled four different ways in the various records. But the linkage of large data files helps to rule out that possibility. Between 1820 and 1860, there were *no* records of two Hazeltines living in Cambridge and Somerville at the same moment. In this, as in many other conclusions, this work relies on careful comparison and educated guesswork. Neither statistics nor local records speak for themselves. Yet they do inform each other. In combination, they allow us to approximate the perspective early nineteenth-century Americans had on their neighbors and their communities and thereby to understand how they created the suburbs.

Notes

Introduction

1. This book deals with American residential suburbs, as distinguished from most suburbs in Europe and from industrial suburbs in the United States. Although European cities experienced growth and population deconcentration in the nineteenth century, they did not produce new suburban communities quite like those that appeared in Jacksonian America. With a few exceptions, the commuter residential suburb developed more slowly in Europe, while suburban municipal independence was curtailed much sooner by strong central governments. There is no adequate comparative study of European and American suburban growth, but the outlines may be gleaned from: David L. Sills, ed., *International Encyclopedia of the Social Sciences* 2 (New York, 1968): 160–61; Dean S. Rugg, *Spatial Foundations of Urbanism* (Dubuque, 1972), 70, 224–43; Frank J. Cappa, "Cities and Suburbs in Europe and the United States," in Philip C. Dolce, ed., *Suburbia: The American Dream and Dilemma* (Garden City, N. Y., 1976), 167–91; G. A. Wissink, *American Cities in Perspective, with Special Reference to the Development of Their Fringe Areas* (Assen, Netherlands, 1962); William Bennett Munro, *The Government of European Cities* (New York, 1909), 12–16, 51–52, 61, 118–19; Peter Hall, *The World Cities* (New York, 1966), 61–69; H. J. Dyos, "The Growth of a Pre-Victorian Suburb: South London, 1580–1836," *Town Planning Review* 25 (1954): 59–78; Asa Briggs, *Victorian Cities* (New York, 1970), 15–16, 27–29; David H. Pinkney, *Napoleon III and the Rebuilding of Paris* (Princeton, 1958), 7–17, 165–71.

In the United States, the growth of twentieth-century industrial satellites and suburban blue-collar housing prompted scholars to distinguish "employing" from "residential" suburbs. See Leo F. Schnore, "The Social and Economic Characteristics of American Suburbs," *Sociological Quarterly* 4 (1963): 122–34; Bennett Berger, *Working Class Suburb: A Study of Auto Workers in Suburbia* (Berkeley, 1960); Herbert J. Gans, "The Suburban Community and Its Way of Life," in Robert Gutman and David Popenoe, eds. *Neighborhood, City, and Metropolis* (New York, 1970). This book

241

does not deal with these later developments, but rather with the basic pattern that preceded and underlay all of them: a ring of legally distinct communities dominated by residential interests, surrounding the city core.

2. The quotation is from Sam Bass Warner, Jr., *Streetcar Suburbs: The Process of Growth in Boston, 1870–1900*, 2d ed. (Cambridge, 1978), viii. The mass-transportation model of growth has influenced nearly all writing about suburbs in one of two ways. In one category are those authors who think of residential suburbs as recent, rail-spawned outgrowths of the city. The most influential works of this sort are Harlan P. Douglass, *The Suburban Trend* (New York, 1925); Robert C. Wood, *Suburbia: Its People and Their Politics* (Boston, 1958); and Warner's *Streetcar Suburbs*, which treats antebellum suburbs as peripheral imitations of the central-city pattern (pp. 18–21). The second category includes works that look further into the past but find there only precursors of the present—identifying well-to-do "commuters" as far back as the Renaissance but ignoring the many transformations of the suburban community in the past two centuries. Good examples are: Lewis Mumford, *The City in History* (New York, 1961), 482–96; and James E. Vance, Jr., "The American City: Workshop for a National Culture," in John S. Adams, ed., *Contemporary Metropolitan America*, part 1: *Cities of the Nation's Historic Metropolitan Core* (Cambridge, 1976), 12–14. Both kinds of writing fail to consider the antebellum suburb on its own terms.

3. Led by Kenneth Jackson, a few historians have done pioneering research on antebellum suburbanization. These studies, though too few, have clearly shown that the roots of the modern suburb lie well before the Civil War. See Jackson, "Urban Deconcentration in the Nineteenth Century: A Statistical Inquiry," in Leo F. Schnore, ed., *The New Urban History: Quantitative Explorations by American Historians* (Princeton, 1975), 110–42; George Rogers Taylor, "The Beginnings of Mass Transportation in Urban America" (2 parts), *Smithsonian Journal of History* 1 (1966): 35–50, and 2 (1967): 31–54; David R. Goldfield and Blaine A. Brownell, *Urban America: From Downtown to No Town* (Boston, 1979), 142–46.

Geographer Richard A. Walker has produced a provocative analysis of the overall relationship between city morphology and nineteenth-century economic change: "The Transformation of Urban Structure in the Nineteenth Century and the Beginnings of Suburbanization," in Kevin R. Cox, ed., *Urbanization and Conflict in Market Societies* (Chicago, 1978), 165–212.

On the distinctive traits of American residential suburbs, see Douglass, *Suburban Trend*, 33, 176–79; Jon Teaford, *City and Suburb: The Political Fragmentation of Metropolitan America, 1850–1970* (Baltimore, 1979), chaps. 1–5; Warner, *Streetcar Suburbs*, Introduction to the Second Edition; and Barry Schwartz, "Images of Suburbia: Some Revisionist Commentary and Conclusions," in Barry Schwartz, ed., *The Changing Face of the Suburbs* (Chicago, 1976), 330.

4. A typical example is the following: "When deconcentration extends beyond the cities' political boundaries, so that a densely settled milieu begins to take shape upon what in a legal sense is extra-city landscape, the phenomenon is known as suburbani-

zation and the settlements are called suburbs"; John Kramer, ed., *North American Suburbs: Politics, Diversity, and Change* (Berkeley, 1972), xi.

5. On the preindustrial faubourg-Vorstadt model and its weaknesses, see Gideon Sjoberg, *The Preindustrial City, Past and Present* (New York, 1960), 97–102; Peter Burke, "Some Reflections on the Pre-Industrial City," *Urban History Yearbook, 1975* (Leicester, 1975), 13–21; and Jackson, "Urban Deconcentration," 127–28.

6. David Ward, *Cities and Immigrants: A Geography of Change in Nineteenth Century America* (New York, 1971), 89–90; Robert Greenhalgh Albion, with the collaboration of Jennie Barnes Pope, *The Rise of New York Port, 1815–1860* (New York, 1939); Walter Muir Whitehill, *Boston: A Topographical History*, 2d ed. (Cambridge, 1968), chaps. 3–4. See also the essays by Rubin, Hutchins, and Brady in David T. Gilchrist, ed., *The Growth of the Seaport Cities, 1790–1825* (Charlottesville, 1967).

7. The quotation is from the single most influential essay in promoting the urban fringe concept: George S. Wehrwein, "The Rural-Urban Fringe," *Economic Geography* 18 (1942): 217–28. Wehrwein also defined the fringe as "the area of transition between well recognized urban land uses and the area devoted to agriculture" (p. 212). Important later elaborations and case study refinements include M. R. G. Conzen, "Alnwick, Northumberland: A Study in Town Plan Analysis," *Transactions of the Institute of British Geographers* 27 (1960); Wissink, *American Cities;* J. W. R. Whitehand, "Fringe Belts: A Neglected Aspect of Urban Geography," *Transactions of the Institute of British Geographers* 41 (1967): 223–33; R. J. Pryor, "Defining the Rural-Urban Fringe," *Social Forces* 47 (1968): 202–15; James H. Johnson, ed., *Suburban Growth: Geographical Processes at the Edge of the Western City* (London, 1974).

8. The myth of sterile uniformity that sprang up around post–World War II suburbs has now been thoroughly debunked. But even those who stress diversity among suburbs regard them as pieces of the metropolis. See Bennett Berger, "The Myth of Suburbia," *Journal of Social Issues* 17 (1961): 38–49; Herbert J. Gans, "Urbanism and Suburbanism as Ways of Life: A Re-Evaluation of Definitions," in Arnold Rose, ed., *Human Behavior and Social Processes* (Boston, 1962), 625–48.

Many writers on the suburbs have been strong advocates of metropolitan unification. For such authors the individual traits of suburban communities were unimportant, since metropolitan interests were paramount. For a good example of the bias at work, see Amos H. Hawley and Basil G. Zimmer, "Resistance to Unification in a Metropolitan Community," in Morris Janowitz, ed., *Community Political Systems* (Glencoe, 1961), 146–84. On suburbs as creations of the central city, see Douglass, *Suburban Trend,* 3–7 and passim.

9. There has lately been a resurgence of interest in communities among both historians and sociologists. Some historians have reacted to the flood of quantitative mobility by reemphasizing the cultural and political dimensions of community. See Josef Barton, *Peasants and Strangers: Italians, Rumanians, and Slovaks in an American City, 1890–1950* (Cambridge, 1975); Susan E. Hirsch, *Roots of the American Work-*

ing Class: The Industrialization of Crafts in Newark, 1800–1860 (Philadelphia, 1978); Virginia Yans-McLaughlin, *Family and Community: Italian Immigrants in Buffalo, 1880–1930* (Ithaca, N. Y., 1977). Influential works by sociologists are Morris Janowitz, *The Community Press in an Urban Setting: The Social Elements of Urbanism,* 2d ed. (Chicago, 1952); Gerald D. Suttles, *The Social Construction of Communities* (Chicago, 1972); and Albert J. Hunter, *Symbolic Communities: The Persistence and Change of Chicago's Local Communities* (Chicago, 1974).

10. Most historians of the antebellum community have not been primarily interested in community development. Rather, they chose their various towns or cities as settings for some larger story. Various communities, because they were representative or centrally important or merely convenient, have become good places for the study of mobility, family and class relationships, migration, or ethnicity. Some scholars have found in community change an explanation for labor militance, revivals, or reform. Works that begin with one or another of these goals, however, sometimes shed light on communities themselves—their form and organization, the motives and perceptions of their residents, the reasons for their particular lines of development. Good examples are: Hirsch, *Roots of the American Working Class;* Kathleen Conzen, *Immigrant Milwaukee, 1836–1860: Accommodation and Community in a Frontier City* (Cambridge, 1976); Paul E. Johnson, *A Shopkeeper's Millennium: Society and Revivals in Rochester, New York, 1815–1837* (New York, 1978); Bruce Laurie, *Working People of Philadelphia, 1800–1850* (Philadelphia, 1980).

This book does not focus on a strike, a revival, or a reform crusade. Centering on the process of community development, it shares a focus with only a few other works on this period: Michael Frisch, *Town into City: Springfield, Massachusetts, and the Meaning of Community, 1840–1880* (Cambridge, 1972); Don H. Doyle, *The Social Order of a Frontier Community: Jacksonville, Illinois, 1825–1870* (Urbana, Ill., 1978); Stuart Blumin, *The Urban Threshold: Growth and Change in a Nineteenth-Century American Community* (Chicago, 1976).

11. George Rogers Taylor, "American Urban Growth Preceding the Railway Age," *Journal of Economic History* 27 (1967): 309–39; Sam Bass Warner, Jr., *The Private City: Philadelphia in Three Periods of Its Growth* (Philadelphia, 1968); Laurie, *Working People;* Paul S. Boyer, *Urban Masses and Moral Order in America, 1820–1920* (Cambridge, 1978); Jon Teaford, *The Municipal Revolution in America: Origins of Modern Urban Government, 1650–1825* (Chicago, 1975).

12. Blumin, *Urban Threshold;* Conzen, *Immigrant Milwaukee;* Doyle, *Social Order;* John C. Schneider, *Detroit and the Problem of Order, 1830–1880: A Geography of Crime, Riot, and Policing* (Lincoln, Neb., 1980).

13. The only overall surveys of annexation history are Kenneth T. Jackson, "Metropolitan Government versus Suburban Autonomy: Politics on the Crabgrass Frontier," in Kenneth T. Jackson and Stanley K. Schultz, eds., *Cities in American History* (New York, 1972); and Teaford, *City and Suburb,* chaps. 1–3.

Chapter 1
Improvement Enterprise
and the Fringe Economy

1. Justin Winsor, ed., *The Memorial History of Boston . . . 1630–1880* (Boston, 1881), 4:97 n; Walter Firey, *Land Use in Central Boston* (Cambridge, 1947).

2. Numerous maps of the inner Middlesex region were prepared for military purposes during the Revolution. A useful descriptive list is given in Winsor, 3:i–vii (the most readily available reproductions will be found there, p. 80); Samuel Adams Drake, *Historic Fields and Mansions of Middlesex* (Boston, 1874), facing p. 1; Edward A. Samuels and Henry H. Kimball, eds., *Somerville Past and Present* (Boston, 1897), 71. Modern maps showing the eighteenth-century topography of Cambridge are to be found in Cambridge Historical Commission, *Survey of Architectural History in Cambridge*, 5 vols. (Cambridge, 1965–77), 2:10, 16; 3:14; 5:18–36 (hereafter cited as CHCS).

3. The locations of the main roads inland, and the degree of their relative importance, have been determined from the following sources: Samuels and Kimball, 30–31, 77, 89–90; Charles Brooks, *History of the Town of Medford, Middlesex County, Massachusetts* (Boston, 1855), 422–25; Elbridge Henry Goss, *The History of Melrose, County of Middlesex, Massachusetts* (Melrose, 1902), 44–45, 47–55; William B. Stevens, *History of Stoneham, Massachusetts* (Stoneham, 1891), 39–42, 60–62; D. Hamilton Hurd, comp., *History of Middlesex County, Massachusetts, with Biographical Sketches of Many of Its Pioneers and Prominent Men,* 3 vols. (Philadelphia, 1890), 1:342, 3:582; Charles Hudson, *History of the Town of Lexington, Middlesex County, Massachusetts, from Its First Settlement to 1868, Revised and Continued to 1912* (Boston, 1913) 1:473; G. Frederick Robinson and Ruth Robinson Wheeler, *Great Little Watertown: A Tercentary History* (Watertown, 1930), 48; Lewis M. Hastings, "An Historical Account of Some Bridges over the Charles River," Cambridge Historical Society, *Publications* 7 (January 1912): 51–63 (hereafter, CHS, *Pub*); Deloraine Pendre Corey, "Life in the Old Parsonage, 1772–1784, from the Diary of the Rev. Peter Thatcher," *Register of the Malden Historical Society*, 1 (1910–11):41.

4. Goss, 56–57.

5. James F. Hunnewell, *A Century of Town Life: A History of Charlestown, Massachusetts, 1775–1887* (Boston, 1888), 508, 11–16; Drake, 187–88; Lucius R. Paige, *History of Cambridge, Massachusetts, 1630–1877* (Boston, 1877), 170, 174; Percy Wells Bidwell, "Rural Economy in New England at the Beginning of the Nineteenth Century," *Transactions of the Connecticut Academy of Arts and Sciences* 20 (April 1916): 293, 306–7, 318, 352–53; Percy Wells Bidwell and John I. Falconer, *History of Agriculture in the Northern United States, 1620–1860* (New York, 1925), 46, 99.

6. Hunnewell, 8–11; Brooks, 350–52, 392; Helen T. Wild, "A Business Man of Long Ago," *Medford Historical Register* 3 (1900): 76–91; Hurd, 3:373–74, 377, 392.

7. Hunnewell, 154; Drake, 95–97; CHCS 2:13–15.

8. See below, chaps. 4–7. On the phenomenon of "regulation without laws," see Warner, *Streetcar Suburbs.*

9. A good introduction to the story of bridge building around Boston is Stanley I. Kutler, *Privilege and Creative Destruction: The Charles River Bridge Case* (New York, 1971). For details on the backing and promotion of each project, see Henry C. Binford, "The Influence of Commuting on the Development of Cambridge and Somerville, Massachusetts, 1815–1860" (Ph.D. diss., Harvard University, 1973), 12–18.

10. Samuel Eliot Morison, *The Maritime History of Massachusetts, 1783–1860* (Boston, 1921), 129; Chistopher Roberts, *The Middlesex Canal, 1793–1860,* Harvard Economic Studies, 61 (Cambridge, 1938), 32; Hunnewell, 22, 30; Oscar Handlin and Mary Flug Handlin, *Commonwealth: A Study of the Role of Government in the American Economy: Massachusetts, 1774–1861,* rev. ed. (Cambridge, 1969), 102; Massachusetts *Statutes 1784,* ch. 53; Whitehill, 49.

Throughout this work, details concerning individual careers have been drawn from files of biographical information compiled by the author. In addition to the sources cited, these files contain data from the genealogical and biographical registers in the standard histories of Charlestown, Cambridge, Somerville, Medford, and Arlington; from selected lists of voters and taxpayers in Cambridge and Somerville; from the Cambridge directories published from 1847 onward; from the Somerville directory of 1851; from Boston directories for 1840, 1846, 1849, 1850, 1855, and 1860; from unpublished town records; and from the manuscript enumerators' schedules of the federal censuses taken in 1820, 1830, 1840, and 1850. For a discussion of these sources, see Appendix.

11. For examples of mercantile investment patterns, see Kenneth Wiggins Porter, *The Jacksons and the Lees: Two Generations of Massachusetts Merchants, 1765–1844,* 2 vols. (Cambridge, 1937), 1:122, 468–69.

12. *Private and Special Statutes of the Commonwealth of Massachusetts,* 6 vols. (Boston, 1805–1848), 3:135–39, 612; Brooks, 52–53, 138–39, 351, 353.

13. *Private and Special Statutes* 3:181–85, 514–15. Wellington was a legendary figure in Cambridge, West Cambridge, and Watertown, and local histories abound with tales about him, some probably apocryphal. On the Wellington family and the facts of Jeduthun's life, see Paige, 683; Mary Isabella Gozzaldi, *History of Cambridge, Massachusetts . . . Supplement and Index* (Cambridge, 1930), 785 and the references cited there; Benjamin Cutter and William R. Cutter, *History of the Town of Arlington, Massachusetts, formerly the Second Precinct in Cambridge . . . 1635–1879* (Boston, 1880), 105, 110, 112, 121, 133, 314–15; Albert Harrison Hall, "Thomas Wellington 'of Cambridge,' His Ancestors and Some of His Descendants," CHS, *Pub.* 8 (October 1913): 21–25; Francis B. Baldwin, *From Pequossette Plantation to the Town of Belmont, Massachusetts, 1630–1953* (Belmont, 1953), 33–34.

14. Hunnewell, 16; Winsor, 3:552, 558–59; *Private and Special Statutes* 1:21–24, 278–79, 286; Josiah Bartlett, *An Historical Sketch of Charlestown, in the County of Middlesex, and Commonwealth of Massachusetts* (Boston, 1814), 9.

15. Rev. David Osgood to an unidentified friend, 26 June 1786, quoted in Brooks, 70–71.

16. Chief Justice Francis Dana (1743–1811) was a member of a family distinguished in Charlestown, Cambridge, and Boston alike. At the time of the bridge promotion, he had already served five terms as a delegate to the Continental Congress and three years as ambassador to Russia. He had been one of the first presidential electors in 1789 and had just begun a fifteen-year period at the head of the Massachusetts Supreme Court. After the Revolution he occupied a mansion off Main Street in Cambridge, which commanded a view of his projected settlement in Cambridgeport, his bridge, and the Boston peninsula beyond. This seat on Dana Hill became a resort for Massachusetts Federalists, and the judge gained a reputation for elegant hospitality. Paige, 491–92, 529, 633; Richard Henry Dana, "Francis Dana," CHS, *Pub.* 3:62–63; Henry Wadsworth Longfellow Dana, "The Dana Saga," CHS, *Pub.* 26 (1940): 83–94; Thomas C. Amory, *Life of James Sullivan with Selections from His Writings,* 2 vols. (Boston, 1859), 1:78–123, 131, 259, 293; 2:391–92; Isaac Livermore, *An Account of Some Bridges over Charles River, as Connected with the Growth of Cambridge* (Cambridge, 1858), 6–9; CHCS 3:17–18.

17 Royal Makepeace (1772–1855), migrated from his native Warren, Massachusetts, to Boston when he was about twenty, served a brief apprenticeship, and joined with a townsman who had accompanied him to set up the store in Cambridgeport. Gozzaldi, *History of Cambridge, Supplement,* 471, 486, 489, 492; Paige, 176 n–177 n, 450, 461, 466, 468, 607; CHCS 2:28; 3:18, 49.

18. Paige, 173, 176–77; CHCS 2:22, 24; 3:17.

19. Paige, 183–86. Andrew Craigie had been apothecary general to the Revolutionary army and had purchased an abandoned Tory residence (later famous as the home of Henry Wadsworth Longfellow) on Brattle Street in 1792. He resided there until his death in 1819. Paige, 183 n; Frederick Haven Pratt, "The Craigies," CHS, *Pub.* 27 (1941): 62–63.

20. Amory, *Life of James Sullivan* 1:369; *Private and Special Statutes* 4:76–81; list of canal shareholders in Roberts, 200.

21. Paige, 186; Carl Seaburg and Stanley Paterson, *Merchant Prince of Boston: Colonel T. H. Perkins, 1764–1854* (Cambridge, 1971), 211–15.

22. J. P. Staniels to the Somerville selectmen, February 1843, Somerville Town and City Papers, Somerville City Vault (hereafter cited as STCP); Paige, 184, 310, 549–50, 700–701; CHCS 2:20–21, 26–27.

23. Seaburg and Paterson, 214–15; Paige, 184–87; *Private and Special Statutes* 4:279–81; John W. Reps, *The Making of Urban America: A History of City Planning in the United States* (Princeton, 1965), 294–96.

24. The bare outline of the controversy is chronicled in Paige, 203–9. But Paige neglected those parts of the struggle that took place outside of Cambridge and consequently offered no explanation for its outcome.

25. Information on the selectmen is derived from the list in Paige, 462–66 and from the biographical sources listed in note 11 above.

26. Paige, 187, 214. Bartlett, writing in 1814, attributed Charlestown's failure to the influence of East Cambridge interests in the legislature; *An Historical Sketch,* 11; Lura Woodside Watkins, *Cambridge Glass, 1818 to 1888: The Story of the New England Glass Company* (Boston, 1930), 5–6.

27. Paige, 206. Throughout the period 1807–19 the county court system was an important element in the escalating patronage struggles between Federalists and Republicans in the state. Each shift in control of the legislature and the governor's office signaled a wholesale restructuring of the courts to create new positions. In 1807 the victorious Republicans had packed the Court of Sessions with their followers, and the Federalists did not succeed in reversing the process until late in June 1809. Reorganizations occurred again in 1811 and 1814. The chronology of these shifts may be traced by comparing the summary of legislation in Hurd, 1:xvii–xviii, with the account in Paul Goodman, *The Democratic-Republicans of Massachusetts: Politics in a Young Republic* (Cambridge, 1964), 150–52.

28. Quoted in Paige, 205. On Perkins, see David Hackett Fischer, *The Revolution of American Conservatism: The Federalist Party in the Era of Jeffersonian Democracy* (New York, 1965), 271.

29. Quoted in Paige, 206. Seaburg and Paterson, in their work on Perkins, portray this struggle as one between Federalists and Republicans within the town of Cambridge; *Merchant Prince,* 212–13. But the party alignments, which were clearly at work in attempts to influence the legislature, did not extend so clearly to local politics. Craigie and his allies were, of course, Federalists, and Elbridge Gerry, one of the authors of the remonstrance, was a Republican. But Francis Dana, Craigie's principal opponent in Cambridge, was as thoroughgoing a Federalist as Craigie himself; Fischer, 247. In this as in most such town struggles, party ties seem to have been subordinate to local interests.

30. See Binford, "Influence," 34–35.

31. Paige, 187–89; Sophia Shuttleworth Simpson, "Two Hundred Years Ago; or a Brief History of Cambridgeport and East Cambridge," CHS, *Pub.* 16 (April, 1922): 43. The county courts did not actually move until 1816, and glass was not a profitable enterprise on Lechmere Point until 1818. Watkins, 6–14. For the later years of Craigie, see Pratt, "The Craigies," 61–67. On changing attitudes of the mercantile-manufacturing investors, see Robert F. Daltzell, Jr., "The Rise of the Waltham-Lowell System and Some Thoughts on the Political Economy of Modernization in Ante-Bellum Massachusetts," *Perspectives in American History* 9 (1975): 229–270.

32. Bidwell, "Rural Economy," 303–5, 318, 352–53, 389–90; Douglass C. North, *The Economic Growth of the United States, 1790–1860* (New York, 1961), 18; James M. Banner, Jr., *To the Hartford Convention: The Federalists and the Origins of Party Politics in Massachusetts, 1789–1815* (New York, 1970), 195; Hurd, 3:184.

33. Christine E. Bishop, "On the Road to Boston: The Development of Eastern Cambridge, 1790–1820" (Seminar paper, Harvard University, January 1969), 17–18. I am grateful to Ms. Bishop for allowing me to read her essay.

34. Albert W. Bryant, "Lexington Sixty Years Ago," *Proceedings of the Lexington Historical Society* 2 (1890): 19–64; Hurd, 2:843–44; Harriet A. Adams, "Neighborhood Sketch No. 7—Winter Hill," Somerville Historical Society (hereafter SHS), *Historic Leaves* 3 (April 1904): 24; Stevens, *History of Stoneham*, 92; James A. Hervey, "Reminiscences of an Earlier Medford," *Medford Historical Register* 4 (July 1901): 61–77; Parker Lindall Converse, *Legends of Woburn, now first Written and Preserved in Collected Form* (Woburn, 1892), 17–18; Brooks, 351; Hunnewell, 95; Henry Smith Chapman, *History of Winchester, Massachusetts* (Winchester, 1936), 96; Bidwell, "Rural Economy," 308.

35. Henry Colman, *Fourth Report of the Agriculture of Massachusetts: Counties of Franklin and Middlesex* (Boston, 1841), 300; Robinson and Wheeler, 81. Nathaniel Hawthorne, on a trip through western Massachusetts, encountered one such drive and recorded the activities of the drover in managing and selling pigs; *Passages from the American Note-Books,* in *The Complete Works of Nathaniel Hawthorne,* ed. George P. Lathrop, 9 (Boston, 1883), 200.

36. Charles Briggs, *A Discourse Delivered at Concord, October the Fifth, 1825* (Concord, 1825), 23–24; Jeremiah Spofford, *A Gazetteer of Massachusetts, containing a General View of the State* (Newburyport, 1828), 166.

37. Paul Wallace Gates, *The Farmer's Age: Agriculture, 1815–1860* (New York, 1960), 279–80, Bidwell and Falconer, 202–3; Hurd, 3:392; Caleb Eddy, *Historical Sketch of the Middlesex Canal, with Remarks for the Consideration of the Proprietors* (Boston, 1843), 19–20; Albert W. Bryant, "The Munroe Tavern," *Proceedings of the Lexington Historical Society* 3 (1904): 151.

38. On the influence of urban demand on agriculture near all New England cities, see Bidwell and Falconer, 200, 227–28, 235–36, 242, 372, 421, 429; Gates, 27–28, 209, 269–70; Spofford, *Gazetteer,* 20; Colman, 197–98.

39. Henry F. Howe, *Salt Rivers of the Massachusetts Shore* (New York, 1951), 86–87; Samuels and Kimball, 26–27; George O. Smith, "The Milk Business and Milk Men of Earlier Days," *Proceedings of the Lexington Historical Society* 2 (1897): 187–96; Colman, 249–54; Bidwell and Falconer, 227–28.

40. Hurd, 3:325; Colman, 353–54; James G. Carter and William H. Brooks, *A Geography of Middlesex County; for Young Children . . .* (Cambridge, 1830), 76.

41. J. K. Hosmer et al., *Memorial of George Washington Hosmer, D. D.* (n. p., 1882), 28–29.

42. George O. Smith, "The Milk Business," 189–92; Cutter and Cutter, *Arlington,* 148.

43. Smith, "The Milk Business," 190.

44. Colman, 257–59; Gates, 233–34.

45. In Cambridge two members of the Hovey family built national fame on growing strawberries and other small fruits, and in Brighton the Winship nurseries and

gardens became locally renowned. *Dictionary of American Biography* 8:272; Gates, 260; John Warner Barber, *Historical Collections . . . relating to the History and Antiquities of . . . Massachusetts* (Worcester, 1839), 313; A. Forbes and J. W. Greene, *The Rich Men of Massachusetts* (Boston, 1851), 91.

46. Colman, 302, gives statistics of sales. For general descriptions of the market in this period, see Barber, *Historical Collections,* 353; Winsor, 3:602, 607–9; Hawthorne, *Works* 9:248–51; John Hayward, *A Gazetteer of Massachusetts* (Boston, 1846), 113–14.

47. Thomas F. O'Malley, "Old North Cambridge," CHS, *Pub.* 20 (1929): 131–32.

48. Hosea Hildreth, *A Book for Massachusetts Children, in Familiar Letters from a Father, for the Use of Families and Schools,* 2d ed. (Boston, 1831), 61; *Bunker Hill Aurora,* 5 January 1928, 1; Carter and Brooks, *Middlesex,* 15; Colman, 299–301.

49. Abram English Brown, *Faneuil Hall and Faneuil Hall Market, or Peter Faneuil and His Gift* (Boston, 1900), 70–73, 79–86, 90, 93–96, 100.

50. Ibid., 149–51; Whitehill, 42, 52, 69; Charles Shaw, *A Topographical and Historical Description of Boston* (Boston, 1817), 180–83.

51. Josiah Quincy, *A Municipal History of the Town and City of Boston, during Two Centuries* (Boston, 1852), 75, 84–85; Brown, *Faneuil Hall,* 179–80.

52. Winsor, 4:60–61; Whitehill, 98, 107–11, 114–18; Quincy, *Municipal History,* 113–16.

53 Nathaniel Dearborn, *Dearborn's Reminiscences of Boston, and Guide through the City Environs* (Boston, 1851), 30.

54. Franklin F. Mendels, "Proto-Industrialization: The First Phase of the Process of Industrialization," *Journal of Economic History* 22 (1972): 241–61.

55. Discussions of the pattern of Boston investments in this period frequently refer to mercantile interests as being primarily "local" or confined to "Boston and its immediate hinterland." But these comments refer to an emphasis on New England as opposed to more distant parts of the country. The same works contain evidence that, within New England, Bostonians passed over the inner suburbs in placing their capital in new venture. See N. S. B. Gras and Henrietta M. Larson, *Casebook in American Business History* (New York, 1939), 119–32; Porter, *The Jacksons and the Lees* 1:466–72, 766–72; Arthur M. Johnson and Barry E. Supple, *Boston Capitalists and Western Railroads: A Study in the Nineteenth-Century Railroad Investment Process* (Cambridge, 1967), 18–19; Oscar Handlin, *Boston's Immigrants: A Study in Acculturation,* rev. ed. (Cambridge, 1959), 9–10.

56. Hurd, 3:402–4, 428–29, 751–52; Caroline Ware, *The Early New England Cotton Manufacture: A Study in Industrial Beginnings* (New York, 1931), 60–66, 80–82, 116; John G. Palfrey, *Statistics of the Condition and Products of Certain Branches of Industry . . . 1845* (Boston, 1846), 59, 78–79. Palfrey's industrial census omits returns for some important industries and contains only incomplete figures for others (see pp. iii–iv). While it is therefore unsafe to use his statistics for detailed analysis, they do provide an indication of gross relationships in the suburban economy.

57. Goss, 81; Robinson and Wheeler, 75; Victor S. Clark, *History of Manufactures in the United States* (New York, 1929), 1:431, 545–46; Samuels and Kimball, 78. The Somerville Bleachery was not incorporated until 1838, but local historians have placed the date of its establishment in 1821. The Charlestown school authorities, in their report for 1823–24, mention the "recent establishment of factories at Milk Row"; *Annual Reports of the Trustees of the Charlestown Free Schools* (1801–38) (Charlestown, 1874), 47 n. See Stat. 1838, ch. 149; Hayward, *Gazeteer*, 272; Cutter and Cutter, 109, 319–20; employment figures from Palfrey, *Statistics*, 63, 71, 78, 79.

58. Hervey, "Reminiscences," 73–76; Fred H. Cooley, "Old Ship Street: Some of Its Houses, Ships, and Characters," *Medford Historical Register* 4 (October 1901): 87–90; Brooks, 359–80; Roberts, 120–21; Palfrey, 65, 362.

59. Henry Hall, "The Ice Industry of the United States with a Brief Sketch of Its History and Estimates of Production in the Different States," in U.S. Department of the Interior, *Tenth Census, 1880* 20 (Washington, D.C., 1888): 2–5; Morison, *Maritime History*, 280–83; Hill, *Trade and Commerce*, 115–16, 130, 143–44; *DAB* 19:47–48, 20:576–77; Ellen S. Bulfinch, "The Tudor House at Fresh Pond," CHS, *Pub.* 3 (October 1908): 105–6; Parker, 288–90; Cutter and Cutter, 146–47; Godley, *Letters* 1:6; William Roscoe Thayer, "Extracts from the Journal of Benjamin Waterhouse," CHS, *Pub.* 4 (January, 1909): 25 (entry for 5 March 1836). James Russell Lowell remembered that he and other boys in Cambridge assisted with the ice harvest in the 1820s. See Lowell to Charles F. Briggs, 8 August 1845, in Charles Eliot Norton, ed., *Letters of James Russell Lowell* (New York, 1894), 1:94–95.

60. Watkins, *Cambridge Glass*, 5–11; Palfrey, 44. The Boston Manufacturing Company was originally incorporated with an authorized capitalization of $400,000. By 1845 the Waltham cotton mills alone absorbed paid-in capital to the amount of $440,000, employing at that date 468 persons. The Lowell complex of cotton mills reported a capitalization of $8,475,000 and employment of 7,196 people in 1845. Hurd, 3:752; Palfrey, 59, 78.

61. Whitehill, 48, 55, 98; Palfrey, 2, 45, 66, 71–72.

62. Bidwell, "Rural Economy," 261–65, 273; Hurd, 1:355, 361; Stevens, 96–97; Clark, *History of Manufactures*, 482.

63. Palfrey, 43, 45, 47, 85, 355; Hunnewell, 34.

64. See the discussion involving a country soapmaker recorded by Hawthorne, *Works* 9:139.

65. CHCS 1:41–42; 3:22; Palfrey, 45, 47, 350. Brushmaking, also an industry dependent on animal by-products for its raw materials, followed a similar course of development. By 1845, Cambridge contained three large brush factories, one in Cambridgeport and two in East Cambridge, which together employed 81 people. The two largest of these, founded by Cambridge residents, opened stores in Boston as outlets for their products. Palfrey, 44; George Adams, *The Cambridge Almanac and Business Directory for the Year 1847* (Boston, 1847), 19, 25; *Stimpson's Boston Directory* (Boston, 1837).

66. Winsor, 4:80; Brooks, 355–56; Carter and Brooks, *Geography,* 15; Samuels and Kimball, 77; Palfrey, vii, 43, 45, 48, 62, 72, 81, 356; CHCS 5:27–30.

67. Ayer, "Medford Turnpike," 16–17; Samuels and Kimball, 460; Drake, *Historic Fields,* 99.

68. Ayer, 16; Charles D. Elliot, "Union Square and Its Neighborhood about the Year 1846," SHS, *Historic Leaves* 4 (April 1907): 5; Thayer, "Extracts," 29.

69. The following discussion is based on a reconstruction of data from the manuscript schedules of the sixth federal census. The printed returns from this enumeration (*Sixth Census* [Washington, D.C., 1841]) provide only aggregate information for the several towns. Subtotals for the major villages have been obtained by retabulating the original data, a process requiring some guesswork and therefore subject to a small margin of error.

Moreover, the 1840 census was a crude instrument, and the original schedules embody important weaknesses. Enumerators collected occupational data according to only seven broad categories (mining, agriculture, commerce, manufacturing, navigation of the ocean, navigation of rivers and inland waters, and learned professions). These were obviously capable of varied interpretations by individual census takers.

In addition, a comparison of the total number of occupations reported with the total population for each of the inner Middlesex towns makes it clear that some enumerators were more careful than others in counting occupations at all. The returns were further weakened by occasional negligence: in East Cambridge the enumerator completely omitted occupational data for some 70 households. See the MS returns for Cambridge, sheets 89–91.

70. Thomas Wentworth Higginson, "Life in Cambridge Town," in Colman, 41. On the Charlestown mainland 125 of the 237 households reported more than one employed member in 1840. And in 37 of these 125 cases, the occupations fell in more than one category.

71. Abiel Holmes, "The History of Cambridge," Massachusetts Historical Society, *Collections,* ser. 1, 7 (1800): 4. The founders of Cambridgeport clearly meant the canal network to become the focus of a commercial center and the meetinghouse square to serve as a civic and religious nucleus. CHCS 1:62–64; 3:18–19, and fig. 13, 15, 16.

72. See, for example, James Fling, "Historical Notices of Reading and South Reading, in an Address delivered . . . May 29, 1844," in *Historical Address and Poem delivered at the Bi-Centennial Celebration of the Incorporation of . . . Reading* (Boston, 1844), 50.

73. Watkins, 159–60.

74. John G. Hales, *A Survey of Boston and its Vicinity* (Boston, 1821), 34, 79, and passim; Hildreth, 59; Hunnewell, 150–53; *Annual Reports of the Trustees of the Charlestown Free Schools* (1800–1838), 46 n, 47 n, 61, 62 (reports for 1823–24, 1829–30, 1830–31).

75. *Bunker Hill Aurora,* 5 January 1828, p. 1; Thomas Whittemore, *The Early Days of Thomas Whittemore: An Autobiography extending from A.D. 1800 to A.D.*

1825 (Boston, 1859), 318; Henry Wadsworth Longfellow to Ferdinand Freiligrath, 19 March 1843, in Andrew Hilen, ed., *The Letters of Henry Wadsworth Longfellow* (Cambridge, 1966), 2:518. See also John Holmes, Introduction to the section on Cambridge in Hurd, 1:3; Bulfinch, "Tudor House," 107.

76. Elliot, "Union Square," 5; "Estimates to show that equal division into three wards can be made without dividing ward three," memorandum in Massachusetts Archives (hereafter MA), original documents relating to Acts of 1846, ch. 109, State House, Boston.

77. Hurd, 1:318; Robinson and Wheeler, 73–74.

78. Godley, 1:11; Levi S. Gould, "Reminiscences of North Malden (Melrose) and Vicinity," *Register of the Malden Historical Society* 4 (1915–16): 83–84.

79. Hunnewell, 94–95; David T. Pottinger, "Thirty-Eight Quincy Street," CHS, *Pub.* 23 (April 1934): 25–26; Thomas Wentworth Higginson, "Address" (at the Cambridge Historical Society Celebration of the Two Hundred and Seventy-Fifth Anniversary of the Founding of Cambridge), CHS, *Pub.* 1 (December 1905): 50–51.

80. Martha Perry Lowe, "Reminiscences of Somerville," in Samuels and Kimball, 439; Elliott, "Union Square," 15; Edward Everett, *Eulogy on Thomas Dowse of Cambridgeport* (Boston, 1859), 19–20; Simpson, 48; Edward Everett Hale, *A New England Boyhood* (New York, 1893), 116–17; Charles Eliot Norton, "Reminiscences of Old Cambridge," CHS, *Pub.* 1 (October 1905): 12–13, 16; Hervey, "Reminiscences," 63–64; Hunnewell, 38; Thomas Wentworth Higginson, *Cheerful Yesterdays* (Boston, 1898), 33–34.

81. Brooks, 424; Stevens, 140; Gould, "Reminiscences," 76.

82. The *Bunker Hill Aurora* described its plans for achieving wider circulation in early issues; see, for example, 27 December 1827, p. 2. But continued poor circulation of this as well as the Boston papers was evident in the controversy over enclosure of the Cambridge Common (see below, chap. 4) when opponents successfully petitioned for a new hearing on the grounds that publication of advertisements in the Boston press was not an adequate means of notification. See the petitions labeled "Lechmere Point," "Concord Road," and "Cambridgeport," and the Report of the Commissioners on Enclosure in MA, original documents relating to Acts of 1830, ch. 6. Cf. Report relating to the Enclosure of Cambridge Common, *Massachusetts Senate Documents, 1832*, No. 32, 7–8.

83. Spofford, 159; Hayward, *Gazetteer,* 41, 47; Shaw, 293; Colman, 197–98, 249, 424–31; Jesse Chickering, *A Statistical View of the Population of Massachusetts, from 1765 to 1840* (Boston, 1846), 8, 12–13, 42–49, 54–77.

Chapter 2
Village Building

1. On the general characteristics of rural towns, see Dwight Sanderson, *Locating the Rural Community,* Cornell Extension Bulletin 413 (Ithaca, 1939), 6–10. Studies

of early nineteenth-century communities affected by external forces include Blumin, *Urban Threshold;* Johnson, *Shopkeeper's Millennium;* Frisch, *Town into City.*

2. A summary of the literature on neighborhoods may be found in Donald I. Warren, "Neighborhoods in Urban Areas," in Roland L. Warren, ed., *New Perspectives on the American Community* (New York, 1977), 224–37. On nineteenth-century neighborhoods, see Warner, *Private City,* 125–57; Michael Feldberg, "Urbanization as a Cause of Violence: Philadelphia as a Test Case," in Allen F. Davis and Mark H. Haller, eds. *The Peoples of Philadelphia: A History of Ethnic Groups and Lower-Class Life, 1790–1940* (Philadelphia, 1973).

3. Gerald D. Suttles, *The Social Construction of Communities,* 3–18; Albert L. Hunter, *Symbolic Communities.*

4. For a discussion of Boston metropolitan population growth, see George R. Taylor, "Comment," in Gilchrist, 38–40.

5. Percy Wells Bidwell, "Population Growth in Southern New England," *Quarterly Publications of the American Statistical Association,* n. s. 120 (December 1917): 813.

6. The traditional conceptions are summarized and critically examined in Janet Abu-Lughod, "The Urban-Rural Differential as a Function of the Demographic Transition: Egyptian Data and an Analytic Model," *American Journal of Sociology* 69 (1964): 476–90; and John Knodel, "Town and Country in Nineteenth-Century Germany: A Review of Urban-Rural Differentials in Demographic Behavior," *Social Science History* 1 (1977): 356–82.

7. Don H. Doyle, "The Social Functions of Voluntary Associations in a Nineteenth-Century American Town," *Social Science History* 1 (1977): 333–55; Kathleen Neils Conzen, *Immigrant Milwaukee.*

8. The census schedules do not contain information on family relationships. I have considered "three-generation" households to be those that contained people aged under 15 *and* over 60.

9. Summaries and interpretations of the literature on geographic mobility: Stephan Thernstrom and Peter Knights, "Men in Motion: Some Data and Speculations about Urban Population Mobility in Nineteenth-Century America," in Tamara K. Hareven, ed., *Anonymous Americans* (Englewood Cliffs, N. J., 1971), 17–47; Howard P. Chudacoff, *Mobile Americans: Residential and Social Mobility in Omaha, 1880–1920* (New York, 1972); Michael B. Katz, *The People of Hamilton, Canada West: Family and Class in a Mid-Nineteenth Century City* (Cambridge, 1975), 119–33.

10. There are two notable exceptions to this general statement: Peter Knights, *The Plain People of Boston, 1830–1860;* and Robert Doherty, *Society and Power: Five New England Towns, 1800–1860* (Amherst, 1977).

11. Chudacoff found variations between neighborhoods in late nineteenth-century Omaha, but most scholars have not followed up his investigation of local differences. See *Mobile Americans,* 36–39.

12. Doyle, "Social Functions," 335.

13. Katz, *People of Hamilton,* 123–24; Doherty, 41–42.

14. These big households sometimes shrank as their heads grew older and children grew up. It seems likely that the census data caught the "stable" residents at the peak of household size. Other studies have suggested a link between mobility and stage in the family cycle. See Doherty, 41–42, 75–77.

15. Based on an examination of occupation data for those who were still there when the census of 1850 collected detailed occupational information.

16. John Whiting Donallan, *History of the Second Baptist Church, Cambridge, Massachusetts* (Lawrence, 1866), 17, 50.

17. See Thernstrom and Knights.

18. See above, p. 27.

19. Livermore (1722–1862) was the eleventh and youngest child of a Revolutionary leader in Waltham. Walter Eliot Thwing, *The Livermore Family of America* (Boston, 1902), 33–34, 78; Gozzaldi, *History of Cambridge, Supplement*, 460; Hurd, 1:208; Simpson, 42, 48, 85; Paige, 307–32. Isaac Livermore (1797–1880) also became a major investor and executive in several railroads and a major figure in statewide politics. See below, chap. 3. William Bond Wheelwright, *Life and Times of Alvah Crocker* (Boston, 1923), 27; Edward C. Kirkland, *Men, Cities, and Transportation: A Study in New England History, 1820–1900*, 2 vols. (Cambridge, 1948) 2.458, CHCS 2.59, Forbes and Greene, 95, Hill, 144. An announcement of his co-partnership with Hugh Kendall of Boston is in the Burlingame Family Papers, Box 1, folder 2, Manuscript Division, Library of Congress. The firm is listed in the *Boston Directory* (Boston, 1830), 196, 209; Robert F. Lucid, ed., *The Journal of Richard Henry Dana, Jr.*, 3 Vols. (Cambridge, 1968) 1:341.

20. DAB 8:272; CHCS 2:27; Brown, 185–86; Gozzaldi, *History of Cambridge, Supplement*, 409.

21. Wyman, 2:964–67; Brooks, 545–50; Report of the Committee of the House of Representatives . . . to inspect the records . . . of Charles River Bridge, *Massachusetts House Documents, 1827*, No. 71, Appendix C; Harriet A. Adams, "Winter Hill," 22; Aaron Sargent, "Neighborhood Sketch, No. 2: The Winter Hill Road in 1842," SHS, *Historic Leaves* 1 (October 1902): 20.

22. Wyman, 2:967–71; Forbes and Greene, 100, 115; *DAB* 19:49; Elliot, "Union Square," 9, 11–12.

23. Wyman, 2:844, 908–9, 966; Samuels and Kimball, 621; Elliot, "Union Square," 7–9.

24. Samuel Eliot Morison, *Harrison Gray Otis, 1765–1848: The Urbane Federalist* (Boston, 1969), 82; Baldwin, *Belmont*, 38; Colman, 259, 399–400; Godley, 2:58–59.

25. Bigelow (1765–1849) served several terms as one of Cambridgeport's first members on the Cambridge Boards of Assessors (from 1810) and Selectmen (from 1812). He lived in the Inman mansion until his death. Gozzaldi, *History of Cambridge, Supplement*, 244; CHCS 2:20–21, 24; Paige, 466, 468; Thomas W. Baldwin, comp., *Vital Records of Cambridge, Massachusetts to the Year 1850* (Boston, 1914–15) 2:467.

Bangs (1786–1859) was a voter in Cambridge as early as 1822. He also became a resident of Cambridgeport and a selectman and served for eighteen years as deacon of the Cambridgeport Parish. Gozzaldi, *History of Cambridge, Supplement,* 28; Paige, 312, 466; Baldwin, *Vital Records* 2:23.

26. Edward M. Cook, Jr., *The Fathers of the Towns: Leadership and Community Structure in Eighteenth Century New England* (Baltimore, 1976), 11–19 and passim.

27. Winsor, 3:471, 560–62; Hunnewell, 55–58. For details on Morse and Holmes, see *DAB* 9:160–61; 13:245–47; Paige 299–302.

28. William G. McLoughlin, *New England Dissent, 1630–1833: The Baptists and the Separation of Church and State* (Cambridge, 1971) 1:685, 692.

29. Inhabitants of the Union Square neighborhood were oriented toward Cambridgeport and especially East Cambridge and attended meetings of congregations in those places. For an account, see Mrs. E. A. Bacon, *Memoir of Rev. Henry Bacon* (Boston, 1857), 49. Farther to the west, many families attended services in West Cambridge. Parker, 74.

30. Hurd, 1:53–54; Simpson, 48, 86; Stat. 1808, ch. 62; John F. W. Ware, *Cambridgeport Parish: A Discourse on the Occasion of the Fiftieth Anniversary of the Settlement of Rev. Thomas B. Gannett, First Minister of the Parish* (Cambridge, 1864), 6–7; Paige, 311–12.

31. Fields of attendance cannot be mapped precisely but their general dimensions are evident in the distribution of names from Stephen P. Sharples, comp., *Records of the Church of Christ at Cambridge in New England, 1632–1830* (Boston, 1906), when compared with local reminiscences.

32. Based on linkage of all 1820 household heads with baptism, marriage, death, and membership records of the First Church, 1790–1830.

33. A seating plan for the First Baptist Church is reprinted in CHCS 3:78.

34. Whittemore, *Early Days,* 301, 322–24; Stat. 1821, ch. 63. On Tufts, see above, p. 62.

35. Paige, 318–19, 322–24.

36. Rev. James S. Hoyt, *The First Evangelical Congregational Church, Cambridgeport, Massachusetts* (Cambridge, 1877), 39.

37. Table of Members, ibid., 195 ff.

38. Hurd, 1:73; Watkins, 7–8, 180–81; Winsor, 3:438–39; Paige, 318–19, 322–24. The principal leader in the organization of the Second Baptist was a shoe dealer named Enos Reed (1796–1881), who had attempted to gather a church since 1824, was elected its first deacon, and served in that capacity for 45 years. Donallan, 4–10; Gozzaldi, *History of Cambridge, Supplement,* 616; Paige, 324.

39. Whitney (1783–1853) was born in Northboro and arrived in Cambridge at some point before 1816, when he became selectman. Gozzaldi, *History of Cambridge, Supplement,* 799; Paige, 304, 306, 466; CHCS 2:18.

Willard (1780–1856) was a professor from 1807 until 1831, a shareholder in the markethouse, an investor in Cambridgeport lands, an assessor, selectman, representative, member of the Governor's Council, and one of the first mayors of Cambridge.

Gozzaldi, *History of Cambridge, Supplement,* 816; Paige, 231 n, 306, 460, 461, 466, 468, 469; CHCS 3:25.

40. An alphabetical list of all deacons, 1704–1860, compiled from Paige, 305–37, and the various church histories cited above, was linked to the census as a basis for this analysis.

41. Acts 6:2. See the discussion of this text and other passages of scripture concerning deacons in the early records of the Second Baptist Church, quoted in Donallan, 12–13.

42. Alexander McKenzie, *The Good Deacons: Sermons in Memory of Stephen T. Farwell and Charles W. Homer, Deacons of the First Church in Cambridge* (Boston, 1873), 4–7. Stephen T. Farwell (1805–1872) moved on from being a store clerk to become the chief financial administrator of the American Education Society in Boston. He also served a total of four terms in local office and six terms as representative and senator. Gozzaldi, *History of Cambridge, Supplement,* 247; *Boston Directory . . . 1851* (Boston, 1851).

43. McKenzie, *Good Deacons,* 7, 9, 12, 25, 27, and passim; Gozzaldi, "Merchants of Old Cambridge in the Early Days," CHS, *Pub.* 7 (1913): 30–40; the "good character" valued and encouraged by such men was discussed in the letters of Deacon Isaac Warren of Charlestown (1758–1834) to his son at school. See Thomas C. Amory, *Class Memoir of George Washington Warren, with English and American Ancestry* (Boston, 1886), 34–75.

44. For examples, see Donallan, 11, 62–63; Alexander McKenzie, *Lectures on the History of the First Church in Cambridge* (Boston, 1873), 175–77.

45. Cutter and Cutter, 139 n; Hurd, 1:135.

46. Samuels and Kimball, 85, 269.

47. Quincy, *Municipal History,* 153–63, 180–92, 203 6.

48. Fire company regulations: Records of the Selectmen of the Town of Cambridge (MS, Cambridge City Hall), 2, October 1835, May 1840 (hereafter cited as CSR).

49. Names of the firemen for 1835 are recorded in CSR, 2, April 1835.

50. Fire company officers, ibid., annual lists for 1833–45.

51. Biographical form for the New England Historic Genealogical Society, Burlingame Papers, Box 2, Folder "1870s."

52. The visiting card, issued in Detroit on 1 April 1844 and endorsed in Cambridgeport on May 27, is among the Burlingame Papers, Box 1, Folder 4. On arrangements for Burlingame to speak before the Odd Fellows in Boston, see the Cambridge Diary kept by his fellow boarder and future brother-in-law Frederick Bruce, entry for 12 February 1846, and the note of thanks from Samuel Wentworth to Burlingame, 31 December 1847, both in the same folder.

53. The markethouse shareholders are listed in Paige, 230–32 and notes.

54. This function of suburban banks was clearly stated in the recollections of John Livermore (1813–98), son of Nathaniel and brother of Isaac, a long-term director of the Cambridge City Bank during the 1850s. Hurd, 1:198; Thwing, 134–35.

55. Banks in Boston and other ports had originally developed as an outgrowth of the credit-making activities of individual merchants. In the early nineteenth century both overseas traders and the various ranks of wholesalers, jobbers, and lesser dealers continued to perform many financial functions commonly performed by banks. Gras and Larson, 162–63; Bray Hammond, *Banks and Politics in America from the Revolution to the Civil War* (Princeton, 1957), 75–76; Albion, 283–86; Fred Mitchell Jones, *Middlemen in the Domestic Trade of the United States, 1800–1860,* Illinois Studies in the Social Sciences, vol. 21 no. 3 (Urbana, Ill., 1937), 21.

56. On Charlestown's early banks, see Binford, "Influence," 89–90, 92–93.

57. *Private and Special Statutes,* 7:450–53.

58. Paige, 230 n, 557.

59. Stat. 1825, ch. 53, in *Private and Special Statutes,* 6:361–64; *Boston Directory . . . 1825* (Boston, 1825).

60. On Chaplin, see above, p. 68; Stat. 1825, ch. 165; *Private and Special Statutes,* 6:450–53; Paige, 557. Early officers are listed in Hurd, 1:167, 198, and in Arthur Gilman, ed., *The Cambridge of Eighteen Hundred and Ninety-six: A Picture of the City and its Industries Fifty Years after its Incorporation* (Cambridge, 1896), 301–3.

61. Stat. 1832, ch. 69, in *Private and Special Statutes,* 7:203–4; Hurd, 1:198–99; Gozzaldi, "Merchants of Old Cambridge," 37; Gilman, *Cambridge,* 304; Edwin P. Conklin, *Middlesex County and Its People: A History* (New York, 1927), 1:197.

62. Hurd, 1:198; Arthur B. Darling, *Political Change in Massachusetts, 1824–1848: A Study of Liberal Movements in Politics* (New Haven, 1925), 15; Winsor, 4:167–68. An investigative report on the failure took pains to point out that the local transactions of the Middlesex were properly conducted and accused Parmenter of betraying both his community and his own directors by neglecting the opportunities present at Lechmere Point. Report . . . relating to the Middlesex Bank, *Massachusetts Senate Documents, 1838,* No. 27, 6–11.

The political character of William Parmenter (1789–1866) does not, however, seem to have suffered from such accusations. First elected a state representative in 1829, he had moved on to become senator in 1836 and a Democratic representative in the U.S. Congress in 1837. Despite the bank scandal in the winter of 1837/38, he was reelected in the fall and also won victories in 1840 and 1842. Moreover, he had been an important figure in town government before his election to Congress and retained a reputation for fairness and parliamentary skill. *Biographical Directory of the American Congress, 1774–1961* (Washington, D.C., 1961), 1427; Gozzaldi, *History of Cambridge, Supplement,* 566; Hurd, 1:224.

63. Little (1799–1869) became a clerk in Hilliard's firm in 1821, junior partner in 1827, and senior partner in 1837. He moved to Cambridge sometime before 1836, when he was elected both selectman and representative. *DAB* 9:297–98; Gozzaldi, *History of Cambridge, Supplement,* 459; Paige, 446, 462.

64. Watkins, 10.

Chapter 3
The Mobility Revolution Begins

1. Turnpikes and bridges charged different rates for various vehicles, for riders, and for pedestrians. The highest tolls were laid on pleasure carriages, the lowest on farm wagons and walkers. Kirkland, 1:42–43; Livermore, 17–18; *Private and Special Statutes,* 3:367–68, 589.

2. Hurd, 2:495; Roberts, 35–36, 39; for examples, see the extracts from the diary of Louisa Higginson in Higginson, "Cambridge Eighty Years Since," 21, 27–30.

3. *Works* 9:117.

4. Kirkland, 1:49, 56–57; Bryant, "Lexington 60 Years," 26–27; Parker, 50.

5. Elliot, "Union Square," 8.

6. John Holmes, "Introduction," to the section on Cambridge in Hurd, 1:3; Higginson, *Cheerful Yesterdays,* 96.

7. Simpson, 51, 59, 62.

8. Norton, "Reminiscences," 18–19; Edmund Quincy, *Life of Josiah Quincy of Massachusetts* (Boston, 1867), 529–30.

9. James P. Munroe, "Elias Phinney," *Proceedings of the Lexington Historical Society* 2 (April 1890): 66–68, 70–75, 80; Colman, *Fourth Report,* 396–99.

10. Handlin and Handlin, *Commonwealth,* 238; Winsor, 3:556.

11. Winsor, 3:555; *Review of the Case of the Free Bridge, between Boston and Charlestown* (Boston, 1827), 4; *Bunker Hill Aurora,* 12 July 1827, p. 2: Governor Levi Lincoln's message accompanying his veto of the bill for a free bridge is quoted in *Review,* 101–2.

12. Winsor, 3:555; *Review,* 93.

13. Livermore, 30–34; *Private and Special Statutes* 8:602–6.

14. *Cambridge Chronicle,* 12 June 1852, p. 2; Hurd, 1:210.

15. Hunnewell, 47. Alson Studley was enumerated among the Neck Village residents in the census of 1840. See the manuscript returns for Charlestown, sheet 59; Hurd 1:211.

16. Early versions are described in George Rogers Taylor, "The Beginnings of Mass Transportation in Urban America: Part 1," 40–43. On the migration of the omnibus from France to England and America, see John Copeland, *Roads and Their Traffic, 1750–1850* (Newton Abbot, 1968), 107–8; *Cambridge Chronicle,* 12 June 1852, p. 2.

17. *Boston Directory . . . 1846* (Boston, 1846), 39; Kirkland, 1:51–54; *Cambridge Chronicle,* 12 June 1852, p. 2.

18. Kirkland, 1:346; *Boston Directory . . . 1846,* 39; *Cambridge Almanac and Business Directory . . . 1847* (Boston, 1847), 4.

19. For the details, see Binford, "Influence," 191.

20. Solomon Sargent, who was for a short time a partner in the New Line, was chosen alderman much later, in 1858.

21. Norton, "Reminiscences," 18–21; Quincy, *Josiah Quincy,* 529–30.

22. Kirkland, 1:112.

23. Kirkland, 1:111, 125, 127–28; Wheelwright, *Crocker,* 13–16, 22–23, 26; *Bunker Hill Aurora,* 26 February 1842, p. 2.

24. *Report of the committee appointed by the Stockholders of the Charlestown Wharf Company* (Boston, 1839), 3–4, 79. George Pierce Baker, *The Formation of the New England Railroad Systems: A Study of Railroad Combination in the Nineteenth Century* (Cambridge, 1949), 100–105; Kirkland, 1:192–95; First Annual Report of the Boston and Maine Railroad Extension Company, *Massachusetts Senate Documents, 1845,* No. 21, 15.

25. Harrison G. Otis, *An Address,* 5 January 1829, in *The Inaugural Addresses of the Mayors of Boston,* I (Boston, 1894), 125; Kirkland, 1:106, 108–11.

26. Chapman, 135; Thomas S. Harlow, "Some Notes of the History of Medford from 1801 to 1851," *Medford Historical Register* 1 (July 1898): 82–93; Kirkland, 1:123, 346; *Daily Evening Transcript,* 23 June 1835, pp. 2, 3.

27. Proceedings of the Directors and Stockholders of the Boston and Worcester Railroad, quoted in Kirkland, 1:346.

28. Undated manuscript draft in Hale Family papers (hereafter Hale MSS), Box 20, folder labeled "Railroad Miscellaneous." Internal evidence places it in October or November 1839; Nathan Hale to John A. Rockwell, 6 February 1840, Hale MSS, binder 2, p. 387, Manuscript Division, Library of Congress.

29. *Boston Post,* 28 October 1839, p. 4; Charles J. Kennedy, "Commuter Services in the Boston Area, 1835–1860," *Business History Review* 36 (1962): 153–69; Seventh Annual Report of the Charlestown Branch Rail-Road Company, *Massachusetts Senate Documents,* 1843, No. 19, 68; *Daily Evening Transcript,* 25 May 1842, p. 3; *Bunker Hill Aurora,* 21 January 1843, p. 2.

30. Eighth Annual Report of the Charlestown Branch Rail-Road Company, *Massachusetts Senate Documents, 1844,* No. 19, 70.

31. Kirkland, 1:103, 104, 107, 111, 119; Kennedy, 157–58. The subscription book is in the Hale MSS, Box 20, folder labeled "Railroad Miscellaneous."

32. Second Annual Report of the Fitchburg Rail-Road Company, *Massachusetts, Senate Documents, 1844,* No. 19, 87–88; Third Annual Report, *ibid., 1845,* No. 21, 56–57, 61.

33. Eleventh Annual Report of the Boston and Maine Railroad Company, *Massachusetts Senate Documents, 1846* No. 21, 16–17; Kennedy 157–58, 160.

34. Charles Hale (1831–1880) went on to become a journalist, politician, diplomat, and assistant secretary of state under Hamilton Fish. *DAB* 8:96–97. Many issues of his journal are in the Hale MSS, Box 17, four folders labeled "Railroad Journal."

35. Railroad Journal, 15 March 1843, 24 April 1843, pp. 5, 12; 5 October 1843, pp. 2, 4; 17 July 1844, p. 4; 27 May 1844, p. 21, Hale MSS.

36. *Bunker Hill Aurora,* 30 October 1830, p. 2; Hurd, 1:211.

37. George S. Hilliard, *Life, Letters, and Journals of George Ticknor* (Boston, 1876), 1:339, 391–92, 395; 2:226; Kirkland, 1:123; Harlow, "Some Notes," 90–91;

Boston Daily Evening Transcript, 25 May 1842, p. 3; 28 May 1842, p. 3; 11 June 1845, p. 3.

38. Hilen (ed.), *Letters* 2:4, 7, 382; MS Journal of John Gorham Palfrey, entries for 15 January, 14 February, 23 June 1843, Palfrey collection, Houghton Library, Harvard University; Brown, 180–81; Caroline H. Gilman, *Recollections of a Housekeeper* (New York, 1836), 45; Gould, "Reminiscences," 83.

39. Mary Isabella Gozzaldi, "Extracts from the Reminiscences of Isabella Batchelder James," CHS, *Pub.* 23 (October 1934): 55; Thayer, "Extracts," 28; Hawthorne, *Works* 9:18.

40. CHCS 5:39–40; plats of Kent and Brastow property, Middlesex County Deeds, 1843, Middlesex County Court house.

41. Petitions submitted to the Cambridge selectmen for street acceptance and street name changes are in CSR, 2, 28 October and 12 December 1834, 31 October 1836. Notes given for lots created from town holdings are recorded in *Annual Report of the Town of Cambridge, 1840,* p. 22. Names from these documents have been checked against the biographical files.

42. Paige, 460; *Report of a Committee . . . to consider . . . a Reorganization of the Public Schools* (Cambridge, 1834).

43. Frank Otto Gatell, *John Gorham Palfrey and the New England Conscience* (Cambridge, 1963), 68–69, 77, 103.

44. CHCS 2:21, fig. 15; "Old Landmarks in Cambridge," undated newspaper clipping in Burlingame MSS, Box 5, following last folder.

45. Handlin, *Boston's Immigrants,* 15, 88–89; *Review of the Case of the Free Bridge,* 14

46. Until the late 1840s, Boston directories omitted many clerical workers and junior staff including in their listings the partners of a firm.

47. Glen Porter and Harold C. Livesay, *Merchants and Manufacturers: Studies in the Changing Structure of Nineteenth-Century Marketing* (Baltimore, 1971).

48. Livermore and Quincy were assessed for $30,000 and $55,000 worth of real and personal estate, respectively. Quincy's wealth was partly hidden, since Harvard provided his housing. But neither man ranked with the forty wealthiest Bostonians, as identified by Edward Pessen. The Boston elite averaged well over $100,000 in assessed valuation. Tax Rolls of the Town of Cambridge, 1840 (microfilm, Cambridge Public Library); Edward Pessen, "Did Fortunes Rise and Fall Mercurially in Antebellum America?" *Journal of Social History* 4 (1971): 348.

Chapter 4
New Model Communities

1. William H. Furber, *Historical Address delivered . . . July 4, 1876* (Boston, 1876), 6–7; M. A. Haley, *The Story of Somerville* (Boston, 1903).

2. Thomas Wentworth Higginson, "Life in Cambridge Town," in Gilman, ed., *Cambridge,* 35–42; Higginson, *Cheerful Yesterdays,* 1–37, 42–46; Charles Eliot Norton, "Reminiscences," 12–13, 18–19.

3. There is no adequate history of American urban government in the nineteenth century. We have many studies of politics but few of structure and administration. Jon C. Teaford, *The Municipal Revolution in America: Origins of Modern Urban Government, 1650–1825* traces the early stages of evolution but ends before the expansion of the mid-century. His *Cities and Suburbs* deals with a later period but is largely concerned with metropolitan relationships.

4. Many of the procedures followed in town government had no specific basis in law until after the Revolution. And even then, the legal requirements were loose and vaguely stated and remained uncodified until well into the nineteenth century. As a result, practices varied enormously between communities, and each town enjoyed a good deal of latitude in deciding how it would conduct its affairs. See John Bacon, *The Town Officer's Guide, containing a Compilation of the General Laws of Massachusetts, relating to the Whole Power and Duty of Towns* (Haverhill, Mass., 1825); Michael Zuckerman, *Peaceable Kingdoms: New England Towns in the Eighteenth Century* (New York, 1972), 156–86.

5. Harlan Updegraff, *The Origin of the Moving School in Massachusetts* (New York, 1908), 124–32; Bacon, 265–68.

6. County governments were strengthened after the Revolution in order to provide a better check on the towns. Handlin and Handlin, *Commonwealth*, 95–96.

7. O'Malley, "Old North Cambridge," 126; Brooks, 52–53; Hurd, 2:844; Paige, 202–3.

8. Division of towns into districts, begun in some places before the Revolution and sanctioned by law in 1789, was the second in a series of innovations undertaken to cope with population dispersion. District schools, which shared the town appropriation of funds and adjusted their schedules to meet the needs of given areas, replaced the system of "moving schools" that had met in different locations for a few months each. Updegraff, chaps. 6 and 8; Paul Munroe, *Founding of the American Public School System: A History of Education in the United States* (New York, 1940), 118–23, 275, 277; Winsor, 3:557–58; Paige, 375–76; *Annual Reports of the Trustees of the Charlestown Free Schools (1801–1838),* 43–44, 60–61.

9. McKenzie, *First Church,* 178–79; *Brief History of the First Baptist Church,* 25 ff.

10. McKenzie, *First Church,* 188–206. The final statements of the two sides to the dispute were both published as pamphlets in 1829. Holmes's supporters issued *An Account of the Controversy in the First Parish in Cambridge, 1827–1829* (Boston, 1829), and the Unitarians countered with *Controversy between the First Parish in Cambridge and the Rev. Dr. Holmes, their late pastor* (Cambridge, 1829).

11. Based on a list of the names of members of the numerous committees appointed by both sides during the course of the dispute. The same old Cambridge householders were reappointed on almost every occasion. *Controversy,* 13–16.

The dispute was not mentioned in any of the Boston newspapers or in the *Bunker Hill Aurora,* nor did it receive notice in the available writings of suburban citizens who were not directly involved.

12. Gozzaldi, *Supplement,* 584; Paige, 225, 677, 702–6.

13. Paige, 230–32.

14. Updegraff, 129–34.

15. Hunnewell, 38.

16. For example, Charlestown in 1830 contained nearly two thousand eligible voters. But the greatest number of votes cast at any meeting that year was 549, on the first ballot in the elections of state representatives. Even on that occasion, the total number of votes cast fell off rapidly in the second and third rounds of balloting. Charlestown Town Records, vol. 12, 99 (MSS on microfilm, Boston Public Library). Cf. also Gould, "Reminiscences," 76–77; *Bunker Hill Aurora,* 2 May 1829, p. 2; 12 February 1842, p. 2.

17. Charles Edward Mann, "Methodist Beginnings in Malden," *Register of the Malden Historical Society* 4 (1915–16): 47–48; Hurd, 2:24–25, 718–19; 3:184.

For examples of sabotage, see Henry Bradshaw Fearon, *Sketches of America: A Narrative of a Journey of Five Thousand Miles through the Eastern and Western States of America* (London, 1818), 97; Amory, *Sullivan* 2:113–14; Paige, 204; CHCS 2:24.

18. The outline of this controversy is sketched in Paige, 235–40, but his discussion of the political issues is superficial.

19. Suburban park planning derived from the improvements undertaken on the Boston Common (see above, p. 34). Wealthy individuals took up the idea not only in Cambridge but also in Medford and Lexington. See Brooks, 58–59; Bryant, "Lexington Sixty Years Ago," 36–37.

20. Christiana Hopkinson Baker, *The Story of Fay House* (Cambridge, 1929), 27–28, 50–52; Thayer, "Extracts," 31.

21. The petition is in MA, original documents relating to Acts of 1830, ch. 6. The activities of the commissioners are described in their report, filed in the same place.

22. See the petitions labeled "Canal Bridge," "Lechmere Point," "Cambridgeport," and "Concord Road," MA, documents of 1830. Cf. the plan of proposed changes in roads, surveyed by James Hayward. MA, Maps and Plans, third series, vol. 46, p. 3.

23. The vote tallies were, respectively, 169 to 119 and 299 to 211. Paige, 237.

24. Paige, 238–39.

25. The relevant documents are filed in MA, documents of 1832, bundle 9173.

26. MA, documents of 1832, bundles 9173/7 and 9173/5. The Sawyer remonstrance consisted of several sheets pasted together. Comparison of the signatures with data from other biographical sources indicates that each sheet contained names from a different neighborhood. It therefore seems likely that the document was the result of widespread systematic canvassing. The quotation is from the remonstrance of James Russell and others, dated December 1831. MA, bundles 9173/8.

27. Thayer, "Extracts," 26. See also Report relating to the Enclosure of Cambridge Common, *Massachusetts Senate Documents, 1832,* No. 23.

28. Paige, 238–39.

29. Robert H. Lord, John E. Sexton, and Edward T. Harrington, *History of the Archdiocese of Boston in the Various Stages of Its Development, 1604 to 1943* (New York, 1944) 2:206–8, 210–21; Louisa G. Whitney, *The Burning of the Convent* (Boston, 1844).

30. Whitney, *Burning,* 114ff.

31. CSR, 12–13 August 1834.

32. Ibid., 21 August, 6 September 1834.

33. Porter and Livesay, *Merchants and Manufacturers;* Handlin and Handlin, *Commonwealth,* 202; Richard P. McCormick, *The Second American Party System* (Chapel Hill, 1966), 35–49; John L. Thomas, "Romantic Reform in America," *American Quarterly* 17 (1965): 656–81.

34. Paige, 326.

35. Hayward (1786–1866) was chosen to survey a rail route from Boston to Providence in 1827 and another route from Boston to Lowell in 1829. In later years he resigned his Harvard professorship in order to give full time to civil engineering. He went on to lay out several railroads to the north and west, to superintend construction of the first part of what eventually became the Boston and Maine, in 1833, and to serve as B&M president during the 1850s. Kirkland, 1:107, 111, 159–61, 172, 193, 395, 399, 2:460–61, 468; Gozzaldi, *Supplement,* 370; *Appleton's Cyclopedia of American Biography* 3 (New York, 1887): 147.

Whittmore (1800–1861) served with Hayward in the legislature in 1831 and 1832 and joined him in promoting the Vermont and Massachusetts Railroad beginning in 1844. Gozzaldi, *History of Cambridge, Supplement,* 812; Paige, 690–91; Kirkland, 2:460; Whittemore, *Early Days,* 300–301, 303–4, 318–20.

Concerning Parmenter, see above, p. 74. Buttrick (b. 1799) joined the Middlesex bar in 1823, practiced in East Cambridge, and served as selectman, representative, and later as alderman. Gozzaldi, *Supplement,* 101; Hurd, 1:xlviii.

36. Quincy, *Municipal History,* 153–63, 180–92, 203–6; *Private and Special Statutes* 7:266–68.

37. *Report of a Committee, appointed August 4, 1834, to consider the Subject of a Reorganization of the Public Schools in the Town of Cambridge* (Cambridge, 1834), 8–9.

38. Ibid., 9–11; Munroe, *Founding,* 253–60.

39. Quincy, *Municipal History,* 194–96; Winsor, 4:45–46; Petition of Israel Porter and others, MA, original documents relating to Acts of 1830, ch. 6.

40. James Hayward, *Report of the Survey of the Roads in Cambridge* (Cambridge, 1838), 4–5, 14–16.

41. For details on Charlestown improvements, see Binford, "Influence," 134–38.

42. Hayward, *Report of the Survey,* 13.

43. Ibid., 14.

44. On dog tags: Records of the Town of Cambridge (MS, Cambridge City Clerk's Office), 8 August 1836 (hereafter cited as CTR); CSR, 13 August 1836.

45. Hayward, *Report of the Survey,* 16.

46. Benjamin F. Thomas, *The Town Officer: A Digest of the Laws of Massachusetts in relation to the Powers, Duties and Liabilities of Towns, and of Town Officers* (Worcester, 1849), 307.

In both towns, reports of committees chosen to consider important issues were occasionally printed for circulation, and in Cambridge the controversy over the Common was probably a stimulus to the institution of an annual series of statements. See James F. Hunnewell, *Bibliography of Charlestown, Massachusetts, and Bunker Hill* (Boston, 1880), 43–44, 50–51.

47. Only the town treasurer was legally required to submit an account to a town meeting. The surveyors of highways, assessors, and members of the school committee all had to return partial records of their doings to the selectmen but were not bound to give a full public report. In practice, such officials seem to have been called upon to speak in the annual meeting, but the surviving evidence of these oral presentations indicates that they were brief and did not involve any strict accounts of duties performed or money spent. See Thomas, *Town Officer,* 44, 212, 293, 307; *Annual Reports of the Board of Trustees in the Charlestown Free Schools* (1801–1838), passim.

48. *Annual Report of the Receipts and Expenditures of the Town of Cambridge, March, 1837* (n.p., n.d.), 10–12.

49. *Annual Report of the Receipts and Expenditures of the Town of Cambridge, March, 1840* (Cambridge, 1840), p. 26.

50. Ibid., 27–28; Bacon, *Town Officer's Guide,* 80–87, 160–61; Charlestown Town Records, vol. 12, 42; *Annual Report of the Receipts and Expenditures of the Town of Cambridge,* March 1844 (Cambridge, 1844), 27; ibid., March 1845 (Cambridge, 1845), 23; *Annual Statement of the Expenses of the Town of Charlestown . . . 1842* (Charlestown, 1842), 2; ibid., 1843 (Charlestown, 1843), 23.

51. *Statement of the Expenses of the Town of Charlestown . . . April, 1829* (Charlestown, 1829), 2–3, 9; *Annual Report of the Receipts and Expenditures of the Town of Cambridge, March, 1840,* 23, 27–29; *Annual Statement . . . Charlestown . . . 1843, 23.*

52. Bartlett, 8; *Annual Reports of the Trustees of the Charlestown Free Schools* (1801–1838), 9–10 (report for 1813).

53. *Bunker Hill Aurora,* 6 December 1827, p. 2. Rodenburgh's *Charlestown Directory* for 1836 contained about 1400 entries, less than 7 percent of which were for citizens resident on the mainland. Even a conservative estimate based on census schedules indicates that the mainland contained more than 10 percent of the heads of households. For Guidebook portraits, see Spofford, 173–74; Hildreth, 58.

54. The most important separations were those of Billerica (1655), Newton (1687), and Lexington (1712) from Cambridge; and of Woburn (1642), Malden (1649), and Stoneham (1725) from Charlestown. See Paige, 4–5; Hurd, 2:462, 3:578.

55. "Sketches of some of the reasons which may be adduced before a committee of the Legislature in favor of a separation of the town of Charlestown," in "Guy C. Hawkins Papers—Number 2," SHS *Historic Leaves* 5 (July, 1906): 40–42.

56. Ibid., 43. Of the 38 landowners known to have supported separation, 34 listed barns and other farming structures among their taxable assets. On the other hand 9 of the 18 known opponents listed stores or factories. "Guy C. Hawkins Papers—Number 1," SHS, *Historic Leaves* 5 (April 1906): 10–14.

57. Petition of Samuel Tufts and others, in MA, documents of 1828, bundle 8605.

58. The names of the 1824 remonstrants are given in "Guy C. Hawkins Papers—Number 1," but the original doucments do not survive. Opponents in 1828 signed their names to the Remonstrance of Melzar Torrey and others, MA, documents of 1828, 8605/2. James Russell, innkeeper in Neck Village, was one of the principal opponents both in 1824 and 1828. He was joined by his cousins and in-laws among the Russells and Teels and by members of the Cutter, Lamson, and Torrey families—nearly all residents of Neck Village. See Wyman, 1:264–71, 2:594–97, 838–40, 935–37.

59. The best overall account of the events leading to Somerville's separation is in Furber, *Historical Address*, 6–8. A much more complete account, written by the first town clerk begins the Records of the Town of Somerville, 1:1–4 (STR, in the vault of the City Clerk's Office, Somerville.).

The *Bunker Hill Aurora*, 1 January 1842, p. 3, identified the organizing committee of the movement:

Clark Bennett (1810–82) migrated from Vermont in the early 1830s, engaged in brickmaking for 25 years, then entered the insurance business, and served many terms in town office after the Civil War. Samuels and Kimball, 495.

James Hill, Jr. (b. 1806), was probably a son of the farming family prominent in West Cambridge. A successful business dealing in vegetables allowed him to buy an estate on the mainland sometime in the late 1830s. Cutter and Cutter, 260–61; Elliott, "Union Square," 9; manuscript schedules of the 1840 census of Charlestown, sheet 59; 1850 census schedules for Somerville, p. 371, dwelling number 251.

John S. Edgerly (1804–72), born in New Hampshire, moved to mainland Charlestown about 1836 and occupied a house on Winter Hill that had previously belonged to Congressman Edward Everett. Edgerly later served twelve terms as Somerville selectman. Helen M. Despeaux, "John S. Edgerly," SHS *Historic Leaves* 3 (July 1904): 36–43; Samuels and Kimball, 526.

For the early career of Francis Bowman (b. 1792), see Bryant, "Lexington Sixty Years Ago," 40–41. Bowman appears on a Cambridge list of registered voters for 1836 and in the manuscript returns of the 1840 census for mainland Charlestown (sheet 62). By 1845 he was the sixth largest taxpayer in Somerville. See "List of Town and County Taxes as Assessed for the year 1845," in *Expenditures of the Town of Somerville (1845–46)* (Somerville, 1846), 9.

60. The petition is in MA, original documents relating to Acts of 1842, ch. 76. The following discussion draws upon a card file of names from this petition, which

has been supplemented by information from the census schedules and other biographical sources for each signer. The distribution of occupations among petition signers and the mainland population as a whole, as indicated by the 1840 census, was as follows:

	petition	total population
mining	6	6
agriculture	98	207
commerce	32	76
manufacturing	127	271
learned professions	6	9
total	269	569

61. *Bunker Hill Aurora,* 8 January 1842, p. 2; STR 1:2–4; Memorial of John C. Bucknam and others, MA, original documents relating to Acts of 1842, ch. 76. The signers included George O. Brastow, George Meacham, Amos Hazeltine, John Davenport, and William Hunnewell, all Cambridge landowners.

62. The Somerville Whigs succeeded only in part. State election data reflect the creation of a slender Whig majority in the new town, as indicated in the returns for governor:

	1836		1840		1843	
	Whig	Democrat	Whig	Democrat	Whig	Democrat
Charlestown	532	477	579	820	622	777
Somerville	—	—	—	—	117	100

But neither Whigs nor Democrats could muster the votes needed to elect a state representative from Somerville's town meeting. Despite many heated contests, Somerville did not send any representative to the legislature until 1848, when real estate entrepreneur George Brastow, a Whig with Free-Soil leanings, finally gained a victory.

63. Changes in support have been determined through a comparison of names on the 1828 remonstrance against separation with those on the 1842 Hawkins petition for. The bargaining over property and boundaries may be traced through the following: *Annual Report of the Board of Trustees of the Charlestown Free Schools* (Charlestown, 1839), 7; Charlestown Town Records, vol. 14, 19–20; *Bunker Hill Aurora,* 29 January 1842, p. 3; *Boston Post,* 4 February 1842, p.2; "Draft of Amendments," in MA, original documents relating to Acts of 1842, ch. 76. A map showing one of the proposed dividing lines is in MA, maps and plans, 3d series, vol. 45, p.8. For the objections of the disappointed Neck Village residents see *Bunker Hill Aurora,* 12 March 1842, pp. 2–3. Cf. the petition of Edward Cutter and others to be reunited to Charlestown, dated 7 January 1843, in Records of the Selectmen of the Town of Somerville, I, 24 (in the vault of the City Clerk's Office, Somerville). The election of Bowman was recorded in STR 1:16.

64. *Bunker Hill Aurora,* 28 January 1843, p. 3.

65. CTR, March 1842. James D. Green (1798–1882) was born in Malden, was graduated from Harvard in 1817 but did not enter the pastorate until 1828, when he

was ordained at Lynn. He arrived in Cambridge in 1830 and served ten years as minister of the Third Congregational Church. Gozzaldi, *Supplement, 326;* Paige, 322; Gilman, *Cambridge,* 62–63.

66. Petition of Jacob H. Bates and others, in MA, documents of 1843–1844, bundle 11577.

Joseph Story (1779–1845) was justice of the U.S. Supreme Court from 1811 until his death and Dane Professor of Law at Harvard, 1828–45. Arthur E. Sutherland, *The Law at Harvard: A History of Ideas and Men, 1817–1967* (Cambridge, 1967), 95–100.

Simon Greenleaf (1783–1853) became Royall Professor of Law in 1833 and Dane Professor in 1846. He was an author of texts and, after Story's death, the most important figure in the Harvard Law School. Sutherland, 122–23, 137, 149–50; Hurd, 1:153; Conklin, 1:200–201.

Jacob Hill Bates (b. 1788) was a painter, son of a Revolutionary soldier, shareholder in the Old Cambridge markethouse, assessor, and selectman. Gozzaldi, *Supplement,* 35; Paige, 231 n, 446, 468.

The career of George Coolidge is obscure. He was a carriage painter resident on North Avenue and appears on a voter list for 1836.

67. Based on a comparison of the Bates and Wyeth petitions from Cambridge with the Hawkins petition from Somerville.

68. Remonstrances of Isaac Livermore, Nathaniel Watson, and Rev. W. S. Stearns, MA, documents of 1843 and 1844, 11577/8, 9, 12–13; Resolves of the Town of Cambridge against the Division of Said Town, ibid., 11577/11; Petition of Morill Wyman and others; Remonstrances of Sidney Willard, John L. Hobbs, and Curtis Davis, MA, documents of 1843 and 1844, 11577/14, 16–18; Preamble and Resolves adopted by the Town of Cambridge, against a Division . . . , ibid., 11577/10.

69. *Report of the Committee appointed to consider the Expediency of Consolidating Certain Boards of Officers of the Town of Cambridge* (Boston, 1846), 6–7.

70. *Annual Report of the Receipts and Expenditures of the Town of Cambmridge* (Boston, 1846), 6–7.

71. On the struggle for a city charter for Boston, see the chapters by James M. Bugbee and John D. Long in Winsor, 3:217–301; Robert A. McCaughey, "From Town to City: Boston in the 1820s," *Political Science Quarterly* 88 (1973): 191–213; Quincy, *Municipal History,* 16–17, 22–33, 40–41, 83–85, 115–16; Amory, *Sullivan,* 1:147, 264–66, 2:58–59, 114–16. Frederick Hathaway Chase, *Lemuel Shaw: Chief Justice of the Supreme Judicial Court of Massachusetts, 1830–1860* (Boston, 1918), 84–85; Brown, *Faneuil Hall,* 179.

72. Paige, 244–46; "Remonstrance of Samuel P. P. Fay and others," MA, original documents relating to Acts of 1846, ch. 109.

73. (Columbus Tyler), Report of a Committee on a Fire Engine, 28 April 1845, STCP.

74. Ibid.

75. Joseph H. Beale, "The History of Local Government in Cambridge," CHS, *Pub.* 22 (January 1932): 17–28.

76. *Cambridge Chronicle,* 7 May 1846 and 1 March 1848.

Chapter 5
Commutation

1. David Ward, *Cities and Immigrants: A Geography of Change in Nineteenth Century America* (New York, 1971), 87–93; Handlin, *Boston's Immigrants,* 101–9.

2. *Boston Directory* (1846), 36.

3. Kennedy, "Commuter Services," 159–60; Charles Hale, Railroad Journal, 27 May 1844, p. 21. Hale MSS, Box 17, folder labeled "Railroad Journal 1843–1849"; Fifteenth Annual Report of the Boston and Lowell Railroad Corporation, *Massachusetts Senate Documents, 1846,* No. 21, 14–15; Fourteenth Annual Report of the Boston and Worcester Railroad Corporation, ibid., 27; Nineteenth Annual Report of the Boston and Lowell Railroad Corporation, ibid., *1849,* Nos. 7–8.

4. *Boston Directory* (1849–50), 43.

5. Quotation from an advertisement for the sale of parts of the Craigie estate in Cambridge, *Boston Post,* 24 June 1850, p. 3. The same issue contained 31 advertisements for real estate, 18 of which offered property outside of Boston.

6. *Boston Directory* (1849–50), 55.

7. Inaugural address, in *Inaugural Addresses of the Mayors,* 353.

8. All nineteenth-century directories listed more well-to-do citizens than poor ones. Working-class persons who "commuted" to work on foot from nearby areas of Charlestown and East Cambridge were therefore less likely to appear than riders of public transportation. Moreover, the directories were intended to be guides to the business comunity of the city. Until the 1840s, Boston's directories listed only the senior partners in each large firm, probably on the assumption that prospective customers and clients would have no interest in the lower-ranking personnel. Information on suburban places of residence was even less necessary, and only in 1846 did the directories list such addresses systematically. For these reasons, all the directories were better guides to "true" commuters than to those who walked, and later directories, whose listings reflected an expanded view of the purposes of such volumes, were probably better guides to all types of commuting than were the ones published in earlier years. These considerations should be borne in mind when evaluating the trends evident in the statistics presented here. On directories in general, see Peter R. Knights, *The Plain People of Boston, 1830–1860: A Study in City Growth* (New York, 1971), Appendix A.

9. Gozzaldi, *History of Cambridge, Supplement,* 661–62; *Boston Directory* (1851), 218–19.

10. Vincent Y. Bowditch, *Life and Correspondence of Henry Ingersoll Bowditch* (Boston, 1902), 1:236–40, 246.

11. Handlin, *Boston's Immigrants,* 63.

12. Samples of every tenth listing in the Cambridge and Somerville directories for 1870 and 1880 indicate 15–20 percent Boston-employed for both years.

13. Samuels and Kimball, 618, 627; Hurd, 3:775–77.

14. Robert F. Lucid, ed, *The Journal of Richard Henry Dana, Jr.* (Cambridge, 1968), 1:64, 101, 2:461, 483.

15. Ibid., 2:536.

16. Ibid., 1:393.

17. Hayward, *Gazetteer,* 193.

18. Brooks, *Medford,* 352.

19. *Daily Evening Transcript,* 2 January 1954, p. 3. For details, see Binford, "Influence," 240–41.

20. Hurd, 3:189; *Boston Directory* (1846), 39; *Bi-Centennial Book of Malden,* 224–25; *Boston Post,* 24 June 1850, p. 5; *Cambridge Chronicle,* 12 June 1852, p. 2; 21 October 1854, p. 2; *Charlestown Directory* (1848), advertisement on back cover.

21. Schedules were printed in the *Boston Directory* (1849–50), 43–44, 47. Cf. Kennedy, "Computer Services," 158–62; Kirkland, 1:345. See also schedules and comments in: *Daily Evening Transcript,* 2 January 1845, p. 1; 19 March 1845, pp. 2, 3; 8 April 1845, p. 1; 1 November 1845, p. 1; *Boston Post, 24 June 1850, p. 7; Boston Directory* (1849–50), 43–44.

22. Fourteenth Annual Report of the Boston and Lowell Railroad, *Massachusetts Senate Documents, 1845,* No. 21. Fifteenth Annual Report 1844, p. 1.

23. Brooks, 158; First Annual Report of the Lexington and West Cambridge Railroad Corporation,*Massachusetts Senate Documents, 1846,* No. 21, 71–72; Second Annual Report, ibid., *1847,* No. 30, 60–61; Fifth Annual Report . . . Fitchburg Railroad, ibid., 51–52; Fifteenth Annual Report . . . Boston and Worcester, ibid., *1847,* No. 30, 18–20.

24. *Daily Evening Transcript,* 2 Jaunary 1845, p. 1; 3 March 1845, p. 1; 11 April 1845, p. 1; 9 May 1845, p. 3; 2 June 1845, p. 1; 1 November 1845, p. 1.

25. *DAB* 8:324–25; Lois Lilley Howe, "Dr Estes Howe, a Citizen of Cambridge," CHS, *Pub.* 25 (1938–39): 123–32.

26. Robert W. Lovett, "The Harvard Branch Railroad, 1849–1855," CHS, *Pub.* 38 (1959–60): 24–40; Gozzaldi, *Supplement,* 363, 800; *Bunker Hill Aurora,* 26 February 1842, p. 2; Brooks, 55.

27. Lovett, 41–50; *Cambridge Directory* (1850), xxii.

28. Kennedy, 162–65.

29. Fifteenth Annual Report . . . Boston and Maine, *Massachusetts Senate Documents, 1850,* No. 30, 19, 24; Nineteenth Annual Report . . . Boston and Lowell, ibid., 14–15; Eighth Annual Report . . . Fitchburg, ibid., 81–82.

30. Norton, "Reminiscences," 21–22; Taylor, "Beginnings," 47.

31. *Cambridge Chronicle,* 31 January 1851, p. 2; 15 November 1851, p. 2.

32. *Cambridge Directory* (1849), 4.

33. Kirkland, 1:102; Thomas Tredgold, *A Practical Treatise on Rail-Roads and Carriages* (London, 1825), 64–92, 144–52. Cf. Thomas Grahame, *A Treatise on In-*

ternal Intercourse and Communication in Civilised States, and particularly in Great Britain (London, 1834), vi–ix, 36–39, 115–17, 126, 153–55.

34. Kirkland, 1:100–101, 108; *Daily Evening Transcript,* 5 June 1835, p. 2; 27 May 1842, p. 3; Twelfth Annual Report . . . Boston and Providence, *Massachusetts Senate Documents, 1844,* No. 19, 59; Kennedy, 157–58; Taylor, "The Beginnings of Mass Transportation in Urban America," Part 2: 34, 38–39.

35. Taylor 2:43; Winsor, 4:63 n; *Cambridge Chronicle,* 12 March 1853, pp. 1–2; 19 March 1853, p. 2; 7 May 1853, p. 2.

36. Howe, "Dr. Estes Howe," 130–32; and biographical file data.

37. Samuels and Kimball, 501.

38. Fisk and his partner David Kimball are listed in Boston directories throughout the late 1840s and early 1850s. Richard Downing was one of the four omnibus proprietors of 1848 and participated in the agreement with the Boston lines to divide the available territory in 1854. Peter Hubbell was listed in Cambridge business directories as a partner in a Fresh Pond brickyard but never appeared in the directory listings of residents or on tax or voting lists. See CHCS 5:28–29.

39. Based on a comparison of street railway promoters with the separatist petitions.

40. Hurd, 3:190, 588, 766, *Cambridge Chronicle,* 21 August 1858, p. 2; 28 August 1858, p. 2; 6 November 1858, p. 2; *Boston Directory* (1861), 583–84.

41. Taylor, "Beginnings," part 2, 50; *Cambridge Chronicle,* 20 June 1857, p. 2.

Chapter 6
Suburban Society:
Goals and Boundaries

1. Livermore, 39–43; Samuels and Kimball, 457; Gozzaldi, *Supplement,* 679; *Cambridge Directory* (1849), 14.

2. De Witt, *Statistical Information,* 293, 340; CHCS 3:113–14.

3. Gilman, 303–4; O'Malley, 131–32.

4. This labor force analysis is based on an analysis of interval samples of households in Cambridge and Somerville census schedules for 1850 and 1860, linked to directory listings. The business directory listings, appearing as supplements to the main directory, were obviously incomplete and biased. But a house-by-house examination of the census schedules, undertaken while reconstructing routes of census takers (see note 8 below), confirms the dispersion of skilled and service jobs. Only a systematic analysis of all census and directory entries would provide conclusive proof, and such an analysis was beyond the scope of this study.

5. The 1860 sample data indicate 3 percent for Somerville, less than 1 percent for Cambridge.

6. The later parts of Peter Hubbell's career are discussed in CHCS 5:28–29. The earlier parts have been filled in with the aid of census schedules, Cambridge and Charlestown directors, and the Middlesex deeds. I am indebted to Arthur J. Krim of

the Cambridge Historical Commission for allowing me to read his unpublished manuscript on the northern Cambridge brickyards.

7. For the pattern of geographical change see CHCS 5, chap. 1. The results were reflected in the three most detailed maps of the Cambridge-Somerville area in the 1850s: The Walling map of Cambridge (1854), the Draper map of Somerville (1851), and an anonymous map in the Somerville Historical Society (c. 1857).

8. The enumerators' routes in Cambridge and Somerville were reconstructed with the aid of directories and contemporary maps. See Appendix.

9. The following discussion is based on an analysis of Somerville and Cambridge tax rolls for 1840, 1850, and 1860. The original assessment books are stored in the Somerville City Hall and in the Cambridge Public Library (on microfilm). Beginning in the late 1840s, Somerville published the list of assessments as part of its annual reports. In Cambridge, the annual city directories included a list of tax payments for all who paid more than $25.00.

The analysis below omits Harvard College and the Boston & Lowell Railroad. These corporations consistently ranked at or near the top of the taxpayer hierarchy because of their landholdings, but they did not play a role in the suburban communities comparable to those of individual landowners, entrepreneurs, or manufacturing and commercial firms.

10. In both 1850 and 1860 this group included about 2 percent of all male taxpayers. The figures omit women, estates, trusts, and corporate taxpayers. The analysis employs both real and personal property because assessors' records sometimes make it difficult to distinguish the two and because the census figures for real property are incomplete and untrustworthy. The $20,000 threshold is arbitrary but in line with categories adopted by both contemporary and scholarly discussions of wealth distribution. A. Forbes, for example, adopted a threshold of $50,000 for inclusion in his *Rich Men of Massachusetts* (Boston, 1851). For a discussion of the problems of wealth ranking, see Michael Katz, *The People of Hamilton, Canada West: Family, and Class in a Nineteenth Century City* (Cambridge, 1975), 24–26 and accompanying notes.

11. Twenty-three of the 72 were employed in Cambridge and Somerville. Six more had workplaces in both Boston and the suburbs, usually because they maintained city sales outlets for suburban manufactures.

12. On speculative railroad villages in the inner suburbs, see Goss, 84, 107, 116; Hurd, 1:361; Brooks, 55.

13. *Cambridge Chronicle,* 7 May, 1853, 19 March 1853, 29 March 1856, 21 June 1856, 26 September 1857.

14. Early complaints about the streetcars: ibid., 22 March 1851, 13 November 1852, 14 May 1853, 14, 28 October 1854, 12 September 1857.

15. Praise for and criticism of the utilities: ibid., 22 March 1851, 13 November 1852, 14 May 1853, 14, 28 October 1854, 12 September 1857.

16. Sam Warner defined the elements of the postwar process in *Streetcar Suburbs.*

17. CHCS 2:24–29; O'Malley, 134; Hayward, *Gazetteer,* 271; CHCS 5:39–41.

18. On Henry Potter: CHCS 5:20, 41–42.

19. Lists of buildings and comments on the value of residential construction: *Cambridge Chronicle*, 1 March 1851, 19 July 1856, 16 May 1857; *Annual Report of the Selectmen of the Town of Somerville . . . 1856* (Boston, 1856).

20. Perceptive and provocative discussions of the modern meaning of neighborhood are Hunter, *Symbolic Communities;* Suttles, *The Social Construction of Communities,* esp. chaps. 1–3; and Constance Perin, *Everything in Its Place: Social Order and Land Use in America* (Princeton, 1977).

21. The technique of cognitive mapping is discussed and exemplified in Kevin Lynch, *The Image of the City* (Cambridge, 1966), Appendixes B, C, and passim; and Charles Tilly, ed., *An Urban World* (Boston, 1974), 9–14.

22. Jenette Teele, "Neighborhood Sketch No. 1" (c. 1836) SHS, *Historic Leaves* 1 (1902): 31–32; Harriet A. Adams, "Neighborhood Sketch No. 7, Winter Hill" (c. 1840), ibid. 3 (1904): 22–24; Aaron Sargent, "Neighborhood Sketch No. 2, the Winter Hill Road in 1842," ibid. 1 (1902): 19–22; Charles D. Elliott, "Union Square and Its Neighborhood about the Year 1846," ibid. 6 (1907): 5–16; John F. Ayer, "Neighborhood Sketch No. 6, Medford and Walnut Streets" (c. 1850), ibid. 2 (1903): 42–46.

23. Kathryn Kish Sklar, *Catharine Beecher: A Study in American Domesticity* (New Haven, 1973), esp. chap. 11; Clifford Clark, "Domestic Architecture as an Index to Social History: The Romantic Revival and the Cult of Domesticity in America, 1840–1870," *Journal of Inderdisciplinary History* 7 (1976): 33–56; David Handlin, *The American Home: Architecture and Society, 1815–1915* (Boston, 1979), chap. 1; Gwendolyn Wright, *Moralism and the Model Home: Domestic Architecture and Cultural Conflict in Chicago, 1873–1913* (Chicago, 1980), chap. 1.

24. *Cambridge Chronicle*, 17 January 1852, 10 February 1855.

25. Ibid., 12 December 1853, 10 February, 4 August 1855, 8 October 1859.

26. George Whitaker, *Historical Address at the Semi-Centennial Anniversary of the First Methodist Episcopal Church, Somerville* (n.p., 1908), 6–8; Hurd, 1:63; Paige, 328–29, 331–34.

27. *A Brief History of the Perkins Street Baptist Church, Somerville* (Somerville, 1887), 6–7.

28. Pope, *Address . . . 1851,* 5, 6, 9, 22.

29. Michael Katz, *The Irony of Early School Reform: Educational Innovation in Mid-Nineteenth Century Massachusetts* (Cambridge, 1968), 42–43.

30. Cambridge *Annual Report of the School Committee . . . 1845* (Boston, 1845), 11–12, 16–20. (Hereafter, Cambridge School Committee reports will be cited: CSchR, date.) CSchR, 1847, 64–65; CSchR, 1848, 86.

31. CSchR, 1848, 81, 85–86. Green was an early advocate of compulsory education. In 1852, Mann and others used arguments similar to his in their successful campaign for legislation making Massachusetts the first state to require primary schooling for all children.

32. Report on the Burning of the Prescott School, STCP, 1856; Report of a Committee on the Milk Row School House, ibid., 1843; Report on the Prescott School,

ibid., 1853. Somerville's town records contain minutes of long arguments over school location in 1843 and 1853. Similar sentiments found expression in Cambridge: CSchR, 1846, 15–16; 1854, 17; 1856, 102–3; 1857, 101–2.

33. CSchR, 1856, 98, 102–3.

34. Arguments for public parks and donations of land for the purpose: *Cambridge Chronicle,* 17 December 1853, 10 February, 4 August 1855, 11 April 1857; *The Mayor's Address at the Organization of the City Government . . . 1857,* 12–13.

35. Letter from "A," *Cambridge Chronicle,* 10 October 1857. Ford's shift: ibid., 12 December 1853, 14 October 1854, 4 August 1855, 22 October 1859.

36. CSchR, 1849, 85; 1854, 9–11; 1857, 96; 1858, 112. Bennett, Minority Report of the School Committee, STCP, 1846; (Tyler) Report of a Committee on a Fire Engine, ibid., 1843.

37. *Cambridge Chronicle,* 9 September 1854, 19 July 1856.

38. Edmund Tufts's first Somerville directory, compiled in 1850 for the following year, did not have a successor until 1870. Thomas Work began advertising his services as a newsdealer in the *Cambridge Directory* for 1851. On shopping: *Cambridge Chronicle,* 19 June 1852.

39. The *Chronicle* reported regularly and at length on crime and disease in Boston and elsewhere. See *Chronicle* 4 March 1847, 26 March 1853, 17 June, 22, 29 July, 21 October 1854. Useful analyses of Jacksonian urban disorder are Roger Lane, *Policing the City: Boston, 1822–1887* (New York, 1971), chaps. 3–5; David Montgomery, "The Shuttle and the Cross: Weavers and Artisians in the Kensington Riots of 1844," *Journal of Social History* 5 (1972): 411–46; and the essays by Michael Feldberg, Bruce Laurie, and David R. Johnson in Davis and Haller, eds., *The Peoples of Philadelphia.*

Some historians have argued that the outbreaks of disease and disorder prevalent in the 1840s and 1850s heightened middle-class awareness of urban poverty. See Katz, *Irony,* 170–77; Carol Smith Rosenberg, *Religion and the Rise of the American City: The New York City Mission Movement, 1812–1870* (Ithaca, N.Y., 1971), chap. 6.

40. *Cambridge Chronicle,* 4 March 1847, 28 May, 4, 13 June 1846, 2 March 1848, 27 December 1851, 28 August, 16 October 1852. On Victorian America's fear of confidence men in general, see Karen Halttunen, *Confidence Men and Painted Women: A Study of Middle-Class Culture in America, 1830–1870* (New Haven, 1983).

41. On urban fears, see Boyer, *Urban Masses and Moral Order;* Feldberg, "Urbanization as a Cause of Violence"; and Laurie, *Working People.*

42. *Mayor's Address . . . 1846,* 14. For an account of the Philadelphia events that provoked his alarm, see Bruce Laurie, "Fire Companies and Gangs in Southwark, the 1840s," in Davis and Haller, eds., *Peoples of Philadelphia,* 71–87.

43. *Cambridge Chronicle,* 8, 15, 22 March 1851.

44. Ibid., 15 March 1851.

45. Ibid., 28 August 1852, 12 April, 10 May 1856.

46. Ibid., 18 September 1852, 12 May 1855, 17 October 1857, 3 November 1860.

47. Letter from "H" in ibid., 28 August 1852; Quincy, *Municipal History,* 153–54. Commentaries on suburban arson: CSR, 2, 21 September 1835, 31 October 1839, 28 January 1840; *Bunker Hill Aurora,* 2, 21 March 1840, 23 March 1842; manuscript records of the Somerville selectmen, in the City Vault, 1:261, 508 (hereafter cited as SSR).

48. The *Chronicle* and its correspondents defended firemen against any hints that they might set fires: 14, 28 August, 18 September 1852.

49. Ibid., 20 May, 11, 18 November 1854, 23 February 1856, 10 October 1857; Report on the Burning of the Prescott School, STCP, 1856.

50. *Cambridge Chronicle,* 28 August, 18 September 1852; SSR, 1:460, 2:66, 189.

51. J. R. Lowell to G. B. Loring, 6 July 1842, in *Letters of James Russell Lowell,* ed. Charles Eliot Norton (New York, 1894), 1:68–69. Temperance petitions from Bennett and others are in STCP, 1843, 1847–49, 1858. See also STR, 1:181–82, 243; and Bennett's angry letter to the selectmen, dated 31 May 1843, also in STR.

52. *Cambridge Chronicle,* 18 June 1846, 20 March 1852, 8 March 1851. Lists of temperance speakers and committee members appeared frequently in the *Chronicle.* These and the petitions in STCP form the basis for my analysis of temperance support.

53. *Cambridge Chronicle,* 31 July 1852. On the Maine law enthusiasm, see Clifford S. Griffin, *Their Brother's Keepers: Moral Stewardship in the United States, 1800–1865* (New Brunswick, 1960) 147–51.

54. *Cambridge Chronicle,* 7, 14, 28 August, 4, 11, 18, 25 September 1852; Dana, *Journal,* 2: 507, 509.

55. *Cambridge Chronicle,* 18 September, 2 October, 6 November 1852, 19 March, 14 May 1853, 8 February, 28 October, 11 November 1854, 12 May, 8 September, 13 October 1855; *Commonwealth v. Zachariah B. Porter,* 4 Gray 261 (70 Mass. Sup. Ct. Rept. 423), 1855.

56. *Cambridge Chronicle,* 15 August, 3 October 1857.

57. Ibid., 18 September 1852, 31 July 1853, 22 January 1853, 24 December 1853.

58. Ibid., 25 September 1854.

Chapter 7
Suburban Government:
Setting, Roles,
and Structure

1. Most historians of American cities have ignored the political crisis of the 1850s, choosing instead to fit events of this decade into long-term interpretations that stress the decline of patrician elites or the persistence of class-stratified power. Examples of the former are: Robert Dahl, *Who Governs? Democracy and Power in an American City* (New Haven, 1961) and Warner, *The Private City,* chap. 5; and of the latter: Edward Pessen, "Who Governed the Nation's Cities in the Era of the Common Man?"

Political Science Quarterly 87 (1972): 591–614. A few historians of politics have produced useful city case studies, but they have generally dealt with local issues only as influences on party evolution, not as ingredients in the shaping of local political culture. Thus for Michael Holt, personality conflicts and hostility toward railroads in Pittsburgh were simply grist for the mills of Democratic and Republican party managers, whose eyes were on the mayoralty and the state house. See Michael Holt, *Forging a Majority: The Formation of the Republican Party in Pittsburgh, 1848–1860* (New Haven, 1969). An exception to these generalizations is Roger Lotchin's study of San Francisco, in which Know-Nothing groups and vigilance committees are treated not only as influences on party formation but as agencies for the coalescence of community loyalties: Lotchin, *San Francisco, 1846–1856: From Hamlet to City* (New York, 1974), chaps. 8 and 9. A thorough and incisive discussion of the literature on community politics is David C. Hammack, "Power in the Cities and Towns of the United States," *American Historical Review* 83 (1978): 323–49.

2. Reassertions of the importance of meetings, nonpartisanship, and voluntarism: *Cambridge Chronicle,* 8, 15 March 1851, 17 January, 21 February, 6 March 1852; G. W. Warren, *Address* (as first mayor of Charlestown), 26 April 1847 (Charlestown, 1847), 19–21.

3. *Cambridge Chronicle,* 7 March 1850, 1, 8 March 1851, 28 February 1852.

4. Ibid., 22 March 1851.

5. Ibid., 7 March 1850.

6. Ibid., 8, 15 March 1851.

7. Ibid., 15 March 1851, 17 January 1852.

8. Ibid. 28 February 1852.

9. Arthur B. Darling, *Political Changes in Massachusetts, 1824–1848* (New Haven, 1925), though dated, remains the best outline of state politics in the Jacksonian period. Later scholars have revised some of his ideas concerning shifts in voting and cast new light on the period of turmoil after 1848. Synthetic accounts which draw on this new research and attempt to place the Massachusetts experience in a national context of party realignment are: Eric Foner, *Free soil, Free Labor, Free Men: The Ideology of the Republican Party before the Civil War* (New York, 1970), esp. 243, 250–53; Richard P. McCormick, *The Second American Party System: Party Formation in the Jacksonian Era* (Chapel Hill, N. C., 1966); Michael F. Holt, *The Political Crisis of the 1850s* (New York, 1978), chap. 5. David M. Potter, *The Impending Crisis, 1848–1860* (New York, 1976), chap. 10. Those interested in Massachusetts politics specifically should also consult the detailed studies listed in note 10.

10. Recent analyses of voting, some by Michael Holt's students, have shown that the issues and the sequence of events in Massachusetts politics were in some ways different from the national pattern. The following account is based on: Dale Baum, "Know-Nothingism and the Republican Majority in Massachusetts: The Political realignment of the 1850s," *Journal of American History* 64 (1978): 959–86; Kevin Sweeney, "Rum, Romanism, Representation, and Reform: Coalition Politics in Massachusetts, 1847–1853," *Civil War History* 22 (1976): 116–37; Michael Brunet, "The Secret Ballot Issue in Massachusetts Politics from 1851 to 1853," *New England*

Quarterly 25 (1952): 354–59; Martin B. Duberman, "Some Notes on the Beginning of the Republican Party in Massachusetts," ibid. 34 (1961): 364–70.

11. *Cambridge Chronicle,* 4 March 1854. Here and elsewhere, statements about the composition of local slates are based on comparison of tickets published in the *Chronicle* with information in the biographical file.

12. Ibid., 2, 9 December 1854.

13. Based on lists of officeholders in Paige, 459 ff. Michael Holt has argued that Know-Nothingism was "overwhelmingly a movement of the laboring and middle classes," who revolted against both Catholics and incumbent political leaders and who not only opened a path for the Republican party but supplied a number of its early candidates for state and local office; Holt, "The Politics of Impatience: The Origins of Know-Nothingism," *Journal of American History* 60 (1973): 309–31. But Baum has demonstrated that in Massachusetts there was little continuity between voting for Know-Nothingism and voting for Republicans and that Republicanism was in part a revolt against nativism; Baum, "Know-Nothingism and the Republican Majority," 965–72. The Cambridge experience supports Baum's viewpoint. Know-Nothingism in Cambridge drew support, briefly, from all five wards, but those nominated for local office after 1855 were not those who had been put forward by the Know-Nothings, and by 1857 the only remaining sources of strong nativist voting (30 percent of ward totals) were northern Cambridge and East Cambridge, where Protestant native-born workers lived in close juxtaposition to large immigrant settlements.

14. *Cambridge Chronicle,* 3, 24 February, 10, 17, 24 March, 14 April 1855.

15. Names of the Whig committeemen: *Cambridge Chronicle,* 3 November 1855.

16. Warner, *Private City,* 152–53; Kenneth Jackson, "Metropolitan Government versus Suburban Autonomy," 442–62. On the history of annexation procedures in general, see Jon C. Teaford *City and Suburb,* esp. chap. 3.

17. E. H. Derby, "Commercial Cities and Towns of the U.S.—No. XII—Boston," *Hunt's Merchant's Magazine and Commercial Review* 13 (November 1850): 483–97; *Report of the Committee in Favor of the Union of Boston and Roxbury* (Boston, 1851), 20–22; *Cambridge Chronicle,* 9 September 1854.

18. *Cambridge Chronicle,* 20 March 1852, 26 March 1853, 29 April, 7, 21 October 1854.

19. Benjamin F. Butler, *Autobiographical and Personal Reminiscences* (Boston, 1892), 1000–1002.

20. As a basis for the following analysis, I have sorted and dated all of the documents in STCP for the period 1842–60 and indexed all the signatures on petitions. I then traced all petitions and memoranda through the relevant entries in the town and selectmen's records.

21. [Luther V. Bell] "Report of the Somerville School Committee, 1844," MS, STCP, 1844; *Cambridge Chronicle,* 10 February 1855, CSchR, 1847, 56–57, 64; 1859, 127–29.

22. *Mayor's Address . . . 1846* (Cambridge), 11; ibid., 1857, 3, 6–7. Samuels and Kimball, 90; Petitions of S. E. Brackett et al., 17 February 1849; Fitch Cutter et al., March 1852, STCP.

23. Samuels and Kimball, 121; SSR 2:190; STR 2:46, 49–51. On Boston's campaign for a water supply, see Nelson Manfred Blake, *Water for the Cities: A History of the Urban Water Supply Problem in the United States* (Syracuse, 1956), chaps. 9 and 10; *Mayor's Address . . . 1850*, 9–10.

24. Given a known persistence rate of at most 40 percent for both decades, a minimum of 6000 adult males lived in Somerville at some time between 1840 and 1860. Only 810 men signed petitions.

25. *Cambridge Chronicle,* 27 March 1852.

26. Drafts of Somerville By-Laws, STCP, 1855. Requests for nuisance abatement: letter from A. Houghton to the Somerville selectmen, 3 November 1858; record of Board of Health notices dated 4 June, 16 July 1859, STCP, 1858, 1859; *Cambridge Chronicle,* 11 November 1854, 30 April 1859. See also the letter from "A. B.," ibid., 4 December 1852.

27. Ibid., 26 September, 24 October 1857.

28. Ibid., 12, 26 September, 14, 21 November, 5, 12 December 1857.

29. CSchR, 1846, 14–15; 1859, 122.

30. *Annual Report of the Selectmen of the Town of Somerville . . . 1856,* 11.

31. MS Report of the Somerville School Committee, 1846, STCP; CSchR, 1846, 5–7, 10; 1861, 125; *Annual Reports . . . Somerville, 1860.*

32. In 1855, out of a total Somerville town debt of $21,674, $5,000 represented a loan from the Middlesex Institution for Savings. The rest of the debt was owed to a few wealthy citizens. *Annual Report of the Selectmen . . . 1856,* 23; (Cambridge) *Mayor's Address . . . 1859,* 5.

33. CSchR, 1851, 18–19; April 1854, 13–14; 1859, 128–29.

34. *Cambridge Chronicle,* 2 March 1848.

35. Ibid., 8 December 1855, 6 December 1856, 12 December 1857.

36. Ibid., 22 December 1855; (Cambridge) *Mayor's Address . . . 1857.* The controversy over changing the boundaries may be traced through the *Chronicle,* 22 August, 12 September, 24 October 1857.

37. *Mayor's Address . . . 1859,* 12.

38. *Annual Report of the Selectmen . . . 1857,* 12–13.

39. Somerville selectmen's efforts to cope with overwork: STR 1:57, and passim.

40. *Cambridge Chronicle,* 14, 21 March, 13 June 1857; (Cambridge) *Mayor's Address . . . 1856,* 10–11.

41. David Brion Davis has emphasized an underlying theme of revolt against presumed conspiracies and irresponsible uses of power in a variety of political movements of the 1850s—anti-corporate, anti-Catholic, and anti-slave power (*The Slave Power Conspiracy and the Paranoid Style* [Baton Rouge, 1969]). Michael Holt suggests that this anti-conspiratorial movement fueled anti-railroad sentiment in many communities and that Know-Nothings, Democrats, and Republicans all tried to exploit it at different times and in different locales ("The Politics of Impatience" and *Forging a Majority*). No one, however, has examined the influence of anti-conspiratorial thinking in movements against horse railroads or municipal utilities.

42. "Memorial" in STCP, 1848; *Cambridge Chronicle*, 10, 31 March 1855; STR 1:478–79.

43. *Cambridge Chronicle*, 1 December 1855, 29 March 1856.

44. Ibid., 5 April 1856, 28 March 1857.

45. Ibid., 3 May 1856.

46. (Cambridge) *Mayor's Address . . . 1855*, 5.

47. *Cambridge Chronicle*, 19 March, 30 April 1859; see also the discussion throughout August 1857.

48. Ibid., 6 November 1858.

49. Ibid., 12, 19 March, 30 April 1859.

50. Bennett, Minority Report . . . 1846, STCP, 1846. See also his economizing moves recorded in STR 1:180–85.

51. (Cambridge) *Mayor's Address . . . 1857*, 3–5; SSR 2:166, 173; STR 2:21.

52. (Cambridge) *Mayor's Address . . . 1859*, 9; *Cambridge Chronicle* 3 December 1859.

53. *Cambridge Chronicle*, 10 December 1859.

54. (Cambridge) *Mayor's Address . . . 1860*, 4–6, 20–21.

55. Ibid., 21.

56. Ibid., 7–15.

57. *Cambridge Chronicle*, 27 July 1861.

58. Livermore, *Some Bridges*, 43.

Epilogue: Civil War and Suburban Identity

1. Conklin, 1:125, 135; Samuels and Kimball, 105–17.

2. (Cambridge) *Mayor's Address . . . 1862*, passim; ibid., *1865*, 6.

3. Hurd, 3:818; Conklin, 2:415–16; Watkins, 30, 36, 38.

4. Hurd, 1:359, 468, 2:494; Goss, 66–67.

5. CHCS 5:29–31, 42–43; Samuels and Kimball, 452–53.

6. (Cambridge) *Mayor's Address . . . 1863*, 12–14.

7. Boston-employed population as a proportion of all listings in the *Cambridge Directory*, estimated from one-in-ten sample data: 1861: 22%; 1871: 18%; 1881: 16%. On expanded streetcar scheduling, see the *Cambridge Directory*, 1881, 347, and similar data in other directories of the period.

8. CHCS 5:41–43. Subdivisions are mapped in fig. 55 of the same volume.

9. Somerville subdivisions have been traced through the records of transactions in Middlesex deeds and the plats filed in the County Registrar's Office, East Cambridge. See especially the transactions involving the Vinal, Houghton, and Bennett families.

10. Conklin 1:135.

11. (Cambridge) *Mayor's Address . . . 1863*, 7.

12. Ibid., 1862, 8–11; 1865, 17.

13. Ibid., 8–10; Hurd, 1:193–94, 217–18, 3:595–96; Hunnewell, 49–50; Conklin, 2:383, 460; Brooks, *Medford,* 333–37.

14. Samuels and Kimball, 134–37; Susan Wade Peabody, *Historical Study of Legislation Regarding Public Health in the States of New York and Massachusetts* (Chicago, 1909), 55–56.

15. *Annual Report of the Selectmen of the Town of Somerville . . . 1869,* 13.

16. Warner, *Streetcar Suburbs,* chap. 6.

17. Hurd, 3:737.

18. Warner, *Streetcar Suburbs,* 41–42, 111–13, 124, 163–65.

19. Walker, "The Transformation of Urban Structure," 192.

Bibliography

Manuscript Collections

Bell Family Papers. 30 File Drawers, Bell Room, National Geographic Society.
Burlingame Family Papers. 5 Boxes. Manuscript Division, Library of Congress.
Hale Family Papers. 20 Binders and 19 Boxes. Manuscript Division, Library of Congress.
John Gorham Palfrey Papers. Houghton Library, Harvard University.

Newspapers and Directories

Boston Daily Evening Transcript, 1835–60.
[Stimpson's] *Boston Directory*. Boston, 1830–45.
[Adam's] *Boston Directory*. Boston, 1846–
Boston Post, 1840–60.
Bunker Hill Aurora, 1827–50.
The Cambridge Almanac and Business Directory for the Year 1847. Boston, 1847.
Cambridge Chronicle, 1846–60.
The Cambridge Directory. Cambridge, 1848–
Charlestown Directory. Charlestown, 1831, 1836, 1848.
Malden Messenger, 1856–60.
The Somerville Directory. Somerville, 1851.

Government Records and Serial Publications

Federal Census Materials

MS Schedules of the Fourth, Fifth, Sixth, Seventh, and Eighth Censuses. Microfilm, U.S. National Archives.
Sixth Census, or Enumeration of the Population. Washington, 1840.

281

Seventh Census. Washington, 1851.
Tenth Census. Washington, 1881–88.

Charlestown and Somerville

Annual Report of the Trustees of the Charlestown Free Schools [1801–38].
Charlestown, 1874.
Annual Report of the Charlestown Free Schools. Charlestown, 1839–60.
Annual Statement of the Expenses of Charlestown. Charlestown, 1820–60.
Charlestown Town Records, vols. 12–14. MSS on microfilm, Boston Public Library.
Records of the Town of Somerville, 1842–70. 2 MS vols. in the vault, City Clerk's
Office, Somerville.
Records of the Selectmen of the Town of Somerville, 1842–70. MS vol. in the vault,
City Clerk's Office, Somerville.
Reports of the Selectmen and Treasurer of the Town of Somerville. Somerville,
1845–70.
Somerville Town and City Papers. MS. 2 boxes in the vault, City Clerk's Office,
Somerville.
Uncataloged Maps and Papers. Somerville Historical Society, Somerville.

Cambridge

Annual Report of the Receipts and Expenditures of the Town of Cambridge.
Cambridge, 1837–60.
Annual Report of the School Committee of Cambridge. Cambridge, 1841–
The Charter and Ordinances of the City of Cambridge. Boston, 1880.
*The Mayor's Address at the Organization of the City Government, and the Annual
Reports made to the City Council.* Cambridge, 1846–.
Records of the Town of Cambridge, 1833–45. 1 MS vol. City Clerk's Office,
Cambridge.
Records of the Selectmen of the Town of Cambridge, 1833–45. 1 MS vol. City
Clerk's Office, Cambridge.

Other

Abstract of the Massachusetts School Returns. Boston, 1838.
Annual Reports of the Railroad Corporations in the State of Massachusetts.
Published annually as part of the Massachusetts Senate Documents. Boston,
1837–

Articles, Pamphlets, and Books

Abu-Lughod, Janet. "The Urban-Rural Differential as a Function of the
Demographic Transition: Egyptian Data and an Analytic Model." *American
Journal of Sociology* 69 (1964): 476–90.

An Account of the Controversy in the First Parish in Cambridge, 1827–1829. Boston, 1829.

Adams, Harriet A. "Neighborhood Sketch No. 7: Winter Hill." Somerville Historical Society, *Historic Leaves*, 3 (April 1904): 22–24.

Address of the Mayor upon the First Organization of the Cambridge City Government, May 4, 1846. Cambridge, 1846.

Albion, Robert Greenhalgh, with the collaboration of Jennie Barnes Pope. *The Rise of New York Port, 1815–1860.* New York, 1939.

Amory, Thomas C. *Class Memoir of George Washington Warren, with English and American Ancestry.* Boston, 1886.

_____. *Life of James Sullivan, with Selections from His Writings.* 2 vols. Boston, 1859.

Ayer, John F. "Neighborhood Sketch No. 6: Medford and Walnut Streets." Somerville Historical Society, *Historic Leaves* 2 (July 1903): 42–46.

_____. "The Old Medford Turnpike" Somerville Historic Society, *Historic Leaves* 1 (July 1902): 7–20.

Bacon, Mrs. E. A. *Memoir of Rev. Henry Bacon.* Boston, 1857.

Bacon, John. *The Town Officer's Guide, containing a Compilation of the General Laws of Massachusetts, relating to the Whole Power and Duty of Towns, Districts, and Parishes, with their several Officers.* Haverhill, 1825.

Baker, Christina Hopkinson. *The Story of Fay House.* Cambridge, 1929.

Baker, George Pierce. *The Formation of the New England Railroad Systems: A Study of Railroad Combination in the Nineteenth Century.* Cambridge, 1949.

Baldwin, Francis B. *From Pequossette Plantation to the Town of Belmont Massachusetts, 1630–1953.* Belmont, 1953.

Baldwin, Thomas W., comp. *Vital records of Cambridge, Massachusetts to the Year 1850.* 2 vols. Boston, 1914–15.

Banner, James M., Jr. *To the Hartford Convention: The Federalists and the Origins of Party Politics in Massachusetts, 1789–1815.* New York, 1970.

Barber, John Warner. *Historical Collections, being a General Collection of Interesting Facts, Traditions, Biographical Sketches, Anecdotes, etc., relating to the History and Antiquities of Every Town in Massachusetts, with Geographical Descriptions.* Worcester, 1839.

Bartlett, Josiah. *An Historical Sketch of Charlestown, in the County of Middlesex and Commonwealth of Massachusetts.* Boston, 1814.

Barton, Josef. *Peasants and Strangers: Italians, Rumanians, and Slovaks in an American City, 1890–1950.* Cambridge, 1975.

Baum, Dale. "Know-Nothingism and the Republican Majority in Massachusetts: The Political Realignment of the 1850s." *Journal of American History* 64 (1978): 959–86.

Beale, Joseph H. "The History of Local Government in Cambridge." Cambridge Historical Society, *Publications* 22 (January 1932): 17–28.

Berger, Bennett. "The Myth of Suburbia." *Journal of Social Issues* 17 (1961): 38–49.
_____. *Working Class Suburb: A Study of Auto Workers in Suburbia*. Berkeley, 1960.
The Bicentennial Book of Malden. Boston, 1850.
Bidwell, Percy Wells. "Rural Economy in New England at the Beginning of the Nineteenth Century." *Transactions of the Connecticut Academy of Arts and Sciences* 20 (April 1916): 241–399.
_____. "Population Growth in Southern New England." *Quarterly Publications of the American Statistical Association*, n.s. 120 (December 1917).
Bidwell, Percy Wells, and Falconer, John I. *History of Agriculture in the Northern United States, 1620–1860*. New York, 1925.
Bigelow, John P. *Statistical Tables Exhibiting the Condition and Products of Certain Branches of Industry in Massachusetts, for the Year Ending April 1, 1837*. Boston, 1838.
Binford, Henry C. "The Influence of Commuting on the Development of Cambridge and Somerville, Massachusetts, 1815–1860." Ph.D. diss., Harvard University, 1973.
Biographical Dictionary of the American Congress, 1774–1961. Washington, 1961.
Bishop, Christine E. "On the Road to Boston: The Development of Eastern Cambridge, 1790–1820." Department of Economics, Harvard University, 1969.
Blake, Nelson Manfred. *Water for the Cities: a History of the Urban Water Supply Problem in the United States*. Syracuse, 1956.
Bliss, Edward P. "The Old Taverns of Lexington." *Proceedings of the Lexington Historical Society* 1 I (1886–89): 72–87.
Blumin, Stuart. *The Urban Threshold: Growth and Change in a Nineteenth-Century American Community*. Chicago, 1976.
Bowditch, Vincent Y. *Life and Correspondence of Henry Ingersoll Bowditch by His Son*. 2 vols. Boston, 1902.
Boyer, Paul S. *Urban Masses and Moral Order in America, 1820–1920*. Cambridge, 1978.
A Brief History of the First Baptist Church in Cambridge. Cambridge, 1870.
Briggs, Asa, *Victorian Cities*. New York, 1970.
Briggs, Charles. *A Discourse Delivered at Concord, October the Fifth, 1825*. Concord, 1825.
Brooks, Charles. *History of the Town of Medford, Middlesex County, Massachusetts*. Boston, 1855.
Brown, Abram English. *Faneuil Hall and Faneuil Hall Market or Peter Faneuil and His Gift*. Boston, 1900.
Brunet, Michel, "The Secret Ballot Issue in Massachusetts Politics from 1851 to 1853." *New England Quarterly* 25 (1952): 354–59.
Bryant, Albert W. "Lexington Sixty Years Ago." *Proceedings of the Lexington Historical Society* 2 (1890): 19–64.
_____. "The Monroe Tavern." *Proceedings of the Lexington Historical Society* 3 (1904): 142–54.

Bulfinch, Ellen Susan. "The Tudor House at Fresh Pond." Cambridge Historical Society, *Publications* 3 (1908): 100–109.

Burke, Peter. "Some Reflections on the Pre-Industrial City." *Urban History Yearbook, 1975* (Leicester, 1975), 13–21.

Butler, Benjamin F. *Autobiographical and Personal Reminiscences*. Boston, 1892.

Cambridge Historical Commission. *Survey of Architectural History in Cambridge*. 5 vols. Cambridge, 1965–77.

Cappa, Frank J. "Cities and Suburbs in Europe and the United States." In Philip C. Dolce, ed., *Suburbia: The American Dream and Dilemma*. Garden City, N.Y., 1976.

Carter, James G., and Brooks, William M. *A Geography of Middlesex County; for Young Children*. Cambridge, 1830.

Chapman, Henry Smith. *History of Winchester Massachusetts*. Winchester, 1936.

Chase, Frederic Hathaway. *Lemuel Shaw: Chief Justice of the Supreme Judicial Court of Massachusetts, 1830–1860*. Boston, 1846.

Chudacoff, Howard P. *Mobile Americans: Residential and Social Mobility in Omaha, 1880–1920*. New York, 1972.

Clark, Clifford. "Domestic Architecture as an Index to Social History: The Romantic Revival and the Cult of Domesticity in America, 1840–1870." *Journal of Interdisciplinary History* 7 (1976): 33–56.

Clark, Victor S. *History of Manufactures in the United States*. 2 vols. New York, 1929.

Conklin, Edwin P. *Middlesex County and Its People: A History*. 2 vols. New York, 1927.

Colman, Henry. *Fourth Report on the Agriculture of Massachusetts: Counties of Franklin and Middlesex*. Boston, 1841.

Controversy between the First Parish in Cambridge and The Rev. Dr. Holmes, Their Late Pastor. Cambridge, 1829.

Converse, Parker Lindall. *Legends of Woburn, Now First Written and Preserved in Collected Form*. Woburn, 1892.

Conzen, Kathleen Neils. *Immigrant Milwaukee, 1836–1860: Accommodation and Community in a Frontier City*. Cambridge, 1976.

Conzen, M. R. G. "Alnwick, Northumberland: A Study in Town-Plan Analysis." *Transactions of the Institute of British Geographers* 27 (1960).

Cook, Edward J. *The Fathers of the Towns: Leadership and Community Structure in Eighteenth Century New England*. Baltimore, 1976.

Copeland, John. *Roads and Their Traffic, 1750–1850*. Newton Abbot, England, 1968.

Corey, Deloraine Pendre. "Life in the Old Parsonage 1772–1784, from the Diary of Rev. Peter Thatcher." *Register of the Malden Historical Society* 1 (1910–11): 38–59.

Cutter, Benjamin, and Cutter, William R. *History of the Town of Arlington, Massachusetts, Formerly the Second Precinct in Cambridge . . . 1635–1879*. Boston, 1880.

Cutter, William R. "Long Bridge." *Winchester Record* 3 (January 1887): 16–24.

Daltzell, Robert F., Jr. "The Rise of the Waltham-Lowell System and Some Thoughts on the Political Economy of Modernization in Ante-Bellum Massachusetts." *Perspectives in American History.* 9 (1975): 229–70.

Dana, Henry Wadsworth Longfellow. "The Dana Saga." Cambridge Historical Society, *Publications* 26 (1940): 63–123.

Darling, Arthur B. *Political Change in Massachusetts, 1824–1848: A Study of Liberal Movements in Politics.* New Haven, 1925.

Davis, David Brion. *The Slave Power Conspiracy and the Paranoid Style.* Baton Rouge, 1969.

Dearborn, Nathaniel. *Dearborn's Reminiscences of Boston, and Guide through the City and Environs.* Boston, 1851.

Derby, E. H., "Commercial Cities and Towns of the U.S.—No. XXII.—Boston." *Hunt's Merchants Magazine and Commercial Review* 23 (November 1850): 483–97.

Despeaux, Helen M. "John S. Edgerly," Somerville Historical Society, *Historic Leaves* 3 (July 1904): 36–43.

De Witt, Francis. *Statistical Information Relating to Certain Branches of Industry in Massachusetts for the Year Ending May 1, 1855.* Boston, 1856.

Doherty, Robert. *Society and Power: Five New England Towns, 1800–1860.* Amherst, 1977.

Donallan, John Whiting. *History of the Second Baptist Church, Cambridge, Massachusetts.* Lawrence, 1866.

Douglass, Harlan Paul. *The Suburban Trend.* New York, 1925.

Doyle, Don H. "The Social Functions of Voluntary Associations in a Nineteenth-Century American Town." *Social Science History* 1 (1977): 333–55.

_____. *The Social Order of a Frontier Community: Jacksonville, Illinois, 1825–1870.* Urbana, Ill., 1978.

Drake, Samuel Adams. *Historic Fields and Mansions of Middlesex.* Boston, 1874.

Duberman, Martin B. "Some Notes on the Beginning of the Republican Party in Massachusetts." *New England Quarterly* 25 (1952): 352–59.

Dyos, H. J. "The Growth of a Pre-Victorian Suburb: South London, 1580–1836." *Town Planning Review* 25 (1954): 59–78.

_____. *Victorian Suburb: A Study of the Growth of Camberwell.* Leicester, 1966.

Eddy, Caleb. *Historical Sketch of the Middlesex Canal, with Remarks for the Consideration of the Proprietors.* Boston, 1843.

Elliot, Charles D. "Union Square and Its Neighborhood about the Year 1846," Somerville Historical Society, *Historic Leaves*, 6 (April 1907): 5–16.

Everett, Edward. *Eulogy on Thomas Dowse of Cambridgeport.* Boston, 1859.

Fearon, Henry Bradshaw. *Sketches of America: A Narrative of a Journey of Five Thousand Miles through the Eastern and Western States of America.* London, 1818.

Feldberg, Michael. "Urbanization as a Cause of Violence: Philadelphia as a Test Case." In Allen F. Davis and Mark H. Haller, eds., *The Peoples of Philadelphia: A History of Ethnic Groups and Lower-Class Life, 1790–1940.* Philadelphia, 1973.

Firey, Walter. *Land Use in Central Boston.* Cambridge, 1947.

Fischer, David Hackett. *The Revolution of American Conservatism: The Federalist Party in the Era of Jeffersonian Democracy.* New York, 1965.

Foner, Eric. *Free Soil, Free Labor, Free Men: The Ideology of the Republican Party before the Civil War.* New York, 1970.

Forbes, A., and Greene, J. W. *Rich Men of Massachusetts, containing a Statement of the Reputed Wealth of about Fifteen Hundred Persons.* Boston, 1851.

Frisch, Michael. *Town into City: Springfield, Massachusetts, and the Meaning of Community, 1840–1880.* Cambridge, 1972.

Furber, William H. *Historical Address Delivered by Ex-Mayor William H. Furber in the High School Building, Somerville, July 4, 1876.* Boston, 1876.

Gans, Herbert J. "The Suburban Community and Its Way of Life." In Robert Gutman and David Popenoe, eds., *Neighborhood, City, and Metropolis.* New York, 1970.

_____. "Urbanism and Suburbanism as Ways of Life: a Re-evaluation of Definitions." In Arnold Rose, ed., *Human Behavior and Social Processes.* Boston, 1962.

Gatell, Frank Otto. *John Gorham Palfrey and the New England Conscience.* Cambridge, 1963.

Gates, Paul Wallace. *The Farmer's Age: Agriculture, 1815–1860.* The Economic History of the United States, vol. 3 New York, 1960.

Gilchrist, David T., ed. *The Growth of the Seaport Cities, 1790–1825.* Charlottesville, 1967.

Gilman, Arthur, ed. *The Cambridge of Eighteen Hundred and Ninety-Six: A Picture of the City and its Industries Fifty Years after its Incorporation.* Cambridge, 1896.

Gilman, Caroline Howard. *Recollections of a Housekeeper.* New York, 1836.

Godley, John Robert. *Letters from America.* 2 vols. London, 1844.

Goodman, Paul. *The Democratic-Republicans of Massachusetts: Politics in a Young Republic.* Cambridge, 1964.

Goss, Elbridge Henry. *The History of Melrose, County of Middlesex, Massachusetts.* Melrose, 1902.

Gould, Levi S. "Reminiscences of North Malden (Melrose) and Vicinity." *Register of the North Malden Historical Society* 4 (1915–16): 65–84.

Gozzaldi, Mary Isabella. "Extracts from the Reminiscences of Isabella Batchelder James." Cambridge Historical Society, *Publications* 23 (October 1934): 49–61.

_____. *History of Cambridge, Massachusetts, 1630–1877, with a Genealogical Register by Lucius R. Paige, Supplement and Index.* Cambridge, 1930.

_____. "Merchants of Cambridge in the Early Days." Cambridge Historical Society, *Publications* 8 (October 1913): 30–40.

Grahame, Thomas. *A Treatise on Internal Intercourse and Communication in Civilized States, and Particularly in Great Britain.* London, 1834.

Gras, N. S. B., and Larson, Henrietta M. *Casebook in American Business History.* New York, 1939.

Griffin, Clifford S. *Their Brothers' Keepers: Moral Stewardship in the United States, 1800–1865.* New Brunswick, 1960.

H. M. *Echoes from Mystic Side: Malden, Melrose, Everett.* Boston, 1890.

Hale, Edward Everett. *A New England Boyhood.* New York, 1893.

Hales, John G. *A Survey of Boston and Its Vicinity.* Boston, 1821.

Haley, M. A. *The Story of Somerville.* Boston, 1903.

Halttunen, Karen. *Confidence Men and Painted Women: A Study of Middle-Class Culture in America, 1830–1870.* New Haven, 1983.

Hammack, David C. "Power in the Cities and Towns of the United States, 1800–1960." *American Historical Review* 83 (1978): 323–49.

Hammond, Bray. *Banks and Politics in America from the Revolution to the Civil War.* Princeton, 1957.

Handlin, David. *The American Home: Architecture and Society, 1815–1915.* Boston, 1979.

Handlin, Oscar. *Boston's Immigrants: A Study in Acculturation.* Cambridge, 1959.

Handlin, Oscar, and Handlin, Mary Flug. *Commonwealth: A Study of the Role of Government in the American Economy—Massachusetts, 1774–1861.* Rev. ed. Cambridge, 1969.

Harlow, Thomas S. "Some Notes of the History of Medford from 1801 to 1851." *Medford Historical Register* 1 (July 1898): 82–92.

Hastings, Lewis M. "An Historical Account of Some Bridges over the Charles River." Cambridge Historical Society, *Publications* 7 (January 1912): 51–63.

Hawley, Amos H., and Zimmer, Basil G. "Resistance to Unification in a Metropolitan Community." In Morris Janowitz, ed., *Community Political Systems.* Glencoe, 1961.

Hawthorne, Nathaniel. *Passages from the American Note-Books.* Vol. 9 of *The Complete Works of Nathaniel Hawthorne*, ed. George P. Lathrop. Boston, 1883.

Hayward, James. *Report of the Survey of the Roads in Cambridge.* Cambridge, 1838.

Hayward, John. *A Gazetteer of Massachusetts, containing Descriptions of All the Counties, Towns and Districts in the Commonwealth.* Boston, 1846.

Hervey, James A. "Reminiscences of an Earlier Medford." *Medford Historical Register* 4 (July 1901): 61–77.

Higginson, Thomas Wentworth. Address at the Cambridge Historical Society Celebration of the Two Hundred and Seventy-Fifth Anniversary of the Founding of Cambridge. Cambridge Historical Society, *Publications* 1 (December 1905 1905): 48–53.

————. "Cambridge Eighty Years Since." Cambridge Historical Society, *Publications* 2 (October 1906): 20–32.

————. *Cheerful Yesterdays*. Boston, 1898.

Hildreth, Hosea. *A Book for Massachusetts Children, in Familiar Letters from a Father for the Use of Families and Schools*. 2nd ed. Boston, 1831.

Hilen, Andrew, ed. *The Letters of Henry Wadsworth Longfellow*. 6 vols. Cambridge, 1967–82.

Hill, Hamilton Andrews. *The Trade and Commerce of Boston, 1630–1890*. Boston, 1895.

Hilliard, George S. *Life, Letters, and Journals of George Ticknor*. 2 vols. Boston, 1876.

Hirsch, Susan E. *Roots of the American Working Class: The Industrialization of Crafts in Newark, 1800–1860*. Philadelphia, 1978.

Historical Address and Poem, delivered at the Bi-Centennial Celebration of the Incorporation of the Old Town of Reading, May 29, A.D. 1844. Boston, 1844.

Holmes, Abiel. "The History of Cambridge." Massachusetts Historical Society, *Collections*, ser 1, vol. 7 (1800): 1–67.

Holt, Michael F. *Forging a Majority: The Formation of the Republican Party in Pittsburgh, 1848–1860*. New Haven, 1969.

————. *The Political Crisis of the 1850s*. New York, 1978.

————. "The Politics of Impatience: The Origins of Know Nothingism." *Journal of American History* 60 (1973): 309–31.

Hosmer, J. K., et al. *Memorial of George Washington Hosmer, D.D.* N.p., 1882.

Howe, Henry F. *Salt Rivers of the Massachusetts Shore*. New York, 1951.

Howe, Lois Lilley. "Dr. Estes Howe: A Citizen of Cambridge." Cambridge Historical Society, *Publications*, 25 (1938–39): 122–41.

Hoyt, Rev. James S. *The First Evangelical Congregational Church, Cambridgeport, Massachusetts*. Cambridge, 1877.

Hudson, Charles. *History of the Town of Lexington, Middlesex County, Massachusetts, from Its First Settlement to 1868, Revised and Continued to 1912*. 2 vols. Boston, 1913.

Hunnewell, James F. *Bibliography of Charlestown, Massachusetts, and Bunker Hill*. Boston, 1880.

————. *A Century of Town Life: A History of Charlestown, Massachusetts, 1775–1887*. Boston, 1888.

Hunter, Albert J. *Symbolic Communities: The Persistence and Change of Chicago's Local Communities*. Chicago, 1974.

Hurd, D. Hamilton, comp. *History of Middlesex County, Massachusetts, with Biographical Sketches of Many of Its Pioneers and Prominent Men*. 3 vols. Philadelphia, 1890.

The Inaugural Addresses of the Mayors of Boston. Boston, 1894.

Jackson, Kenneth T. "Metropolitan Government versus Suburban Autonomy: Politics on the Crabgrass Frontier." In Kenneth T. Jackson and Stanley K. Schultz, eds., *Cities in American History*. New York, 1972.

————. "Urban Deconcentration in the Nineteenth Century: A Statistical Inquiry."
In Leo F. Schnore, ed., *The New Urban History: Quantitative Explorations by
American Historians*. Princeton, 1975.

Janowitz, Morris, ed., *Community Political Systems*. Glencoe, 1961.

————. *The Community Press in an Urban Setting: The Social Elements of
Urbanism*. 2nd ed. Chicago, 1952.

Johnson, Arthur M., and Supple, Barry E. *Boston Capitalists and Western
Railroads: A Study in the Nineteenth-Century Investment Process*. Cambridge,
1967.

Johnson, James H., ed., *Suburban Growth: Geographical Processes at the Edge of
the Western City*. London, 1974.

Johnson, Paul E. *A Shopkeeper's Millennium: Society and Revivals in Rochester,
New York, 1815–1837*. New York, 1978.

Jones, Fred Mitchell. *Middlemen in the Domestic Trade of the United States, 1800–
1860*. Illinois Studies in the Social Sciences, vol. 21, no. 3. Urbana, Ill., 1937.

Katz, Michael B. *The Irony of Early School Reform: Educational Innovation in Mid-
Nineteenth Century Massachusetts*. Cambridge, 1968.

————. *The People of Hamilton, Canada West: Family and Class in a Mid-
Nineteenth Century City*. Cambridge, 1975.

Kennedy, Charles J. "Commuter Services in the Boston Area, 1835–1860." *Business
History Review* 37 (1962): 153–69.

Kirkland, Edward Chase. *Men, Cities, and Transportation: A Study in New
England History, 1820–1900*. 2 vols. Cambridge, 1948.

Knights, Peter R. *The Plain People of Boston, 1830–1860: A Study in City Growth*.
New York, 1971.

Knodel, John. "Town and Country in Nineteenth-Century Germany: A Review of
Urban-Rural Differentials in Demographic Behavior." *Social Science History* 1
(1977): 356–82.

Kramer, John, ed., *North American Suburbs: Politics, Diversity, and Change*.
Berkeley, 1972.

Kutler, Stanley I. *Privilege and Creative Destruction: The Charles River Bridge Case*.
New York, 1971.

Labaree, Benjamin W. *Patriots and Partisans: The Merchants of Newburyport,
1764–1815*. Cambridge, 1962.

Lane, Roger. *Policing the City: Boston, 1822–1887*. New York, 1971.

Laurie, Bruce. *Working People of Philadelphia, 1800–1850*. Philadelphia, 1980.

List of Streets and Ways in the City of Cambridge, Massachusetts, January 1, 1932.
Cambridge, n.d.

Livermore, Isaac. *An Account of Some Bridges over the Charles River, as connected
with the Growth of Cambridge*. Cambridge, 1858.

Lord, Robert H., Sexton, John E., and Harrington, Edward T. *History of the
Archdiocese of Boston in the Various Stages of Its Development, 1604–1943*. 3
vols. Boston, 1945.

Lotchin, Roger. *San Francisco, 1846–1856: From Hamlet to City*. New York, 1974.

Lovett, Robert W. "The Harvard Branch Railroad, 1849–1855." Cambridge Historical Society, *Publications* 38 (1959–60): 23–50.

Lowell, James Russell. *Letters of James Russell Lowell*. Ed. Charles Eliot Norton. 2 vols. New York, 1894.

Lucid, Robert F., ed., *The Journal of Richard Henry Dana, Jr.* 3 vols. Cambridge, 1968.

Lynch, Kevin. *The Image of the City*. Cambridge, 1966.

McCaughey, Robert A. "From Town to City: Boston in the 1820s." *Political Science Quarterly* 88 (1973): 191–213.

McCormick, Richard P. *The Second American Party System: Party Formation in the Jacksonian Era*. Chapel Hill, 1966.

McKenzie, Alexander. *The Good Deacons: Sermons in Memory of Stephen T. Farwell and Charles W. Homer, Deacons of the First Church in Cambridge*. Boston, 1873.

———. *Lectures on the History of the First Church in Cambridge*. Boston, 1873.

McLaughlin, William G. *New England Dissent, 1630–1833: The Baptists and the Separation of Church and State*. 2 vols. Cambridge, 1971.

Middlesex County Agricultural Society. *Transactions*. N.p., 1852–.

Montgomery, David. "The Shuttle and the Cross: Weavers and Artisans in the Kensington Riots of 1844." *Journal of Social History* 5 (1972): 411–46.

Morison, Samuel Eliot. *Harrison Gray Otis, 1765–1848: The Urbane Federalist*. Boston, 1969.

———. *The Maritime History of Massachusetts, 1783–1860*. Boston, 1921.

Mumford, Lewis. *The City in History*. New York, 1961.

Munro, William Bennett. *The Government of American Cities*. New York, 1909.

Munroe, James P. "Elias Phinney." *Proceedings of the Lexington Historical Society* 2 (April 1890): 65–84.

Munroe, Paul. *Founding of the American Public School System: A History of Education in the United States*. 2 vols. New York, 1940.

Newell, William. *The Pastor's Remembrances: A Discourse Delivered before the First Parish in Cambridge on Sunday, May 27, 1855*. Cambridge, 1855.

North, Douglass C. *The Economic Growth of the United States, 1790–1860*. New York, 1961.

Norton, Charles Eliot, "Reminiscences of Old Cambridge." Cambridge Historical Society, *Publications* 1 (October 1905): 11–23.

O'Malley, Thomas F. "Old North Cambridge." Cambridge Historical Society, *Publications* 20 (1929): 121–35.

Paige, Lucius R. *History of Cambridge, Massachusetts, 1630–1877*. Boston, 1877.

Palfrey, John G. *Statistics of the Condition and Products of Certain Branches of Industry in Massachusetts for the Year ending April 1, 1845*. Boston, 1846.

Parker, Charles S. *Town of Arlington, Past and Present*. Arlington, 1907.

Perin, Constance. *Everything in Its Place: Social Order and Land Use in America*. Princeton, 1977.

Perry, Bliss. *Life and Letters of Henry Lee Higginson*. Boston, 1921.

Pessen, Edward. "Did Fortunes Rise and Fall Mercurially in Antebellum America? The Tale of Two Cities: Boston and New York." *Journal of Social History* 4 (1971): 339–57.

———. "Who Governed the Nation's Cities in the Era of the Common Man." *Political Science Quarterly* 87 (1972): 591–614.

Pinkney, David H. *Napoleon III and the Rebuilding of Paris*. Princeton, 1958.

Pope, Augustus R. *An Address Delivered at the Laying of the Corner Stone of a House of Worship for the Allen Street Congregational Society, 1851*. Cambridge, 1851.

Porter, Glenn, and Livesay, Harold C. *Merchants and Manufacturers: Studies in the Changing Structure of Nineteenth Century Marketing*. Baltimore, 1971.

Porter, Kenneth Wiggins. *The Jacksons and the Lees: Two Generations of Massachusetts Merchants, 1765–1844*. Cambridge, 1937.

Potter, David. *The Impending Crisis, 1848–1861*. New York, 1976.

Pottinger, David T. "Thirty-Eight Quincy Street." Cambridge Historical Society, *Publications* 23 (April 1934): 24–28.

Pratt, Frederick Haven, "The Craigies." Cambridge Historical Society, *Publications* 27 (1941): 43–86.

Private and Special Statutes of the Commonwealth of Massachusetts. 6 vols. Boston, 1805–48.

Pryor, R. J. "Defining the Rural-Urban Fringe." *Social Forces* 47 (1968) 202–15.

Quincy, Edmund, *Life of Josiah Quincy of Massachusetts*. Boston, 1867.

Quincy, Josiah. *A Municipal History of the Town and City of Boston, during Two Centuries*. Boston, 1852.

Records of the First Church, see Stephen C. Sharples, comp.

Report and bill relative to the Middlesex Bank. *Massachusetts Senate Documents, 1838*, no. 27.

Report of a Committee, appointed August 4, 1834, to Consider the Subject of a Reorganization of the Public Schools in the Town of Cambridge. Cambridge, 1834.

Report of the Committee Appointed by the Stockholders of the Charlestown Wharf Company, at the Last Annual Meeting. Boston, 1839.

Report of the Committee Appointed to Consider the Expediency of Consolidating Certain Boards of Officers of the Town of Cambridge. Boston, 1846.

Report of the Committee in Favor of the Union of Boston and Roxbury. Boston, 1851.

Report of the Committee of the House of Representatives who were instructed to inspect the records and proceedings of the Charles River Bridge. *Massachusetts House Documents, 1827*, no. 71.

Report of the Majority of the Committee appointed by the Town of Charlestown, to consider the Expediency of Obtaining a City Charter. Charlestown, 1846.

Reps, John W. *The Making of Urban America: A History of City Planning in the United States*. Princeton, 1965.

Review of the Case of the Free Bridge, between Boston and Charlestown. Boston, 1827.

Roberts, Christopher. *The Middlesex Canal, 1793–1860.* Cambridge, 1938.

Robinson, G. Frederick, and Wheeler, Ruth Robinson. *Great Little Watertown: A Tercentenary History.* Watertown, 1930.

Rosenberg, Carroll Smith. *Religion and the Rise of the American City: The New York City Mission Movement, 1812–1870.* Ithaca, N.Y., 1971.

Rugg, Dean S. *Spatial Foundations of Urbanism.* Dubuque, 1972.

Samuels, Edward A., and Kimball, Henry H., eds. *Somerville Past and Present.* Boston, 1897.

Sanderson, Dwight. *Locating the Rural Community.* Cornell Extension Bulletin 413. Ithaca, N.Y., 1939.

Sargent, Aaron, "Neighborhood Sketch No. 2: The Winter Hill Road in 1842." Somerville Historical Society. *Historic Leaves* 1 (October 1902): 19–22.

Schneider, John C. *Detroit and the Problem of Order, 1830–1880: A Geography of Crime, Riot, and Policing.* Lincoln, Neb., 1980.

Schnore, Leo. "The Growth of Metropolitan Suburbs." *American Sociological Review* 22 (1957): 165–73.

————. "The Social and Economic Characteristics of American Suburbs." *Sociological Quarterly* 4 (1963): 122–34.

Schwartz, Barry, ed. *The Changing Face of the Suburbs.* Chicago, 1976.

Seaburg, Carl, and Paterson, Stanley. *Merchant Prince of Boston: Colonel T. H. Perkins, 1764–1854.* Cambridge, 1971.

Sharples, Stephen P., comp. *Records of the Church of Christ at Cambridge in New England, 1632–1830.* Boston, 1906.

Shaw, Charles. *A Topographical and Historical Description of Boston, from the first Settlement of the Town to the Present Period; with some Account of its Environs.* Boston, 1817.

Simpson, Sophia Shuttleworth. "Two Hundred Years Ago; or, A Brief History of Cambridgeport and East Cambridge." Originally published in 1859. Reprinted in Cambridge Historical Society, *Publications* 16 (April 1922): 27–96.

Sjoberg, Gideon. *The Preindustrial City: Past and Present.* New York, 1960.

Sklar, Kathryn Kish. *Catharine Beecher: A Study in American Domesticity.* New Haven, 1973.

Smith, George O. "The Milk Business and Milk Men of Earlier Days." *Proceedings of the Lexington Historical Society* 2 (1897): 187–96.

Spofford, Jeremiah. *A Gazetteer of Massachusetts; Containing a General View of the State.* Newburyport, 1828.

Stevens, William B. *History of Stoneham, Massachusetts.* Stoneham, 1891.

Sutherland, Arthur E. *The Law at Harvard: A History of Ideas and Men, 1817–1967.* Cambridge, 1967.

Suttles, Gerald D. *The Social Construction of Communities.* Chicago, 1972.

Sweeney, Kevin. "Rum, Romanism, Representation, and Reform: Coalition Politics in Massachusetts, 1847–1853." *Civil War History* 22 (1976): 116–37.

Taylor, George Rogers. "American Urban Growth Preceding the Railway Age." *Journal of Economic History* 27 (1967): 309–39.

———. "The Beginnings of Mass Transportation in Urban America" (2 parts). *Smithsonian Journal of History* 1 (1966): 35–50; 2 (1967): 31–54.

Teaford, Jon C. *City and Suburb: The Political Fragmentation of Metropolitan America, 1850–1970.* Baltimore, 1979.

———. *The Municipal Revolution in America: Origins of Modern Urban Government, 1650–1825.* Chicago, 1975.

Thayer, William Roscoe. "Extracts from the Journal of Benjamin Waterhouse." Cambridge Historical Society, *Publications* 4 (January 1909): 22–37.

Thernstrom, Stephan, and Knights, Peter. "Men in Motion: Some Data and Speculations about Urban Population Mobility in Nineteenth-Century America," In Tamara K. Hareven, ed., *Anonymous Americans.* Englewood Cliffs, N.J., 1971.

Thomas, Benjamin F. *The Town Officer: A Digest of the Laws of Massachusetts in relation to the Powers, Duties and Liabilities of Towns, and of Town Officers; with the Necessary Forms.* Worcester, 1849.

Thwing, Walter Eliot. *The Livermore Family of America.* Boston, 1902.

Tredgold, Thomas. *A Practical Treatise on Railroads and Carriages, Shewing the Principles of Estimating Their Strength.* London, 1825.

Updegraff, Harlan. *The Origin of the Moving School in Massachusetts,* New York, 1971.

Vance, James E., Jr. "The American City: Workshop for a National Culture." In John S. Adams, ed., *Contemporary Metropolitan America,* part 1: *Cities of the Nation's Historic Metropolitan Core.* Cambridge, 1976.

Walker, Richard A. "The Transformation of Urban Structure in the Nineteenth Century and the Beginnings of Suburbanization." In Kevin R. Cox, ed., *Urbanization and Conflict in Market Societies.* Chicago, 1978.

Ward, David. *Cities and Immigrants: A Geography of Change in Nineteenth Century America.* New York, 1971.

Ware, Caroline F. *The Early New England Cotton Manufacture: A Study in Industrial Beginnings.* New York, 1931.

Ware, John F. W. *Cambridgeport Parish: A Discourse on the Occasion of the Fiftieth Anniversary of the Settlement of Rev. Thomas B. Gannett, First Minister of the Parish.* Cambridge, 1864.

Warner, Oliver. *Statistical Information Relating to Certain Branches of Industry in Massachusetts, for the Year ending May 1, 1865.* Boston, 1866.

Warner, Sam Bass, Jr. *Streetcar Suburbs: The Process of Growth in Boston, 1870–1900.* 2d ed. Cambridge, 1978.

———. *The Private City: Philadelphia in Three Periods of Its Growth.* Philadelphia, 1968.

Warren, Donald I. "Neighborhoods in Urban Areas." In Roland L. Warren ed, *New Perspectives on the American Community.* New York, 1977.

Warren, George W. *Review of the Opinion of the Supreme Court.* Charlestown, 1855.

Watkins, Lura Woodside. *Cambridge Glass, 1818 to 1888: The Story of the New England Glass Company.* Boston, 1930.

Wehrwein, George S. "The Rural-Urban Fringe." *Economic Geography* 18 (1942): 217–28.

Wheelwright, William Bond. *Life and Times of Alvah Crocker.* Boston, 1923.

Whitaker, George. *Historical Address at the Semi-Centennial Anniversary of the First Methodist Episcopal Church, Somerville.* N.p., 1908.

Whitehand, J. W. R. "Fringe Belts: A Neglected Aspect of Urban Geography." *Transactions of the Institute of British Geographers* 41 (1967): 223–33.

Whitehill, Walter Muir. *Boston: A Topographical History.* 2d ed. Cambridge, 1968.

Whitney, Louisa G. *The Burning of the Convent.* Boston, 1844.

Whittemore, Thomas. *The Early Days of Thomas Whittemore: An Autobiography extending from A.D. 1800 to A.D. 1825.* Boston, 1859.

Winsor, Justin, ed. *The Memorial History of Boston, including Suffolk County, Massachusetts, 1630–1880.* 4 vols. Boston, 1881–83.

Wissink, G. A. *American Cities in Perspective, with Special Reference to the Development of their Fringe Areas.* Assen, Netherlands, 1962.

Wood, Robert C. *Suburbia: Its People and Their Politics.* Boston, 1958.

Wooley, Frederick H. C. "Old Ship Street: Some of Its Houses, Ships, and Characters." *Medford Historical Register* 4 (October 1901): 87–100.

Wright, Gwendolyn. *Moralism and the Model Home: Domestic Architecture and Cultural Conflict in Chicago, 1873–1913.* Chicago, 1980.

Wyman, Thomas Bellows. *The Genealogies and Estates of Charlestown in the County of Middlesex and Commonwealth of Massachusetts, 1629–1818.* 2 vols. Boston, 1879.

Yans-McLaughlin, Virginia. *Family and Community: Italian Immigrants in Buffalo, 1880–1930.* Ithaca, N.Y., 1977.

Zuckerman, Michael. *Peaceable Kingdoms: New England Towns in the Eighteenth Century.* New York, 1970.

Index